Targum Pseudo-Jonathan:
Genesis

THE ARAMAIC BIBLE
• THE TARGUMS •

PROJECT DIRECTOR
Martin McNamara, M.S.C.

EDITORS
Kevin Cathcart • Michael Maher, M.S.C.
Martin McNamara, M.S.C.

EDITORIAL CONSULTANTS
Daniel J. Harrington, S.J. • Bernard Grossfeld

The Aramaic Bible

Volume 1B

Targum Pseudo-Jonathan: Genesis

Translated, with Introduction and Notes

BY

Michael Maher, M.S.C.

A Michael Glazier Book
THE LITURGICAL PRESS
Collegeville, Minnesota

About the Translator:

Michael J. Maher, M.S.C., is Lecturer in Scripture at the Mater Dei Institute of Religious Education, Dublin. He studied at Hebrew Union College, Cincinnati, and earned his Ph.D. in Semitic Languages at University College Dublin. His publications include *Genesis* (Old Testament Message, 2).

First published in 1992 by The Liturgical Press, Collegeville, Minnesota 56321.
Copyright © 1992 by The Order of St. Benedict, Inc., Collegeville, Minnesota. All rights reserved.

Library of Congress Cataloging-in-Publication Data

Bible. O.T. Genesis. English. Maher. 1992.
   Targum Pseudo-Jonathan, Genesis / translated, with introduction
and notes by Michael Maher.
      p.   cm. — (The Aramaic Bible ; v. 1B)
  "A Michael Glazier book."
  Includes bibliographical references and indexes.
  ISBN 0-8146-5492-4
  1. Bible. O.T. Genesis. Aramaic. Targum Pseudo-Jonathan-
-Translations into English. 2. Bible. O.T. Genesis. Aramaic.
Targum Pseudo-Jonathan—Criticism, interpretation, etc. I. Maher,
Michael, 1933- . II. Title. III. Series: Bible. O.T. English.
Aramaic Bible. 1987 ; v. 1B.
BS709.2.B5 1987 vol. 1B
[BS1233]
221.4'2 s—dc20
[222'11042]   92-6452
                    CIP

Logo design by Florence Bern.
Typography by Graphic Sciences Corporation, Cedar Rapids, Iowa.
Printed in the United States of America.

iv

TABLE OF CONTENTS

Dedicated to the memory of
PROFESSOR ALEJANDRO DÍEZ MACHO, M.S.C.

EDITORS' FOREWORD

While any translation of the Scriptures may in Hebrew be called a Targum, the word is used especially for a translation of a book of the Hebrew Bible into Aramaic. Before the Christian era Aramaic had in good part replaced Hebrew in Palestine as the vernacular of the Jews. It continued as their vernacular for centuries later and remained in part as the language of the schools after Aramaic itself had been replaced as the vernacular.

Rabbinic Judaism has transmitted Targums of all books of the Hebrew Canon, with the exception of Daniel and Ezra-Nehemiah, which are themselves partly in Aramaic. We also have a translation of the Samaritan Pentateuch into the dialect of Samaritan Aramaic. From the Qumran Library we have sections of a Targum of Job and fragments of a Targum of Leviticus, chapter 16, facts which indicate that the Bible was being translated in Aramaic in pre-Christian times.

Translations of books of the Hebrew Bible into Aramaic for liturgical purposes must have begun before the Christian era, even though none of the Targums transmitted to us by Rabbinic Judaism can be shown to be that old and though some of them are demonstrably compositions from later centuries.

In recent decades there has been increasing interest among scholars and a larger public in these Targums. A noticeable lacuna, however, has been the absence of a modern English translation of this body of writing. It is in marked contrast with most other bodies of Jewish literature for which there are good modern English translations, for instance the Apocrypha and Pseudepigrapha of the Old Testament, Josephus, Philo, the Mishnah, the Babylonian Talmud and Midrashic literature, and more recently the Tosefta and Palestinian Talmud.

It is hoped that this present series will provide some remedy for this state of affairs.

The aim of the series is to translate all the traditionally-known Targums, that is those transmitted by Rabbinic Judaism, into modern English idiom, while at the same time respecting the particular and peculiar nature of what these Aramaic translations were originally intended to be. A translator's task is never an easy one. It is rendered doubly difficult when the text to be rendered is itself a translation which is at times governed by an entire set of principles.

All the translations in this series have been specially commissioned. The translators have made use of what they reckon as the best printed editions of the Aramaic Targum in question or have themselves directly consulted the manuscripts.

The translation aims at giving a faithful rendering of the Aramaic. The introduction to each Targum contains the necessary background information on the particular work.

In general, each Targum translation is accompanied by an apparatus and notes. The former is concerned mainly with such items as the variant readings in the Aramaic texts, the relation of the English translation to the original, etc. The notes give what explanations the translator thinks necessary or useful for this series.

Not all the Targums here translated are of the same kind. Targums were translated at different times, and most probably for varying purposes, and have more than one interpretative approach to the Hebrew Bible. This diversity between the Targums themselves is reflected in the translation and in the manner in which the accompanying explanatory material is presented. However, a basic unity of presentation has been maintained. Targumic deviations from the Hebrew text, whether by interpretation or paraphrase, are indicated by italics.

A point that needs to be stressed with regard to this translation of the Targums is that by reason of the state of current targumic research, to a certain extent it must be regarded as a provisional one. Despite the progress made, especially in recent decades, much work still remains to be done in the field of targumic study. Not all the Targums are as yet available in critical editions. And with regard to those that have been critically edited from known manuscripts, in the case of the Targums of some books the variants between the manuscripts themselves are such as to give rise to the question whether they have all descended from a single common original.

Details regarding these points will be found in the various introductions and critical notes.

It is recognized that a series such as this will have a broad readership. The Targums constitute a valuable source of information for students of Jewish literature, particularly those concerned with the history of interpretation, and also for students of the New Testament, especially for those interested in its relationship to its Jewish origins. The Targums also concern members of the general public who have an interest in the Jewish interpretation of the Scriptures or in the Jewish background to the New Testament. For them the Targums should be both interesting and enlightening.

By their translations, introductions and critical notes the contributors to this series have rendered an immense service to the progress of targumic studies. It is hoped that the series, provisional though it may be, will bring significantly nearer the day when the definitive translation of the Targums can be made.

Kevin Cathcart   Martin McNamara, M.S.C.   Michael Maher, M.S.C.

PREFACE

Since Targum Pseudo-Jonathan of the Pentateuch was first printed in the second Rabbinic Bible (Venice, 1591), it has held its place in the body of traditional literature that attracted attention in Jewish learned circles. Although it never achieved the quasi-canonical status enjoyed by Onqelos, it has continually exercised the minds of scholars and commentators who have tried to clarify its meaning and to resolve the difficulties it raises. In our time several writers have dedicated important works to the study of this intriguing document, and this volume owes much to their discoveries and to their clarifications.

We are now in the fortunate position of possessing excellent texts of Pseudo-Jonathan in the editions of Rieder, Díez Macho, and Clarke listed in the Bibliography. The second edition of Rieder's work adds a Hebrew translation of the Aramaic text, and the Díez Macho edition contains a Spanish translation. R. Le Déaut and J. Robert have produced a French translation of Pseudo-Jonathan with an introduction and notes (see Bibliography). An English translation of this Targum, that of Etheridge, also mentioned in the Bibliography, appeared almost one hundred and thirty years ago.

The present translation, in line with the directions of the editors, "aims at giving a faithful rendering of the Aramaic" (see above, p. vii). It remains as close to the original as correct English will allow. In these days when we have become accustomed to translations of the Bible into current idiomatic English, one might question the wisdom of offering a rather old-fashioned translation of a Targum. But the justification for such a translation is that it helps to give the reader who does not know Aramaic the flavor of the Targumic idiom, and it brings him or her as close as possible to the original.

Due to the limitations of space, the notes are rather telegrammatic. But it is hoped that the many references they give to the sources from which Pseudo-Jonathan has drawn, the many indications to his method of interpretation and translation, and to the secondary literature on that Targum, will be of help to those who want to delve deeper into the secrets of Pseudo-Jonathan. In the notes we frequently mention themes which were of special interest to Pseudo-Jonathan and which occur at different places in his text.

I would like to round off this Preface with a little anecdote. Mrs. Chrissie Moore, who typed the manuscript of my translation of Pseudo-Jonathan as well as the manuscript of Martin McNamara's rendering of Targum Neofiti, and who knew nothing about Targums except what she picked up in the course of typing our manuscripts, remarked to Father McNamara that Pseudo-Jonathan was by far the most interesting of the two Targums. I could, of course, only agree with her judgment and commend her taste, although some Targumic scholars might disagree. It is my hope that the readers of the present work will find it interesting and stimulating, and that it will give them some insights into Jewish biblical interpretation and into the place of the Bible in the Jewish community.

MICHAEL MAHER, M.S.C.

Blackrock, Ireland

ABBREVIATIONS

Abod. Zar.	Abodah Zarah
Ant.	Josephus, *Jewish Antiquities*
Arak.	Arakin
ARN A	*The Fathers According to Rabbi Nathan.* Trans. J. Goldin.
ARN B	*The Fathers According to Rabbi Nathan.* Trans. A. J. Saldarini.
b.	Babylonian Talmud
B. Bat.	Baba Bathra
Bek.	Bekhoroth
Berak.	Berakhoth
B. Mez.	Baba Mezia
B. Qam.	Baba Qamma
CTg (A,B,E, etc.)	Cairo Genizah (Pal.) Tg. Manuscript
Deut. R.	Deuteronomy Rabbah
Ed. pr.	*Editio princeps* of Tg. Ps.-J. (Venice, 1598).
Erub.	Erubin
Exod. R.	Exodus Rabbah
Frg.Tg(s).	Fragment Targum(s)
Gen. R.	Genesis Rabbah
Gitt.	Gittin
Hag.	Hagigah
Hor.	Horayoth
HT	Hebrew Text
Hul.	Hullin

j.	Jerusalem (Palestinian) Talmud
Jon.	Jonathan
Ketub.	Ketuboth
L	Frg.Tg. Leipzig MS
LAB	Pseudo-Philo's *Liber Antiquitatum Biblicarum*
Lam. R.	Lamentations Rabbah
Lev. R.	Leviticus Rabbah
Lond.	British Library MS 27031 of Pseudo-Jonathan
LXX	Septuagint
m.	Mishnah
Mak.	Makkoth
Meg.	Megillah
M. Qat.	Mo'ed Qatan
N	Nürnberg Frg.Tg. MS
Ned.	Nedarim
Nf	Neofiti
Nfi	Neofiti interlinear gloss
Nfmg	Neofiti marginal gloss
Nid.	Niddah
Num. R.	Numbers Rabbah
Ohol.	Oholoth
Onq.	Onqelos
P	Paris BN Frg.Tg. MS
Pal. Tg(s).	Palestinian Targum(s)
Pesah.	Pesahim
Pesh.	Peshitta
Ps.-J.	Targum Pseudo-Jonathan
PRE	*Pirqe de Rabbi Eliezer*
PRK	*Pesiqta de Rab Kahana*
Qidd.	Qiddushin
Quaest. hebr.	Jerome, *Quaestiones hebraicae in libro Geneseos*
1 QGenApoc	*The Genesis Apocryphon of Qumran Cave 1*
Rosh. Hash.	*Rosh Ha-Shanah*

Sam.	Samaritan Targum
Sanh.	Sanhedrin
Shabb.	Shabbath
Shebu.	Shebu'oth
t.	Tosefta
Ta'an.	Ta'anith
Tanḥ.	Midrash Tanḥuma
Tanḥ. B.	Midrash Tanḥuma, ed. S. Buber
Tg.	Targum
V	Vatican Library Frg. Tg. MS
Vulg.	Vulgate
Yebam.	Yebamoth
Zebah.	Zebahim

Journals and Series

AJSL	American Journal of Semitic Languages and Literature
EJ	Encyclopaedia Judaica
HUCA	Hebrew Union College Annual
JAOS	Journal of the American Oriental Society
JJS	Journal of Jewish Studies
JNES	Journal of Near Eastern Studies
JNSL	Journal of Northwest Semitic Languages
JPS	Jewish Publication Society
JQR	Jewish Quarterly Review
JStJ	Journal for the Study of Judaism.
JSS	Journal of Semitic Studies
JTS	Journal of Theological Studies
MGWJ	Monatsschrift für Geschichte und Wissenschaft des Judentums
PAAJR	Proceedings of the American Academy of Jewish Research
RB	Revue Biblique
REJ	Revue des Études Juives
RHPR	Revue d'histoire et de philosophie religieuses.

RSO	Rivista degli Studi orientali
SBL	Society of Biblical Literature
SR	Studies in Religion/Sciences Religieuses
VT	Vetus Testamentum
VTSupp	Supplement to Vetus Testamentum
ZDMG	Zeitschrift der Deutschen Morgenländischen Gesellschaft
ZNW	Zeitschrift für die Neutestamentliche Wissenschaft

INTRODUCTION

Since Ps.-J. is essentially a Pal. Tg., much of what M. McNamara says in his "General Introduction to the Palestinian Targums" in Volume 1A is applicable to Ps.-J. The reader is referred to that Introduction, and we limit ourselves here to some remarks on the specific character of Ps.-J.

The first reference to a Targum of the Pentateuch that is attributed to Jonathan ben Uzziel comes to us from the Italian kabbalist Menahen Recanati (c. 1320).[1] Azariah de Rossi, in his work *Me'or 'Enayim* (1573–75), noted that this Targum was also known as Targum Yerushalmi, but in the *editio princeps* (Venice, 1590–91) the title Targum Jonathan ben Uzziel was used. This latter title seems to be due to the fact that some scribes mistakenly interpreted the abbreviation TY (Targum Yerushalmi) as Targum Yonathan.[2] This fictitious Yonathan was then identified with Jonathan ben Uzziel, the reputed author of the Targum of the Prophets. In order to correct this mistaken identification and to avoid confusion, it has become customary to use the word "Pseudo" when referring to the Jonathan ben Uzziel to whom a Targum of the Pentateuch was attributed.

Pseudo-Jonathan (Ps.-J.) provides us with a translation of almost every verse of the Pentateuch.[3] It is a unique piece of literature, quite different from the other Targums of the Pentateuch. It is different not only from Onq., which, according to the view more commonly held today, received its final form in Babylon,[4] but also from Nf, the Frg. Tgs., and the Genizah Fragments, which represent the genuine Palestinian Pentateuchal Targum tradition. Yet Ps.-J. is closely related both to Onq. and to the Pal. Tgs. of the Pentateuch, for it is essentially a branch of the Palestinian Targumic tradition that has been strongly influenced by Onq.[5] The haggadic material in Ps.-J. is essentially

---

[1] See W. Bacher, "Targum," in *Jewish Encyclopedia* XII (1906) 60; D. M. Splansky, *Targum Pseudo-Jonathan,* 17.

[2] This theory was proposed by L. Zunz, *Die Gottesdienstlichen Vorträge,* 71, and it has been commonly accepted by scholars.

[3] Further on in this Introduction we shall mention that verses or parts of verses have been omitted by mistake in the British Library manuscript (Lond.) and/or in the *editio princeps* (*ed. pr.*), and we shall draw attention to these omissions in our translation.

[4] See, e.g., the summary of the arguments about the origins of Onq. in R. Le Déaut, *Introduction à la Littérature Targumique,* Première Partie, 1966, 78–88; Grossfeld, *The Targum Onqelos to Genesis,* 1988, 30–35.

[5] All scholars agree that there are many similarities between Ps.-J. and Onq. How these similarities are explained is, however, a matter of debate. The view more commonly held today, and the one to which we would subscribe, is that Ps.-J. is a Palestinian Targum that has been modified under the influence of Onq. Among the authors who held this

1

Palestinian,[6] and its hybrid language is a mixture of Palestinian forms with linguistic elements that are characteristic of Eastern Aramaic.[7] Yet, although Ps.-J. is a composite work, it has its own individuality, and the author-editor has composed his work with skill and initiative.

The Halakah in Ps.-J.

Like all the Pentateuchal Targums, Ps.-J. contains halakic material.[8] What is surprising, however, is the great number of halakic elements we find in Ps.-J., and the fact that so many of these run counter to the accepted halakah. It is true, of course, that we find much halakic material in the Pal. Tgs. that runs counter to the Mishnah and to the generally accepted views of the Rabbis, but this happens much more frequently in Ps.-J. S. Gronemann examined much of the halakah in this Targum and tried to discover the system followed by the *meturgeman* in his choice of halakic interpretations.[9] Gronemann formulates five "rules" which, in his opinion, guided Ps.-J.'s halakic choices.[10] However, Gronemann's "rules" are rather vague, and the fifth and final "rule" simply states that when halakic views were disputed, Ps.-J. chose one or other opinion, not following any particular principle but guided by some chance inspiration.[11] Gronemann's "rules" are so general that they cannot be said to clarify the principles that Ps.-J. followed when inserting halakic material into the biblical text,[12] but

---

view were the following: Ginsburger, *Pseudo-Jonathan* XII, XVII; Bloch, "Note sur l'utilisation des fragments" *REJ* 14 (1955) 30–31; Díez Macho, "The Recently Discovered," 239–245; Le Déaut, *Introduction à la Littérature Targumique,* 97–101. Other authors maintained that Ps.-J. is simply Onq. to which elements from the Palestinian Targumic tradition have been added. Among the proponents of this theory we may name Kahle, *Masoreten des Westens,* II, 12*; however, in *The Cairo Geniza,* 2nd ed., 202, Kahle leaves the question open; Grelot, "Les Targums du Pentateuque," *Semitica* 9 (1959) 88. Splansky maintains that Onqelos provided a basic text for Ps.-J.; cf. Splansky, *Targum Pseudo-Jonathan,* 40. Vermes proposes the view that Onq. depends on Ps.-J., either directly (Onq. being a revised version of a proto-Ps.-J.), or indirectly (Onq. and Ps.-J. deriving from a common Targumic source); cf. Vermes, "The Targumic Versions of Genesis IV 3–16," 98. Kuiper maintains that Ps.-J. is a strand of the Pal. Tg. tradition and that it has only minor contacts with Onq. Kuiper believes that these contacts are probably due to the transmission of the MSS by scribes who were acquainted with Onq. It is his view that Onq. is a redaction of the Pal. Tg. tradition of which Ps.-J. is a strand; cf. Kuiper, *The Pseudo-Jonathan Targum,* 106. See Kaufman's review of this work in *JNES* 35 (1976) 61–62. For further literature on the question of the relation of Ps.-J. to Onq., see Le Déaut, *Introduction à la Littérature Targumique,* 98–100.

[6]Shinan, "On the Characteristics of the Pseudo-Jonathan Targum," 111, maintains that the author or editor of Ps.-J. had at his disposal a Targumic text that was very similar to what we now find in Nf.

[7]Cf., e.g., Tal, *The Language of the Targum of the Former Prophets,* Introduction, 22–23. We shall reflect briefly on the language of Ps.-J. later on in this Introduction (p. 8).

[8]On the halakah in Onq., see P. Churgin, "The Halakah in Targum Onqelos" (in Hebrew), *Talpiyot* 2 (1945–46) 417–430; the same article appears in *Horeb* 9 (1946) 79–93. See also Berliner, *Targum Onkelos,* 224–245. In his article "Halakic Elements in the Neofiti Targum," *JQR* 66 (1975) 27–38, B. J. Bamberger studies the halakic material in Nf to the last three books of the Pentateuch.

[9]Cf. S. Gronemann, *Die Jonathan'sche Pentateuch-Uebersetzung in ihrem Verhältnisse zur Halacha,* 1879. Apart from Gronemann, and Revel, whom we shall mention later on, there were, until recently, no extended studies of the halakah in Ps.-J.; cf. Y. Maori, "The Relationship of Targum Pseudo-Jonathan to Halakic Sources" (in Hebrew), *Te'uda* 3 (1983) 235, n. 5.

[10]Ibid., 112–154.

[11]Ibid., 144.

[12]For a short critique of Gronemann's work, see the article by Maori (referred to in n. 9 above), p. 240.

his work has the merit of drawing attention to the great amount of halakic material in Ps.-J. and to the fact that a considerable amount of this material runs counter to accepted rabbinic positions.[13]

D. Revel has claimed that Ps.-J. was written with a view to counteracting the Karaites, who rejected the oral Torah and the traditions of the Rabbis.[14] The author maintained that in recording in the Targum halakot that were only commandments of the Sages, Ps.-J. gave these halakot the support of the biblical text, and thus counteracted the position of the Karaites.[15] However, Y. Maori[16] and E. Itzchaky[17] have shown conclusively that Revel's theory cannot be supported. Yet Revel's work is interesting in that it shows an awareness of the special nature of the halakah in Ps.-J. and tries to find a reason for the insertion of this halakic material in a Targum.

In the work just mentioned,[18] E. Itzchaky examined all the halakic material to be found in Ps.-J. and compared it with the halakah in parallel sources (in the other Targumim, the Mishnah, the halakic Midrashim, the Tosefta, the Talmuds, etc.). He found that there are about 120 halakot in Ps.-J. that differ from the accepted halakah.[19] He lists 120 texts where these unusual halakot occur,[20] and in the body of his work he studies the 120 texts, following the order in which these texts occur in the Bible. The author points out that since Ps.-J. deviates so frequently from the official halakah, this Targum may not have been intended for the ordinary uncultured Jew but for the Sages and for cultivated Jews.[21] This is an interesting point that fits in with Maori's view that Ps.-J. was not originally intended for an ordinary synagogue congregation, and with what Shinan says about Ps.-J.'s use of certain popular haggadic themes that would not be altogether suitable in the context of synagogue worship.[22] Itzchaky has done students of Ps.-J. a great service by identifying those texts where this Targum deviates from the accepted halakah, and by identifying the sources where we find parallels to these halakot.

Y. Maori has also studied the relationship between Ps.-J. and the halakic sources.[23] He has pointed out that the amount of halakic material in Ps.-J. far exceeds that which we find in Nf, for example, and that the halakic additions in Ps.-J. deviate from the normative halakah much more frequently than the halakic elements in the other Targums.[24] Ps.-J. adds specifications in verses where the other Targums do not (cf., e.g., Exod 22:22, 26; Lev 5:2; Deut 22:16). Ps.-J. usually produces a smooth text, even though what it adds to a verse may not be in complete harmony with the true meaning

---

[13]See, e.g., Gronemann, pp. 67, 69, 82, 96, and 113, where the author notes that Ps.-J. expresses halakic views that were not accepted by official Judaism.

[14]D. Revel, "Targum Jonathan to the Torah" (in Hebrew), *Ner Ma'aravi* 2 (1924–25) 77–122.

[15]Cf., e.g., ibid., 85–86.

[16]Cf. *art. cit.* (see above, n. 9), 241–244.

[17]E. Itzchaky, *The Halacha in Targum Jerushalmi I* (in Hebrew), Introduction, 7–10.

[18]See the preceding note.

[19]*Op. cit.* (see n. 17), Introduction, 18.

[20]Ibid., Introduction, 29–44.

[21]Ibid., 107.

[22]A brief discussion of Maori's view follows immediately. For Shinan's view see below pp. 5–8.

[23]See the article referred to in n. 9 above.

[24]Ibid., 236, 247.

of the scriptural text. Sometimes, however, the flow of the text is interrupted because of the wording of a halakah that has been introduced into the text (cf., e.g., Lev 22:13; 19:10; 20:10; 25:45).[25] It is difficult to find any consistency in Ps.-J.'s method of adding halakic regulations to the biblical text. Thus, for example, Ps.-J., in accord with the halakah, specifies that a widow and her brother-in-law who perform the duty of a levir must both make their declarations *in Hebrew* (cf. Ps.-J. Deut 25:7–8). In other contexts, however, where the Mishnah also says that Hebrew should be used Ps.-J. makes no reference to Hebrew. In Exod 21:6, Ps.-J., following the halakah, states that the slave's *right* ear is to be pierced. In the parallel text in Deut 15:17, the same Targum does not make this specification.[26]

The lack of consistency in Ps.-J. in the area of halakah is due to the fact that the author chose elements from different halakic sources and inserted them into a Palestinian Targum which was the basis of his work. Ps.-J. used written sources for his halakic additions, as one can gather from the fact that these additions are similar, not only in content but also in formulation, to the halakic midrashim. Ps.-J.'s wording in several texts indicates that the author borrowed from halakic midrashim (e.g., *Mekilta, Sifre*) which had already received a developed or even a definitive formulation. Ps.-J. is often so close to the *Mekilta* that we must conclude that the author knew that work in a form very similar to that which has come down to us. Thus, for example, the halakic elements in Ps.-J. Exod 21:2–11 are so similar to the *Mekilta* to the same verses that one cannot attribute the similarity to chance. Ps.-J. is much closer to the *Mekilta* than to any other halakic midrash that we know. With regard to the Babylonian Talmud, it is not clear that Ps.-J. knew this source in the form in which it exists today.[27]

Maori believes that Ps.-J. was from the beginning intended as a literary work that would be read by individuals rather than proclaimed in the synagogue. Consequently one cannot conclude that the anti-halakic material in that Targum is a proof that Ps.-J. dates from before the formulation of an authoritative halakah. The author of Ps.-J., even if the date of his work is late, could have used ancient sources, and could even have made his personal additions to the text.[28]

Ps.-J.'s halakic additions make it difficult for one who simply hears the text to understand it. Only one who reads the Targum can understand Ps.-J.'s method of interpretation. The halakic additions which Ps.-J. makes are often complicated and would not be understood by an ordinary synagogue congregation, which would be largely composed of simple people.[29] Maori ends his study by stating that many of the halakic additions in Ps.-J. may be the fruit of the *meturgeman's* independent thought, and he admits that much work remains to be done before we understand Ps.-J.'s system of incorporating halakic elements into his Targum.[30]

---

[25] Ibid., 237–239.

[26] Ibid., 240.

[27] Ibid., 244–246.

[28] Ibid., 247.

[29] Ibid., 247–248. These latter statements of Maori agree with Itzchaky's view that Ps.-J. was intended for the Sages rather than for uncultured Jews (see above, p. 3), and with Shinan's view that Ps.-J. contains certain haggadic elements that are unlikely to have been included in a Targum that was intended for use in the synagogue; see below, pp. 5–8.

[30] Ibid., 250.

The Haggadah in Ps.-J.

Although Ps.-J. shares many haggadic additions with the other Pal. Tgs., this Targum frequently handles this common haggadic material in a unique fashion. Besides, Ps.-J. contains hundreds of haggadic expansions that are not found in the other Targums, and it preserves many haggadic traditions whose sources are unknown.[31] A. Shinan, who has done much original work in the study of the haggadah in Ps.-J., and especially in Ps.-J. to Genesis, has contributed greatly to our appreciation of the manner in which the author of this Targum has incorporated haggadic elements into his work.[32]

Shinan notes, for example, that unlike the other Targums Ps.-J. frequently adds haggadic material *before* it begins the actual translation of the biblical text. Shinan calls such additions "pre-translation haggadot," and he notes that they occur occasionally in all the Pal. Tgs. (but not in Onq.); cf. e.g., Gen 28:10 (Nf,P,V,N,L,Ps.-J.); 30:22 (Nf,Nfmg,P,V,N,Ps.-J.). However, they are much more frequent in Ps.-J., and Shinan has studied twenty-eight texts in Genesis alone where Ps.-J. inserts "pre-translation haggadot." Furthermore, there is a qualitative difference between the "pre-translation haggadot" that are common to several Targums and those that are special to Ps.-J.[33]

Ps.-J. often takes up *the same haggadic tradition on several occasions,* adding elements of that tradition to different verses (which might be quite distant from each other). When joined together, these scattered elements form a self-contained story. See, for example, the haggadah about the seventy angels that Ps.-J. attaches to Gen 11:7, 8; Deut 32:8, 9; or the haggadah about a conspiracy to kill the Pharaoh which we find in Ps.-J. Gen 40:1, 21, 22. Such combinations would seem to be the product of systematic editing, and they belong to a later written stage in the development of the Targumic tradition.[34] Ps.-J. can also occasionally combine haggadic elements from different sources, or even from sources that are unknown to us, and weave them into a little narrative that forms a unit in itself. See, e.g., Ps.-J. Gen 14:13.[35]

Like several authors before him, Shinan notes that we sometimes find *contradictions* in the haggadic material that is incorporated into Ps.-J.[36] This is remarkable, since the *meturgeman* who translated the text in the synagogue would have tried to eliminate contradictions from the biblical text rather than create contradictions by adding opposing haggadic traditions to it. The fact that such contradictions are found in verses that are close to each other is particularly surprising. See, e.g., Gen 37:32 against 38:25, on the question of who took Joseph's coat to Jacob; or 45:4, which says that the mark of Joseph's circumcision was the sign by which his brothers would recognize him, against v. 12, which uses the fact that Joseph spoke Hebrew as a proof of his identity. Such contradictions in such limited contexts show that the author-editor of Ps.-J. was out of

[31]See M. M. Brayer, 1964, 201–231.
[32]See especially A. Shinan, 1979. We shall later refer to several articles by this same author, most of which are slightly modified versions of sections of the work just referred to.
[33]Ibid., 1, 39–83.
[34]Ibid., 1, 119–131; see also Shinan, 1985, 77–82.
[35]Cf. Brayer, 1964, 217–218.
[36]Shinan, 1979, 1, 132–146; idem, 1985, 82–86; cf. Ginsburger, *Pseudo-Jonathan*, XX; E. Levine, 1969, 118–119; idem, 1971A, 91–92.

touch with the reality of live presentation of the Targum in the synagogue, and that he composed his work at a relatively late date.

Ps.-J. differs from the Pal. Tgs. in that it *repeats haggadic traditions,* sometimes adding these traditions to verses that offer no basis for such additions.[37] We find, for example, that Ps.-J. says that Reuben "disarranged" the bed of Bilhah not only in Gen 35:22 and 49:4, where the Hebrew text offers an occasion for mentioning this crime, but also in Gen 37:29, where the biblical text does not invite the targumist to refer to Reuben's sin. Ps.-J. often incorporates into one verse of the Bible a haggadah which both Ps.-J. and the other Targums quote in connection with different verse. Thus, for example, Ps.-J., Nf (cf. Nfmg), P, V, N and L state in Gen 40:23 that Joseph trusted in Pharaoh's chief butler rather than in God. Ps.-J. alone records this tradition in Gen 40:14.

Since the *meturgeman* in the synagogue spoke to an audience that included simple, uneducated people, he had to speak in a language that was clear and unambiguous. When, for example, he wished to insert a haggadic element into the text, he had to present a full version of the haggadah so that it would be understood by all, and he could not be satisfied with mere *allusions* to it. This situation is reflected in the Pal. Tgs., which incorporate haggadic traditions that are clear and understandable. These Targums do not give fragmentary haggadot on the presumption that the audience who are familiar with the traditions will pick up the allusions. Ps.-J. is an exception, and in this Targum we find haggadic references which can be understood only by one who knows the whole haggadah. In Gen 18:21, for example, the reference to "the complaint of the maiden Peletith" makes no sense unless one knows the story in *PRE* which tells that Peletith, daughter of Lot, cried out to the Lord when the citizens of Sodom were about to burn her for giving bread to a poor man.[38] Such allusions to haggadot would not be made by a *meturgeman* in the synagogue, but by one who addressed an educated audience.[39]

The *content* of the haggadic material in Ps.-J. is often different from that which we find in the other Targums. Ps.-J. mentions many *popular beliefs,* including superstitious beliefs, and it presents material that is meant to edify the simple people and to encourage them in the practice of their religious observances. Thus, for example, though all the Targums tell of *miracles and wonders,* Ps.-J. distinguishes itself from the other Targums in that it shows a far greater interest in the miraculous and the wonderful. Thus, Ps.-J. alone tells of miracles that happened to Noah (Gen 9:20), Rachel (Gen 30:21), and Phinehas (Num 25:8). Ps.-J.'s interest in the miraculous is all the more intriguing, since the attitude of the Rabbis to the miraculous was ambivalent.[40]

Magic and witchcraft, which always had a fascination for the populace, have no place in the Targums. Ps.-J. is an exception, and we find, for example, that it mentions the "evil eye" (cf. Gen 42:5; Num 33:55), that it believes in the efficacy of a curse (cf. Gen 42:37; Num 21:24), and that it accepts that certain individuals have extraordinary powers (cf., e.g., Exod 7:15; 9:14).[41]

---

[37]Shinan, 1979, 1, 113–118; idem, 1985, 74–77.

[38]Cf. *PRE* 25 (182–183).

[39]Cf. Shinan, 1979, 1, 160–171; idem, 1982, 69–77.

[40]Cf. idem, 1979, 2, 247–252; idem, 1983B, 2, 419–423.

[41]Cf. idem, 1979, 2, 253–256; idem, 1983B, 424–425.

All the Targums mention *angels,* either to avoid anthropomorphisms or to solve theological problems to which the biblical text gives rise. Ps.-J. goes further and mentions unnamed ministering angels even where the verse being translated does not require this. This happens about thirty times in Ps.-J. (cf., e.g., Gen 1:26; Exod 14:24), whereas it occurs very rarely in the other Targums (see Gen 22:10 Ps.-J., Nf, P, V, N, L; 30:22 Nf, Nfmg, P, V, N; Deut 32:3 Nf, P, V, N, L). Unlike the other Targums, Ps.-J. attributes miraculous interventions on behalf of humans to angels (cf., e.g., Gen 27:25; Exod 15:2). Ps.-J. also mentions angels' names, e.g., Zagnugel in Exod 3:2, that are not known from traditional rabbinic texts, while the other Targums use only the names that are known from the Book of Daniel and from rabbinic literature in general. All the Targums mention destructive angels or demonic beings (cf., e.g., the different Pal. Tgs. of Exod 4:24-26), but Ps.-J. does so even in places where mention of such angels is not required by the text being translated (cf., e.g., the reference to "Sammael, the Angel of Death" in Gen 3:6). Ps.-J. thus shows a fondness for angels, both good angels and destructive beings, and in this it sets itself apart from the other Targums.[42]

The Targums, apart from Ps.-J., rarely use the *Ineffable Name* except when the biblical verse calls for this. See, however, Exod 32:25 and 33:6, where Ps.-J., Nf, and Frg. Tgs. all mention the Divine Name. Ps.-J. often mentions the Ineffable Name in contexts where the text being translated does not require this (see, e.g., Gen 4:15; Num 20:8), sometimes attributing supernatural powers to it (cf., e.g., Exod 2:21; Num 20:8). Thus it can be said that Ps.-J. distinguishes itself from the other Targums by the frequency with which it refers to the Ineffable Name and in the way in which it attributes miraculous power to that Name.[43]

Since the Targums were intended to be read in the synagogue in the presence of a devout congregation which included women and children, the targumists were careful to *avoid coarse and vulgar language,* especially in matters related to sex. In this matter, too, Ps.-J. goes its own way and introduces rather indelicate expressions into the text when these could easily have been omitted. Thus, for example, Ps.-J. alone says that Potiphar bought Joseph with the intention of indulging in homosexuality with him (cf. Gen 39:1), and in Gen 49:24 this Targum is alone in making explicit reference to Joseph's *membrum virile.* The fact that the author-editor of Ps.-J. incorporates such elements into his text shows that he did not intend it to be used in the synagogue, where the unnecessary mention of coarse or indelicate matters would be out of place.[44]

Ps.-J. sometimes makes statements that run *counter to beliefs that are commonly accepted* in all the other Targums. The Targums are careful to proclaim *the virtue of the Fathers* and to avoid any comment that might denigrate them. Ps.-J. however, can, for example, refer to Abraham's failure to believe (cf. Ps.-J. Gen 15:13), and that Targum's mention of the sin of the Golden Calf in Lev 16:4 does not add to the dignity of either the people or of Aaron.[45]

Ps.-J. sometimes uses names for God which do not occur in the other Targums. See,

[42]Cf. idem, 1979, 2, 256–279; idem, 1983C, 181–198; idem, 1983A, 143–150.
[43]Cf. idem, 1979, 2, 279–283; idem, 1983A, 151–153; idem, 1986, 112.
[44]Cf. idem, 1979, 2, 284–285; idem, 1983A, 153–154; idem, 1986, 112.
[45]Cf. idem, 1979, 2, 316–321; idem, 1986, 112.

for example, "The Place" (Exod 17:15), "Lord of the World" (cf. Gen 22:1, 5; 27:1; Exod 12:11, etc.), "Heaven" (Num 20:21; 26:1).[46]

Having considered the many differences that one finds between Ps.-J. and all the other Targums, Shinan concludes that Ps.-J. is not, strictly speaking, a Targum. It is based on a Palestinian Targum very similar to Neofiti, but the author-editor has added material that circulated in the schools or in popular lore, and he has produced a work very similar to a literary genre that can be called the "rewritten Bible."[47] *PRE*, the work on which Ps.-J. often depended, is basically a midrash, but it shares many of the characteristics of the "rewritten Bible." Similarly, Ps.-J. is basically a Targum, but it is moving in the direction of the genre "rewritten Bible" (in Aramaic).[48]

Shinan's conclusions are therefore very similar to those drawn by Itzchaky and Maori, who maintain that from the beginning Ps.-J. was not intended for the ordinary uneducated Jew who attended the synagogue, but was rather conceived as a literary work that was addressed to a more sophisticated audience.[49] The studies of these Israeli scholars show that Ps.-J. is a very special kind of work and that it deserves to be studied not just as a Targum among the Targums, but as a piece of literature that has its own special characteristics. The text of Ps.-J. as a whole must be examined with a view to discovering linguistic features of the work, its relationship to the midrashic and halakic sources which it uses, its relationship to the other Pal. Tgs. and to Onq.

The Language of Ps.-J.

We have already noted in passing that Ps.-J. is written in a hybrid language that combines elements of Palestinian Aramaic with features that are characteristic of Eastern Aramaic (see above, pp. 1–2). H. Seligsohn and J. Traub asserted that the dialect of the Fragment Targum and of Ps.-J. is Palestinian Aramaic, although this dialect, besides revealing many linguistic elements that are characteristic of Palestinian Aramaic, is also very similar to the language of Onq. The authors describe the dialect in question as a hybrid combination of Eastern and Western Aramaic.[50] G. Dalman concluded that the

---

[46]Cf. idem, 1979, 2, 339–340; idem, 1982–1983, 12–13.

[47]The term "Rewritten Bible" is used by Vermes in his study of the Life of Abraham as described in *Sefer Ha-Yashar*, see G. Vermes, 1961, 68–95. Shinan, "The Chronicles of Moses" (in Hebrew), *Ha-Sifrut* 24 (1977) 100–101, assigns *The Chronicles of Moses* to the genre "rewritten Bible." The authors of such works as *Sefer Ha-Yashar* and *The Chronicles of Moses* "rewrite" the Bible in that they deal very freely with the scriptural story, inserting haggadic developments, anticipating questions, and solving problems. Such ancient works as *Genesis Apocryphon* and the *Book of Jubilees* also belong to this genre of literature; cf. J. Dan, "The Hebrew Story at the Beginning of the Middle Ages" (in Hebrew), *Molad* 27 (1971) 129–130. See also G.W.E. Nickelsburg, "The Bible Rewritten and Expanded" in M. E. Stone (ed.), *Jewish Writings of the Second Temple Period* (Assen: Van Gorcum; Philadelphia: Fortress, 1984) 89–156.

[48]Cf. Shinan, 1979, 1, 130–131; 2, 355–356; idem, 1986, 114–115; idem, 1985, 81–82, 87. See also M. M. Brayer, "The Aramaic Pentateuch Targums and the Question of Avoiding Anthropomorphisms" (in Hebrew), *Talpiyot* 8 (1963) 521, who says of Ps.-J. that so much haggadic material has been added to it that it has become a midrash. E. Levine, 1972, 12, says that Ps.-J. "is closer to a commentary than to a translation."

[49]See above pp. 3 and 4.

[50]H. Seligsohn and J. Traub, 1857, 99.

language of Ps.-J. (and that of the Fragment Targum) does not consistently exhibit the characteristics of Palestinian Aramaic. It is rather a mixture of different dialects.[51] M. Neumark held that the language of Ps.-J. and the Fragment Targum is basically Palestinian Aramaic, although it contains some Babylonian elements also.[52] Neumark, who studied the vocabulary of the Pal. Tgs.—which, for him, included Ps.-J. and the Fragment Targum—accepted that these Targums used many words that are also found in Onq.[53]

J. A. Foster says that the language of Ps.-J. does not constitute a single dialect but rather combines elements of the dialects of the Targums and late rabbinic literature to create an artificial dialect of its own. Ps.-J. cannot be said to be a member of the Palestinian Targum family, although it utilizes Palestinian material.[54]

E. M. Cook has recently dedicated his doctoral dissertation to the study of the language of Ps.-J.[55] After a general discussion of the Pentateuchal Targums and their language (pp. 1–39), the author studies the relationship of Ps.-J. to Onq. (pp. 40–53), and reasserts what is the consensus among scholars, namely, that there is impressive evidence for Ps.-J.'s use of Onq. (p. 52). The author then offers a detailed examination of Ps.-J. to Deut 32 (pp. 54–106), and, among other things, he says in the conclusion of this study that although Ps.-J. and Nf/Frg. Tgs. show a common interpretative tradition, Ps.-J. at almost every turn shows the influence of Onq. even when the resulting conflate paraphrase is inelegant. Hence, Ps.-J. cannot be taken as a reliable witness to any other Targum text; it is completely reformed and recast (p. 105). The rest of Cook's work offers what the author calls a "Grammatical Sketch" of Ps.-J., examining, e.g., the morphology, the syntax, and the vocabulary of the text (pp. 107–265), and then compares the language of Ps.-J. with that of the Targums of the Writings (pp. 266–280).

Cook asserts that while Western Aramaic is very much to the fore in Ps.-J.,[56] there are many linguistic features in that Targum that are common in Eastern Aramaic. Thus, for example, Ps.-J., like Onq. and Tg. Jon., prefers to use the pronominal suffixes attached to the verb rather than denote the direct object by using the particle *yt* followed by the pronominal suffixes, as do the Pal. Tgs.[57] The form of the infinitive in the derived stems used by Ps.-J. is that employed by Onq. and Tg. Jon. rather than that of Western Aramaic, where the preformative *mem* is used in this form.[58] In the *Pe'al* imperfect form of the root *hwy*, "to be," the Pal. Tgs. use the longer form (*yhwy, thwy,* etc.) while Onq. and Tg. Jon. use the shorter form (*yhy, thy,* etc.). In Ps.-J. the shorter form predominates.[59] In the vocabulary of Ps.-J. we find many words that are characteristic of Eastern Aramaic.[60]

[51]G. Dalman, 1927, 32.
[52]M. Neumark, 1905, 13–16.
[53]Ibid., 19.
[54]Cf. J. A. Foster, 1969, 104, 112.
[55]See E. M. Cook, 1986.
[56]Ibid., 249, 259.
[57]Ibid., 135–136.
[58]Ibid., 193–194.
[59]Ibid., 209–210.
[60]Ibid., 249–259.

The numerous conflate readings to be found in Ps.-J. show that this Targum used Onq.[61] Ps.-J. is *not always consistent* in its translation of Hebrew words and expressions. Thus, for example, the Hebrew verb *ngd* (Hif.), "to tell, show," is translated in Onq. by the Pa'el of *hwy*, in the Pal. Tgs. by the Pa'el of *tny*, while Ps.-J. uses both words. Yet there is *a certain consistency* in Ps.-J.'s translations. For example, Hebrew *šwb*, "return," is regularly translated by *twb* in Onq., and by *hzr* in the Pal. Tgs. Ps.-J. almost always uses *twb*, rarely *hzr*. For the verb "to see" Ps.-J. prefers *hm'*, which is used in the Pal. Tgs., to *hz* of Onq. Onq. and Tg. Jon. use the particle *'ry*, "for, because," while the Pal. Tgs. use *'rwm*. Against 990 occurences of *'rwm* in Ps.-J., there are only six of *'ry*. Thus, some of the features used by Ps.-J. are typical of Onq./Tg. Jon., while others are typical of the Pal. Tgs., and others still are peculiar to Ps.-J.[62] Such a mixture of different features is peculiar to Ps.-J. among the Targums.[63]

Cook asserts that the Targums of the Writings bear a demonstrable linguistic relationship to Ps.-J.[64] The language of Ps.-J. (and of the Targums of the Writings) is a mixture of elements from several Aramaic dialects, and it can only be described as "artificial." That is to say, it is "a literary language concocted out of other literary languages, and bearing no relationship to any known Aramaic vernacular."[65] Yet this language is not a random mixture of elements from different dialects but a consistent mixture of such elements that constitutes a new dialect.[66]

Cook states that his study of the language of Ps.-J. leads him to conclusions that confirm the views of Shinan and Itzchaky, who, as we noted above, studied the contents of Ps.-J. The internal unity and self-consistency, coupled with contradiction, which Shinan noted for the contents of this Targum, are also found in its language. The language of Ps.-J. is that of educated laymen who lived after the Muslim conquest and who did not know any living Aramaic tradition. The author-editor wrote outside the sphere of rabbinic influence, and this would explain not only the considerable amount of halakah in Ps.-J., which, as Itzchaky shows, runs counter to accepted rabbinic views, but also the folkloristic elements (miraculous events, magic, lore about angels and demons) and the indelicate language to which Shinan drew attention.[67]

Cook does not mention that, as is the case with all the Pal. Tgs., we find that Greek

---

[61]Ibid., 46–48. On this question see also Splansky, *Targum Pseudo-Jonathan*, 1981, 23–40, who notes that these conflates occur throughout the entire Torah, and that they constitute undeniable evidence of the dependency of Ps.-J. on Onq. (39–40).

[62]The present writer has observed that Ps.-J. frequently differs from both Onq. and the Pal. Tgs. in its choice of word to translate a particular Hebrew word. We take the following examples from Genesis 1 alone. In Gen 1:9 Ps.-J. has *dwkt'*, "place," while Nf, P, and Onq. have *'tr'*; in Gen 1:10 Ps.-J. alone uses the word *ngybt'* for "dry land," while Nf, P, and Onq. have *ybšt'*; in 1:17 Ps.-J. uses *sdr*, "arranged," to translate Heb. *ntn*, "set" (RSV), whereas Nf and P employ *šwy*, and Onq. has *yhb*; in 1:24 Ps.-J. twice uses the word *bryy'*, lit. "created thing," to translate Heb. *hyh*, "living," whereas Nf, P, and Onq. use the Aramaic cognate of *hyh*; in 1:26 Ps.-J. alone translates Heb. *dmwt*, "likeness," by *dyywqn'*; in 1:27 Ps.-J. uses the same word, written *dywqn'*, to translate *ṣlm*, "image," against *ṣlm* of Onq., and *dmwt* of Nf, P, V, N, L.

[63]Cf. Cook, ibid., 48–51, 108, 272.

[64]Ibid., 109, 266, 276.

[65]Ibid., 277–278.

[66]Ibid., 36.

[67]Ibid., 36–37, 278–280.

words are frequently used in Ps.-J. Here we may content ourselves with drawing attention to what M. McNamara has said on this matter.[68]

The Date of Ps.-J.

Opinions expressed on the date of Ps.-J. range from the time of Ezra, or shortly after it,[69] to the time of the Crusades.[70] My purpose here is not to record or discuss all the views that have been expressed on this matter[71] but rather to state what is the more commonly accepted view today.

Although Ps.-J. certainly contains ancient traditions,[72] many recent authors argue that this Targum received its final form after the Arab conquest of the Middle East. D. M. Splansky believes that Ps.-J. dates from the ninth or tenth century. His main arguments may be summarized as follows: The reference to Adisha and Fatima in Ps.-J. Gen 21:21 should not be seen as an insertion. The source of the midrash could not have originated before 633 C.E at the earliest.[73] Ps.-J. makes use of *PRE* and both *Tanḥumas,* a fact which points to the ninth or tenth century as the time of Ps.-J.'s compilation.[74] The way in which Ps.-J. presents the midrash about Abraham's refusal to bless Ishmael in Gen 25:11 betrays an anti-Moslem polemic, and the reference to the blemish of Ishmael and the blemish of Esau in Ps.-J. Gen 35:22 can best be explained against the background of a world divided between Arabs and Christians.[75] There are possible indications in other texts in Ps.-J. (e.g., Gen 16:12; 25:13; 49:26; Num 7:87) that they date from a time after the Arab conquest.[76] The precise reference to calendar matters in Ps.-J. Gen 1:16 shows that this Targum was written in the second half of the ninth century at the earliest.[77]

Shinan has also stated his conviction that Ps.-J. depends on *PRE* and that it is the work of an author-editor who was active in the seventh or eighth century.[78] Le Déaut affirms that the final redaction of Ps.-J. could not have taken place before the eighth century.[79] Cook's examination of the language of Ps.-J. leads him to conclude that there are a number of indications which place Ps.-J. after the Muslim conquest of the East.[80]

---

[68]See vol. 1A, pp. 16–23.

[69]Cf. M. M. Kasher, *Torah Shelemah,* vol. 24, Introduction, p. 5, and p. 11 in the body of the work.

[70]Cf. D. Rieder, in the Introduction (p. 1) to his edition of the British Library MS of Ps.-J., to which we shall refer later on in this Introduction.

[71]This has been done by other writers; cf., e.g., Y. Komlosh, 1973, 43–46; Splansky, *Targum Pseudo-Jonathan,* 1981, 81–105. On the problem of dating the Targums in general, see A. York, 1974, 49–62; Le Déaut, 1974, 22–24.

[72]See the summary in Le Déaut, *Introduction,* 1966, 92–96.

[73]Cf. Splansky, *Targum Pseudo-Jonathan,* 1981, 89.

[74]Ibid., 91.

[75]Ibid., 92–94. Shinan, 1979, 1, 52; 2, 348–349, also sees a certain anti-Moslem polemic in Ps.-J. Gen 25:11. See also M. Ohana, 1975, 367–387.

[76]Splansky, ibid., 94–99.

[77]Ibid., 100–105.

[78]Cf. Shinan, 1979, 1, 171; 2, 356–357; idem, 1986, 113.

[79]Le Déaut, *Targum du Pentateuque,* 1978, *Genèse,* 37.

[80]Cook, *Rewriting the Bible,* 1986, 278; cf. also 36.

J. A. Foster, on the basis of the language of Ps.-J., states that this Targum may date from the eighth or ninth century.[81] The findings of these and other scholars who have dedicated special studies to both the content and the language of Ps.-J. allow us to accept with confidence the view that this Targum in its final form cannot be dated before the seventh or eighth century.

Manuscript and Editions

The only surviving MS of Ps.-J. is British Library Aramaic Additional MS 27031, and it is the text of this MS that is translated in the present work. The MS has been described by E. Levine[82] as follows:

> Br. Museum MS 27031 contains 231 folios written in a characteristic Italian hand.[83] The paper is well preserved, and except for the fact that the letters *Aleph* and *Mem, Ayin* and *Tet* are barely distinguishable, the manuscript is well written and easily read. There is neither punctuation nor vocalization of the Aramaic. Each verse begins with the first Hebrew word of the corresponding verse in the Hebrew Bible. . . .

On folio 231b we find the signature of the censor, Dominico Gierosolomitano, with the date 1598.[84] The MS was probably written in the sixteenth century,[85] and it belonged to the collection of Joseph Almanzi, a rich merchant of Padua who died in 1860. In this work we will refer to this MS as Lond. (London). One of the characteristics of Lond. is that in it the name *Elohim* is regularly written as *Eloqim*; see below n. 2 to Gen 1:1 (Ps.-J.). The Tetragram is represented either by the letter *he* or by a triple *yod*. Levine is quite right in stating, as we have just read, that the text of Lond. is unvocalized. Yet we do find occasional uses of vowel signs; cf., e.g., Gen 7:10 (*thw*); 38:25 (*'nnqy*); in Exod 4:7, where the word *ḥwbyh* occurs twice the vowel *sere* is placed under *beth* on both occasions; Exod 4:25 (*ḥtn'*); 15:10 (*šbt*); 23:24 (*qmty*); Lev 6:5 (*wylpy*).

The *editio princeps* of Pseudo-Jonathan (referred to in this work as *ed. pr.*) was printed in Venice in 1591 by Asher Forins for the publisher Juan Bragadin, and was re-

---

[81]Foster, 1969, 112. R. Hayward, 1989A, 1989B contests the view of those who claim that Ps.-J. must be regarded as post-Islamic in origin, and he believes that the evidence they use to support their claim is patient of other interpretations.

[82]E. Levine, "British Museum Aramaic Additional MS 27013," *Manuscripta,* 16 (1972) 3–13. The text quoted is on p. 3. The note (83) is added by the present writer.

[83]Cf. H. Barnstein, "A Noteworthy Targum MS. in the British Museum," *JQR* 11 (1899) 167–171, who says (p. 169) that the MS "is written in the peculiar and characteristic Italian hand." Cf. also M. Ginsburger, *Pseudo-Jonathan.* (Thargum Jonathan ben Usiël zum Pentateuch). Nach der Londoner Handschrift (Brit. Mus. Add. 27031), 1903, II. M. Steinschneider, *Hebraeische Bibliographie,* V (Berlin: Asher, 1862) 44, under no. 137, indicates, mistakenly, it would seem, that the script in the MS is German.

[84]Neither the name of the censor nor the date is clear. For some facts about the censor in question, see Le Déaut, 1978, *Genèse,* 32, n. 3. See also Dalman, "Die Handschrift zum Jonathantargum des Pentateuch, Add. 27031 des Britischen Museum," *MGWJ* 41 (1897) 455.

[85]Thus, e.g., Ginsburger, *Pseudo-Jonathan,* 1903, II. Contemporary scholars also assign a sixteenth-century date to the MS; cf., e.g., Le Déaut, 1978, *Genèse,* 31; E. Levine, "A Study of Targum Pseudo-Jonathan to Exodus," *Sefarad* 31 (1971) 28. Shinan, 1979, Introduction, 16, says that it dates from the fifteenth century.

printed several times.[86] It is not based on Lond. but on a MS that belonged to the Foa family of Reggio. This latter MS was similar to but not identical with Lond. Le Déaut says that there are so many omissions and so many errors common to the two MSS that they must both derive from the same source, not in the sense that they were both copied from the same MS, but in the sense that they both derive, through a process of copying, from the same original.[87] Yet there are verses or parts of verses that are omitted in Lond. but present in *ed. pr.,* and vice versa, and the two MSS have different readings on occasion.[88] In the edition of Lond. produced by E. G. Clarke et al., to which we shall later refer, the verses that are omitted from Lond., or from Lond. and *ed. pr.,* are listed on pp. xiii–xiv.

Lond. was published for the first time in 1903 by M. Ginsburger.[89] This edition contained many errors to which scholars have drawn attention,[90] and Ginsburger frequently omitted words or modified the text without alerting the reader. But although Ginsburger's text of Ps.-J. cannot be relied on to offer a faithful copy of Lond., his work still remains valuable because of the detailed Introduction (pp. I–XX) and because of the footnotes, which often refer to parallels to Ps.-J.'s additions to the biblical text.

D. Rieder undertook a new edition of Lond.,[91] which has been well received by the reviewers in spite of a few flaws that can be found in it.[92] Rieder's work has only a short Introduction, and even that is elementary in character and of no help to scholars. Rieder also takes some liberties with the text, but he always draws attention to his emendations, so that the reader always knows the exact text of Ps.-J. The editor's frequent references to the *ed. pr.* enables the reader to recognize the best reading in cases of doubt.

Another recent edition of Lond. is that of Díez Macho in the *Biblia Polyglotta Matritensia,* Series IV.[93] In an ample apparatus the editors give variants from the *ed. pr.,* drawing attention even to such things as the variations in the use of *matres lectionis* between Lond. and *ed. pr.* They often note that the reading of *ed. pr.* is to be preferred

---

[86]I. H. Petermann, *De Duabus Pentateuchi Paraphrasibus Chaldaicis,* 1829, 1, 5–6, lists all the known editions of Pseudo-Jonathan.

[87]Le Déaut, 1978, *Genèse,* 33–34.

[88]Cf. Dalman, 1897, 455; Ginsburger, 1903, *Pseudo-Jonathan,* III–IV; Levine, 1971B, 29–30; idem, 1972, 4–5; Le Déaut, 1978, *Genèse,* 33–34.

[89]M. Ginsburger, *Pseudo-Jonathan,* 1903 (see above n. 83).

[90]Cf., e.g., P. Esterlich, "El Targum Pseudojonthán o Jerosolimitano," in *Studi sull' Oriente e la Bibbia offerti a P. Giovanni Rinaldi* (Genoa: Studio e Vita, 1967) 191–195; D. Rieder, "On the Ginsburger Edition of the 'Pseudo-Jonathan' Targum of the Torah" (in Hebrew), *Leshonenu* 32 (1968) 298–303.

[91]D. Rieder (ed.), *Pseudo-Jonathan: Targum Jonathan Ben Uziel on the Pentateuch Copied from the London MS. British Museum add. 27031* (Jerusalem: Salomon, 1974). This edition has been republished, together with a Hebrew translation and notes, in two volumes (Jerusalem, 1984–85).

[92]Cf. M. L. Klein, "A New Edition of Pseudo-Jonathan," *JBL* 94 (1975) 277–279; N. Allony, "The Jerusalem Targum Pseudo-Jonathan. Rieder's Edition" (in Hebrew), *Beth Miqra* 62 (1975) 423–425.

[93]A. Díez Macho, *Biblia Polyglotta Matritensia. Series IV. Targum Palaestinense in Pentateuchum. Additur Targum Pseudojonatan ejusque hispanica versio.* Vol. 1 *Genesis,* 1989; vol. 2 *Exodus,* 1980; vol. 3 *Leviticus,* 1980; vol. 4 *Numeri,* 1977; vol. 5 *Deuteronomium,* 1980. Editio critica curante A. Díez Macho, adjuvantibus L. Díez Merino, E. Martínez Saiz. Targum Palaestinensis testimonia ex variis fontibus: R. Griño (Madrid: Consejo Superior de Investigaciones Científicas, 1977–1989).

to that of Lond. They print the exact text of Lond., and where they consider that defective, they place a dot under the particular letter or letters to show that the reader should consult the apparatus. They often refer to Rieder's edition, especially with a view to drawing attention to his emendations of Lond. The fact that the text of Ps.-J. is printed in conjunction with Nf and the Frg. Tgs. makes comparison with these texts very easy. The Spanish translation of Ps.-J. given alongside the Aramaic text is very reliable, and it is accompanied by brief notes that help even those who do not read Aramaic to get an idea of the text that is being translated.

A third modern edition of Ps.-J. has been produced by E. G. Clarke and others in conjunction with the publishing of a Concordance to Ps.-J.[94] Clarke, in his Introduction (pp. vii–viii) mentions Rieder's edition and notes that it is not free from errors. Although the Introduction is dated October 1983, Clarke does not inform his readers that Díez Macho had produced an edition of Ps.-J., although he refers in p. xviii, footnote 8, to vol. 4 (Numbers) of Díez Macho's work. Clarke states that his main purpose in presenting the text of Ps.-J. was to enable his readers to know what text was used as a basis for the concordance. The editors have aimed at providing a faithful reproduction of the London MS, even to the extent of reproducing errors. They do, however, list in the Introduction (pp. ix–xiv) textual errors, and they draw attention to places where sections of the translation are omitted in the MS. Abbreviations in the MS have been completed according to the readings of the *ed. pr.* It is to be noted that neither Rieder nor Díez Macho nor Clarke reproduces the lemmata that are present in the MS.

---

[94]E. G. Clarke, with collaboration by W. E. Aufrecht, J. C. Hurd, and F. Spitzer, *Targum Pseudo-Jonathan of the Pentateuch: Text and Concordance* (Hoboken, New Jersey: Ktav, 1984).

Targum Pseudo-Jonathan: Genesis
Translation

CHAPTER 1

1. At the beginning[1] God[2] created the heavens and the earth. 2. The earth was without form and void, *desolate of people*[3] *and empty of all animals;*[4] darkness was upon the surface of the deep and a *merciful* wind[5] *from before* God was *blowing* over the surface of the water. 3. God said: "Let there be light *to illuminate the world:*[6] and *immediately*[7] there was light. 4. God saw[8] that the light was good; and God separated the light from the darkness. 5. And God called the light Day,[9] *and he made it so that the inhabitants of the world might labor during it:*[10] and he called

Notes, Chapter 1

[1]Lit.: "From the beginning" (*mn 'wwl'*). Ps.-J. is alone among the Targums in using the idiom *mn 'wwl'* to translate Heb. *br'šyt*. We find this Aramaic idiom in Gen 13:3 (Ps.-J.), in Tg. Jon. Isa 1:26; 40:21; 41:26 and in Tg. Job 20:4; Ps 37:20. See also Tg. Ezek 16:55 (where we find *l'wl'* twice) and Hos 9:10 (*b'wl*). On the Targumic renderings of *br'šyt*, see P. Schäfer, 1971–72, 9; Shinan, 1979, 2, 203–204; R. Kasher, 1986, 3–4. On the rabbinic interpretation of *br'šyt*, see J. Bowker, 1969, 100–102; Schäfer, 1971, 161–166. On some interpretations of Gen 1:1 in patristic literature, see P. Prigent, 1974, 391–397, especially 394–397.

[2]*Ed. pr.*: "The Lord (*yy*)." When Elohim refers to the God of Israel, the Targums usually replace it by the Tetragrammaton in order to avoid the plural form "Elohim," which might be taken by some to indicate a plurality of Gods; cf. Maybaum, 1870, 26–28; Chester, 1986, 330–338. Lond. employs the name Elohim more frequently than the other Targums, but it uses the reverential form Eloqym (*'lqym*). M. Eskhult (1981, 137–139) maintains that *'lqym* was read as *'el qayyam*, "the living, eternal God," or (less likely) *'el qeyam*, "the God of the Covenant." I do not find Eskhult's proposal convincing.

[3]Lit.: "children of men."

[4]Ps.-J., like Nf, P, V, and N, gives an Aramaic transcription of the words *tôhu wabôhu*. These Targums then explain each of these terms, using "desolate and empty," the words used by Onq. to translate *tôhu wabôhu*. Shinan claims that the additions made by Ps.-J. and the Pal. Tgs. are prompted by Ps 104:14 (which mentions grass, cattle, plants and men who cultivate the earth), and possibly by Gen 2:5; cf. Shinan, 1977B, 229–230. See also Jer 4:23, 25; 33:10. On the translation of *tôhu wabôhu* in the Targums, see Schäfer, 1971–72, 10.

[5]Or possibly, "a spirit *of mercy*." But since the verb used with this phrase is "blow," I prefer "wind" to "spirit." Onq.: "a wind from before the Lord." None of the Targums gives a literal translation of *ruaḥ Elohim*, "a mighty wind" (*New American Bible*), a phrase which the Targumists regarded as too anthropomorphic. The phrase "a merciful wind" occurs again in Gen 8:1 (Nf, P, V, N, L, CTg B, Ps.-J.).

[6]Instead of *'lm'*, "the world," *ed. pr.* has *'l'h*, "the upper regions." Ps.-J. is alone in making this addition to the biblical verse. The rabbis debated whether the light created on the first day (Gen 1:3) was the same as the light of the heavenly bodies that were created on the fourth day (vv. 14–15). R. Eleazer held that the two lights were essentially different, while the Sages held that they were identical; cf. *b. Hag.* 12a (64). See also *j. Berak.* 8, 12b; *Gen. R.* 3,6; 42,3. Since the heavenly bodies mentioned in Gen 1:14-15 were made "to give light upon the earth" (v. 15), it would seem that Ps.-J.'s addition of the words "to illuminate the world" in v. 3 was made in the light of the opinion attributed to the Sages in the *Hagigah* text just referred to. J. Cook (1983, 47–49) suggests that Ps.-J.'s addition may have been made with a view to refuting the heretical doctrine of emanation which finds expression in *Gen. R.* 3,4.

[7]The word "immediately" is added only by Ps.-J. By adding this word, Ps.-J., like *b. Hag.* 12a (64) (see preceding note), is asserting that light was created on the first day, even though the heavenly bodies were not created until the fourth day.

[8]Ps.-J., like Onq., does not avoid the anthropomorphic statement "God saw." The Targums are not consistent in translating the verb *r'h* when it has God as subject. They sometimes translate it as *gly qdm*, "it was manifest before," as do Nf and P in our present verse; cf. M. Klein, 1982, 95–96.

[9]The word *ymm'* used by Ps.-J. and Onq., and the word *'ymm'* used by Nf and P, mean "daytime" rather than "day" (a period of twenty-four hours), for which the Targums use *ywm'*. See Jastrow, 51 and 580; Grossfeld, 1988, 43, n. 4.

[10]The words "so that they might labor during it" are omitted by the scribe of Lond., but they are added in the margin.

the darkness Night, *and he made it that creatures might rest during it.*[11] And there was evening and there was morning, one day.[12] 6. God said, "Let the firmament be in the midst of the waters, and let it separate the *upper* waters from the *lower* waters."[13] 7. God made[14] the firmament—*its thickness being three finger breadths*[15]—*between the limits of the heavens and the waters of the ocean,* and he separated the waters that were under the firmament from the waters that were above *in the reservoir*[16] of the firmament. And it was so. 8. And God called the firmament Heaven. And there was evening and there was morning, a second day. 9. God said, "Let the *lower* waters *that remain* under the heavens be gathered together to one place, and let *the earth be dried up*[17] *so that* the dry land may appear." And it was so. 10. And God called the dry land[18] Earth, and the *gathering place* of the waters he called Seas. And God saw that it was good.[19] 11. God said, "Let the earth grow vegetation, plants *whose seed*[20] *is sown,* and fruit trees that produce fruit in which is their seed, each according to its kind, upon the earth." And it was so. 12. The earth brought forth vegetation, plants *whose seed is sown,* <according to their kinds,>[21] and *fruit* trees producing fruit <in which is their seed>, according to their kinds. And God saw that it was good. 13. And there was evening and there was morning, a third day. 14. God said, "Let there be lights in the firmament of the

Notes, Chapter 1

[11]According to *b. Erub.* 65a (453), Rab Judah observed that "Night was created for nought but sleep." It is probable, however, that the two statements in Ps.-J. (daytime for humans to work, nighttime for creatures to rest) are based on Ps 104:20-23. Ps.-J.'s first assertion is similar to v. 23 of the psalm, while his second statement, if taken to mean that wild animals are at ease at night and can go in search of food, corresponds to vv. 21-22; cf. Schmerler, 1932, 11; Shinan, 1977B, 231.

[12]Ps.-J. and Onq. translate the words "one day," literally, while Nf, P, V, and N translate them as "the first day," thus bringing "one day" (cf. v. 5) into line with "second day," "third day," etc., of vv. 8, 13, etc. The use of "one day" in v. 5 was the occasion of some speculation (cf. *Gen. R.* 3, 8; Josephus, *Ant.* 1 § 29; *Gen. R.* 3,9; *b. Nazir* 7a (21).

[13]Onq. translates "the waters from the waters" literally. The Pal. Tgs. and Ps.-J. specify that "the *upper* waters and the *lower* waters" are being referred to. *Gen. R.* 4,3 refers to the "upper waters" that are above the firmament. *PRE* 4 (21) explains that the firmament separates "the waters above and the waters below."

[14]Onq. and Ps.-J. translate Heb. *'sh,* "make," by the corresponding Aramaic verb *'bd,* while Nf and P use the verb *br',* "create." The same happens in vv. 16, 25, and 26. But in v. 31 all the Targums employ *'bd,* "make."

[15]Ben Zoma concluded that there is "only a bare three fingers' breadth" between the waters above and the waters below; cf. *b. Hag.* 15a (92); see also *Gen. R.* 2,4, where the figure given is "two or three fingerbreadths," and *j. Hag.* 2, 77a-b, where the measurement is "about a wide handsbreadth." Different opinions about the thickness of the firmament are expressed in *Gen. R.* 4,5 and *b. Pesah.* 94a (502–503).

[16]*bqwbt'. b. Ta'an.* 8b (34) records the opinion of a Tanna who taught that "there is in heaven a kind of chamber (*kmyn qwbh*) from which the rain issues."

[17]The addition "let the earth be dried up," which is special to Ps.-J., implies that even when the waters were gathered into one place, the earth needed to be dried up before it was fit to be inhabited.

[18]Onq., Nf, and P translate Heb. *ybsh,* "dry land," by its Aramaic cognate *ybst'.* Ps.-J. uses the synonym *ngybt'* (read thus with *ed. pr.* rather than *ngbyt'* of Lond.), from the root *ngb,* "be dry," which the same Targum had used in v. 9 (see preceding note).

[19]Ps.-J., following Onq., translates *ky twb,* "that it was good," literally. Compare Nfmg and P. See below, n. 55 to v. 31.

[20]The word for "seed" (*byzr'*), which Ps.-J. uses twice in this verse and again in vv. 12 and 29ab, is an Eastern Aramaic form which is frequent in the Babylonian Talmud; cf. Jastrow, 154; Levy 1, 89; Cook, 1986, 251.

[21]The phrases "according to their kinds" in the first part of this verse and "in which is their seed" in the second part are omitted in Lond. and *ed. pr.,* probably through scribal error.

heavens to separate the day from the night, and let them serve as signs[22] and as *festival times,*[23] *and for counting*[24] *the reckoning* of days, and for *sanctifying the beginnings of months and the beginnings* of years,[25] *the intercalations of months and the intercalations of years, the solstices, the new moon, and the cycles (of the sun).*[26] 15. And let them serve as lights in the firmament of heaven to give light upon the earth." And it was so. 16. God made the two great lights, *and they were equal in glory*[27] *for twenty-one hours*[28] *less six hundred and seventy-two parts of an hour. After that the moon spoke with a slanderous tongue*[29] *against the sun, and it was made smaller. And he appointed the sun which was* the greater light to rule over the day, and *the moon which was* the lesser light <to rule over the night>,[30] and the stars. 17. And God *arranged* them *in their courses* in the firmament of heaven to give light upon the earth, 18. and to *minister*[31] in the day and in the night, and to separate the light *of the day* from the darkness *of the night.* And God saw that it was

Notes, Chapter 1

[22]While Onq., Nf, P, V, and N translate Heb. *'tt,* "signs," by its Aramaic cognate (*'tyn*), Ps.-J. goes its own way and uses the word *symnyn,* which is the Gr. *semeion.* On the translation of Heb. *'wt* in the Pentateuchal Targums, see Maher, 1988, 1, 313–315.

[23]*Gen. R.* 6, 1 takes HT *lmw'dym,* "for seasons," to refer to the three pilgrimage festivals.

[24]*lmmny bhwn* = Onq. The final part of this verse in Onq. reads: "and *for counting* the days and the years." The interpretation of Onq. is therefore of the same type as that of the Pal. Tgs. and Ps.-J., although Onq. does not add details to the text as do the other Targums.

[25]*Gen. R.* 6,1 states that the moon was created "in order to sanctify new moons and years thereby" (cf. *PRK* 5,1). According to *b. Hul.* 60b (331), Israel is to reckon the days and the years by the moon. According to *Gen. R.* 6,1, "for days and years" refers to the beginnings of the months and to the sanctification of the years.

[26]Ps.-J. mentions four things (the intercalation of years, the solstices, the new moon, and the cycles of the sun) which are not mentioned in any of the other Targums of this verse. The "intercalation of months" is mentioned in Ps.-J. and Nf. Of the four things that are special to Ps.-J., three (the intercalation of years, the solstices, and the cycles) are mentioned (among other terms) in *PRE* 8 (52), and the technical terms used are the Heb. cognates of those used in Ps.-J. The fourth term, *mwld syhr',* "the new moon," occurs several times in its Hebrew form in *PRE* 7 (41–51). See also Tg. 1 Chron 12:33, where several of the technical terms used by Ps.-J. in our present verse also occur. On the words *mhzwr,* "cycle of the sun," and *tqwpwt (šmš'),* "solstices," used here by Ps.-J., see Cook, 1986, 241, 247. On the Targumic renderings of Gen 1:14, see M.M. Kasher, *Torah Shelemah,* vol. 24, 225–227.

[27]Lit.: "in their glory." The equality of the two lights is implied in HT: "the two great lights." *PRE* 6 (31) says of the two luminaries that "one was not greater than the other. They were equal in height, in appearance, and in brilliance." *1 Enoch* 72,37 says that the sun and moon were originally equal in size. *Gen. R.* 6,3 expresses the view that by speaking of "the lesser light" (Gen 1:16) God cast a slur on the moon.

[28]We read "hours" (*š'yn*) with Lond., rather than "years" (*šnyn*) of *ed. pr.* On the calendar details expressed in this verse in Ps.-J., see Splansky, 1981, 100–105. According to Splansky, Ps.-J.'s version of Gen 1:16 shows that the author had precise knowledge of calendar calculations which were not known to the Jews before 835 C.E. There is no known source for Ps.-J.'s statement that the sun and moon were equal for twenty-one hours less 672 parts of an hour; cf. Brayer, 1964, 204.

[29]Lit.: "with triple tongue." The same idiom occurs in Ps.-J. Gen 49:23; Lev 9:2, 3; 19:16; Deut 27:24. In *b. Arak.* 15b (89) the idiom is explained as follows: "(the triple tongue) kills three persons: him who tells (the slander), him who accepts it, and him about whom it is told."

[30]The words "to rule over the night" are omitted in the text of Lond. and in *ed. pr.,* but they are added in the margin of Lond. *PRE* 6 (31) says that it was as a result of rivalry between the two luminaries that God made one larger than the other (see above, n. 27) and appointed the lesser one to rule the night. According to *Gen. R.* 6,4, the moon humbled itself to rule by night; cf. also *b. Hul.* 60b (331), which says that God ordered an atonement to be made for him for making the moon smaller. This tradition is mentioned in Ps.-J. Num 28:15.

[31]Both Lond. and *ed. pr.* use the verb *šmš,* "minister," which is also the verb used in P. But the verb *šlt,* "rule," is used in the marginal gloss in Lond. This latter verb is also used in Onq. and Nf.

good. 19. And there was evening and there was morning, the fourth day. 20. God said, "Let *the alluvial mud*[32] *of* the waters swarm forth a swarm of living creatures, and birds that fly, *whose nests are* on the earth, and *the course of their flight* across *the air of*[33] the firmament of heaven."[34] 21. God created the great sea monsters, *Leviathan and his mate,*[35] *that are designated for the day of consolation,*[36] and all living creatures that creep, that the *clear* waters[37] swarmed forth, according to their kinds, *kinds that are clean and kinds that are not clean,*[38] and all birds *that fly with wings,* according to their kind, *kinds that are clean and kinds that are not clean.* And God saw that it was good. 22. [39] 23. And there was evening and there was morning, a fifth day. 24. God said, "Let the *clay*[40] *of* the earth bring forth living creatures according to their kind, *kinds that are clean and kinds that are not clean,*[41] cattle and creeping things, and creatures of the earth according to their kind." And it was so. 25. God made the beasts of the earth according to their kind, *kinds that are clean and kinds that are not clean,* and the cattle according to their kind, and all the creeping things of the earth according to their kinds, *kinds that are clean and kinds that are not clean.* And God saw that it was good. 26. And God said to *the angels who minister before him,*[42] *who were created on the second day of the*

Notes, Chapter 1

[32] The Hebrew form of the word used here by Ps.-J. (*rqq*) occurs in *b. Hul.* 27b (141) and *b. Erub.* 28a (191), where the view is expressed that birds were created out of the alluvial mud (*hrqq*).

[33] Onq. and P translate *'lpny* (RSV: "across") by the corresponding Aramaic idiom (*'l 'py*). Ps.-J. uses *'l 'wyr,* "across *the air.*" Nf combines the reading of Onq.-P with that of Ps.-J.

[34] Having referred to the birds that fly, Ps.-J. explains that the biblical words "above the earth," which might seem unnecessary, mean that the birds build their nests on the earth. The author then balances his sentence by explaining that "across the firmament" refers to the course of the birds' flight in the air.

[35] Since the biblical text says that God created the "sea monsters" (plur.), the midrash takes the monsters to be Leviathan and Behemoth, the monsters mentioned in Job 40:15, 25 (English: 41: 1); see *Gen. R.* 7,4; *1 Enoch* 60,7–8; *2 (Syriac) Baruch* 29,4.

[36] See *b. B. Bat.* 75a (299): "The Holy One ... will in time to come make a banquet for the righteous from the flesh of Leviathan." Cf. *ibid.* 74b (296), where it is said that the flesh of the female monster will be preserved "in salt for the righteous in the world to come." See also *PRE* 10 (70, 72); *2 (Syriac) Baruch* 29,4; *4 Ezra* 6,49-52. On the time of consolation, see M. Pérez Fernández, 1981, 109–111. The reference in Nf (Gen 1:21) to *two* monsters and Ps.-J.'s expansion about Leviathan and his mate show that these two Targums knew the traditions that are recorded in the midrashic and apocalyptic texts mentioned in this and the preceding notes; cf. R. Bascom, "The Targums: Ancient Reader's Helps?" *The Bible Translator* 36 (1985) 301–316, especially 305–308.

[37] "*Clear* waters," as opposed to "*alluvial mud of* the waters" in the preceding verse.

[38] *PRE* 9 (60) says that on the fifth day God created all kinds of winged fowl, unclean and clean, all kinds of fish, unclean and clean, all kinds of locusts, unclean and clean. In our present verse Ps.-J. explains that *lmynhm* and *lmynhw,* "according to their/its kind," both refer to clean and unclean creatures. This Targum follows the same procedure in vv. 24a, 25ab, but not in other similar texts; cf., e.g., v. 24b ("creeping things" which are mentioned here are all unclean; cf. *PRE* 11 [75]); 6:20; 7:14.

[39] Omitted in Lond. and *ed. pr.*

[40] The word *grgyšt',* which we translate as "clay," is used again by Ps.-J., and only Ps.-J., in additions to the biblical text in Gen 4:10; Lev 6:21; 15:19. The same word is used in Tg. Jon. 1 Kings 7:46. According to Ps.-J., living creatures were created from three different materials: from "*the alluvial mud* of the waters" (Gen 1:20), from "*clear* waters" (v. 21), and from "*clay of the* earth" (v. 24).

[41] *PRE* 11 (74): "On the sixth day (God) brought forth from the earth all kinds of animals, male and female, clean and unclean." See above, n. 38.

[42] The fact that God's words, "let us make," are in the plural, and might be taken to indicate that there is a plurality in the Godhead, gave rise to the opinion that God spoke these words to the angels; cf. *Gen. R.* 8,4; *b. Sanh.* 38b (242). Of the

creation of the world, [43] "Let us make man in our image, in our likeness, [44] and let them have dominion over the fish [45] of the sea, and over the birds *that are in the air of the heavens,* and over the cattle, and over all the earth, and over every creeping thing that creeps upon the earth." 27. And God created Adam in his own likeness, in the image of God he created him, *with two hundred and forty-eight members,* [46] *with six* [47] *hundred and sixty five nerves, and he formed a skin over him, and filled it with flesh and blood;* [48] male and female *in their appearance* [49] he created them. 28. God blessed them, and God said to them, "Increase and multiply and fill the earth *with sons and daughters,* and become powerful *in possessions* [50] upon it, and have dominion over the fish of the sea and over the birds of the heavens, and over every *creeping* animal [51] that creeps upon the earth." 29. God said, "Behold I have given to you every plant whose seed is sown, that is upon the face of all the earth, and every *unfruitful* tree *for the requirements of building and for burning; and (every tree)* on which there is fruit [52] whose seed is sown shall be yours for food. [53] 30. To

Notes, Chapter 1

four Targums (Onq., Nf, P, Ps.-J.) of Gen 1:26, only Ps.-J. has been influenced by this midrash. On other occasions, too, Ps.-J. specifies that words of God which are recorded in the plural in the Bible, were, in fact addressed to angels (cf. Ps.-J. Gen 3:22; 11:7; see also 18:20, where Ps.-J. tells us that God spoke to the angels). Rabbinic sources explained the words "let us make" in such a way as to exclude the Christian claim that these words pointed to the Trinity. Besides the texts from *Gen. R.* and *b. Sanh.* just mentioned, see *Gen. R.* 8,3; 8,9; *j. Berak.* 9,12d. See further, Bowker, 1969, 106–108; Schäfer, 1975, 88–89; J. Cook, 1983, 51–52.

[43]The day on which the angels were created was a matter of dispute. Ps.-J.'s view that they were created on the second day is also expressed in *Gen. R.* 1,3; 3,8 and *PRE* 4 (20). See further L. Ginzberg, *Legends,* 5, 20–21, n. 61; Bowker, 1969, 108.

[44]Ps.-J. differs from the other Targums (Onq., Nf, P) in its translation of the words "after our likeness." According to Jastrow (297), the word used by Ps.-J. (*dyywqn'*) is a reverential transformation of *'yqwn',* which, in turn corresponds to Gr. *eikôn,* "image." Levy's view (1, 170) is that Ps.-J.'s word is composed of two Greek words, *dyo,* "two," and *eikôn.* Ps.-J., and Ps.-J. alone, uses *dywqn'* again as a translation of *dmwt* in Gen 5:1, and as a translation of *ṣlm,* "image," in Gen 1:27; 9:6, and in Targumic additions to Lev 26:1 and Deut 21:23.

[45]Lond. uses the same word (*nwn*) as Onq., Nf, and P. *Ed. pr.* has *kwwr,* a word which occurs again in Ps.-J. Gen 48:16, in both Lond. and *ed. pr.,* and which is an Eastern Aramaic form (cf. Cook, 1986, 254).

[46]The belief that there are 248 members in the human body is expressed in *m. Ohol.* 1,8; *b. Mak.* 23b (169); *Ned.* 32b (98); *ARN* A 16.

[47]Both Lond. and *ed. pr.* read "six." Later editions (e.g., Walton) read "three." We know of no source for the view that there are 665 (365) nerves in the human body. J. Cook (1983, 52–53) believes that Ps.-J. introduced the view that the human body is made up of 248 members and 365 nerves in order to draw a parallel between human beings and the Torah, which contains 248 commands and 365 prohibitions. By drawing this parallel, Ps.-J., according to Cook, was showing that men and women, like the Torah, are good. Thus Ps.-J. was disproving the Christian teaching of the sinfulness of all human beings.

[48]Cf. Ezek 37:6.

[49]There was a tradition that God created the first man with two faces (and that one of these was destined for the woman); cf. *Gen. R.* 8,1; *b. Berak.* 61a (381); *Erub.* 18a (123).

[50]The source of this addition is unknown; cf. Schmerler, 1932, 21.

[51]See *b. Sanh.* 59b (405), where it is said that the words "every living creature that moves upon the earth" (Gen 1:28) refer to the serpent.

[52]Schmerler, 1932, 21–22, and Schäfer, 1971–72, 24, explain that although the biblical verse refers only to fruit trees ("every tree with seed in its fruit"), Ps.-J. focuses on "*every*" tree and takes the text to refer also to trees that do not bear fruit. Shinan does not accept this explanation of Ps.-J.'s addition. He notes that *Jubilees* (2,7) also states that all trees were created on the third day, and he suggests that Ps.-J.'s addition was made under the influence of the words "fruit trees and all cedars" in Ps 148:9, where "all cedars" may be taken to represent trees that do not bear fruit (cf. Shinan, 1977B, 230).

[53]*lmykl*; = Onq.; Nf, P: *lmzwn.* On the translation of Heb. *'kl,* "food," in the Targums, see Cowling, 1968, 167–168.

every beast of the earth, to every bird of the heavens, and to everything that creeps upon the earth, in which there is the breath of life, (I give) every green plant." [54] And it was so. 31. And God saw all that he had made, and behold, it was very good. [55] And there was evening and there was morning, a sixth day.

CHAPTER 2

1. Thus the *creatures* [1] of the heavens and of the earth and all their hosts were completed. [2] 2. And on the seventh day God completed [3] the work which he had done, *and the ten things he had created at twilight;* [4] and he rested on the seventh day from all the work which he had done. 3. God blessed the seventh day, *more than all the days of the week,* [5] and he sanctified it, because on it he rested from all his work which God had created *and was to* do. [6] 4. These are the generations [7] of the heavens and of the earth when they were created. When the Lord God [8] made

Notes, Chapter 1 (Cont.)

[54] Both Lond. and *ed. pr.* omit "for food."

[55] *ṭb;* Onq.: *ṭqyn,* "good," "in order," "proper." In vv. 4, 10, 12, 18, 21, 25 Ps.-J. followed Onq. in translating Heb. *ṭb* by its Aramaic cognate. In our present verse Ps.-J. again uses *ṭb* while Onq. employs *ṭqyn,* possibly for purely stylistic reasons; see J. A. Loader, 1978, 200–201.

Notes, Chapter 2

[1] Nf, P, and Ps.-J. add "creatures," or possibly "creation." However, the verb ("were completed") is in the plural in each of these three Targums, as it is in the underlying Hebrew.

[2] Nf, P, and Ps.-J. use the verb *šlm,* whereas Onq. employs *škll* (Ithpa.), "be finished, decorated."

[3] Nf, Ps.-J. and a variant reading in the margin of P again (see n. 2) use the verb *šlm,* while Onq. uses *šyṣy,* "cease, finish." On this latter translation cf. B. Grossfeld, "Targum Onkelos and Rabbinic Interpretation to Gen 2:1, 2," *JJS* 24 (1973) 176–178; cf. also M. Aberbach and B. Grossfeld, 1982, 26–27. The editor of the text of P avoided a translation that might be taken to mean that God worked on the Sabbath. He translates Heb. *wykl,* "finished," by *ḥmd,* "desire," as if the Hebrew verb were derived from *klh,* which also has this meaning. Cf. Bowker, 1969, 113. See *PRE* 19 (141), which says that God created seven days but chose the seventh day only. Cf. also *PRK* 23,10.

[4] Many rabbinic sources list a number (6, 7, 10, or more) of things that were created on the eve of the first Sabbath; cf., e.g., *m. Aboth* 5,6; *Mekilta* to Exod 16:32 (2, 124–125); Ps.-J. Num 22:28. See further W. S. Towner, 1973, 66–71; *ARN* B, pp. 306–310. The Targum Tosefta of our present verse which was published by R. Kasher gives a list of the items created on the eve of the Sabbath; cf. R. Kasher, 1976–77, 9–17, and see especially pp. 15–16.

[5] This addition is also in the Targum Tosefta to this verse (see preceding note), p. 17, ll. 22–23. *Gen. R.* 11,2-4 tells of many ways in which God blessed the Sabbath.

[6] The Heb. phrase *'šr br' 'lhym l'śwt,* lit. "which God created to make," is syntactically difficult. The midrashim explained it in different ways. *Gen. R.* 11,10 explains that God rested from the work of creating but not from the work of punishing the wicked. Le Déaut (1978, *Genèse,* 85, n. 3) thinks that Ps.-J. may be referring to this tradition. Shinan (1977A, 189–190) thinks that the reference is to the tradition recorded in *Gen. R.* 11,9, which teaches that whatever God was to have made on the seventh day he made on the sixth.

[7] *twldt* = Onq.

[8] When *Elohim* is used in conjunction with *Yahweh,* as often happens in Gen 2, it can only refer to the God of Israel, and the Targums can translate it by their different forms of Elohim (see above, n. 2 to Gen 1:1).

the earth and the heavens 5. And no *trees*[9] of the field[10] were yet on the earth, and no plant of the field had yet sprouted, because the Lord God had not sent rain upon the earth, and there was no man to till the soil. 6. But a cloud *of glory*[11] *came down from beneath the throne of glory,*[12] *and was filled with water from the ocean,* went up *again* from the earth, *and sent rain down*[13] and watered the whole surface of the ground. 7. The Lord God *created Adam with two inclinations.*[14] *And he took* dust *from the site of the sanctuary*[15] *and from the four winds of the world,*[16] *and a mixture of all the waters of the world*[17] *and created him red, black and white.*[18] And he breathed into his nostrils the breath of life, *and the breath* became *in the body of Adam* a spirit *capable of speech,*[19] *to give light to the eyes and to give hearing to the ears.* 8. *Before the creation of the world*[20] a garden *had been* planted by *the Memra*

Notes, Chapter 2

[9]Cf. *Gen. R.* 13,2.

[10]*hql';* = Onq.; Nf: *'py br'.* Onq. usually translates Heb. *śdh,* "field," by *ḥql',* while the Pal. Tgs. use *'py br'.* In many cases Ps.-J. follows Onq., although it sometimes uses *'npy br';* cf., e.g., Gen 24:63; Lev 26:4; Deut 20:19; 22:27; Ps.-J. uses *br'* in Gen 4:8.

[11]Ps.-J. frequently mentions "the cloud(s) of glory." Besides the many texts where this Targum mentions "the cloud(s) *of glory*" when the biblical text speaks only of "the clouds" (cf., e.g., Gen 9:14a; Exod 16:10; 19:9; 24:15, 16; 33:9; 34:5; 40:34) we also read of "the cloud(s) of glory" in additions to the biblical text that are usually special to Ps.-J.; cf. Gen 2:6; 22:4; Exod 12:37; 13:20; 17:9; 18:7; Lev 23:43 (also Nf); Num 10:28; 12:14; 12:16 (also Nf, P, V, N, L); 14:42; 20:29; 22:28, 41; 33:5; Deut 1:31; 10:6; 32:10; 33:3 (Onq., Nf, and P, V, N, L mention "clouds" but not "clouds of glory"). We know of no source for the statement in our present verse that the cloud of glory came down from beneath the throne of glory to gather water that would become rain; cf. Brayer, 1964, 207.

[12]Ps.-J. mentions "the throne of Glory" more frequently than other Targums; cf. Gen 2:6; 27:1; 28:12 (also Nf, P, V, N, L); 28:17; Exod 4:20; 15:17; 17:16 (also Nf, P, V, N); 31:18; Num 11:26; Deut 30:2; 33:26. "The throne of Glory" is mentioned on a few occasions in Targums other than Ps.-J.; cf. Gen 15:17 (Nfmg 2); Exod 20:11 (P; *Mahzor Vitry,* Hurwitz, 341).

[13]Onq. and Nf understand Heb. *'d,* "mist," to mean "cloud" (cf. *j. Ta'an.* 3,66c). The idea, expressed in Ps.-J., that the clouds gather up water from the ocean and then send rain on the earth is found in several rabbinic sources; cf., e.g., *Gen. R.* 13,10; *b. Ta'an* 9b (40-41); *Qoh. R.* 1,7.1; *Midrash Psalms* 18,16 (1,245).

[14]The presence of two *yods* in the Heb. *wyyṣr,* "and (the Lord God) formed," gave rise to the midrashic view that God created man with two *yezers,* or inclinations—a good inclination and a bad one. (Cf., e.g., *Gen. R.* 14,4; *b. Berak.* 61a [381].)

[15]Cf. *j. Nazir* 7,56b; *Gen. R.* 14,8. *PRE* 11 (78) says that when God created man, he was in a clean place, in the navel of the earth. According to *Jubilees* 8,19, Mount Sion was in the navel of the earth. See below, v. 15 and 3:23.

[16]*b. Sanh.* 38a (241); *PRE* 11 (76-77). According to *2 Enoch* 30,13 and *Sibylline Oracles* 3,24-26, God composed man of four letters—east, west, south, and north. E. B. Levine claims that in this verse Ps.-J. has combined two contradictory traditions: (a) Adam was created from dust from the Temple site; (b) he was created from dust gathered from the four corners of the earth; cf. E. B. Levine, 1969, 118; idem, 1968, 37. However, Shinan asserts that Ps.-J. unites the two traditions and thus creates a new view; cf. Shinan, 1979, 1, 136; idem, 1985, 84, n. 45.

[17]We know of no source for this idea; cf. Schmerler, 1932, 23; Brayer, 1964, 207.

[18]According to *PRE* 11 (76-77), the dust from which the first man was created was red, black, white, and green.

[19]= Onq., Nf. The Targums probably mention the gift of speech in order to show man's superiority over the beast.

[20]Heb. *mqdm* (RSV: "in the east") can mean either "in the east" or "from of old." The Targums (Onq., Nf, Ps.-J.) understand the term in the latter sense in our present verse. The view expressed here by Ps.-J. (see also Nf, P, V, N, L, Ps.-J., Gen 3:24) that the Garden of Eden was created before the creation of the world is debated in *Gen. R.* 15,3. The Garden of Eden is included among the ten things that were created on the eve of the first Sabbath (see above, n. 4 to v. 2). According to *Jubilees* 2,7 and *2 Enoch* 30,1, the Garden of Eden was created on the third day.

of the Lord God [21] *from* [22] Eden *for the righteous,* [23] and he made *Adam* dwell there *when* he created *him.* 9. And the Lord God caused to grow from the ground every tree that is desirable [24] to see and good to eat, and the tree of life in the middle of the garden *whose height was a journey of five hundred years,* [25] and the tree *whose fruit enables those who eat it to distinguish* [26] *between* good and evil. 10. A river goes out from Eden to water the garden, and from there it divides and becomes four *river*-heads. [27] 11. The name of one is Pishon; it is the one that encircles the whole land of *India* [28] where there is gold. 12. The gold of that land is *choice*; bdellium is there, and *precious* stones *of beryl.* [29] 13. The name of the second river is Gihon; it is the one that encircles the whole land of Cush. 14. The name of the third river is Tigris; it is the one that flows to the east of Asshur. And the fourth river is the Euphrates. 15. The Lord God took [30] *Adam from the mountain of worship, the place* [31] *whence he had been created,* [32] and made him dwell in the garden of Eden to *labor in the law* and to keep *its commandments.* [33] 16. And the Lord God commanded *Adam* saying, "You may surely eat of every tree of the garden; 17. but of

Notes, Chapter 2

[21] Onq.: "the Lord God." Onq. and Nf do not try to avoid the anthropomorphism involved in saying that God planted a garden. Ps.-J. and Nfmg attribute the act of planting to the *Memra.*

[22] If the translation *"from* Eden" in Lond. and *ed. pr.* is not a mistake for "*in* Eden," perhaps Ps.-J.'s statement that the garden was created from Eden may have been influenced by the rabbinic opinion that Adam's garden and Eden were not the same (see, e.g., *b. Berak.* 34b (215)).

[23] Cf. Ps.-J., Nf, P, V, N, L Gen 3:24. *2 Enoch* 8,1-8 describes Paradise and goes on in 9,1 to say that it had been prepared for the righteous. Compare Matt 25:34. *PRE* 18 (128) has Adam speak of "the place of the abode of the righteous in the garden of Eden."

[24] *mrgg* = Onq.

[25] *Gen. R.* 15,6; *j. Berak.* 1,2c and *Song R.* 6,9.3 state that the tree of life covered a five hundred years' journey.

[26] Lit.: "and the tree *of which those who eat its fruit know*"; = Onq., except that Onq. uses the verb *ḥkmyn*, "are perceptive," instead of *yd'yn,* "know," which we have in Ps.-J. See also Nf, P, V, N, L, which add a similar explanatory gloss at this point. The addition is made in the light of Gen 3:5.

[27] The Targums (Nf, Ps.-J., Onq.) take "four rivers" (RSV), lit. "four heads," to refer to *river*-heads, which seems to mean main rivers rather than four branches of one river; cf. Grossfeld, 1988, 45, n. 7. *Gen. R.* 16,1 (Theodor-Albeck, 142), which says that Adam opened up four *river-heads,* uses the Heb. form (*r'šy nhrwt*) of the idiom used in our present verse by the Targums.

[28] Onq.: Havilah. See Gen 25:18, where Onq. again takes over the Heb. word "Havilah." Jerome records the view that Pishon is the Ganges, the river of India (*Quaest. hebr. in Gen.* 2:11).

[29] Onq.: *beryl* stones. Ps.-J. mentions the precious stones from Pishon in Exod 14:9; 35:27 in haggadic additions. The tendency to repeat traditions about a particular topic gives to Ps.-J. a certain internal unity. On this topic see Shinan, 1979, 1, 119–131; idem, 1985, 77–82. See above, Introduction, p. 6.

[30] *dbr* = Onq. Nf, P, V, N, L: *ns(y)b*. In translating Heb. *lqḥ,* "take," Onq. uses *nsb* with impersonal objects, but *dbr* with humans. Ps.-J. generally follows the same practice. The Pal. Tgs. generally avoid using *dbr* except for actual leading. See Cowling, 1968, 169–183; Cook, 1986, 234.

[31] Lit.: "a place."

[32] *PRE* 12 (84) explains the words "The Lord God took the man and put him in the Garden of Eden" to mean that he took the man "from the place of the Temple, and He brought him into His palace, which is Eden." See above, v. 7, and n. 15 to that verse.

[33] The phrase "to till it and keep it" raised problems, since the garden of Eden needed no one to till it. The Targums, apart from Onq., took the biblical phrase to refer to labor in the Law. See also *Sifre* to Deut 11:13; *ARN* B 21 (131); *PRE* 12 (84-85); *2 Enoch* 31,1.

the tree *of which those who eat its fruit have the wisdom to distinguish*[34] good and evil, you shall not eat, because[35] on the day on which you eat <of it>[36] you shall *incur the* death-*penalty."*[37] 18. And the Lord God said, "It is not *right*[38] that *Adam* should *sleep* alone; I will make for him *a woman who will be* a support alongside him."[39] 19. So the Lord God *created* from the ground every beast of the field and every bird of the heavens, and brought (them) to *Adam* to see what *name* he would call them; and whatever *Adam* called each living creature, that was its name. 20. And *Adam* gave their names to all the cattle and to *all*[40] the birds of the heavens, and to all the beasts of the field; but for Adam, no support alongside him was *yet* found. 21. The Lord God cast a *deep* sleep upon Adam, and he slept. And he took one of his ribs—*it was the thirteenth rib of the right side*[41]—and he closed[42] *its place*[43] with flesh. 22. And the Lord God built the rib he had taken from *Adam* into a woman and brought her to *Adam.* 23. And *Adam* said, "This time, *but never again will woman be created from man as this one had been created from me*[44]— bone of my bones and flesh of my flesh. *It is fitting* to call this one woman, for she[45] has been taken from man." 24. Therefore a man shall leave *and be separated from the bedroom*[46] of his father and of his mother, and he shall *be united* to his

Notes, Chapter 2

[34]Lit.: *"are wise to* know," (*ḥkmyn lmyd'*). In Lond. *lmyd'* has been erased. Onq.: *ḥkmyn,* "are wise, or perceptive." See above, v. 9 and n. 26 to that verse.

[35]*'ry.* This is one of the rare occasions on which Ps.-J. uses *'ry* (which is the usual form of this particle in Onq. and Tg. Jon.) rather than *'rwm* (which is usual in the Pal. Tgs.). See also Ps.-J. Gen 19:2; 20:7b; 26:16; 32:26; Deut 11:22 (*ed. pr.: 'rwm*).

[36]Omitted in Lond. and *ed. pr.*

[37]*ḥyyb qṭwl.* See *Tanḥ., Bemidbar* 23 (495), where a similar Heb. phrase (*nthyyb myth,* "he incurred the death penalty") is used with reference to Adam, who disobeyed the command given in our present verse (Gen 2:17). See also *PRK* 14,5 (271); *Midrash Psalms* 92,14 (2,123). Since Adam did not die immediately after his sin (cf. Gen 3), as one might expect from the wording of our present verse (HT), Ps.-J. (and the midrashim) modify the threatening words "in the day that you eat of it you shall die," and explain them to mean that if Adam sinned, he would incur the death penalty and would therefore be subject to death.

[38]= Onq. The Targums do not translate Heb. *ṭwb* by the corresponding Aramaic word in order to avoid the apparent contradiction between this verse and Gen 1:31, which states that everything God made was good (cf. Bowker, 1969, 120).

[39]Or: "opposite him"; = Onq.

[40]= Pesh., LXX, Vulg.

[41]The source of this addition is unknown; cf. Brayer, 1964, 208. Rieder (1965, 116–117) notes that *m. Ohol.* 1,8 says that man has eleven ribs, and he claims that Ps.-J. originally read "twelfth rib," thus implying that Eve was made from one of man's twelve ribs. A copyist, by mistake, wrote "thirteenth" for "twelfth."

[42]Onq., LXX: "filled." Ps.-J. is the only one of the Targums to translate Heb. *wysgr,* "and (God) closed," literally.

[43]Lond.: *'t';* read: *'tr';* omitted in *ed. pr.*

[44]See *Gen. R.* 8,9: "In the past Adam was created from dust and Eve was created from Adam; but henceforth it shall be *In our image, after our likeness* (Gen 1:26); neither man without woman nor woman without man. . . ." The same tradition is repeated in *Gen. R.* 22,2.

[45]Lit.: "this one."

[46]Onq.: "a man shall leave the *sleeping abode* of." All the Targums (Onq., Nf, P, V, N, L, CTg B, Ps.-J.) mention "bed" or "bedroom" in their translations of this verse. On the possible reasons for this addition, see Aberbach-Grossfeld, 1982, 33, n. 24; Grossfeld, 1988, 45, n. 11.

wife, and the *two of them*[47] shall become one flesh. 25. And the two of them were *wise,* [48] Adam and his wife, but they did not *remain in their glory.* [49]

CHAPTER 3

1. Now the serpent was more skilled *in evil*[1] than all the beasts of the field which *the Lord* God had made. And he said to the woman, "*Is it true* that the Lord God said, 'You shall not eat of any tree of the garden'?" 2. And the woman said to the serpent, "We *are allowed* to eat of the fruit of the *other* trees of the garden;[2] 3. but of the fruit of the tree in the middle of the garden *the Lord* said, 'You shall not eat of it and you shall not touch it, lest you die.' " 4. *At that moment* the serpent *spoke slander*[3] *against his creator, and* said to the woman, "You shall not die. *But every craftsman hates his fellow craftsman.*[4] 5. For *it is manifest before the Lord* that on the day on which you eat of it[5] you shall be like the *great angels,*[6] who *are able to*

Notes, Chapter 2 (Cont.)

[47]Cf. Pesh., Sam., LXX, Vulg., Matt 19:5.

[48]Onq.: "naked." Heb. *'rwm* can mean both "naked" and "shrewd." See the play on this word in Gen 2:25 and 3:1 (HT). Ps.-J., who often introduces indelicate themes into the text he is translating (see above, Introduction, p. 7), avoids saying that Adam and Eve were naked and says instead that they were wise.

[49]Midrashic texts frequently use the words of Ps 49:13 ("Man does not abide in his honor [*byqr*]") to prove that Adam was deprived of his glory when he was expelled from Eden; cf. *Gen. R.* 12,6; *ARN* A 1. *b. Sanh.* 38b (242); see also *Gen. R.* 18,6. Cook maintains that Ps.-J.'s version of our present verse was intended to prove that the sin of Adam and Eve was one of disobedience, not of sexual intercourse; cf. J. Cook, 1983, 54–55.

Notes, Chapter 3

[1]The corresponding Heb. phrase, *ḥkm lhr',* is applied to the serpent in *PRE* 13 (92; Luria 31b). Onq.: "cunning."

[2]Lit.: "We are allowed to eat of the rest of the fruit of the trees of the garden."

[3]Ps.-J. uses the Latinism *dlṭwr* (read: *dlṭwr'*), "information, accusation." In the corresponding passage in *Gen. R.* 19,4 (Theodor-Albeck 172; see next note) the same Latinism (in the form *dylṭwryh*) is used.

[4]Comp. *Gen. R.* 19,4 (Theodor-Albeck 172-173): "He (the serpent) began speaking slander (*dylṭwryh*) of his Creator, saying, 'Of this tree did he eat and then create the world; hence He orders you, ye shall not eat thereof, so that you may not create other worlds, for every person hates his fellow craftsmen (*br 'wmnwtyh*).' " See also *Gen. R.* 20, 1-2; *Tanḥ., Bereshith* 8 (22); *PRE* 13 (94). Ps.-J.'s addition to our present verse merely summarizes the *Gen. R.* text just quoted. The term for "his fellow craftsman" used by Ps.-J. is exactly the same as that used in *Gen. R.* See also what we said in the preceding note about *dlṭwr.*

[5]The translation of the phrase "your eyes will be opened" is omitted in Lond. and *ed. pr.*

[6]Lit.: "like great angels." Onq.: "like (the) great ones." Ps.-J. combines the reading of Onq. with "angels," which we find in Nf and CTg B. All the Targums of our present verse avoid suggesting that Eve could become like God.

distinguish[7] good *from* evil." 6. And the woman saw *Sammael the angel of death*[8] *and she was afraid.*[9] *She knew* that the tree was good to eat, that *it was a cure* for *the light* of the eyes,[10] and that the tree was desirable as a source of wisdom.[11] And she took of its fruit and ate; and she also gave to her husband (who was) with her, and he ate. 7. Then the eyes of both of them were *enlightened* and they knew that they were naked *because they were stripped of the clothing of fingernails*[12] *in which they had been created, and they saw their shame;* and they sewed fig leaves *for themselves,* and they made girdles[13] for themselves. 8. They heard the voice of *the Memra of* the Lord God strolling in the garden at the *decline*[14] of the day; and *Adam* and his wife hid themselves from before the Lord God in the midst of *the trees in* the garden. 9. The Lord God called to *Adam* and said to him,[15] *"Is not the whole world which I created manifest before me, the darkness as well as the light?*[16] *How*[17] *then do you imagine in your heart that you can hide yourself from before me? Do I not see the place where you are hiding? And where*[18] *are the commandments*

Notes, Chapter 3

[7]Lit.: "who are wise to know." Onq.: "who are wise."

[8]The angel Sammael is mentioned twice (in our present verse and in 4:1) in Ps.-J. See also the Targum Tosefta to Gen 38:25 (CTg FF), where Sammael is said to have concealed the three witnesses from Tamar. Many roles have been given to this hostile and destructive being. See Ginzberg, *Legends* 7 (Index), 414–415; Bowker, 1969, 125–126; A Caquot, "Bref Commentaire du 'Martyre d'Isaïe,'" *Semitica* 23 (1973) 72.

[9]This addition seems to recall a tradition which is also recorded in *PRE* 13 (95) and which states that when Eve touched the tree, she saw the angel of death and said, "Woe is me! I shall now die. . . ." See also *ARN* B, 1 (34). In *3 Baruch* (Greek) 4,8 and 9,7 Sammael features in the story of Adam and Eve. Note that in our present verse Ps.-J. translates Heb. *wtr',* "so when (the woman) saw," three times, twice with a meaning derived from *r'h,* "see" ("saw, knew"), and once as if the Heb. word were derived from *yr',* "fear" ("she was afraid"). See Shinan, 1979, 2, 272–273; idem, 1983C, 192–193.

[10]Onq.: "a *cure* for the eyes." The idea that the tree had curative powers may be inspired by Ezek 47:12 (cf. Rev 22:2). Besides, since the effect of eating the fruit was that "the eyes of both of them were opened" (Gen 3:7) one could conclude, as do Onq. and Ps.-J., that the tree had a curative effect.

[11]Lit.: "desirable to become wise *therewith*"; = Onq.

[12]Jastrow (525–526) proposes that we read *šwpr',* "beauty, grace" rather than *twpr',* "fingernail." In v. 21 *ed. pr.* reads *šwpryhwn* rather than *twpryhwn* of Lond. Le Déaut (1978, *Genèse,* 91) reads *vêtement de splendeur* in our present verse. However, since Ps.-J. has "fingernail" in both v. 7 (Lond. and *ed. pr.*) and v. 21 (Lond.), and since *PRE* 14 (98; Luria 33b) says that the first man was dressed in "a skin of nail" (*'wr šl spwrn*), and that the nail skin was stripped of him when he sinned, I prefer to translate the text as it stands. See also *Gen. R.* 20, 12 (Theodor-Albeck, 196), which says that Adam's garments were "as smooth as a fingernail (*ħlqym kṣypwrn*). Bowker (1969, 121) reads "clothing of onyx" (see Levy, 1, 316).

[13]Ps.-J. differs from all the other Targums of this verse in that it translates Heb. *ħgrt,* "aprons," by *qmwryn.*

[14]= Onq. "At the decline of the day" probably reflects the true meaning of the underlying Heb. phrase; see Speiser, 1964, 24.

[15]Nf, P, V, N, L (cf. also Nfmg), and Ps.-J. have all added essentially the same material at this point. These Targums avoid a direct translation of the phrase "Where are you?" which might give the impression that God's knowledge was limited. Onq. translates the biblical question literally. Rabbinic literature had different ways of resolving the problem raised by God's question; see, e.g., *Gen. R.* 19,9; *b. Sanh.* 38b (244).

[16]According to Brayer (1964, 209), there is no known source for the reference to darkness and light in the Targums (Nf, P, V, N, L, Ps.-J.) of this verse. Shinan (1979, 1, 224–225) suggests that the *meturgemanim* may have been influenced by Ps 139 (see vv. 5, 7, 15, and esp. v. 11), which was sometimes associated with Adam; cf., e.g., *Midrash Psalms* 139 (2, 342–347).

[17]The Targums (Nfmg, P, V, N, L, Ps.-J.) translate Heb. *'ykh ('ayyekah),* "where are you?" as if it were *'eykah,* "how?"

[18]Having already translated *'ykh* as "how?" (see preceding note), the Targums now translate that word literally, but they modify the biblical question. "The commandments" to which Ps.-J. Nfmg and P refer are probably the Noachide commandments (cf. *b. Sanh.* 59a-b [402–404]). Nf, V, N and L mention "the commandment," that is, the commandment not to eat of the forbidden tree (cf. Díez Macho, *Neophyti 1,* III, 1971, 32*).

that I commanded you?" 10. He said, "I heard the voice *of your Memra* in the garden and I was afraid, for I was naked, *because I neglected the commandment you gave me,*[19] and I hid myself *for shame."*[20] 11. He said, "Who told you that you were naked? *Perhaps* you have eaten of *the fruit of* the tree from which I commanded you not to eat?" 12. And *Adam* said, "The woman you put beside me, she gave me of *the fruit of* the tree, and I ate." 13. The Lord God said to the woman,[21] "What is this you have done?" And the woman said, "The serpent lured[22] me *with his cleverness and led me astray in his wickedness,* and I ate." 14. Then the Lord God *brought the three of them to judgment,*[23] *and* he said to the serpent, "Because you have done this, cursed are you above all cattle, and above all beasts of the field. Upon your belly you shall go about, *and your feet shall be cut off,*[24] *and you will cast off your skin once every seven years,*[25] *and the poison of death will be in your mouth,*[26] and you shall eat dust all the days of your life. 15. And I will put enmity between you and the woman, between the offspring *of your children* and the offspring *of her children. And when the children of the woman keep the commandments of the Law, they will take aim and strike you on your head. But when they forsake the commandments of the Law you will take aim* and wound them on *their heels.*[27] *For them, however, there will be a remedy; but for you there will be no remedy; and they are to*

Notes, Chapter 3

[19]Lit.: "because I let the commandment you gave me pass from me." Compare *PRE* 14 (Luria 33a; not in Friedlander's version): ". . . I was afraid on account of my deeds, for I was naked of my commandments." See also *b. Shabb.* 14a (57) and *Gen. R.* 19,6, where "naked" is taken to mean naked of good deeds or of precepts.

[20]Ps.-J. alone adds "for shame." The word used, *kyswp',* belongs to Eastern Aramaic; cf. Cook, 1986, 254–255. The same word occurs in Ps.-J. (and in Ps.-J. alone) Num 16:4. Ps.-J. twice uses a verbal form of the same root in Num 12:14 in an addition that is special to this Targum.

[21]= *ed. pr.*; Lond.: "his wife."

[22]Reading *'syyny* with *ed. pr.*; Lond.: *'tyyny.* Ps.-J. translates Heb. *hśy'ny,* "beguiled me," twice, first as *'syyny,* which we have translated as "lured me," and then as *'t'yyny,* (Onq.: *'t'yny*), "led me astray." *Gen. R.* 19,12 (Theodor-Albeck, 182) translates the Heb. word in question three times: "He incited me (*gyrny*), he incriminated me (*ḥyybny*), and he beguiled me (or: led me astray) (*ht'ny*)." Ps.-J.'s first rendering ("lured") seems to correspond to the first interpretation in *Gen. R.* ("incited me"), while Ps.-J.'s second rendering ("led me astray") agrees with the third interpretation in *Gen. R.* With Ps.-J.'s first translation ("lured") compare *PRE* 14 (99): "the serpent enticed my mind to sin. . . ."

[23]*PRE* 14 (99): "He brought the three of them and passed sentence of judgment upon them. . . ." See also *Gen. R.* 20,2; Josephus, *Ant.* 1 § 49-50.

[24]*Gen. R.* 20,5: "ministering angels descended and cut off his hands and feet"; (further on in the same passage *Gen. R.* says that God had created the serpent to walk upright like a man); see *PRE* 14 (99); Josephus, *Ant.* 1 § 50. Ps.-J. refers to this tradition in Exod 7:9.

[25]*PRE* 14 (99): ". . . (God) decreed that it (the serpent) should cast its skin and suffer pain once in seven years. . . ."

[26]*PRE* 14 (99): ". . . and the gall of asps, and death is in its (the serpent's) mouth. . . ;" Josephus, *Ant.* 1 § 50: "He (God) also put poison beneath his tongue. . . ." See Job 20:16.

[27]The idea of "keeping" (Nf, Ps.-J.) or "toiling in" (Nfmg, P, V, N, L) the Law seems to have been introduced into this verse because the *meturgemanim* took the verb *šwp* in *yšwpk r'š,* "he shall bruise your head," to be derived from *š'p,* "gasp, pant," which they took to refer to the striving and the effort required in the observance of the Torah. By then linking the verb *šwp* with the same verb *š'p* in the sense of "pant after, long for," and thus "strive to reach a goal," the *meturgemanim* (Nf, P, V, N, L, Ps.-J.; cf. Nfmg) derive the idea of "take aim" from *yšwp(k)* and *tšwp(nw),* "he/you shall bruise." The Targums (Nf, P, V, N, L, Ps.-J.; cf. Nfmg) translate *šwp* in those latter words a second time, taking it to mean "strike" (Aramaic: *mḥy*) in *yšwp(k),* and "wound" or "bite" (Aramaic: *nkt*) in *tšwp(nw).* See Díez Macho, *Neophyti 1,* III, 32*, n. 1; Shinan 1979, 2, 211–212; Pérez Fernández 1981, 40–45. The underlying theory in the Targums of this verse, namely, that Israel's prosperity depends on her observance of the Law, is commonplace in the Targums; see below, v. 24, and nn. 58 and 60 to that verse.

make peace in the end, in the days of the King Messiah." [28] 16. To the woman <he said>, [29] "I will greatly multiply your affliction *in the blood of virginity* [30] and (in) your pregnancies; in pain you shall bear children, yet your desire shall be for your husband; he shall rule over you *both for righteousness and for sin."* [31] 17. And to Adam he said, "Because you listened to *the word* [32] *of* your wife, and ate of *the fruit of* the tree concerning which I commanded you saying, 'You shall not eat of it,' cursed be the earth because *it did not show you your guilt;* [33] by toil you shall eat of it all the days of your life. 18. Thorns and thistles it shall sprout *and produce* [34] because of you; and you shall eat the plants that are upon the surface of the field." *Adam answered and said, "I beseech by the mercy before you, O Lord,* [35] *Let me not be reckoned* [36] *before you as cattle, that I should eat the grass of the surface of the field.* [37] *I will arise and labor with the labor of my hands, and I will eat of the food* [38] *of the earth; and thus let there be a distinction before you between the children of men and the offspring of cattle."* 19. "By the *labor of your hand* [39] you shall eat *food* until you return to the *dust* from which you were *created,* because dust you are, and

Notes, Chapter 3

[28]The word *špywt',* which also occurs (with spelling variations) in Nf, P, V, N, L, and which we translate as "peace" (see Jastrow, 1615; Levy 2, 506) was derived from Heb. *šwp* (see preceding note), with which it has at least an external similarity. The Heb. *'qb,* "heel," is taken in the metaphorical sense of "end (of time)," and translated *b'yqb',* "in the end," which is then explained to mean "in the days of the King Messiah." Pérez Fernández, however, (see preceding note), 43 (cf. also pp. 45, 47), prefers to translate the last part of this verse as *"y ellos curarán el talón en los días del Rey Mesías,"* "but they shall cure the heel in the days of the King Messiah." There are no rabbinic parallels for the idea that there will eventually be peace between the serpent and human beings (cf. S. H. Levey, 1974, 2–3. *Gen. R.* 20,5 states that in the Messianic age all will be healed except the serpent.

[29]Omitted in Lond and *ed. pr.*

[30]Cf. *b. Erub.* 100b (697); *ARN* A 1. *PRE* 14 (100) includes the afflictions arising from menstruation and the tokens of virginity among nine curses imposed on the first woman.

[31]Lit.: "whether to be innocent or to sin." We know of no direct source for this addition. But see *b. Berak.* 17a (102–103): "Whereby do women earn merit? By making their children go to their synagogue . . . and their husbands to the Beth Hamidrash. . . ."

[32]Lit.: *"accepted the word."*

[33]*PRE* 14 (101). This tradition in our present verse contradicts Ps.-J. Gen 5:29, where it is said that the earth was cursed "because of the sins of the children of men." As A. Geiger (1928, 456) pointed out, other ancient versions (LXX, Syriac, Theodotion) try to explain why the earth should be cursed.

[34]Onq.: "sprout"; Ps.-J. combines the reading of Onq. with that of the Pal. Tgs.

[35]This prayer formula (see also Nf, P, V, N, L) occurs frequently (sometimes with slight variations) in the Targums; see, e.g., Gen 15:2 (Nf, V, N, L, CTg H); 18:3, (Ps.-J., cf. Nf), 27,31 (Ps.-J.); 24:42 (Nf); 38:25 (Nf, P, V, N, L, Ps.-J., CTg E). This particular formula does not occur in Jewish liturgical prayers (see Shinan, 1979, 2, 334).

[36]*nthsb.* The preformative *nun* which is characteristic of the first person plural is sometimes used for the first person singular in the Pal. Tgs. and in Ps.-J.; cf. Le Déaut, 1978, *Genèse,* 95, n. 13; Cook, 1986, 180.

[37]*Gen. R.* 20,10; *b. Pesah.* 118a (607); *ARN* A 1. See also Philo, *Legum Allegoriae* 3, § 251. The Targums (Nf, P, V, N, L, Ps.-J.) develop this tradition at greater length. The tradition resolves the apparent contradiction between v. 18 ("you shall eat the plants of the field") and v. 19 ("you shall eat bread"). According to the haggadah, the latter command was given as a result of Adam's urgent prayer which is recorded in the Targums of v. 18; cf. Schmerler, 1932, 37.

[38]Lit.: "I will eat food of the food."

[39]Lit.: "the palm of your hand." Ps.-J., and Ps.-J. alone, takes the biblical phrase "the sweat of your face" (RSV) to mean "the labor of your hand."

to dust you will return; *but from the dust you are destined to arise*[40] *to render an account and a reckoning of all you have done, on the day of great judgment."*[41] 20. Adam named his wife Eve, because she was the mother of all *human beings.*[42] 21. And the Lord God made *garments of glory*[43] for Adam and for his wife *from the* skin *which the serpent had cast off*[44] (to be worn) *on the skin of their flesh,*[45] *instead of their (garments of) fingernails*[46] *of which they had been stripped,*[47] and he clothed them. 22. And the Lord God said *to the angels who minister before him,*[48] "Behold, Adam was *alone on the earth as I am alone in the heavens on high.*[49] *From him*[50]

Notes, Chapter 3

[40]According to *Gen. R.* 20,10, the phrase "and to dust you shall return" hints at resurrection. We find references to the resurrection of the dead in such Targumic texts as our present verse 3:19 (Nf, P, Ps.-J.); Gen 19:26 (Nf, Nfmg, P, V, N, L); 25:34 (Nf, Nfmg, P, V, N, L; cf. Ps.-J.); Deut 32:39 (Nf, V, N); cf. also Gen 25:32 (Ps.-J.); 30:22 (Nf, Nfmg, P, V, N); Num 11:26 (Ps.-J.); Deut 28:12 (Ps.-J.); 33:6 (Nf, P, V, N, L, Ps.-J., CTg DD, Onq.). See further Rodríguez Carmona, 1978, 21–59.

[41]"The day of (great) judgment" is mentioned frequently in the Targums. Besides our present text (Ps.-J.) see, e.g., Gen 4:7 (Nf, P, V, N, L, CTg B, Ps.-J., Onq.); 9:6 (Ps.-J.); 39:10 (Ps.-J.); Exod 15:12 (Ps.-J., Nf: "the judgment of the great day"); 20:7 (Nf, Nfmg, CTg F, Ps.-J.); 34:7 (Nf, V, N, Ps.-J.); Num 14:18 (Nf, V, N); 15:31 (Ps.-J.); 31:50 (Nf, P, V, N, Ps.-J.); Deut 5:11 (Nf, Ps.-J.); 32:34 (Nf, P, V, N, L, Onq.); also Targumic Tosefta to Gen 2:3 (cf. R. Kasher, 1976–77, 17). On the use of similar phrases in the New Testament, see McNamara, 1972, 135–136; Rodríguez Carmona, 1978, 17, 20.

[42]Lit.: "all the children of man"; = Onq. Nf and P retain the play on the words *ḥwh* ("Eve"), and *ḥy* ("living thing"). Onq. and Ps.-J. specify that Eve is the mother of all humans, not of all living things.

[43]= Onq. Cf. *PRE* 20 (144; Luria 46a): "coats of glory." *Gen. R.* 20,12 says the garments of Eve were made of light (*'wr*) rather than skin (*'wr*), as the biblical text says. Garments made of light would, of course, be garments of glory. In translating "garments of skin," Ps.-J. first follows this tradition, but then goes on to interpret the biblical phrase literally, *"from* the skin. . . ." See further, Komlosh, 1973, 170–171; Bowker, 1969, 129–130.

[44]See above, v. 14 and n. 25.

[45]= Onq.

[46]= Lond.; *ed. pr.*: "their beauty." See above, v. 7, and n. 12.

[47]See above, v. 7.

[48]Cf. *Gen. R.* 21,5; *Mekilta* to Exod 14:29 (1, 248); *PRE* 12 (85). Ps.-J. alone adds the words "to the angels who minister before him." This addition was made to resolve the problem raised by the biblical phrase "like one of us," which might seem to indicate a plurality of gods (see above, n. 42 to 1:26). The addition does not fit very well with the phrase "as I am alone in the heavens," which occurs later in the verse. See further M. Pérez Fernández, 1984, 457–475. Bowker (1969, 130) claims that when adding the words "to the angels who minister before him," Ps.-J. also intended to counteract the claim of Christian writers that this verse supports the doctrine of the Trinity.

[49]Or: "unique on the earth . . . unique in the heavens. . . ." The Targums (Nf, P, V, N, L, Ps.-J.) took Heb. *'ḥd,* "one," to mean "alone" (or "unique"), and they made a comparison between God, who is alone (or, unique) in heaven (cf., e.g., *Gen. R.* 98, 13; 99, 11; *Tanḥ., Shemoth* 18 [174]; *Song R.* 1, 9.2), and Adam, who was alone (or, unique) in the world (cf. *Mekilta* to Exod 14:15 [1, 216]; *PRE* 12 [85]; *m. Sanh.* 4, 5). If we do read "unique" rather than "alone," as does Hayward (1981, 138), we may take it to mean that Adam was unique in that God revealed to him the ways of life and death, so that he was free to choose between them; cf. *Gen. R.* 21, 5. The Targums apply the term *yḥyd,* "singular, unique," as a title of honor to Abraham and Isaac (Gen 22:10 Nf, P, V, N, L, Ps.-J.) to Abraham (Tg. Isa 51:2; Ezek 33:24); and to Israel (Ps.-J. Num 23:24; 29:36; Deut 26:18). See further Lentzen-Deis, 1970, 228–240; Pérez Fernández, 1984, 463–467.

[50]Since the Heb. *mmnw* can mean "(one) of us" or "from him," the Targums (Nf, P, V, N, L, Ps.-J.) understand it in this latter sense and take "from him" to refer to Adam. Of those who are to arise from Adam, Ps.-J. mentions only "those who know how to distinguish between good and evil" (compare Nf, P, V, N, L), referring, apparently, to the Jews. The rather mysterious translation of Onq. ("Adam has become the only one in the world knowing good and evil by himself") seems to be an abbreviated version of the tradition recorded in the Pal. Tgs. and Ps.-J.; see Vermes, 1963B, 164–165; = 1975, 132–134.

there will arise those who will know *how to distinguish* between good and evil. *If he had kept the commandments (which) I commanded him he would have lived and endured like the tree of life* [51] *forever.* But now, *since he has not observed what I commanded him, let us decree against him, and let us banish him from the Garden of Eden,* before he puts forth his hand and takes (also) *of the fruit* of the tree of life. *For behold, if* he eats of it, he will live *and endure* forever." [52] 23. And the Lord God drove him *out* of the Garden of Eden, *and he went and settled on Mount Moriah* [53] to till the soil from which he had been *created.* [54] 24. And he drove *Adam out of (the place) where, from the beginning,* [55] he had caused *the Glory of his Shekinah* to dwell *between the two* cherubim. [56] *Before he had yet created the world, he created the Law.* [57] He *established* the garden of Eden *for the righteous, that they might eat and take delight in the fruit of the tree, for having during their lives cherished the instruction of the Law in this world and fulfilled the precepts. For the wicked he established Gehenna, which is like a sharp two-edged* sword. [58] *Within it he established sparks of fire and burning coals* [59] *with which to judge the wicked, who during their lives re-*

Notes, Chapter 3

[51]Cf. Tg. Isa 65:22. In the *Psalms of Solomon* 14 the pious ones of God are called "the trees of life."

[52]Lit.: *"and endure* until the ages." Ps.-J. alone adds "and endure," and Ps.-J. alone has *'d l'lmyn,* while the other Targums (Nf, P, V, N, L, Onq.) have *l'lm.*

[53]*PRE* 20 (143); *Midrash Psalms* 92,6 (2,113).

[54]See above 2:7, 15 and n. 15 on 2:7.

[55]Heb. *mqdm,* "at the East" (RSV), can also mean "from the beginning" (see above, n. 20 to 2:8). Nf, V, N and L use both translations in our present verse. Ps.-J. and P use only "from the beginning."

[56]The reference to the Shekinah was occasioned by the use of the verb *škn* (*wyškn*), "he placed" (RSV). Ps.-J.'s view that the Shekinah dwelt between the cherubim may be inspired by such texts as 1 Sam 4:4; 2 Sam 6:2; 2 Kings 19:15; Isa 37:16. The terms "Glory (of the Lord)" and "Shekinah" are used to refer to God's presence or to divine manifestations. The combination of these terms which we have in our present verse is frequent in the Pal. Tgs. and in Ps.-J. Onq. uses the terms "Shekinah" and "Glory," but it does not combine them, except in Num 14:14. See Goldberg, 1963 and 1969.

[57]See above n. 4 to 2:2. The Law was identified with Wisdom, which was created at the beginning of time (cf. Prov 8:22-31). According to Nf and P, V, N, L, the law was created two thousand years before the creation of the world; cf., e.g., *Gen. R.* 8, 2; *Lev. R.* 19, 1, while Ps.-J. says only that it was created before the world; cf., e.g., *Gen. R.* 1,8; *PRE* 3 (10-11). Gehenna is mentioned in the present verse because the "flaming sword" of the biblical text was taken to refer to Gehenna, where the wicked are punished; cf. *Gen. R.* 21, 9; *Tanh. B., Bereshith* 25 (1, 18).

[58]The belief that the righteous would be rewarded for their good deeds and that the wicked would be punished for their sins was, of course, commonplace in Jewish literature; see Urbach, 1975, 1, 436–444; M. Melinek, "The Doctrine of Reward and Punishment in Biblical and Early Rabbinic Writings," in *Essays Presented to Chief Rabbi Israel Brodie on the Occasion of His Seventieth Birthday,* ed. H.J. Zimmels, J. Rabbinowitz and L. Finestein (London: Soncino, 1967) 275–290. This same belief is frequently expressed in the Targums; see, besides our present verse, Gen 3:24 (Nf, P, V, N, L, Ps.-J.); 4:8 (Nf, P, V, N, Ps.-J.; Targum Toseftas CTg I, FF, X); 15:1 (Nf, Nfmg, P, V, N, L, CTg H, Ps.-J.); 17 (Nf, Nfmg 1 and 2, P, V, N, L, Ps.-J.); 38:25(26) (Nf, P, V, N, L, CTg D, E, Ps.-J.; Targum Toseftas CTg X, FF); 39:10 (Nf, P, CTg E, Ps.-J.); 49:1 (Nf, P, V, N, Ps.-J., Targum Tosefta CTg T-S); 49:22 (Nfmg, P); Lev 26:43 (P, V, N, Ps.-J.; cf. Onq.); Num 12:16 (Nf, P, V, N, L, Ps.-J.); 23:23 (Nf, P, V, N, L); 24:23 (Nf, P, V, N); Deut 7:10 (Nf, Nfmg, P, V, N, Ps.-J.). See also Tg. Jon. Judg 5:2,4; 1 Sam 2:8.

[59]Lit.: "coals of fire." The fire of Gehenna is mentioned, e.g., in 4 Macc 12:12; in the Pseudepigrapha (*Testament of Zebulun* 10, 3; *2* [Syriac] *Baruch* 85, 13) in rabbinic literature (e.g., *b. Pesah.* 54a [265]; *B. Mez.* 85a [489]; *Gen. R.* 26,6) and in the N.T. (cf., e.g., Matt 5:22; 18:8–9; 25:41); See further Strack and Billerbeck, 1961, IV, 2, 1075–1078. Besides our present verse, Gen 3:24 (Nf, P, V, N, L, Ps.-J.), we find reference to the fire of Gehenna, or to burning in Gehenna or in the world to come, in such texts as Gen 15:17 (Nf, Nfmg 1 and 2, P, V, N, L, Ps.-J.); 27:33 (Ps.-J.); 38:25(26) (Nf, P, V, N, L, CTg D, E, Ps.-J.; Targum Toseftas CTg X, FF); Deut 32:35 (Nf, P, V, N, L, CTg DD).

belled against the instruction of the Law. The Law is better for him who toils in it than the fruit of the tree of life, (that Law) which the Memra of the Lord established to be kept so that people might endure and walk in the paths of the way of life *in the world to come.* [60]

CHAPTER 4

1. *Adam* knew[1] his wife Eve *who* had conceived *from Sammael, the angel of the Lord.*[2] 2. Then, *from Adam her husband* she bore *his twin sister*[3] and Abel. Abel was a keeper of sheep, and Cain was *a man* tilling the earth.[4] 3. After a certain time,[5] *on the fourteenth of Nisan,*[6] Cain brought of the produce of the land, *of the seed of flax,*[7] as an offering *of first fruits before*[8] the Lord. 4. Abel, on his part,

Notes, Chapter 3 (Cont.)

[60]The Targums frequently stress the importance of observing the Law; cf. J. Ribera i Florit, "Elementos comunes del Targum a los Profetas y del Targum Palestinense," in *Simposio Bíblico Español* (Salamanca, 1982), ed. N. Fernández Marcos *et al.,* (Madrid: Universidad Complutense, 1984) 477–493, especially pp. 487–491. "The world to come" is mentioned several times in the Targums; cf., e.g., Gen 15:1 (Nf, Nfmg, P, V, N, L, Ps.-J.); 39:10 (Nf, P, Ps.-J.); 49:22 (Nfmg); Exod 15:12 (Nf, P, V, N, Tg. Tosefta CTg FF, W; Ps.-J.); Num 23:23 (Nf, P, V, N); 31:50 (Nf, Nfmg, P, V, N, Ps.-J.); Deut 7:10 (Nf, Nfmg, P, V, N, Ps.-J.). See further R. P. Gordon, "The Targumists as Eschatologists," *VTSupp* 29 (Congress Volume Göttingen, 1977) 113–130.

Notes, Chapter 4

[1]*yd‘* = Onq.; Nf: *ḥkm.*

[2]This verse could also be translated as follows: "Adam knew that his wife Eve. . . ." *Ed. pr.* has a different version of this verse: "Adam knew Eve his wife, who desired the angel, and she conceived and bore Cain. And she said, 'I have acquired a man, the angel of the Lord.' " The belief that Cain was the child of Sammael (see above, n. 8 to 3:6) was derived from the fact that Gen 5:3 says that Seth was in the likeness and image of Adam. Since this is not said of Cain in 4:1, the conclusion was drawn that he was not Adam's son. Ps.-J. states explicitly in 5:3 that Eve bore Cain, who was not from Adam and who did not resemble him. *b. Shabb.* 146a (738), *Yebam.* 103b (711), *Abod. Zar.* 22b (114) say that the serpent copulated with Eve and/or infused her with lust, but they do not say that he fathered Cain. *PRE* 21 (150) says that he (i.e., Sammael) came to her riding on the serpent, and she conceived. We conclude that the "he" in question was Sammael, since *PRE* 13 (92) tells us that Sammael mounted the serpent and rode upon it. In effect, then, Ps.-J. is the earliest text that explicitly identifies Sammael as the father of Cain (cf. Cashdan, 1967, 33). See further Ginzberg, *Legends* 1, 105; Bowker, 1969, 136; Schäfer, 1975, 100–101; Shinan 1979, 2, 273–274; idem, 1983A, 148; idem, 1983C, 193.

[3]This is a reference to the traditions which explain that (twin) sisters were born to Cain and Abel. We can thus understand how these two could marry. Cf., e.g., Josephus, *Ant.* 1 § 52; *Jubilees* 4,1 and 8; *Gen. R.* 22,3; *j. Yebam.* 11,11d; *b. Sanh.* 38b (242); *PRE* 21 (152). See further Bowker, 1969, 137. Ps.-J. in our present verse simply makes an allusion to these well-known traditions; (see above, Introduction, p. 6).

[4]In Gen 4:2 Cain is described as "a tiller of the soil," and in 9:20 Noah is called "a man of the soil." Ps.-J. combines both descriptions in both verses. See Klein, 1982A, 136*.

[5]Lit.: "at the end of the days," which is a literal translation of HT.

[6]*Gen. R.* 22,4; *PRE* 21 (153). Ps.-J. often specifies times that are vague in the biblical text; cf., e.g., Gen 4:3, 25; 7:11; 8:4, 5, 13, 14, 22; 14:13; 17:26; 25:24; 33:17; see Petermann, 1829, 55.

[7]*Tanḥ., Bereshith* 9 (22); *PRE* 21 (153).

[8]*qdm* = Nfmg, Onq.; Nf: "to the name of"; HT: "to." When HT speaks of making an offering "to" God, the Tgs. frequently replace "to" (*l-*) by *qdm* ("before"). The Pal. Tgs. sometimes use "to the name of" instead of "before," as does Nf in our present verse; cf. also, e.g., Nf Num 15:8, 19, 21.

brought of the firstlings of the flock and of their fat parts. *It was pleasing*[9] *before the Lord, and he turned a friendly face* towards Abel and his offering, 5. but to Cain and his offering he did not turn a friendly face.[10] This grieved Cain very much,[11] and *the expression*[12] *of* his face was downcast. 6. The Lord said to Cain, "Why are you angry, and why is *the expression of* your face downcast? 7. If you perform *your deeds* well *your guilt*[13] *will be forgiven*[14] *you.* But if you do not perform *your deeds* well *in this world your sin will be retained for the day of great judgment.*[15] Sin crouches at the gates *of your heart, but in your hand I have placed power over the evil inclination.*[16] Its desire will be towards you, but you will have dominion over it, *whether to be innocent or to sin.*" 8. Cain said to his brother Abel, "*Come, let us both go outside.*"[17] When *the two of them had gone* outside *Cain spoke up*[18] *and said to Abel, "I see that the world was created with mercy,*[19] *but it is*

Notes, Chapter 4

[9]Lit.: "There was favor." Ps.-J. gives a double translation of the biblical phrase "had regard for." The first translation, lit. "there was favor before," agrees with Onq., which is similar to Nf and CTg B. The second translation, (*sbr 'pyn*), may be taken as a nominal construction and rendered "acceptance," or it may be seen as a verbal form (see v. 5) and translated as "and he (God) turned a friendly face;" cf. Levy, 1, 52; 2, 139.

[10]In our present verse Ps.-J. translates "had no regard" only once (see preceding note). It differs from Onq., Nf, and CTg B, which translate that phrase as they did the corresponding formula in v. 4.

[11] = Onq. Lit.: "It lay very heavily on Cain."

[12]*'yqwnyn* = Gr. *eikôn*, "likeness." The idiom *'yqwnyn d'(n)pyn*, which is used by Ps.-J. here and in v. 6, occurs in this same Targum, and in Exod 34:29, 30, 35.

[13]By attributing guilt to Cain, the Targum explains why his gift was not accepted by God. The LXX suggests that Cain did not divide the sacrifice correctly. According to *Gen. R.* 22,5, Cain offered inferior produce to the Lord. Philo (*The Sacrifices of Abel and Cain*, XIII, § 52) says Cain was doubly guilty in that he did not make his offering immediately and in that he did not offer the first-fruits.

[14]In translating Heb. *ś't*, "you will be accepted" (RSV), the Targums understand the verb *nś'* as if it were used in the idiom *nś' 'wn*, "take away one's guilt"; cf., e.g., Exod 34:7; Lev 10:17; Num 14:18. Ps.-J. and Onq. have only "forgive." Compare Pal. Tgs.

[15]See above, n. 41 to 3:19 (Ps.-J.).

[16]The Targums paraphrase the words "its desire is for you, but you must master it." The Pal. Tgs. and Ps.-J. take "desire" to refer to the evil inclination, and they state that Cain has the power to master it; cf. *Gen. R.* 22,6; *ARN* A 16; *b. Sukk.* 52b (249). Ps.-J. adds a literal translation of the phrase in question. The phrase "whether to be innocent or to sin," which is added in Ps.-J. and in the Pal. Tgs., has been used by Nf and Ps.-J. in Gen 3:16.

[17]HT does not tell us what Cain said to Abel. The Targums, Pesh., LXX, and Vulg. put words on Cain's lips. The Pal. Tgs. and Ps.-J. record a discussion which took place between the two brothers in the field. Another version of the discussion is found in the Targum Tosefta of Gen 4:8 from Cod. Ox. 2305 which has been printed many times; cf., e.g., M. Ginsburger, *Das Fragmententhargum* (Berlin: Calvary, 1899) 72; Sperber, 1959, 354. The Targumic addition gives us to understand that Cain concluded that the God who rejected his gift was unjust, and it explains that Cain killed his brother because of a difference of opinion on theological matters. No source that is earlier than the Targums records this dispute at length, although a dispute is mentioned in Philo (*Quod deterius potiori insidiari soleat* 1,1); *Gen. R.* 22,7; *Tanḥ., Bereshith* 9 (22–23). Many scholars think that the dispute may reflect the controversy between the Sadducees and the Pharisees concerning the world to come (Vermes, 1963A, 103; Isenberg, 1970, 433–444). A. Y. Brayer (1971, 583–585) rejects Isenberg's view and says that the Targumic addition may be very late, even as late as the eighth or ninth century. Others think that it contains an anti-Epicurean polemic (H. A. Fischel, *Rabbinic Literature and Greco-Roman Philosophy*, Studia Post Biblica 21 [Leiden: Brill, 1973] 35–50), while J. M. Bassler ("Cain and Abel in the Palestinian Targums. A Brief Note on an Old Controversy," *JStJ* 17 [1986] 56–64) believes that the different versions of the Pal. Tgs. reflect different polemical situations.

[18]Lit.: "answered."

[19]Cf., e.g., *Gen. R.* 8,4; 12,15.

not governed according to the fruit of good deeds, and there is partiality in judgment. Therefore your offering was accepted with favor, but my offering was not accepted from me with favor." Abel answered and said to Cain, *"The world was created with mercy, it is governed according to the fruit of good deeds,* [20] *and there is no partiality in judgment. Because the fruit of my deeds was better than yours and more prompt than yours my offering was accepted with favor."* Cain answered and said to Abel, *"There is no judgment, there is no judge, there is no other world, there is no gift of good reward for the righteous, and no punishment for the wicked."* Abel answered and said to Cain, *"There is judgment, there is a judge,* [21] *there is another world,* [22] *there is the gift of good reward for the righteous, and there is punishment for the wicked."* Concerning these matters they were quarreling in the open country. And Cain rose up against Abel his brother *and drove a stone into his forehead* [23] and killed him. 9. The Lord said to Cain, "Where is your brother Abel?" He said, "I do not know. Am I, *perhaps,* my brother's keeper?" 10. Then he said, "What have you done? The voice of the blood *of the murder* of your brother *which has been swallowed up by the clay,* [24] cries out *before* me from the earth. 11. And now, [25] *because you have killed him,* cursed are you [26] from the earth which has opened its mouth to receive your brother's blood from your hand. 12. When you till the earth it shall not continue to yield the strength *of its fruit* to you. You shall be a wanderer and an exile [27] on earth." 13. Cain said *before* the Lord, "My *rebellion* [28] is *much* too great [29] to bear, [30]

Notes, Chapter 4

[20]Cf. *m. Abot* 3,16.

[21]Cf. *Gen. R.* 26,6; *Lev. R.* 28,1.

[22]*m. Berak.* 9,5. The Sadducees denied the resurrection and the doctrine of reward and punishment (cf. Isenberg, 1970, 441–443). The Targums often give expression to belief in both these doctrines; see above 3:19 (Ps.-J.) and n. 40 to that verse; 3:24 (Ps.-J.) and nn. 58 and 60 to that verse.

[23]*Gen. R.* 22, 8; *PRE* 21 (154). Ps.-J. is the only Targum to add the phrase "and drove a stone into his forehead." Ps.-J.'s words correspond exactly to those of *PRE* in the text just referred to. Ps.-J. uses the Hebraism *myṣḥ* for "forehead," apparently taking it over directly from *PRE* (cf. Cook, 1986, 242).

[24]Ps.-J. differs from all the Targums in its rendering of the phrase "your brother's blood." Onq. reads: "The voice of the blood *of the descendants who would have come forth from* your brother," which is essentially the same as the paraphrase which we find in the Pal. Tgs. They take the plur. *dmy,* "bloods," of HT to refer to Abel's descendants. This midrashic interpretation is well known; cf. *m. Sanh.* 4, 5; *Gen. R.* 22, 9 (189); *ARN* A 31. Ps.-J. ignores this interpretation; cf. Díez-Macho, *Neophyti 1,* I, 1968, 105*. With Ps.-J.'s phrase "which has been swallowed up by the clay," which anticipates v. 11 to a certain extent, compare Pseudo-Philo, *LAB* XVI, 2: "... *et festinans terra deglutivit sanguinem eius.*" See also the interpolated haggadah in *m. Sanh.* 4, 5: "his blood was cast over the trees and the stones."

[25]*wk'n* = Onq.; Nf, CTg B: *wkdwn.* Onq. uses *k'n* to translate the exhortative particle *n',* or *'th,* "now." Nf usually uses *k'n* to translate *n'* (cf., e.g., Gen 12:11, 13; 13:8, 9, 14; 15:5; 16:2 [twice]; 18:4) and *kdw(n)* to translate *'th* (cf., e.g., Gen 4:11; 19:9; 22:12; 26:22 [Nf: *k'n*; Nfmg: *kdwn*]; 26:29). Ps.-J. translates both *n'* and *'th* by *kdwn,* but it uses *k'n* only rarely, and then possibly under the influence of Onq. Cf. J. Ribera i Florit, "Evolución morfológica y semántica de las partículas *k'n* y *'ry* en los diversos estadios del arameo," *Aula Orientalis* 1 (1983) 227–233; Tal, 1975, 51; Cook, 1986, 164–165.

[26]Ps.-J. and Onq. translate "cursed are you" directly, while the Pal. Tgs. wish to avoid this phrase, which might be taken to refer to the congregation (cf. Shinan, 1979, 1, 198).

[27]= Onq.; Nf, CTg B: "an exile and a wanderer."

[28]Onq.: "my sin," or "my guilt" (*ḥwby*). Ps.-J. alone has "my rebellion."

[29]Ps.-J. has a double translation, of "great," reading lit. "great mighty." Onq.: "too great."

[30]Onq.: "to be forgiven."

but you are able[31] *to forgive it.*[32] 14. Behold, you have driven me out this day from the face of the earth. Is it possible (for me) to hide from you?[33] And *if* I am a wanderer and an exile[34] upon the earth any *righteous person*[35] who finds me will kill me." 15. And the Lord said to him, "*Behold* therefore,[36] whoever kills Cain, revenge shall be taken *on him* for seven *generations.*"[37] Then the Lord *traced* on Cain's *face* a *letter of the great and glorious Name,*[38] so that anyone who would find him, *upon seeing it on him,* would not kill him. 16. Cain went out from the presence of the Lord and settled in the land of *the wandering of his exile which had been made on his account from the beginning in the Garden of* Eden.[39] 17. Cain knew his wife, and she conceived and bore Enoch. He built a city, and named the city after the name of his son Enoch. 18. To Enoch was born Irad,[40] and Irad begot Mehujael, and Mehujael begot Methushael, and Methushael begot Lamech. 19. Lamech took two wives; the name of the one was Adah, and the name of the other was Zillah. 20. Adah bore Jabal; he was *chief*[41] of *all* who dwell in tents and of cattle-*owners.*[42] 21. His brother's name was Jubal; he was *chief* of all *who are appointed*[43] *to play* the harp and the flute. 22. As for Zillah, she bore Tubal-Cain, the *chief of all craftsmen who are skilled in the working of* bronze and iron. And the

Notes, Chapter 4

[31]Lit.: "(there is) ability before you."

[32]See *Gen. R.* 22, 11; *b. Sanh.* 101b (687–688). The words "to bear" and "to forgive" in this verse represent a play on the Heb. *ns'*, "to bear;" see above n. 14 to v. 7. The rabbis regarded Cain's words in Gen 4:13 as an expression of repentance (cf., e.g., *Lev. R.* 10, 5; *PRE* 21 [155–156]). This tradition was known to Josephus (*Ant.* 1 § 58). See below, v. 24. See Ginzberg, *Legends,* 1, 111; 5, 140, n. 24.

[33]None of the Targums accepts the idea that one can hide from God. Onq., Nf, and CTg B have Cain proclaim that it is impossible to hide from God, thus making a statement that contradicts the biblical verse; cf. Klein, 1976, 517–518.

[34]= Onq.; Nf, CTg B: "an exile and a wanderer." See above n. 27 to v. 12.

[35]Cf. *PRE* 21 (156).

[36]Heb. *lkn,* "therefore," is awkward. Pesh., LXX, and Vulg. read "not so." Onq. follows HT, and Ps.-J. adds "behold."

[37]= Onq.

[38]Cf. *PRE* 21 (156). The rabbis gave several different answers to the question: "What sign did God place on Cain?" Cf. *Gen. R.* 22, 12. Ps.-J. (and *PRE*) took Heb. *'wt,* "sign," to mean "letter" (*'t'*), and gave us an interpretation that is not known in the Targums or in rabbinic sources that are earlier than *PRE* and Ps.-J.; cf. Shinan, 1976, 148–150. Unlike the other Targums, Ps.-J. frequently mentions the Divine Name, often attributing magical powers to it. See above, Introduction, p. 7.

[39]Onq.: "and dwelt in the land of exile and wandering which had been made on his account east of the Garden of Eden." In translating "Nod," the Targums were influenced by their translations of the idiom *n' wnd,* "a fugitive and a wanderer," in vv. 12 and 14. The addition ("which had been made ... beginning") in Ps.-J. and Onq. shows that these Targums took *qdmt,* "east of," to mean "from the beginning." See above, n. 55 to 3:24. On Onq.'s version of our present verse, see Bowker, 1967, 54–56. None of the sources which list things that were created on the eve of the first Sabbath (see above, n. 4 to Gen 2:2) mentions the land of Cain's wandering.

[40]HT uses the unusual construction of a passive verb followed by the sign of the accusative, *'t.* Although the Targums sometimes avoid this construction, they (Nf, Ps.-J., Onq.) translate HT directly in our present verse, using a passive verb followed by *yt.* Ps.-J. sometimes retains this construction (cf. Gen 4:18; 17:5; 21:5; 27:42; 46:20; Exod 10:8; Num 11:22; 26:60), but that Targum often modifies the syntax in order to avoid the awkward Heb. construction (cf., e.g., Gen 17:25; 21:8; 29:27; 40:20). See further Klein, 1981, 176–177; idem, 1982, 100–103.

[41]= Onq.; HT: "father."

[42]*mry* = Onq.; HT: "cattle." The Targums clarify the text, as do Pesh., LXX, and Vulg.

[43]Onq.

sister of Tubal-Cain was Naamah; *she was a composer*[44] *of dirges and songs.* 23. Lamech said to his wives Adah and Zillah: "Hearken to my voice, wives of Lamech; listen to my word:[45] I have *not* killed a man so *that I should be killed for him: neither* have I *wounded* a young man so *that my offspring should be exterminated*[46] *because of him.*[47] 24. If for Cain *who sinned and repented*[48] *(judgment) was suspended for* seven *generations, it is surely right that* for Lamech, his *grand*son, *who did not sin, (judgment) should be suspended* for seventy seven." 25. Adam knew his wife again *at the end of a hundred and thirty years after Abel had been killed,*[49] and she bore a son and called his name Seth, for *she said,*[50] *"The Lord has given*[51] me another son* instead of Abel, for Cain killed him." 26. And to Seth also a son was born, and he called[52] his name Enosh. *That was the generation in which*[53] they began *to go astray, making idols for themselves and* calling *their idols* by the name of the *Memra* of the Lord.[54]

Notes, Chapter 4

[44]Lit.: "mistress." The Pal. Tgs. and Ps.-J. associate Naamah with songs, because they derive her name from *n'm,* "be pleasant"; cf. *Gen. R.* 23, 3.

[45]*mymry* = Onq. The Targums sometimes use *memra* in conjunction with a subject other than God; cf., e.g., Gen 9:17 (Ps.-J.); 41:40 (Onq., Ps.-J., CTg C); 45:21 (Onq., Ps.-J., Nfmg); Exod 38:21 (Onq., Ps.-J., Nfmg).

[46]Lit.: "so that they should exterminate (or destroy) my seed."

[47]The Targums give us to understand that Lamech was not guilty of murder and violence. In this they contradict the biblical verse. (See also above, v. 14 and n. 33 to that verse). The Targums make this change in order to harmonize this verse with v. 24, where Lamech argues that if Cain was avenged seven times, then he, Lamech, should be avenged seventy-seven times. The implication of v. 24 is that Lamech's offense was much less serious than Cain's; cf. *Gen. R.* 23, 4. See further Klein, 1976, 518–519.

[48]On Cain's repentance see above, v. 13 and n. 32.

[49]*b. Erub.* 18b (127) explains that when Adam saw that through him death was ordained as a punishment, he separated from his wife for 130 years; see also *Gen. R.* 20:11; 23, 4.

[50]= Onq.

[51]The Targums lose the assonance which we find in HT between the name Seth and the verb *št,* "appointed" (RSV). Ps.-J. and Onq. use the verb *yhb,* while Nf and Nfmg have *šwy,* lit. "placed."

[52]Lond. and *ed. pr.,* influenced by the preceding verse, read "she called."

[53]Lit.: "in whose days."

[54]All the Targums, including Onq. ("the sons of men *were lax in praying* in the name of the Lord") offer a midrashic interpretation of v. 26b. The Pal. Tgs. and Ps.-J. first translate Heb. *hwhl,* "(men) began," literally. They then understand it as if it were derived from *hll,* "profane," and take this to mean that the generation of Enosh profaned the name of God by making idols and calling them by God's name. It is sometimes said that the Targumists intended to eliminate what they saw as a contradiction between 26b and Exod 3:15 and 6:3 (cf. Bowker, 1967, 59; idem, 1969, 140–141; R. Le Déaut, "Un Phénomène spontané de l'herméneutique juive ancienne: le 'targumisme'," *Biblica* 52 (1971) 517; Díez Macho, 1972, 24). It is, however, more probable that the Targumists, following rabbinic tradition, simply wished to portray the contemporaries of Enosh as a wicked generation (Shinan, 1979, 2, 208–210; S. D. Fraade, *Enosh and His Generation* [Chico, Calif.: Scholars Press, 1984] 112–119, 200–201). On different translations and interpretations (ancient and modern) of Gen 4:26b, see S. Sandmel, "Genesis 4:26b," *HUCA* 32 (1961) 19–29.

CHAPTER 5

1. This is the record of the genealogical *line*[1] of Adam. On the day that *the Lord* created Adam, in the likeness[2] of *the Lord* he made him. 2. Male and female he created them. He blessed them *in the name of his Memra,* and called their name Adam on the day they were created. 3. When Adam had lived a hundred and thirty years, he begot *Seth,* who *resembled* his image and likeness. *For before that, Eve had borne Cain, who was not from him and who did not resemble him.*[3] *Abel was killed by Cain, and Cain was banished, and his descendants are not recorded in the book of the genealogy of Adam.*[4] *But afterwards he begot one who resembled him and he called his name Seth.* 4. The days of Adam after he had begotten Seth were eight hundred[5]. . . . 7. . . . and seven years, and he begot sons and daughters. 8. All the days of Seth were nine hundred and twelve years; and he died. 9. Enosh lived ninety years and begot Kenan. 10. After he had begotten Kenan, Enosh lived eight hundred and fifteen years, and he begot sons and daughters. 11. All the days of Enosh were nine hundred and five years; and he died. 12. Kenan lived seventy years and begot Mahalalel. 13. After he had begotten Mahalalel, Kenan lived eight hundred and forty years, and he begot sons and daughters. 14. All the days of Kenan were nine hundred and ten years; and he died. 15. Mahalalel lived sixty-five years and begot Jared. 16. After he had begotten Jared, Mahalalel lived eight hundred and thirty years, and he begot sons and daughters. 17. All the days of Mahalalel were eight hundred and ninety-five years; and he died. 18. Jared lived a hundred and sixty-two years, and he begot Enoch. 19. After he had begotten Enoch, Jared lived eight hundred years, and he begot sons and daughters. 20. All the days of Jared were nine hundred and sixty-two years; and he died. 21. Enoch lived sixty-five years, and he begot Methuselah. 22. Enoch *worshiped in truth before the Lord*[6] after he had begotten Methuselah three hundred years, and he begot sons and daughters. 23. All the days of Enoch *with the inhabitants of the earth*[7] were three hundred and sixty-five years. 24. Enoch *worshiped in truth before the Lord,* and be-

Notes, Chapter 5

[1]Onq.: "the genealogy."

[2]See above, n. 44 to 1:26.

[3]See above, n. 2 to 4:1. Cf. also *b. Erub.* 18b (127); *PRE* 22 (158).

[4]Cf. *PRE* 22 (158–159): "From Cain arose and were descended all the generations of the wicked, who rebel and sin. . . ."

[5]The end of v. 4, vv. 5-6, and the first part of v. 7 are omitted in both Lond. and *ed. pr.* The copyist jumped from the number eight hundred in v. 4 to the same number in v. 7.

[6]HT: "walked (*hlk*; Hithp.) with God." In texts where the verb "walk" is used of humans in relation to God, Nf (see also P, V, N, L Gen 5:24) translates as here: "served (*or:* "worshiped," *plḥ*) in truth before"; thus Nf Gen 5:22, 24; 6:9; 17:1; 24:40. In Gen 48:15, however, the verb "walked" is retained: "your fathers walked before me in truth." Onq. translates in Gen 5:22, 24; 6:9 as "walked in the fear of the Lord." When referring to the patriarchs, Onq. renders as: "worshiped before" (Gen 17:1; 24:40; 48:15). Ps.-J. is inconsistent translating like Nf in Gen 5:22, 24 but translating like Onq. in 6:9; 17:1; 24:40 and 48:15.

[7]This addition is made in Ps.-J. in the light of the following verse, where the phrase "with the inhabitants of the earth" also occurs.

hold he was not *with the inhabitants of the earth* because he was taken away[8] and *he ascended to the firmament at the command of the Lord, and he was called*[9] *Metatron, the Great Scribe.*[10] 25. Methuselah lived a hundred and eighty-seven years, and he begot Lamech. 26. After he had begotten Lamech, Methuselah lived seven hundred and eighty-two years, and he begot sons and daughters. 27. All the days of Methuselah were nine hundred and sixty-nine years; and he died. 28. Lamech lived a hundred and eighty-two years, and he begot a son, 29. and he called him Noah, saying, "Out of the ground which the Lord has cursed *because of the sins of the children of men,* this one will bring us relief from our work *which does not succeed,*[11] and from the toil of our hands." 30. After he had begotten Noah, Lamech lived five hundred and ninety-five years, and he begot sons and daughters. 31. All the days of Lamech were seven hundred and seventy-seven years; and he died. 32. Noah was five hundred years old, and Noah begot Shem, Ham and Japheth.

CHAPTER 6

1. When *the children of* men began to multiply on the face of the earth and *beautiful*[1] daughters were born to them, 2. the sons of *the great ones*[2] saw that the

Notes, Chapter 5 (Cont.)

[8]HT: "(God) took him." The verb used by Ps.-J. is *ngd* (Ithpe.); = Nf, V, N, L. This verb is used by Ps.-J. to translate Heb. *gw'*, "expire, perish," in Gen 6:17; 25:8, 17; 35:29; 49:33. Since in our present verse Ps.-J. goes on to say that Enoch now lives as Metatron, this Targum must be taken to mean that Enoch did not die, but that he was transferred to a new existence; cf. the LXX version of Gen 5:24; *Jubilees* 4, 23; *1 Enoch* 70; *Ethiopic Ascension of Isaiah* 9, 9. On the numerous traditions about Enoch, cf. Ginzberg, *Legends* 1, 125–140; 5, 156–164, nn. 58-61. Bowker, 1969, 143–150; L. R. Ubigli, "La Fortuna di Enoc nel giudaismo antico: valenze e problemi," *Annali di Storia dell Esegesi,* 1 (1984) 153–163 (includes Tgs.); K. Luke, "The Patriarchal Enoch," *Indian Theological Studies* 23 (1986) 125–153.

[9]Lit.: "by a word (or: command) from before the Lord, and he called his name."

[10]The identification of Enoch with Metatron seems to have taken place sometime after 450 C.E.; cf. P. S. Alexander, "The Historical Setting of the Book of Enoch," *JJS* 28 (1977) 156–180, especially 163–165. On Enoch-Metatron traditions, see J. T. Milik, *The Books of Enoch: Aramaic Fragments of Qumran Cave 4* (Oxford: Clarendon, 1976) 125–135. On Metatron, see further S. Lieberman, "Metatron, the meaning of his name and his functions." Appendix 1 to I. Gruenwald, *Apocalyptic and Merkavah Mysticism* (Leiden: Brill, 1980) 235–241.

[11]After the sin of Adam neither the soil nor the animal kingdom was responsive to man's efforts. After the birth of Noah, however, the soil became productive and there was order in the animal world; cf. *Tanḥ., Bereshith* 11 (25); *Gen. R.* 25, 2.

Notes, Chapter 6

[1]By adding "beautiful," Ps.-J. anticipates what is said in v. 2.

[2]= Onq.; Rabbinic tradition considered it blasphemous to translate the phrase "sons of God" literally; cf. *Gen. R.* 26,5; but see *LAB* 3,1. The most ancient interpretation took the sons of God to be "angels" (cf., e.g., *1 Enoch* 6–11; *Jubilees* 5,1). This latter view is retained in Nfmg and *PRE* 22 (160), and it seems to be reflected in Ps.-J.'s version of v. 4, where Shamhazai and Azael are mentioned (see below, n. 10). From the second century C.E. rabbinic and Christian authors, probably reacting against esoteric groups that gave excessive importance to angels, rejected the view that the "sons of God" were angels. On the ancient translations and interpretations of "the sons of God," see P. S. Alexander, 1972, 60–71, with ample bibliography; Bowker, 1969, 153–154.

daughters of men were beautiful, *that they painted their eyes and put on rouge,*[3] *and walked about with naked flesh.*[4] *They conceived lustful thoughts,*[5] and they took wives to themselves from among all who pleased them. 3. The Lord said *in his Memra, "None of the evil generations that are to arise (in the future) will be judged*[6] *according to the order of judgment applied to the generation of the Flood, (that is) to be destroyed and wiped out from the world.*[7] *Did I not put my holy* spirit[8] *in them that they might perform good deeds? But behold, their deeds are evil. Behold, I gave them an extension of* a hundred and twenty years *that they might repent, but they have not done so."*[9] 4. *Shamhazai and Azael*[10] fell *from heaven and* were on earth in those days, and also after the sons of *the great ones*[11] had gone in to the daughters of men, who bore them children; *these are called* the heroes of old, the men of renown. 5. The Lord saw[12] that the wickedness of man increased on earth, and that every impulse of his heart's designs was nothing but evil every day. 6. And the Lord regretted[13] *in his Memra* that he had made man on earth, and *he debated in his Memra about them.*[14] 7. Then the Lord said, "I will wipe out from the face of the earth the men whom I created, man and beast and creeping things and birds of the air, for I regret[15] *in my Memra* that I made them." 8. But Noah *because he was a*

Notes, Chapter 6

[3]Or, perhaps: "curled (or combed) their hair." See Jastrow, 1209; Levy 2, 284. According to *1 Enoch* 8, 1-2, Azaz'el (see Ps.-J. v. 4 and n. 10 below) taught the people the art of "decorations (shadowing of the eye) with antinomy, ornamentation, the beautifying of the eyelids . . . and all coloring tinctures and alchemy."

[4]*PRE* 22 (160; Luria 50b–51a): "The angels . . . saw the daughters of the generations of Cain walking about naked, with their eyes painted (*mkhlwt 'ynyhn*). . . ." For "painted their eyes" Ps.-J. uses the corresponding Aramaic verb *khl.* (*ed. pr.*; Lond.: *ksl*). See also *Tanna debe Eliyyahu* 31(29) (384), which says that the men of the generation of the flood walked about naked in the marketplace.

[5]Cf. *Gen. R.* 26,7.

[6]This paraphrase about judgment in the Pal. Tgs. and Ps.-J. was triggered by the obscure Heb. word *ydwn* (RSV: "abide in"), which was linked with the word *dyn,* "judgment." Cf. *m. Sanh.* 10,3; *b. Sanh.* 108a (739); Bowker, 1969, 154–155; J. Schlosser, "Les jours de Noé et de Lot," *RB* 80 (1973) 13–36, especially 16.

[7]Thus, even before the Flood takes place, God promises that there will never be another Flood. Cf. *Gen. R.* 26:6: "Never again will I judge man with this judgment," i.e., with a flood. Compare Gen 9:11.

[8]Ps.-J. and the Pal. Tgs. take "my spirit (*rwhy*)" to be God's spirit enabling humans to do good deeds. On the Holy Spirit in the Targums, see vol. 1A, Introduction, pp. 38–39.

[9]Onq.: ". . . *their deeds are evil; let an extension be granted to them for 120 years (to see) if they will repent.*" Cf. *Mekilta* to Exod 15:6 (2,39-40); *Tanh., Beshallah* 15 (229); *ARN* A 32; see also Jerome, *Quaest. hebr.* in Gen. 6:3. It is to be noted that Ps.-J. Gen 7:4 gives a further opportunity (seven days) for repentance to the generation of the Flood.

[10]Lond.: *'z'l*; *ed. pr.*: *'wzy'l.* Onq.: "mighty ones" or "giants" (*gbry'*). Ps.-J. interprets Nephilim as if it were derived from *npl,* "fall," and takes it to refer to angels who fell from heaven. Ps.-J. then identifies the fallen angels as Shamhazai and Azael, who were among the leaders of the fallen angels (cf. *1 Enoch* 6, 3.7; 8, 1; 9,6.7; 10,8.11; see also *b. Yoma* 67b (316). *PRE* 22 (160) identifies the Nephilim as "the angels who fell," but does not name the angels. Ps.-J. often names individuals who are not named in the Bible; see, e.g., Gen 14:13 (Og); 21:21 (Adisha, Fatima); 22:3 (Eliezer, Ishmael); 42:27 (Levi); Exod 2:1 (Amram, Jochebed). See further H. Petermann, 1829, 53–54; Cashdan, 1967, 31–39. On the role of fallen angels in the fall of the human race, see Bowker, 1969, 157–158.

[11]= Onq.

[12]= HT and Onq.; Nf: "it was revealed before."

[13]*wtb* = Onq.; Nf, V, N, L: "there was regret before"; Nfmg: "regret." Whereas Ps.-J. agrees with Onq. against Nf in our present verse and in v. 7b (cf. n. 15), in Exod 32:12, where there is again reference to the Lord's repenting, Ps.-J. agrees with Nf against Onq.

[14]RSV: "and it grieved him to his heart." The Targums avoid the anthropopathism of this statement. Onq. reads: "and he was determined to break their power according to his will."

[15]*tbyt* = Onq.; Nf as in v. 6 ("there was regret before"); Nfmg: "regret." See n. 13 to v. 6.

righteous man [16] found favor *before* the Lord. [17] 9. This is the genealogy of *the family of* Noah: Noah was an *innocent* man, he was perfect *in good works*, [18] in his age. Noah walked *in the fear of the Lord*. [19] 10. Noah begot three sons, Shem, Ham and Japheth. 11. The earth became corrupt *because of its inhabitants who strayed from the ways that are right* before *the Lord*, and the earth was filled with (acts of) robbery. [20] 12. *The Lord* saw the earth, and behold, it was corrupt, because all flesh, *without exception*, [21] had corrupted its ways upon the earth. 13. So *the Lord* said to Noah, "The end of all flesh has come, for the earth is full of (acts of) robbery, *because of their evil deeds*. [22] Behold, I shall destroy them with the earth. 14. Make yourself an ark of cedar wood; you shall make *a hundred and fifty* compartments [23] for the ark *on the left, and thirty-six in its breadth, and ten cabins in the middle in which food may be stored, and five reservoirs on the right and five on the left*. [24] And you shall plaster it inside and out with bitumen. 15. . . . . . [25] 16. *Go to Pishon and from there take a gem*, [26] *and put it* in the ark to *give you light*. You shall complete it

Notes, Chapter 6

[16]HT: "And Noah found favor in the eyes of God," without reference to his righteousness. Ps.-J. asserts, without qualification, that Noah was a righteous man (cf. *Jubilees* 5,19; 1 *QGenApoc* 6,2; Tg. Isa 65:8). The midrashim say that he was righteous (only) in (comparison with) his generation; cf. Gen 6:9; *Gen. R.* 30,9; *b. Sanh.* 108a (741–742). In Gen 9:20, after the Flood, the Pal. Tgs. call Noah righteous, but Ps.-J. does not. On rabbinic attitudes to Noah, see Ginzberg, *Legends* 1, 159; 5, 178, n. 28; J. C. Vanderkam, "The Righteousness of Noah," in *Ideal Figures in Ancient Judaism*, ed. S.W.E. Nickelsburg and J. J. Collins (Chico, Calif.: Scholars Press, 1980) 13–27; E. G. Clarke, 1986, 337–345.

[17]HT: "in the eyes of the Lord." For the use of paraphrases in order to avoid anthropomorphism, see Introduction, vol. 1A, pp. 33–35. The Targums generally translate the phrase "in the eyes of the Lord" as "before the Lord"; cf., besides our present verse, the Targums of Gen 38:7, 10; Exod 33:12, 17 (in v. 17 Nf has "in my sight," lit. "in my face"); Lev 10:19; Num 23:27; 24:1; 32:13; Deut 4:25; etc.; see further Aberbach-Grossfeld, 1982, 54, n. 12.

[18]= Nf; Onq.: "perfect." When HT refers to someone as "blameless" (*tm, tmym*), Nf regularly translates that word as "perfect in good works." Ps.-J. agrees with Nf in our present verse. In 25:27 Ps.-J. reads "perfect in his works." In Deut 18:13 Ps.-J. agrees with Onq. ("perfect in the fear [of the Lord]") against Nf and Nfmg. In Gen 17:1, Ps.-J. differs from both Nf and Onq. See also Gen 33:18 (Nf) and 34:21 (Nf, Ctg C), where "in good works" is added in the translation of *šlm*, "safe, friendly." According to Num 12:1, Zipporah (Nf, P, V, N, L) and Saul (P) were distinguished by their good works. Exod 13:18 (Nf, P, V, N) says that the Israelites left Egypt "armed with good works." Abel declared that the world is governed by the fruit of good works (Gen 4:8 V, N, Ps.-J.). Compare the term "good works" in Eph 2:10; Titus 2:14.

[19]HT: "Noah walked with God"; see n. 6 to Gen 5:22.

[20]"(Acts of) robbery" = Onq.

[21]Onq.: "all human flesh." Onq. explains that "all flesh" of HT refers only to humans. Ps.-J.'s addition conveys the idea that all living things acted corruptly; *Gen. R.* 28,8. See also *b. Sanh.* 108a (742).

[22]= Onq.

[23]*Gen. R.* 31,9 explains that Heb. *qnym*, "rooms," means *qylyn wmdwryn*, "cells and chambers" (Theodor-Albeck, 281). Ps.-J. translates *qnym* as *qwlyn*, while Onq. and Nf use *mdwryn/mdwrwnyn*.

[24]*PRE* 23 (164) says that there were to be fifty rooms on the left side of the ark and thirty-three across its width, and that there were to be five cisterns on the right of the ark and fifty (or five) on the left side. It would seem that Ps.-J. knew this tradition.

[25]V. 15 is omitted in Lond. and *ed. pr.*

[26]The obscure word *ṣhr* of HT (RSV: "roof" or "window") is understood in different ways in the midrash. According to *Gen. R.* 31,11, R. Abba b. Kahana said it means a skylight or window (*ḥlwn*), while R. Levi took it to be a precious stone (*mrglyt*), and another view asserted that Noah had a polished gem (*mrglyt*) which provided him with light. See also *b. Sanh.* 108b (744); *j. Pesaḥ.* 1,27b; *PRE* 23 (166-167). Compare *LAB* 25,12. Onq. ("Make a light") and Nf are in line with the first interpretation given in *Gen. R.* Ps.-J. follows the other views expressed in *Gen. R.* and takes *ṣhr* to be a kind of precious stone which gave light to the inhabitants of the ark. Symmachus renders the Hebrew word as *diaphanes* ("transparent"), in which Jerome sees "window" implied (Jerome, *Quaest. hebr.* in Gen 6:16). There is no parallel in rabbinic literature for Ps.-J.'s words "Go to Pishon . . . gem." However, Ps.-J. refers to the precious stones of Pishon (cf. Gen 2:11-12) not only in our present verse but also in Exod 14:9 and 35:27. Cf. Shinan, 1979, 1, 43.

to a cubit from the top. Put the door of the ark in its side. With lower, second, and third *compartments*[27] shall you make it. 17. For my part, behold, I will bring flood-waters upon the earth to destroy all flesh under the heavens in which there is the breath of life; everything on earth shall perish.[28] 18. But I will establish my covenant with you, and you shall enter the ark, you, your sons, your wife and your sons' wives with you. 19. Of all that lives, of all flesh, you shall take two of each into the ark to keep alive with you; they shall be male and female. 20. From birds according to their kinds, from the animals according to their kinds, from every creeping thing of the earth according to its kind, two of each shall come to you, *(brought) by an angel that will catch them and bring them to you*[29] to keep (them) alive. 21. For your part, take of every food that is eaten,[30] so that it may serve as food for you and for them." 22. Noah did according to all that *the Lord* had commanded him.[31]

CHAPTER 7

1. The Lord said to Noah, "Go into the ark, you and all *the members of*[1] your household, for I have seen that you are *innocent*[2] before me in this generation. 2. Of every clean animal you shall take seven pairs, *male* and *female,*[3] and of the animals that are not clean, two, *male* and *female;*[3] 3. of the birds of the heavens also, seven pairs, male and female, to keep *their* seed alive upon <the face of all>[4] the earth. 4. For *behold I will give them*[5] *an extension of seven days; if they repent it shall be forgiven them;*[6] *but if they do not repent,* after a further *period* of seven days

Notes, Chapter 6 (Cont.)

[27]= Onq., Nf.

[28]All the Targums translate Heb. *ygw'*, "shall die" (RSV) differently. Ps.-J uses the verb *ngd* (Ithpe.) (see above, n. 8 to ch. 5); Onq. employs *mwt, "die,"* and N has *šyṣy* (Ishtaf.).

[29]According to *PRE* 23 (166), when God commanded Noah to bring all the animals into the ark, Noah said, "Have I then the strength to collect them unto me to the ark?" The text then continues: "The angels appointed over each kind went down and gathered them...." Ps.-J. seems to have abbreviated this tradition. Cf. Shinan 1979, 2, 261 and n. 92; Ginzberg, *Legends,* 5, 177, n. 24).

[30]Both Lond. and *ed. pr.* omit the words "and store it up" (RSV).

[31]Both Lond. and *ed. pr.* omit the words "so he did."

Notes, Chapter 7

[1]Where Hebrew *byt* means "household," the Targums, especially Nf, frequently make this meaning clear by adding "the members (lit.: the men) of." See, e.g., Gen 12:17; 18:19; 34:30; 35:2; 41:51; 45:2, 8, 11, 18; 46:27; 47:12; 50:4, 22; Exod 1:1.

[2]= Onq. See n. 16 to 6:8.

[3]= Onq.

[4]Omitted in Lond. and *ed. pr.*

[5]= Lond.; *ed. pr.:* "to you."

[6]Cf. *Gen. R.* 32, 7; *b. Sanh.* 108b (744); *ARN* A 32; Philo, *Quaestiones in Genesim* II, 13; Ephraem in his commentary on Gen 7:6 (cf. R. M. Tonneau, *Sancti Ephraem Syri in Genesim et in Exodum Commentarii* [*Corpus Scriptorum Christianorum Orientalium* 153], Louvain: Durbecq, 1955, 47). Ps.-J. is the only Targum of Gen 7:6 to recall this tradition. See above, 6:3 and n. 9 to that verse.

I will cause rain to come down upon the earth forty days and forty nights, and all *the bodies of men and beasts* <that I have made> I will blot out <from the face of>[7] the earth." 5. And Noah did according to all that the Lord had commanded him. 6. Noah was six hundred years old when the Flood came, the waters upon the earth. 7. Noah and his sons and his wife and his sons' wives with him went into the ark because of the waters of the Flood. 8. Of animals that are clean and of animals that are not clean, of birds, and of everything that creeps upon the earth, 9. two of each, male and female, came to Noah into the ark, as *the Lord* had commanded Noah. 10. *After* seven days, *when the mourning for Methuselah*[8] *had been completed, the Lord saw, and behold the children of men had not repented;*[9] and the waters of the Flood *came down boiling*[10] *from the heavens* upon the earth. 11. In the six hundredth year of Noah's life, in the second month, *that is the month of Marcheshvan,*[11] *for until then months had been counted only from Tishri which was the beginning of the year according to the completion of the world*[12]—in the seventeenth day of the month, on that day all the springs of the great abyss were rent; *and the sons of the giants placed their children there and shut them up;*[13] *but afterwards* the windows of the heavens were opened. 12. The rain *came down*[14] upon the earth forty days and forty nights. 13. That same day[15] Noah, Shem, Ham, and Japheth, Noah's sons, and Noah's wife, and the three wives of his sons with *him,* went into the ark, 14. they and all wild beasts according to their kinds, and all the cattle according to their kinds, and every creeping thing that creeps upon the earth according to its kind, every fowl according to its kind, every bird, everything *that flies.*[16] 15. They came to Noah into the ark, two each of all flesh in which there was the breath of life. 16. And they that entered, male and female of all flesh, entered as *the Lord* God[17] commanded him; and *the Memra of* the Lord *protected the door of the ark before him.*[18] 17. The Flood continued forty days upon the earth, and the

Notes, Chapter 7

[7] The words "that I have made" and "from the face of" are omitted in Lond. and *ed. pr.*

[8] *t. Sotah* 10, 3; *Gen. R.* 32, 7; *b. Sanh.* 108b (744); *ARN* A 32; Philo, *Quaestiones in Genesim* II, 13. Nf and P mention the mourning for Methuselah, but they do not go on, as does Ps.-J. (and *Gen. R.*) to state that the generation of the Flood had failed to repent.

[9] Reading *tbw* for *thw* of Lond.; *ed. pr.: tbn.*

[10] *j. Sanh.* 10, 29b; *b. Rosh Hash.* 12a (43); *Sanh.* 108b (743); *PRE* 22 (162).

[11] *b. Rosh Hash.* 11b (43); *PRE* 23 (167). Ps.-J. often specifies the dates on which events took place; cf. above n. 6 to Gen 4:3.

[12] According to *Gen. R.* 22, 4 and *b. Rosh Hash.* 10b (39), R. Eliezer said that the world was created in Tishri. According to this reckoning, Marcheshvan is the second month. On the Jewish calender see, Schürer, 1973, 587–601; *EJ* 5, 43–50.

[13] *Tanh., Noah* 7 (36); *Tanh.* B., *Noah* 10 (1, 35–36).

[14] = Onq.

[15] Ps.-J. and Onq. usually agree in translating Heb. *b'ṣm hywm hzh,* "on the very same day," as *bkrn ywm' hdyn*; see Gen 7:13; 17:23, 26. Exod 12:17, 41, 51; Lev 23:14, 21 (in 21 Ps.-J. has a conflate rendering), 28, 29, 30; Deut 32:48. The Pal. Tgs. normally use the formula *bzmn ywm' (h)dyn.*

[16] = Onq.

[17] *Ed. pr.*: "the Lord."

[18] In the Heb. phrase *wysgr yhwh b'dw,* lit. "and the Lord closed for him" (RSV: "and the Lord shut him in"), the verb *sgr* has no direct object. LXX supplies an object and reads "and the Lord God shut the ark outside of him." The Targums paraphrase. Onq.: "and the Lord protected him" (comp. *Gen. R.* 32:8). With Ps.-J.'s version compare *PRE* 23 (166), which says that God "closed and sealed with his hand the gate (or door) of the ark."

waters increased and lifted up the ark so that it was raised above the earth. 18. The waters swelled and increased greatly upon the earth, and the ark went *floating*[19] on the surface of the waters. 19. The waters swelled greatly upon the earth, and all the high mountains that are under the whole heavens were covered. 20. The waters swelled fifteen cubits higher, and the mountains were covered. 21. And all flesh that creeps upon the earth perished,[20] birds and cattle, and (wild) beasts, and all creeping things that creep upon the earth, and all *the children of* men. 22. Everything that has the breath of the spirit of life in its nostrils, everything (on) the dry land, died. 23. He blotted out every *body of man and beast* that was upon the face of the earth—man, cattle, creeping things, and the birds *that fly in the air* of the heavens; they were blotted out from the earth, and only Noah was left and those who were with him in the ark. 24. And the waters swelled upon the earth a hundred and fifty days.

CHAPTER 8

1. *The Lord in his Memra* remembered Noah and all the beasts and all the cattle that were with him in the ark. And God caused a merciful wind[1] to cross over the earth, and the waters abated. 2. The fountains of the deep and the windows of the heavens were closed, and the rain was held back *from coming down* from the heavens; 3. the waters receded gradually from upon the earth. At the end of a hundred and fifty days the waters had diminished, 4. and in the seventh month, *that is the month of Nisan,*[2] on the seventeenth day of the month, the ark came to rest upon the mountains of *Kardun;*[3] *the name of one mountain is Cordyene and the name of another mountain is Armenia. There the city of Armenia was built in the land of the east.* 5. The waters gradually diminished until the tenth month, *the month of*

Notes, Chapter 7 (Cont.)

[19]*Gen. R.* 32:9.
[20]Lit.: "melted away," = Nfmg. Onq.: "died."

Notes, Chapter 8

[1]Ps.-J. and the Pal. Tgs. render *rwh,* "wind, spirit" as "wind (or spirit) (*rwh*) of mercy," as in Gen 1:2; see above n. 5 to Gen 1:2.
[2]On the duration of the Flood, see *Gen. R.* 33,7. Ps.-J., alone among the Targums, identifies the seventh month (of the year) as Nisan. This agrees with 7:11 (see above n. 12 on that verse), where Ps.-J. states that the months were counted from Tishri. But see Ps.-J. Lev 16:29; 23:24; Num 29:1, 7, where Tishri is regarded as the seventh month.
[3]*Ed. pr.* reads Kadrun. Onq., CTg B, and Pesh. have Kardu. Ararat is frequently identified with Kardu, which Neubauer (1868, 379) takes to be Kurdistan. See Josephus, *Ant.* 1 § 93); *Gen. R.* 33,4; Tg. Jon. 2 Kings 19:37; Isa 37:38; Jer 51:27. See further, Ginzberg, *Legends,* 5, 186, n. 48.

Tammuz.[4] *In Tammuz* on the first of the month, the tops of the mountains were seen. 6. At the end of forty days Noah opened the aperture[5] of the ark which he had made, 7. and he sent forth the raven. It went to and fro[6] until the waters had dried up from the earth. 8. Then he sent forth the *clean*[7] dove from him to see if the waters had subsided from the face of the earth. 9. But the dove did not find a resting place for the sole of her foot[8] and she returned to him to the ark, *thus making known* that there was water upon the face of all the earth. So he put out his hand and took her and brought her to him into the ark. 10. So he waited[9] another seven days, and again he sent out the dove from the ark. 11. The dove came to him at evening time, and behold, an olive leaf plucked off, *broken off*[10] *and placed*[11] in her beak, *which she had taken from the Mount of Olives.*[12] Then Noah knew that the waters had subsided from upon the earth. 12. He waited[9] yet another seven days and sent forth the dove; but she did not return to him again. 13. In the six hundred and first year, *in Tishri,*[13] on the first of the month, *at the beginning of the year,* the waters had dried up from upon the earth. Then Noah removed the covering of the ark, and looked <and behold> the face of the earth had dried up. 14. In the month of *Marcheshvan,*[14] on the twenty-seventh day of the month, the earth was dried up. 15. Then *the Lord* spoke to Noah, saying: 16. "Go forth from the ark, you and your wife, your sons and your sons' wives with you. 17. Bring forth with you every living thing of all flesh that is with you: birds, animals, and every creeping thing that creeps upon the earth. Let them reproduce on the earth, and let them increase and multiply upon the earth." 18. So Noah went forth, together with his sons, his wife and his sons' wives. 19. Every beast, every creeping thing, and every bird, <everything> that creeps upon the earth, went forth from the ark by families. 20. Then Noah built an altar *before the Lord—it is the altar which Adam built*

Notes, Chapter 8

[4]Ps.-J., alone among the Targums, identifies the tenth month. When identifying the seventh month in v. 4, Ps.-J counted from Tishri, the first month of the year (see n. 2). The author follows the same procedure in v. 5. Counting from Tishri, he identifies Tammuz as the tenth month. According to Tg. Jon. Ezek 1:1, which regards Nisan as the first month, Tammuz is the fourth month.

[5]= Onq.

[6] = Onq.; comp. Nf., CTg B.

[7]Lond.: *dkyyt',* "clean"; *ed. pr.: dbyyt',* "domestic." The fact that *PRE* 23 (168) (see also *b. Sanh.* 108b [745-746]) focuses on the fact that the dove was clean, whereas the raven was unclean, would support the reading "clean." See Rieder, 1965, 117.

[8]*prst rygl' (rglh)* = Onq.; Nf: *kp rglh.*

[9]*'wryk* = Onq.; Nf: *šry.*

[10]Ps.-J. gives a double translation of Heb. *ṭrp,* "plucked off," first using *lqyṭ,* "plucked off, gleaned," to which it adds *tbyr* (= Onq.), "broken, plucked off." Nf uses *qṭym,* "cut off."

[11]= Onq. Lit.: "resting, lying."

[12]= Nfmg. Some rabbis held that the dove brought the olive branch from the land of Israel, while others said from the Mount of Olives, and still others asserted that she took it from the Garden of Eden (cf. *Gen. R.* 33,6; *Lev. R.* 31,10; *Song R.* 1,15,4; 4,1,2. Cf. Bowker, 1969, 170.

[13]= Nfmg 2; Nfmg 1: "in Nisan." See above 7:11, with n. 11 to that verse, and 8:4 with n. 2. For the view that Nisan was the first month (Nfmg 1), cf. Exod 12:2; *m. Rosh Hash.* 1,1; cf. *b. Rosh Hash.* 11b (42); *Abod. Zar.* 8a (37).

[14]= Nfmg. If Tishri is the first month (see v. 13 and n. 13), Marcheshvan is the second.

at the time he was banished from the garden of Eden and on which he offered an of-
fering, and upon which Cain and Abel offered their offerings. But when the waters of
the flood came down it was destroyed. Noah rebuilt it and took of all clean animals
and of all clean birds, and offered *four* burnt offerings[15] upon *that*[16] altar. 21. The
Lord *accepted his offering with favor,*[17] and the Lord said *in his Memra:*[18] "I will
never again curse the earth on account of *the sins of the children of* men,[19] for the
inclination of man's heart is evil from his youth, and I shall never again strike
everything *that* lives, as I have done. 22. As long as the earth endures, sowing *in the*
season of Tishri, and harvest *in the season of Nisan,* cold *in the season of Tebeth,*
and heat *in the season of Tammuz,*[20] summer and winter, day and night, shall not
cease."

CHAPTER 9

1. God blessed Noah and his sons, and said to them, "Increase and multiply and
fill the earth. 2. The fear of you and the dread of you shall be upon every beast of
the earth, and upon every bird of the heavens, on everything with which the earth
swarms, and on all the fish of the sea; into your hand they *shall be* delivered.[1] 3.
Every moving thing that lives shall be yours for food; like the green plants, I have
given all (these) to you. 4. But flesh *that has been torn from a living beast while* its
life *is still in it,*[2] or that has been torn from a slaughtered animal before all its breath
has gone forth,[3] you shall not eat. 5. Moreover, for your lifeblood I will require a
reckoning; of every beast *that kills a man* I will require it, *so that it be killed on his*

Notes, Chapter 8 (Cont.)

[15]"Burnt offerings" omitted in *ed. pr.*

[16]*ARN* A 1 records that Adam built altars and offered a burnt offering. According to *Gen. R.* 34, 9, Noah offered a sacrifice "on the great altar in Jerusalem, where Adam sacrificed." *PRE* 23 (171) records that Noah built up the altar upon
which Cain and Abel had brought offerings, and brought *four* burnt offerings. See below, Ps.-J. Gen 22:9.

[17]= Onq., Nf; cf. *LAB* 3,8. The Targums avoid the anthropomorphism of the biblical phrase "the Lord smelled the
pleasing odor." This is usual in Onq. and Ps.-J. (cf., e.g., Lev 1:9, 13, 17; Num 15:3, 7, 10, 13, 14, 24). In these texts Nf
speaks of a "pleasing odor before the Lord."

[18]= Onq. Ps.-J. and Onq. avoid the anthropomorphism of the biblical phrase "the Lord said to himself (lit.: "to his
heart").

[19]= Onq.: "man's sins."

[20]*Gen. Rab.* 34,11; *b. B. Mez.* 106b (608-609); *PRE* 8 (53). This latter passage offers the closest parallel to Ps.-J.'s text.

Notes, Chapter 9

[1]Onq. (Sperber): "have been delivered." But some versions of Onq. read "shall be delivered"; cf. Sperber, 1959, 13.

[2]*Gen. R.* 34, 13; *b. Sanh.* 57a (386); 59a-b (400, 404). The eating of flesh cut from a living animal was one of the seven
things forbidden to the children of Noah; cf. *b. Sanh.* 56a (381–382); *t. Abod. Zar.* 8, 4.6 (Zuckermandel, 473).

[3]*b. Hul.* 121b (675-6); *Sanh.* 63a (430).

account. Of man, too, of the man *who sheds* his brother's *blood,*[4] I will demand the life of man. 6. Whoever sheds the blood of man *in the presence of witnesses, the judges*[5] *shall condemn him to death; but whoever sheds (it) without witnesses, the Lord of the world will take revenge of him on the day of the great judgment;*[6] because in the likeness[7] of God he has made man. 7. And you, increase and multiply; reproduce on the earth and multiply on it." 8. And God said to Noah and to his sons with him, 9. "As for me, behold I establish my covenant with you and with your *children*[8] after you, 10. and with every living thing that is with you—birds, *and* cattle, and every beast of the earth *that is* with you—all that came out of the ark, every beast of the earth. 11. I will establish my covenant with you, and never again will all flesh be blotted out by the waters of the flood, and never again shall there be a flood to destroy the earth." 12. And God said: "This is the sign of the covenant which I am establishing[9] between *my Memra* and you, and every living thing that is with you, for eternal generations.[10] 13. I have set my bow in the cloud, and it shall be a sign of the covenant between *my Memra* and the earth. 14. When I *spread* clouds *of Glory* over the earth the bow shall be seen *in the daytime, as long as the sun has not sunk*[11] in the cloud, 15. and I will remember my covenant which is between *my Memra* and you and every living thing of all flesh, and the waters shall never again become a flood to destroy all flesh. 16. The bow will be in the cloud, and I will see it and remember the eternal covenant between *the Memra of* God and every living thing of all flesh that is upon the earth." 17. And God said to Noah: "This is the sign of the covenant which I have established between *my Memra* and *the Memra of* all flesh that is upon the earth." 18. The sons of Noah who went out of the ark were Shem, Ham, and Japheth. Ham is the father of Canaan. 19. These three were the sons of Noah, and from them (the peoples) were scattered abroad[12] *to dwell in* all the earth. 20. Noah[13] began *to be a man tilling* the earth.[14] *And he found a vine which the river had brought from the garden of Eden,*[15] and he planted *it in order (to have)* a vineyard. *That same day it sprouted and ripened grapes, and he pressed them.* 21. He drank of the wine and became drunk, and he uncovered himself within his tent. 22. Ham, the father of Canaan, saw his fa-

Notes, Chapter 9

[4]= Onq.

[5]Onq.: "in the presence of witnesses, by sentence of the judges." By referring to witnesses and judges, Ps.-J. and Onq. rule out the possibility of private blood-vengeance; cf. *Gen. R.* 34:14; *b. Sanh.* 57b (390).

[6]*Mekilta* to Exod 23:7 (3,171–172); *Gen. R.* 34, 14; *Deut. R.* 2, 25.

[7]*dywqn'.* See above, n. 44 to 1:26.

[8]= Onq.; HT: "your seed."

[9]Onq., CTg E: "place, set," lit. "give," = HT.

[10]= Onq. Ps.-J. and Onq. give a direct translation of the Heb. idiom. Nfmg reproduces the Heb. words.

[11]The source of this obscure addition is unknown; cf. Brayer, 1950, 20; idem, 1964, 214.

[12]= Onq. HT reads "all the earth was scattered abroad." Ps.-J. and Onq. wish to clarify the text by using a plural form of the verb. Compare Nf and CTg E.

[13]Nf, P, V, N, CTg E call Noah "righteous." Onq. and Ps.-J. do not. See above, n. 16 to 6:8.

[14]See above, n. 4 to 4:2.

[15]*PRE* 23 (170); *3 Baruch* 4, 9–13. Philo (*Quaestiones in Genesim* II, 67) had asked where could Noah have found a vine after the Flood. According to *b. Sanh.* 70a (478), the tree from which Adam ate was a vine.

ther's nakedness and told his two brothers in the street.[16] 23. But Shem and Japheth took a mantle,[17] placed (it) on both their shoulders, and going backwards, covered their father's nakedness; their faces were *turned away* so that they did not see their father's nakedness. 24. When Noah awoke from his wine, he knew *by being told in a dream*[18] what had been done to him by *Ham* his son, *who was* slight in merit[19] *because he was the cause of his not begetting a fourth son.*[20] 25. And he said, "Cursed be Canaan, *who is his fourth son.*[21] A slave *reduced to slavery* shall he be to his brothers." 26. He said, "Blessed be the Lord, the God of Shem, *whose conduct was righteous; therefore* Canaan shall be *his* servant. 27. May God *adorn*[22] the *borders of* Japheth. May *his sons become proselytes and* dwell *in the schoolhouse*[23] of Shem; and let Canaan be a slave to them. 28. Noah lived three hundred and fifty years after the flood. 29. And all the days of Noah were nine hundred and fifty years; and he died.

CHAPTER 10

1. These are the generations of the sons of Noah, <Shem, Ham, and Japheth>;[1] sons were born to them after the Flood. 2. The sons of Japheth: Gomer, Magog,

Notes, Chapter 9 (Cont.)

[16]Or "in the marketplace"; = Onq. Ephraem also knew the reading "in the street;" cf. S. Brock, 1979, 219. The Targums usually translate Heb. *ḥwṣ*, "outside," literally as *br'* (cf., e.g., the Targums of Gen 15:5; 19:16, 17; 24:29, 31), although they sometimes translate it by "the street"; (cf. the Targums of Gen 39:12, 13, 15, 18 and Deut 24:11ab (Ps.-J., Nfmg) and 25:5 (Ps.-J.). By translating Hebrew "outside" as "in the street" in our present verse (9:22), the Targums emphasize the shameful nature of Ham's deed. See Aberbach-Grossfeld, 1982, 67, n. 11; Grossfeld, 1988, 59, n. 4.

[17]*'sṭl';* = *ed. pr.;* Lond.: *'skṭl'.* Greek/Latin: *stolê/stola;* = Nf.

[18]Lit.: "by the narration of a dream." Ps.-J., alone among the Targums, explains how Noah could have known what had happened to him when he was drunk. The source of Ps.-J. 's addition is not known; cf. Brayer, 1964, 214. Ps.-J. sometimes tells how hidden things were revealed to different people (cf. Exod 1:15; 32:20, 28; Num 31:18; Deut 21:8).

[19]The statement that Ham was "slight (or little) in merit" is based on a play on the biblical words "his youngest (lit. little) son." *Gen. R.* 36, 7 explains that "his youngest son" means "his worthless son."

[20]See *Gen. R.* 36, 7; *b. Sanh.* 70a (477-8); *PRE* 23 (170). The texts from *b. Sanh.* and *PRE* say that Ham castrated Noah. See further, Ginzberg, *Legends,* 1, 168; 5, 191 n. 60. Ps.-J. is the only Targum to hint at the rather crude idea that Ham castrated his father. On Ps.-J.'s tendency to use coarse language, see above, Introduction, p. 7.

[21]Cf. Gen 10:6. Canaan, Ham's fourth son, is cursed because Ham prevented Noah from having a fourth son; see v. 24 and the texts from *Gen. R.* and *b. Sanh.* 70a referred to in n. 20.

[22]Ps.-J. links the name Japheth with the Heb. verb *yph,* "be beautiful." Compare the interpretations of Gen 9:27 in *b. Meg.* 9b (50); see especially the words of *R. Hiyya:* "let the chief beauty (*ypwt*) of Japheth (i.e., the Greek language) be in the tents of Shem."

[23]= Nfmg. Apart from Ps.-J. and Nfmg, we know of no other source which uses Gen 9:27 to support the idea that the sons of Japheth (the Greeks) would become proselytes; cf. Shinan, 1979, 2, 343, n. 210. The mention of "the schoolhouse (here simply *mdrš';* see also Ps.-J. Deut 23:17; 29:5) of Shem" is due to the fact that the biblical word "tent" was taken to refer to the *beth ha-Midrash* or schoolhouse; cf., e.g., Onq., Nf, Ps.-J. Gen 25:27 (*Gen. R.* 63, 10); Nf, Nfi, Ps.-J. Num 24:5. "The schoolhouse of Shem" is mentioned in the Targums of Gen 22:19 (Ps.-J.); 25:22 (Nf, Nfmg, Ps.-J., P, V, N, L). See also n. 34 to Gen 22:19 below.

Notes, Chapter 10

[1]Omitted in Lond. and in *ed. pr.*

Madai, Javan, Tubal, Meshech, and Tiras. *And the names of their provinces:*[2] *Phrygia,*[3] *Germania,*[4] *Media,*[5] *Macedonia, Bithynia, Asia,*[6] *and Thrace.* 3. The sons of Gomer: Ashkenaz, Riphath, and Togarmah. 4. <The sons of Javan: Elishah>:[7] *Hellas, Tarsus,*[8] *Achaia,*[9] *and Dardania.*[10] 5. From these *the families* of the coastland peoples[11] spread out <in their lands>,[1] each with its language, according to their lineage, in their nations. 6. The sons of Ham: Cush, Mizraim, Put, and Canaan. *And the names of their provinces: Arabia, Egypt, Allihroq,*[12] and Canaan. 7. The sons of Cush: Seba, Havilah, Sabtah, Raamah, and Sabteca. <The sons of Raamah: Sheba and Dedan>.[13] *And the names of their provinces: Sinirites,*[14] *Indians,*[15] *Semarites,*[16] *Lybians, Zingites* and the sons of *Mauritanos, Zemargad, and Mezag.* 8. Kush begot Nimrod; he began to be a mighty *sinner and rebel* on earth *before the Lord.*[17] 9. He was a mighty *rebel*[18] before the Lord. Therefore it is said: "*From the day the world was created there has not been* a mighty hunter *and rebel* like Nimrod before the Lord." 10. The beginning of his kingdom was Babylon *the Great, Edessa, Nisibis, and Ctesiphon,*[19] in the land of *Pontus.*[20] 11. From that land *Nimrod* went forth *and ruled over* Assyria, *because he did not*

Notes, Chapter 10

[2]Ps.-J., Nf, V, and N borrow the Greek word *eparchia,* which corresponds to the Latin *provincia.* In this chapter the Targumists take the biblical place-names to refer to peoples and places of the Greco-Roman world. The identifications made find parallels in the Targum of 1 Chron 1. See Le Déaut-Robert, 1971, 1, 39–40. These texts give us important insights into the ancient Jewish understanding of geography. Our summary notes on this chapter are based on Alexander, 1974; Neubauer, 1868; Epstein, 1892; Krauss, 1895; McNamara, 1972; Grelot, 1972. See vol. 1A, pp. 21–23.

[3]*'pryqy* does not refer to Africa, as some (e.g., Krauss, 1895, 2) would have it, but to Phrygia (McNamara, 1972, 198).

[4]Probably a region of Asia Minor (Grelot, 1972, 135; McNamara 1968, 194–195). See also Tg. Ezek 38:6.

[5]*hmdyy;* Nfmg and Tg 1 Chron 1:5: *hmd'y;* Nf., *Gen. R.* 37, 1 (Theodor-Albeck 1, 343); *j. Meg.* 1,71b: *mdy.* Nf probably gives the correct reading, and we therefore translate Ps.-J. 's text as Media (cf. Grelot, 1972, 135).

[6]Lond. and *ed. pr.*: *'wsy'.* We find the same reading in Tg. 1 Chron 1:5. See vol. 1A, Introduction, p. 22 (Mysiake). On the identification of the Roman province of Asia, see Grelot, 1972, 136.

[7]Both Lond. and *ed. pr.* have the Hebrew lemma without translation.

[8]Capital of Cilicia. Cf. Krauss, 1895, 53–55; McNamara, 1972, 201.

[9]For *'kzy'* of Lond. and *ed. pr.* we read *'kyy'.* Nf, P, V, N, and *Gen. R.* 37,1 (cf. Tg. 1 Chron 1:7) have *Italia,* which refers to *Magna Graecia,* the southern part of Italy; cf. Krauss, 1895, 53–55; McNamara, 1972, 196.

[10]An area in northern Mysia (cf. Krauss, 1895, 55; McNamara, 1972, 193).

[11]Lit.: "the coastlands of the nations"; = HT.

[12]= Tg. 1 Chron 1:8. Probably the Egyptian name Heracleotes. Authors have identified Allihroq with many different places; cf. Epstein, 1892, 87–89; Krauss, 1895, 55–56.

[13]Omitted in Lond. and *ed. pr.*

[14]Not identified with certainty. See Krauss, 1895, 56; Epstein, 1892, 91–92.

[15]See vol. 1A, Introduction, p. 22 (*Indikê*). Ps.-J. uses this place-name in Gen 2:11; 25:18. Tg. Jon. translated Cush (= Ethiopia) as India; cf. Tg. Jon. Isa 11:11; 18:1; Jer 13:23; Zeph 3:10.

[16]Cannot be identified with certainty, although several identifications have been proposed; cf. Epstein, 1892, 93–94; Krauss, 1895, 56.

[17]Lit.: "he began to be a mighty man in sin and rebellion on earth before the Lord." Since, according to popular etymology, the name Nimrod was associated with the root *mrd,* "rebel," Nimrod was portrayed in rabbinic literature as a rebel against God and as a sinner; cf., e.g., *Gen. R.* 23,7; 37,2-3; 42,4; *b. Pesah.* 94a-b (504-505); *Erub.* 53a (368); *Hag.* 13a (74); *LAB* 4,7; Philo, *De Gigantibus* 66. On Nimrod's role in the building of the tower of Babel, see Josephus *Ant.* 1 § 113-114 and *PRE* 24 (174–175). See below 11:28. But see v. 11 (Ps.-J.) in our present chapter. See further Ginzberg, *Legends,* 1, 177–178, 5, 198–199 n. 77; Bowker, 1969, 179–180.

[18]Lit.: "a mighty man of rebellion."

[19]On the eastern bank of the Tigris, often mentioned in rabbinic literature; Krauss, 1895, 59; McNamara, 1972, 193.

[20]= Nfmg. Ps.-J. again translates Heb. Shinar as Pontus in Gen 14:1, 9.

wish to participate in the scheme of the generation of the Division.[21] *So he left those four cities.*[22] *Therefore the Lord gave him (another) place and he built four (other) cities,* Nineveh, Streets-of-the-City,[23] *Hadiath,*[24] 12. and *Talsar, which is built* between Nineveh and *Hadiath; that is the great city.* 13. Mizraim begot the *Nivatites,*[25] *the Mareotians,*[26] *the Lybians,*[27] *and the Pentasekenites,*[28] 14. *the Casiotites,*[29] *the Pentapolitanians*[30] whence came forth the Philistines, and *the Cappadocians.*[31] 15. Canaan begot Sidon his first-born, and Heth, 16. the Jebusites and the Amorites, the Girgashites, 17. the Hivites, the Arkites, the *Anthosites,*[32] 18. the *Arethusians*[33] the *Emesans,*[34] and the *Antiochenes.* Afterwards the descendants of the Canaanites spread out. 19. The territory of the Canaanites extended from *Bothneas*[35] in the direction of Gerar, as far as Gaza, (and) in the direction of Sodom, Gomorrah, Admah, and Zeboiim as far as *Callirrhoe.*[36] 20. These are the sons of Ham, according to *the descendants of* their clans, according to their languages, by *their settlements* in their lands, by *the families of* their nations. 21. To Shem also *a son* was born. He is the father of all the children of the *Hebrews,* the brother of Japheth, great *in the fear of the Lord.*[37] 22. The sons of Shem: Elam,

Notes, Chapter 10

[21]Lit.: "did not wish to be in the counsel of. . . ." The division referred to is the confusion of languages and the scattering of the peoples mentioned in Gen 11:9; cf. Ps.-J. Deut 32:8.

[22]This addition, which we find only in Ps.-J., paints a positive picture of Nimrod, thus contradicting what has been said in v. 9 (Nf, P, V, N, Ps.-J.) and in v. 8 (Ps.-J.). Since *Gen. R.* 37,4 on Gen 10:11 says that Asshur dissociated himself from the scheme of those who planned to build the tower and that God gave him a new land, Ps.-J., by mistake, may have been applying to Nimrod what is said of Asshur in the *Gen. R.* text; cf. Rappaport, 1930, 98–99 n. 72; Gottlieb, 1944, 29, n. 16.

[23]A direct translation of the Heb. words *rḥbt 'yr,* Rehoboth-ir. See Ps.-J. Num 13:21, where the place-name *rḥb,* Rehob, is translated by Ps.-J. as "Streets."

[24]Lond.: *ḥdywt;* cf. also v. 12, where Lond. and ed. pr. both have *ḥdyyt.* In v. 11 ed. pr. has *prywt.* The reading *ḥdyyt* (*ḥdywt*) is a corrupt form of *ḥdyyb* (*ḥdyyb*), Adiabene, an area in ancient Assyria east of the Tigris; cf. McNamara, 1972, 190–191.

[25]Perhaps the Nabataeans (Levy 2, 97).

[26]District in Lower Egypt, south of Alexandria; cf. Alexander, 1974, 156.

[27]See Krauss, 1895, 60.

[28]According to Alexander (1974, 156) Pentaschoinon is a station between Casius and Pelusium on the road from Palestine to Egypt.

[29]Correcting Nasiotites of both Lond. and *ed. pr.* Casiotis is situated in the area west of modern Al-Arish; cf. Le Déaut, *Genèse,* 1978, 139, n. 34.

[30]Pentapolis is identified with Cyrenaica; cf. Alexander, 1974, 158.

[31]The Targums usually translate Caphtor as Cappadocia (cf. Onq., Nf, Ps.-J. Deut 2:23; Tg. Jon. Jer 47:4; Amos 9:7. According to G. A. Wainwright ("Caphtor-Cappadocia," *VT* 6 [1956] 199–210), Cappadocia was Caphtor.

[32]= Onq. and some MSS of *Gen. R.* 37,6 (cf. Theodor-Albeck 1, 348 apparatus). The Anthosites, or Orthosians, are the inhabitants of Orthosia (cf. 1 Macc 15:37), north of Tripoli (cf. Pliny, *Natural History* 5,17).

[33]Ps.-J. and Nfmg have *lwṭs'y;* see v. 13 (V, N): *lwsṭ'y.* This name is unidentifiable. Jastrow (697) tentatively suggests Arethusians, Arethusia being located between Epiphania and Emesa (modern Homs).

[34]*hwmṣ'y;* the people of Hamas, Greek Emesa, present-day Homs.

[35]Krauss (1895, 62–63) wonders why such a well-known city as Sidon should have to be given another name. According to Tg. 1 Chron 1:13, Bothneas was the founder of Sidon.

[36]*Gen. R.* 37, 6; *j. Meg.* 1,71b. Callirrhoe was well known for its warm springs. The name occurs again in Ps.-J. in an addition to Deut 1:7, and in Nfmg Deut 2:32 as a translation of Hebrew Jahaz.

[37]HT says that Shem was the older (*gdwl,* lit. greater) brother of Japheth. Ps.-J. takes *gdwl* to refer to greatness in virtue, thus paying tribute to Shem, the ancestor of the Hebrews.

Asshur, Arpachshad, Lud, and Aram. 23. . . . .[38] 24. Arpachshad begot Shelah, and Shelah begot Eber. 25. To Eber were born two sons: the name of one was Peleg, for in his days the earth was divided. And his brother's name was Joktan. 26. Joktan begot Almodad, *who measured the earth with cords,* Sheleph, *who diverted the waters of the rivers,* Hazarmaveth,[39] and Jerah, 27. Hadoram, Uzal, Diklah, 28. Obal, Abimael, Sheba, 29. Ophir, Havilah, and Jobab. All these were the sons of Joktan. 30. *The place* where they settled extended from Mesha as far as *the Sepharvaim,*[40] the mountain of the east. 31. These are the sons of Shem, according to their lineage <and their languages>[41] by *their settlements* in their lands, according to *the families of* their nations. 32. These are the genealogies of the sons of Noah according to their genealogies, by their nations. From these the nations were spread abroad over the earth after the Flood.

CHAPTER 11

1. The whole earth had one language, one manner of speaking, *and one counsel.*[1] *They spoke in the language of the Sanctuary,*[2] *(the language) in which the world was created in the beginning.*[3] 2. And when they moved from the east they found a plain in the land of *Babel*[4] and settled there. 3. They said to one another: "Come, let us *cast*[5] bricks and bake[6] them in the *furnace.*"[7] And they had bricks for stone,

Notes, Chapter 10 (Cont.)

[38]V. 23 is omitted in Lond. and *ed. pr.*

[39]Ps.-J. derives Almodad from *mdd,* "measure," and Sheleph from *šlp,* "draw out." The same derivations are found in Tg. 1 Chron 1:20, but they are not known from traditional rabbinic sources. On the other hand, the popular explanation of the name Hazarmaveth in our present verse which we find in *Gen. R.* 37, 8 is ignored by Ps.-J.; cf. Cashdan, 1967, 35–36.

[40]2 Kings 17:24 mentions a place called Sepharvaim.

[41]Omitted in Lond. and *ed. pr.*

Notes, Chapter 11

[1]Nfmg, V, N. Rashi explains that "few words" (RSV) mean that "they came with one plan (*'sh*)."

[2]This phrase is often used in the Targums to refer to Hebrew; besides our present text see, e.g., Gen 2:19 (Nf); 22:1 (Nf); 22:11 (P, V, N, L); 31:11 (V, N, CTg E, Nfmg); 31:46 (Nfmg); 31:47 (Nf, Ps.-J., CTg C); 32:3 (Ps.-J.); 35:18 (Nf, P, V, N, L); 42:23 (Ps.-J., P, V, N, L); 45:12 (Ps.-J., Nf) 46:2 (Nfmg). On this expression see Schäfer, 1972, 138; Shinan, 1975–76, 472–474.

[3]The tradition that God used Hebrew when creating the world is known, e.g., from *Gen. R.* 18,4; 31,8; *Jubilees* 12,26. The tradition that the generation of the Tower of Babel spoke Hebrew is found, e.g., in *j. Meg.* 1,71b; *Tanh., Noah* 19 (47); *Tanh.* B., *Noah* 28 (1,56). Cf. Ginzberg, *Legends,* 1, 181; 5, 204–205, n. 91.

[4]HT: Shinar. See 10:10 (Ps.-J.) and n. 20 to that verse.

[5]Onq. and Ps.-J. use the verb *rmy,* "cast," while Nf uses the verb *lbn,* thus retaining the alliteration of the Heb. *nlbnh lbnym,* "let us make bricks." Onq. and Ps.-J. again use *rmy* in Exod 5:7, 14, where there is mention of casting bricks. In both these verses Nf again has *lbn.*

[6]Reading *nyzy,* from the verb *'zy,* "to heat"; cf. Dan 3:19, 22, and see *nzy,* which is the reading in Nf in our present verse, instead of *nywy* of Lond. and *ed. pr.*; see Klein 1974, 219–220. Onq. uses the verb *srp,* "burn."

[7]Onq.: "the fire."

and *clay* for mortar. 4. And they said: "Come, let us build ourselves a city and a tower with its top *reaching towards* the heavens. *Let us make ourselves an idol at its top, and let us put a sword in its hand,*[8] *and let it draw up battle formations against (him)*[9] *before* we are scattered *from*[10] upon the face of the earth." 5. The Lord *revealed himself to take revenge on them for the work of*[11] the city and the tower which the sons of man had built. 6. And the Lord said: "Behold they are one people, and they have all one language, and they have *planned* to do this! And now, nothing they plan to do can be withheld from them." 7. *Then the Lord said to the seventy angels that stand before him:*[12] "Come *then*, let us go down,[13] and confuse their language there, so that they will not understand one another's language." 8. *The Memra of* the Lord *was revealed against the city, and with it seventy angels corresponding to seventy nations, each having the language of his people and the characters of its writing in his hand.* He scattered them thence upon the face of all the earth *into seventy languages, so that one did not know what the other said, and they killed one another.*[14] And they stopped building the city. 9. That is why it was called Babel, because there the Lord confused the language of all *the inhabitants* of the earth; and from there the Lord scattered them upon the face of the whole earth. 10. This is the line of Shem: Shem was a hundred years old when he begot Arpachshad, two years after the Flood. 11. Shem lived five hundred years after he had begotten Arpachshad, and he begot sons and daughters. 12. Arpachshad lived thirty-five years, and he begot Shelah. 13. Arpachshad lived four hundred and *thirty*[15] years after he had begotten Shelah, and he begot sons and daughters. 14. Shelah lived thirty years, and he begot Eber. 15. Shelah lived four hundred and three years after he had begotten Eber, and he begot sons and daughters. 16. Eber lived thirty-four years, and he begot Peleg. 17. Eber lived four hundred and thirty years after he had begotten Peleg, and he begot sons and daughters. 18. Peleg lived thirty years, and

Notes, Chapter 11

[8]*Gen. R.* 38, 6. The idolatrous tendencies of the generation of the Flood are also mentioned, e.g., in *Mekilta* to Exod 23:13 (3, 180–181); *b. Sanh.* 109a (748); see further, Ginzberg, *Legends,* 1, 180; 5, 201–202, n. 88; Bowker, 1969, 183–184; Vermes, 1961, 76.

[9]Reading thus (*lqwblyh*); cf. Nf, Nfmg, P, V, N. Lond. and *ed. pr.*: *lqw(y)bl'*. See *Gen. R.* 38:6. The idea that the generation of the Flood planned to wage war with God is expressed, e.g., in *b. Sanh.* 109a (748); *Tanḥ., Noah* 18 (46).

[10]= P.

[11]Onq.: "The Lord revealed himself in connection with the work of the city." The Targums avoid the anthropomorphic phrase "the Lord came down to see." See also the Targums of Gen 18:21; Exod 19:11, 18, 20; 34:5; Num 11:25 and 12:5, where HT also refers to the Lord's coming down; cf. Muñoz-León, 1977, 172–173.

[12]*PRE* 24 (177); *Jubilees* 10,22–23; *Sefer Ha-Yashar* 9 (24). Here, as in 1:26, Ps.-J., alone among the Tgs., introduces the angels, lest the words "let us go down" be taken to suggest plurality in God; cf. Bowker, 1969, 184–185; see above, n. 42 to 1:26. Ps.-J. mentions "the seventy angels" again in v. 8 and later in Deut 32:8 (and cf. v. 9), thus forming a complete short story about the seventy angels; cf. Shinan, 1979, 1, 120–121; idem, 1985, 77–78. On Ps.-J.'s tendency to add elements of a haggadic tradition to different verses, see above, Introduction, p. 5.

[13]Surprisingly, Ps.-J. does not avoid the anthropomorphism as do Onq. and Nf, and as Ps.-J. did in the preceding verse.

[14]*PRE* 24 (177); *LAB* 7,5. Ps.-J.'s addition to this verse is similar to the passage in *PRE. Testament of Naphtali* (Hebrew) 8,4-5 says that God came down with seventy angels, who taught each of the seventy nations its own language. According to *Sefer Ha-Yashar* 9 (24), many people were killed because of the confusion of tongues.

[15]= LXX; HT, Onq.: "403."

he begot Reu. Peleg lived two hundred and nine years after he had begotten Reu, and he begot sons and daughters. 20. Reu lived thirty-two years, and he begot Serug. 21. Reu lived two hundred and seven years after he had begotten Serug, and he begot sons and daughters. 22. Serug lived thirty years, and he begot Nahor. 23. Serug lived two hundred years after he had begotten Nahor, and he begot sons and daughters. 24. Nahor lived twenty-nine years, and he begot Terah. 25. Nahor lived a hundred and *sixteen*[16] years after he had begotten Terah, and he begot sons and daughters. 26. Terah lived seventy years, and he begot Abram, Nahor, and Haran. 27. This is the *line* of Terah: Terah begot Abram, Nahor, and Haran; and Haran begot Lot. 28. *It came to pass, when Nimrod cast Abram into the furnace of fire*[17] *because he would not worship his idol, the fire had no power to burn him. Then Haran was undecided, and he said: "If Nimrod triumphs, I will be on his side; but if Abram triumphs, I will be on his side." And when all the people who were there saw that the fire had no power over Abram, they said to themselves: "Is not Haran the brother of Abram full of divination and sorcery? It is he who uttered charms over the fire so that it would not burn his brother.*[18] *Immediately fire fell from the heavens on high*[19] *and consumed him;* and Haran died in the sight of Terah his father, *being burned* in the land of his birth *in the furnace of fire which* the Chaldeans *had made for Abram his brother.* 29. And Abram and Nahor took wives to themselves; the name of Abram's wife was Sarai, and the name of Nahor's wife Milcah, the daughter of Haran the father of Milcah and the father of Iscah—*she is Sarai.*[20] 30. Now Sarai was barren; she had no child. 31. Terah took his son Abram, his grandson Lot, the son of Haran, and his daughter-in-law Sarai, the wife of his son Abram, and they went forth together from *the fire* of the Chaldeans to go to the land of Canaan; and they came to Haran and settled there. 32. The days of Terah were two hundred and five years; and Terah died in Haran.

Notes, Chapter 11

[16]HT: 119; LXX: 129.

[17]*Gen. R.* 34,9; 38,13; *ARN* A 33; *Exod. R.* 23,4; *PRE* 26 (188); *Sefer Ha-Yashar* 12 (32–34); *LAB* 6,16. The well-known legend of Abraham in the furnace is based on the interpretation of the place-name Ur (Gen 15:7) as "fire." See Gen 15:7 (Nf, Ps.-J., V, N, L); 16:5 (Ps.-J., Nf, P, V, N, L). Vulg. Neh 9:7; Jerome, *Quaest. hebr.* in Gen 15; see further, Ginzberg, *Legends* 1, 198–201; 5, 212–213, nn. 28-34; Bowker, 1969, 187–189; Vermes, 1961, 85–90.

[18]Ps.-J. acknowledges the power of sorcery and magic. Besides our present text, see Ps.-J. Gen 31:19; Exod 7:15; 9:14; Num 31:8. All the Pal. Tgs. (Nf, Nfmg 1 and 2, P, V, N, L, CTg DD, Ps.-J.) of Deut 24:6 refer to an obscure magical practice. On Ps.-J.'s interest in magic and witchcraft, see above, Introduction, p. 6.

[19]The phrase "the heavens on high" occurs in the following texts in Ps.-J., without a parallel in the other Targums unless otherwise stated: Gen 3:22 (also Nf, P, V, N, L); 11:28; 18:16; 24:3, 7; 28:12; Exod 2:23; 16:15; 24:10; Num 21:6; Deut 4:36; 28:15; 34:5; see also 33:26.

[20]b. *Meg.* 14a (82); *Sanh.* 69b (471); *Midrash Psalms* 118,11 (2,239); *Sefer Ha-Yashar* 12 (34); Josephus *Ant.* 1 § 151. Ps.-J. here takes Sarai to be Abraham's niece, which contradicts Ps.-J. Gen 20:12, where Sarai is identified as Abraham's cousin. Vermes claims that Ps.-J. (and the parallel texts) take Sarai to be Abraham's niece, so that it could not be said that the patriarch violated the stipulations of Lev 18:9 and 20:17; cf. Vermes, 1961, 75–76. Shinan (1985, 85, n. 46) says that the opinion of Vermes does not seem likely.

CHAPTER 12

1. The Lord said to Abram, "Go from your country. *Depart* from your native land. *Go forth* from your father's house (and) go to the land that I will show you. 2. I will make of you a great people, and I will bless you, and make your name great, and *you will be blessed.*[1] 3. I will bless *the priests who stretch out their hands in prayer* and bless *your children;*[2] but Balaam who will curse *them* I will curse,[3] *and they will kill him*[4] *at the edge of the sword;*[5] and in you all the families of the earth will be blessed." 4. Abram went as the Lord had told him: and Lot went with him. And Abram was seventy-five years old when he went forth from Haran. 5. Abram took Sarai his wife, and Lot his brother's son, and all the possessions which they had acquired, and all the persons whom they had *converted*[6] in Haran, and they went forth to go to the land of Canaan. When they came to the land of Canaan, 6. Abram passed through the land to the site of Shechem, to the *plain that had been pointed out.*[7] The Canaanites were then in the land; *for the time had not yet come for the children of Israel to take possession of it.*[8] 7. And the Lord *revealed himself* to Abram, and said, "To your *children* I will give this land." And he built an altar there *before* the Lord, who *revealed himself* to him. 8. From there he went up to the mountain *which is* to the east of Bethel and pitched his tent, with Bethel to the west and Ai to the east. And he built an altar there *before* the Lord and *prayed*[9] in the name of the Lord. 9. Then Abram moved on, going gradually to the south. 10. Now

Notes, Chapter 12

[1] = LXX, Vulg.; cf. Pesh.

[2] *b. Hul.* 49a (265); *Sotah* 38b (189). Besides Num 6:22–27, where the biblical text treats of the Priestly Blessing, Ps.-J. again refers to this Blessing in Num 7:88. On Ps.-J.'s version of Gen 12:3, see Díez Macho, *Neophyti 1*, II, 1970, 45*–46*.

[3] Cf. *Num. R.* 20,19; *Tanḥ.* B., *Balak* 17 (2, 142). See Tg. Gen 27:29 (Nf, P, V, N, L, Ps.-J.); Num 24:9 (Nfmg, P, V, N, Ps.-J.).

[4] Cf. Num 31:8. The reference to Balaam in our present verse anticipates events, as is often the case in midrashic literature.

[5] Lit.: "according to the word (*ptgm*) of the sword." The Aramaic phrase occurs in the Targums as a translation of Heb. *lpy ḥrb*. See also the Targums of Gen 34:26; Exod 17:13; Num 21:24; Deut 13:16; 20:13. Ps.-J. modifies the formula in Exod 17:13 and Num 21:24.

[6] *Gen. R.* 39,14; 84,4; *ARN* A 12; *ARN* B 26 (156–157); *Sifre Deut* to 6:4 (Finkelstein, 54). Cf. Onq. Gen 12:5: "and the persons whom they had subjected to the Law." The proselytizing activity of Abraham is mentioned again in Gen 21:33 (Nf, Nfmg, P, V, N, L, Ps.-J.). According to Ps.-J. Exod 18:7,27, Moses converted Jethro, and the latter converted his fellow countrymen. The verb *gwr*, which is used in our present verse, can, according to the context, mean either "become a proselyte" or "dwell"; cf. Ohana (1974, 317–332); Díez-Macho (1972, 59); Delcor (1970, 106–108); M. Goodman, "Proselytising in Rabbinic Judaism," *JJS* 40 (1989) 175–185, especially pp. 178–179, which deal with Abraham's missionary role.

[7] Onq.: "the plains of Moreh." We take the word *myyry* in Ps.-J.'s phrase *dhwh myyry* to be derived from *'ry*, "point, throw, discuss"; cf. Jastrow, 772. Levy (2, 33) derives *myyry* from *'mr*, and understands Ps.-J. to refer to the place where the curses and blessings were spoken (cf. Deut 11:29-30, and see Rashi's commentary on Gen 12:6). See below, n. 13 on 13:18.

[8] Cf. *Gen. R.* 39,15; 41,5; see Gen 15:16.

[9] The Targums usually take the formula "call on the name of the Lord" (RSV) to mean "*pray* in the name of the Lord"; cf., e.g., Gen 12:8 (Onq., Nf, Ps.-J.); 13:4 (Onq., Nf, Nfmg, Ps.-J.); 21:33 (Onq., Nf, P, V, N, L); 26:25 (Onq., Nf, Ps.-J.). Gen 4:26 is an exception; see above, n. 54 on that verse. See Maher, 1990, 239–242.

there was a famine in the land, and Abram went down to Egypt to dwell there because the famine was severe in the land. 11. When he was about to enter *the territory of* Egypt, *they came to the river and uncovered their bodies to cross over. Abram* said to Sarai his wife, "Behold *until now I have not looked at your body;*[10] *but now* I know that you are a woman of beautiful appearance. 12. And when the Egyptians *look at* you and see *your beauty,* they will say, 'This is his wife'; and they will kill me and let you live. 13. Say, I pray, *that* you are my sister, that it may go well with me because of you, and that my life may be spared on your account."[11] 14. So when Abram entered Egypt, the Egyptians saw that the woman was very beautiful. 15. The nobles of Pharaoh saw her and praised her to Pharaoh, and the woman was taken to Pharaoh's *royal* house. 16. And because of her *Pharaoh* treated Abram well, and, *of what belonged to him* he acquired[12] sheep, oxen, asses, menservants, maidservants, she-asses, and camels. 17. But *the Memra of* the Lord *unleashed*[13] great plagues against Pharaoh and *the members of* his household on account of Sarai, the wife of Abram. 18. Pharaoh called Abram and said; "What is this you have done to me? Why did you not tell me that she was your wife? 19. Why did you say, 'She is my sister,' so that I took her as my wife? *But immediately a plague was unleashed against me, and I did not approach her.*[14] And now, here is your wife. Take (her) and go." 20. And Pharaoh commanded men concerning him; and they *escorted* him[15] and his wife and all that he possessed.

CHAPTER 13

1. Abram went up from Egypt, he and his wife, and all that he possessed, and Lot with him, *to go* to the south. 2. Now Abram was very rich in flocks, in silver, and in gold. 3. He went on his journeys from the south as far as Bethel, and *returned* to the place where he *had pitched* his tent at the beginning,[1] between Bethel and Ai, 4. to the site of the altar which he had made there in the beginning; and there Abram

Notes, Chapter 12 (Cont.)

[10]*b. B. Bat.* 16a (80); *Tanḥ., Lek-Leka* 5 (50). 1 *QGenApoc* 20,2-7 describes Sarai's beauty at length but does not say that Abram became aware of her beauty for the first time at the river.

[11]Onq.: "through your words."

[12]Lit.: "he had."

[13]Onq.: "brought"; lit: "caused to come."

[14]PRE 26 (189–190); 1 *QGenApoc* 20,16-17; Josephus, *Ant.* 1 § 164. Ps.-J.'s addition, in line with the Targums' tendency to preserve the dignity of the ancestors (cf., e.g., Aberbach, 1969, and see above, Introduction, p. 7), makes it clear that Sarai was not subjected to any indignity in the house of Pharaoh.

[15]= Onq. This is more dignified and more worthy of the patriarch than the Hebrew "sent him off."

Notes, Chapter 13

[1]*mn 'wwl';* see above, n. 1 to Gen 1:1.

prayed in the name of the Lord. 5. Lot, *who was supported by the merits of* Abram,[2] also had sheep and oxen and tents, 6. so that the land could not support them dwelling together, because their possessions were great, and they were not able to dwell together. 7. And there were disputes between the herdsmen of Abraham's cattle and the herdsmen of Lot's cattle. *The herdsmen of Abram had been commanded by him not to go among the Canaanites and the Perizzites, because they still had authority over the land. They used to muzzle their cattle so that they would not eat anything that had been stolen until they had arrived at their grazing grounds. But the herdsmen of Lot allowed (their cattle) to go about freely and to eat in the fields*[3] of the Canaanites and the Perizzites *who* were *still* dwelling in the land. 8. Abram said to Lot: "Let there not, I pray, be a quarrel between me and you, nor between my herdsmen and your herdsmen, for we are kinsmen. 9. Is not the whole land before you? Separate yourself, I pray, from me. If you (go) to the *north,* I (will go) to the *south;* if you (go) to the *south,* I (will go) to the *north.*" 10. And Lot lifted up[4] his eyes *with lustful desire*[5] and saw that the whole plain of the Jordan was all irrigated—(that was) before the Lord *in his anger* destroyed Sodom and Gomorrah. *That land was renowned for (its) trees* like the garden of the Lord, *and for (its) produce*[6] like the land of Egypt, as you come towards Zoar.[7] 11. And Lot chose for himself all the plain of the Jordan; and Lot journeyed *from* the east, and they separated one from the other. 12. Abram dwelt in the land of Canaan, and Lot dwelt in the cities of the plain and *pitched his tent* towards Sodom. 13. And the men of Sodom were evil *towards one another with their wealth,* and sinful *with their bodies*[8] *through sexual immorality, by shedding innocent blood, and by the practice of idolatry, and rebelling* greviously against *the name of* the Lord.[9] 14. And the Lord said to Abram after Lot had separated from him, "Lift up, I pray, your eyes and look from the place where you are, to the north and to the south and to the east and to the *west,* 15. for all the land that you see I will give to you and to your *children* for-

Notes, Chapter 13

[2]*Gen. R.* 41,3; *b. B. Qam.* 93a (537–538).

[3]*Gen. R.* 41,5; compare Ps.-J. Gen 24:32, and n. 22 to that verse.

[4]*zqp* = Onq.; Nf: *nṭl.* Ps.-J. usually follows Onq. in translating *nś'* in the idiom *nś' 'ynym,* "lift up one's eyes," by *zqp.* The only exception is Deut 4:19, where Ps.-J. joins Nf and uses *tly.* See L. Díez-Merino, 1984, 23–41, especially p. 29. But Ps.-J. can use the idiom *tly 'ynyn* in additions to the biblical text; cf., e.g., Gen 38:25; 49:22 (twice); Exod 1:19; Num 31:50.

[5]Lit.: "for unchastity," or "for voluptuousness." Cf. *Gen. R.* 41,7; *b. Nazir* 23a (82); *Hor.* 10b (73). Since the phrase "lift up one's eyes" refers to lustful desire in Gen 39:7, the midrashim take it to have the same meaning in our present verse.

[6]*Gen. R.* 41,7; *Sifre* to Deut 11:10 (edition Finkelstein, 75).

[7]The place-name Zoar is usually written as *z(w)'r* in Ps.-J. and Nf; cf., besides our present verse, 14:2,8; 19:22,23,30. See also Ps.-J. 18:24,28,29,30. In our present verse *ed. pr.* has *ṣw'r.* The form in Onq., as in HT, is *ṣ(w)'r.*

[8]= Onq. Cf. *b. Sanh.* 104b (711); 109a (749); *Mekilta* to Exod 15:1 (2,14) *PRE* 25 (181–182). Ezek 16:49 condemns Sodom for failing to share its possessions with the poor. The following phrase in Ps.-J. ("through sexual immorality") is literally "by revealing (their) nakedness."

[9]*Gen. R.* 41,7; *t. Sanh.* 13,8 (Zuckermandel, 435); *b. Sanh.* 109a (749); *ARN* A 36. The three cardinal sins of Judaism (sexual immorality, murder, idolatry; cf., e.g., *b. Sanh.* 74a [502]; *Shabb.* 33a [152]; *m. Aboth* 5,9) which are mentioned here are referred to in Tgs. Gen 24:31 (Nfmg); 25:29 (Ps.-J.); 28:20 (Ps.-J.); Num 35:25 (Ps.-J.); Deut 23:10 (Ps.-J.); cf. also Gen 49:12 (Nf, V, N, Ps.-J.). The sinfulness of Sodom is described at length in *b. Sanh.* 109a-b (749–752). See further Ginzberg, *Legends* 1, 245–250; 5, 237–238, nn. 155-156; Bowker, 1969, 190–192.

ever. 16. And I will make your *children as numerous* as the dust of the earth; for if one can [10] count the dust of the earth, so *will it be possible* to have your children counted. 17. Arise, walk about in the land and *take possession of it* [11] in its length and in its breadth, for I will give it to you." 18. Abram pitched tents *for oxen and sheep* [12] and he came and dwelt in the *vision* [13] of Mamre which is in Hebron, and there he built an altar *before* the Lord.

CHAPTER 14

1. In the days of Amraphel—*he is Nimrod who ordered* [1] *Abram to be thrown into the fire, he is* the king of *Pontus* [2]—Arioch, *who was tall* [3] *like* [4] *the giants,* king of *Telassar,* [5] Chedorlaomer, *who was short (and) turned like sheaves,* [6] the king of Elam, and Tidal, *a deceiver* [7] *like the fox,* king of the peoples [8] *(who were) subject to him,* 2. made war with Bera king of Sodom, *whose deeds were evil,* [9] and with Birsha

Notes, Chapter 13 (Cont.)

[10] Lit.: "just as it is possible for one"; Nf, Onq.: "just as it is impossible for one."

[11] *Gen. R.* 41,10; *b. B. Bat.* 100a (418); *j. Qidd.* 1,59d. The same Aramaic idiom (*'bd hzqt'*) occurs in Ps.-J. Num 13:20. The noun *hzqt'* seems to be a Hebraism; cf. Cook, 1986, 237–238.

[12] We follow the later printed editions. Lond. and *ed. pr.* are unintelligible; cf. Geiger, 1928, 457; Brayer, 1964, 215.

[13] The Targums offer different renderings of HT "the oaks of Mamre (Moreh)" (RSV). Onq. regularly translates this phrase as "the plains of Mamre (Moreh)" (Gen 12:6; 13:18; 14:13; 18:1; Deut 11:30). Nf has "the plain of the Vision" in all these texts. Where the Frg. Tg. is preserved V, N, and L have "the plain of Hazozah" (Gen 12:6 and 18:1), and P has the "Plain of the Vision" (Gen 18:1). Ps.-J. reads "the Vision of Mamre" in Gen 13:18; 14:13; 18:1; Deut 11:30. See above Gen 12:6 (Ps.-J.) and n. 7 to that verse. Ps.-J. uses the term "the Vision of Mamre" in an addition to Deut 34:6. See further F. Stummer, " 'Convallis Mambre' und Verwandtes," *Journal of the Palestine Oriental Society* 12 (1932) 6–21; Delcor, 1970, 108–112; Le Déaut, 1978, *Genèse,* 157, n. 7.

Notes, Chapter 14

[1] Lit.: "said" (*'mr*). The name Amraphel is read as *'mr* "say," and *pl* (root *npl,* "fall"); cf. *Gen. R.* 42,4; *b. Erub.* 53a (368); *Tanh., Lek-Leka* 6 (52). On the legend of Abram's being thrown into the fire, see above 11:28 and n. 17 to that verse.

[2] Nfmg and Vulg. make the second king (Arioch) king of Pontus. Cf. also Nf v. 9. In v. 9 V, N, L and Ps.-J. identify Amraphel as king of Pontus. On the place-names mentioned in Gen 14, see Fitzmyer, 1971, 158–174; Kuiper, 1968, 149–161; Delcor, 1970, 113–118.

[3] Ps.-J. links the name Arioch with *'rwk,* "long, tall." The source for Ps.-J.'s interpretation is unknown; cf. Brayer, 1964, 216.

[4] Reading *k* with Lond., rather than *b,* "among," of *ed. pr.*

[5] = Pesh. Ps.-J. and Pesh seem to confuse Ellasar of HT with Telassar (Isa 37:12).

[6] Ps.-J.'s interpretation, which has no parallel (Brayer, 1964, 216), is unintelligible. The author links the second part of the name Chedorlaomer with Heb. *'mr,* (*'omer*), "sheaf." If in Ps.-J. we read *qysr,* "a band" with *ed. pr.* (instead of *qsyr,* "short," of Lond.), we may surmise that the Targumist linked the first element of the king's name (Chedor) with *kdwr,* "something that goes around, a ball, a band," and in this case a band that goes around sheaves; cf. Cashdan, 1967, 36, n. 25.

[7] There is no known source for Ps.-J.'s interpretation; cf. Brayer, 1964, 217.

[8] = Onq., LXX. The Targums treat the Hebrew place-name Goiim as a plural noun meaning "peoples, nations (*gwym*)."

[9] Lit.: "in evil." Ps.-J. reads the place-name Bera as *br',* "in evil." Cf. *Gen. R.* 42,5.

king of Gomorrrah, *whose deeds were wicked,* [10] Shinab king of Admah, *who hated even his father,* [11] and Shemeber king of Zeboiim, *who destroyed his member with unchastity,* [12] and (with) the king of *the city that swallowed its inhabitants,* [13] that is Zoar. 3. All these joined together in the plain of *the Orchards,* [14] *that is the place that springs forth streams* [15] *of water and empties them* [16] into the Salt Sea. 4. Twelve years they had served Chedorlaomer, but *in the thirteenth* year [17] they rebelled. 5. And in the fourteenth year Chedorlaomer and the kings who were with him came and wiped out the *giants who were* in Ashteroth-karnaim, *the powerful ones who were* in Hamta, and *the fearsome ones* [18] *who were* in Shaveh-Kiriathaim, 6. and the Horites *who were* in the *high* mountains of *Gabla* [19] as far as *the plain* [20] of Paran, which *is near the edge* of the desert. 7. Then they returned and came to *the place where the judgment of Moses the prophet was decided by the fountain of the Waters of Contention,* [21] that is *Reqem.* [22] And they destroyed all the fields of the Amalekites, and also the Amorites who dwelt in *En-gedi.* [23] 8. The king of Sodom, the king of Gomorrah, the king of Admah, the king of Zeboiim, and the king of *the city that swallowed its inhabitants,* that is Zoar, went out and engaged in battle with them [24] in the plain of *the Orchards,* 9. with Chedorlaomer king of Elam, and Tidal king of the nations *(who were) subject to him,* and Amraphael king of *Pontus,* and

Notes, Chapter 14

[10]Lit.: "in wickedness." Ps.-J. reads the place-name Birsha as *brš'*, "in wickedness." Compare *Gen. R.* 42,5.

[11]Ps.-J. reads the name Shinab as *śn' 'b*, "he hated his father." See *Tanḥ., Lek-Leka* 8 (53), where a comment on the name Shinab says that "he hated the Father in Heaven."

[12]Ps.-J. derives the name Shemeber from *šmm* (Pi.), "lay waste, ruin," and *'br* (*membrum*). We know of no source for Ps.-J.'s rather crude interpretation. On Ps.-J.'s use of vulgar language see above, Introduction, p. 7.

[13]The place-name Bela of HT is taken to the Heb. verb *bl'*, "swallow." Cf. *Gen. R.* 42,5.

[14]The Pal. Tgs. (Nf, V, N, L, Ps.-J.) use the word *prdysy(y)'*, "Orchards," whereas Onq. has *ḥqly'*, "fields." The Targums translate the place-name Siddim as if it were derived from *śdh*, "field"; cf. *Gen. R.* 42,5.

[15]The word *prqṭwn*, which Ps.-J. uses here, occurs again in Ps.-J. Num 21:34 and 24:6 in additions to the biblical text. In these latter texts Nf and P, V, N have essentially the same addition as Ps.-J., but instead of *prqṭwn* they use the word *mbw'*, "spring."

[16]See *Gen. R.* 42,5.

[17]HT reads "and for thirteen years," which Onq. translates literally; cf. Grossfeld, 1988, 67, n. 3.

[18]The names of the three peoples, Rephaim, Zuzim, and Emim, mentioned in this verse are treated as common nouns in the Targums. The Rephaim become "Giants," or "mighty ones"; see also Ps.-J. 15:20. Cf. Deut 3:11, where HT describes the giant stature of Og, who was one of the Rephaim; see also Deut 2:10-11, 20-21. The Zuzim become "the powerful ones" (Onq., Ps.-J.), as if the name were derived from *'zz*, "be strong." See LXX: "strong nations." The Emim are called the "fearsome ones," those who instill fear, *'ymh* (Schmerler, 1932, 120; Fitzmyer, 1971, 164–165).

[19]See also, e.g., Gen 32:4; 36:8, 9. Cf. *1 QGenApoc* 21,29: "in the mountains of Gebal (*gbl*)." Gabla is an area in Edom that was known to Josephus (*Ant.* 2 § 6; 3 § 40; 9 § 188) as Gobolitis or Gebalene (cf. Delcor, 1970, 116; McNamara, 1972, 194). Like Onq. (also Pesh., LXX, Vulg.), Ps.-J. regards Heb. *hrrm*, "their mountain," in our present verse as a plural. Ps.-J. also understood *hrrm* as *hr rm*, "high mountain." No source for this latter interpretation is known.

[20]= Onq. *Gen. R.* 42,6. Onq. and Ps.-J., like *Gen. R.*, understood Heb. *'yl*, "El-(paran)," as *'lwn*, "oak," which they regularly render as "plain." See above, n. 13 to 13:18.

[21]Onq.: "to plain where judgment was decided." Cf. *Num. R.* 19,14; *Tanḥ., Lek-Leka* 8 (53); ibid., *Hukkat* 11 (568). The midrash identifies the place-name En-mishpat (lit. "well of Judgment") with "the waters of Meribah," where Moses and Aaron were judged (cf. Num 20:12-13).

[22]The Targums translate Kadesh by Reqem (cf. Gen 14:7; 16:14; 20:1; Num 13:26; 20:1, 14, 16, 22; 33:36, 37; Deut 1:46. Josephus (*Ant.* 4 § 161) identified Reqem with Petra. See further G.I. Davies, "Hagar, El-Hagra and the Location of Mount Sinai," *VT* 22 (1972) 160–163.

[23]= Onq. Cf. 2 Chron 20:2; *Gen. R.* 42,7; Jerome, *Quaest. hebr.* in Gen 14:7.

[24]Lit.: "arranged battle array with them."

Arioch king of *Telassar*—four kings *engaged in battle*[25] against five. 10. Now, (in) the valley of the *Orchards* there were many wells *full of* bitumen; and as the kings of Sodom and Gomorrah fled, they fell into them, and the rest fled to the mountains. 11. They took all the possessions of Sodom and Gomorrah, and all their provisions, and departed. 12. They captured Lot, the son of Abram's brother, and his possessions, and departed; he had settled in Sodom. 13. Then came *Og, who had* escaped *from among the giants who died in the Flood;*[26] *he had ridden upon the ark, and there was a cover over his head, and he was sustained from Noah's provisions.*[27] *He had not escaped because of his own merit, but that the inhabitants of the world might see the power of the Lord and say, "Did not the giants who were there from the beginning rebel against the Lord of the world,*[28] *and he wiped them out from the earth?" When these kings waged war, Og was with them. He said to himself: "I will go and inform Abram concerning Lot who has been captured, so that when he comes to rescue him from the hands of the kings, he himself will be given into their hands.*[29] *So he came on the eve of the day of the Passover*[30] *and found him making unleavened cakes,*[31] and he told Abram the Hebrew, who was dwelling in the *Vision*[32] of Mamre the Amorite, brother of Eshcol and Aner. These were allies of Abram. 14. When Abram heard that his brother had been captured, he armed his *young men whom* he had trained *for war,*[33] *(who had been) brought up in* his house, *but they did not wish to go with him.*[34] *So he chose from among them Eliezer, son of Nimrod,*[35] *who was equal in strength to all* three hundred and eighteen *of them;*[36] and he pursued (them) as far as Dan. 15. The night was divided *for* them *on the way; one part fought against the kings, and the other part was kept in reserve for the smiting of the first-born in Egypt.*[37] *He arose,* he and his servants, and smote them and pursued

Notes, Chapter 14

[25]Lit.: "arranged battle."

[26]The Legend that Og was a giant that survived the Flood is based on Deut 3:11. Og's survival is mentioned in *b. Zebah.* 113b (560); *Niddah* 61a (433); *Num. R.* 19,32; *PRE* 23 (167); Ps.-J. Deut 3:11. The legend is introduced here because Ps.-J. identified the "one who had escaped" of HT with Og who escaped the Flood. Cf. *Gen. R.* 42,8; *Deut. R.* 1,25.

[27]*PRE* 23 (167).

[28]Ps.-J. is the only one of the Pal. Tgs. to use this divine title; cf., e.g., Ps.-J. Gen 22:1, 5; 27:1, 6; 32:27; 49:20; Exod 12:11; 19:17; 24:10).

[29]Cf. *Gen. R.* 42,8; *Deut. R.* 1,25.

[30]Other events which, according to Ps.-J., took place at Passover were the circumcision of Abraham (cf. Ps.-J. Gen 17:26); Isaac's call to Esau, whom he intended to bless (Ps.-J. Gen 27:1); the covenant with Abraham (cf. Ps.-J. Exod 12:40).

[31]*Gen. R.* 42,8.

[32]See above, Gen 13:18 and n. 13 to that verse.

[33]Ps.-J. takes the obscure *ḥnykyw*, "his trained men" (RSV), to mean "*his young men whom* he had trained (*ḥnyk*) for war."

[34]In *Gen. R.* 43,2 one explanation of Heb. *wyrq,* "he led forth," is that Abraham thinned (lit. "emptied," *hryqn*) the numbers of his followers when he warned them that he needed only those whose hearts were not faint (*rk*).

[35]According to *PRE* 16 (111), when Abraham was leaving Ur, Nimrod gave him his first-born son Eliezer as a slave.

[36]The idea that of the 318 men in Abraham's household Eliezer alone accompanied the patriarch on his campaign to save Lot occurs in many sources; cf., e.g., *Gen. R.* 43,2; *Num. R.* 18,21; *b. Ned.* 32a (97); *PRK* 8,2 (158); *PRE* 27 (194). It is based on the fact that the numerical value of the name Eliezer is 318.

[37]Ps.-J. reads the difficult HT as "and the night was divided for them." This was taken to mean that Abraham's enemies were destroyed at midnight, and the rest of the night was reserved for the destruction of the Egyptians. See *Gen. R.* 43,3; *Tanḥ., Lek-Leka* 9 (54); *PRE* 27 (195); and compare *Mekilta* to Exod 12:29 (1,96). See M. R. Lehmann, 1958–1959, 261.

those of them that remained until *he remembered the sin that was to be (committed) in Dan,* [38] which is *north* of Damascus. 16. He brought back all the possessions; he also brought back Lot his kinsman and his possessions, as well as the women and (the rest of) the people. 17. When he returned from defeating Chedorlaomer and the kings who were with him, the king of Sodom came out to meet him at the *leveled* plain, which is the king's *racecourse.* [39] 18. *The righteous king* [40]—*that is Shem, the son of Noah* [41]—king of *Jerusalem,* [42] *went out to meet Abram,* [43] and brought *him* bread and wine; *at that time he was ministering before* God Most High. [44] 19. He blessed him and said, "Blessed be Abram *from (before)* [45] God Most High, who created the heavens and the earth *for the sake of the righteous.* [46] 20. And blessed be God Most High, who *has made* those who hate you *like a shield that receives a blow."* [47] And he gave him a tithe of all that he had *brought back.* 21. The king of Sodom said to Abram, "Give me the *human* persons *of my people whom you brought back,* and the possessions take for yourself." 22. Abram said to the king of Sodom, "I have raised my hand *in an oath* [48] *before* the Lord, the Most High God, who for the *sake of the righteous* created *as his possession* [49] the heavens and the

Notes, Chapter 14

[38]Ps.-J. links the place-name Hobah with the Aramaic *ḥwb'* "sin." According to *b. Sanh.* 96a (647); *PRE* 27 (194); *Tanḥ., Lek-Leka* 13 (56–57), when Abraham reached Dan and thought of the idolatry that would take place there (cf. 1 Kings 12:28-29), he lost courage; cf. also *Gen. R.* 43,2.

[39]"*Leveled* plain. . . . racecourse" = Onq. The place-name Shaveh is translated as if it were Heb. *šwh,* "equal." The "racecourse of the king" refers to the hippodrome of Solomon, which was known in Jewish legend (cf. Ginzberg, *Legends,* 4,160–162), and which eclipsed the hippodrome of Herod in popular memory; cf. J. T. Milik, "Saint-Thomas de Phordêsa et Gen 14:17," *Biblica* 42 (1961) 82–83. The "king's racecourse" is mentioned in Tg. Jer 31:40. Cf. also the reference to "the racecourse" in Ps.-J. Num 33:21, and see *Testament of Joseph* 20,3.

[40]Josephus, *Ant.* 1 § 180; *Jewish War* 6 § 438; Philo, *Legum Allegoriae,* 3 § 79; cf. Heb 7:2.

[41]*b. Ned.* 32b (98–99); *PRE* 8 (53); 27 (196); *Midrash Psalms* 76,3 (2,15); see *Gen. R.* 56,10; *Tanḥ., Lek-Leka* 15 (57). See further, Ginzberg, *Legends* 5, 225–226, n. 102; Bowker, 1969, 196–199.

[42]= Onq. Salem was frequently identified with Jerusalem; cf., e.g., *1 QGenApoc* 22,13; Josephus, *Ant.* 1 § 180, *J.W.* 6 § 438; Tg. Ps. 76:3; cf. *Gen. R.* 43,6.

[43]*Sefer Ha-Yashar* 16 (45). The phrase added by Ps.-J. corresponds to what is said of the king of Sodom in the HT of v. 17. See a similar phrase in Heb 7:1.

[44]Melchizedek is given the title priest in HT. Onq. ("and he ministered before God Most High") and Ps.-J. deprive him of the title priest. The Targums generally apply the title priest to Aaron, to the Levitical priests, and, in Exod 19:6, to the people of Israel. People like Potiphera (Gen 41:45, 50; 46:20), Jethro (Exod 2:16; 3:1; 18:1) are not called priests in the Targums (cf. A. Rodríguez Carmona, 1980, 71–74; Vermes, 1963B, 167; idem, 1975, 135). By depriving Melchizedek of the title priest, Onq. and Ps.-J. invalidated the arguments of the author of Hebrews (Heb 5–7) and of later Christian writers who draw a comparison between Melchizedek and Jesus in order to show the superiority of the priesthood of Jesus. See further A. Rodríguez Carmona, "La figura de Melquisedec en la literatura targúmica," *Estudios Bíblicos* 37 (1978) 79–102.

[45]Lond. leaves a space after *mn,* "from"; *ed. pr.* has "from the Lord God." With Ginsburger (*Pseudo-Jonathan,* 24) we should probably add "before," in Lond., so that we have the usual Targumic idiom "from before."

[46]This addition is special to Ps.-J. See also Ps.-J. v. 22. Compare *Gen. R.* 12,9; *Tanḥ.* B. *Lek-Leka* 4 (1, 61–62); *Midrash Psalms* 104,15 (2, 173); *b. Shabb.* 88a (417); *b. Sanh.* 98b (667). See also the Targums of Num 22:30 (Nf, P, V, N, Ps.-J.). See further A. Marmorstein, *The Doctrine of Merits in Old Rabbinical Literature,* London, 1920, 108–128.

[47]The verb *mgn,* "delivered" (RSV), of HT is taken to mean "shield"; cf. *Gen. R.* 43, 8; 44,4.

[48]HT reads "I raised my hand," and clearly means "I have sworn" (cf. also Dan 12:7). Ps.-J. correctly interprets the Heb. idiom; see also *Gen. R.* 43,9. Onq. takes it to mean "I have raised my hand *in prayer."*

[49]Ps.-J. gives a double translation of Heb. *qnh,* "maker," combining the reading of Nf ("who created") with that of Onq. ("whose possessions").

earth: 23. I will not take even a thread or a sandal-strap[50] of all that is yours, lest you *boast and* say 'I have enriched Abram *from what was mine.*' 24. *Is it not true that I have no claim to any of the booty,* (except) what the young men, apart from me,[51] have eaten, and the portion of the men who went with me? Aner, Eshcol, and Mamre, they *too*[52] shall take their portion."

CHAPTER 15

1. After these things,[1] *after the kings had gathered together and had fallen before Abram, and (after) he had killed*[2] *four kings and brought back nine encampments, Abram thought in his heart and said, "Woe to me now! Perhaps I have received the reward of my (observance of the) commandments*[3] *in this world, and there will be no portion for me in the world to come. Or perhaps the brothers and relatives of these slain will go and join in legions and come against me. Or perhaps at that time the reward of some minor merits was found with me, so that they fell before me. But the second time the reward (of good deeds) will not be found with me, and the name of heaven will be profaned in me." Therefore a* word of the Lord was addressed to[4] Abram in a vision, saying, "Fear not <A'bram>;[5] *for even if they join in legions and come against you, my Memra* will be a shield for you; *and even if these have fallen before you in this world,* the reward *of your good works is kept and prepared before me for the world to come,*[6] a very great (reward)." 2. But Abram said, "Lord God, *you have given me much, and there is (still) much before you to* give me. But

Notes, Chapter 14 (Cont.)

[50]Lond. and *ed. pr.: sndlt rṣw'h;* read *rṣw'h dsndl* with P, V, N, L.

[51]Ps.-J. interprets Heb. *bl'dy* twice. The author first reads that word as two words *bl 'dy,* "not my booty." He then translates it literally as "apart from me."

[52]Aner, Eschol, and Mamre (cf. v. 13) had not accompanied Abram on his campaign (v. 14). The midrash presumed they remained with the baggage, so that they *too* deserved a share in the booty; cf. *Gen. R.* 43,9.

Notes, Chapter 15

[1]The Targums sometimes inserted long additions at the beginning of *sedarim* (sections of the Bible that were read in the synagogue); cf., e.g., Gen 18:1 (Nf, P, V, N, L; Ps.-J. has this addition in v. 2); 28:10 (Nf, P, V, N, L, Ps.-J.). See above, Introduction, p. 5 ("pre-translation haggadot"). Gen 15:1 marks the beginning of a *seder,* and the addition which the Pal. Tgs. (Nf, P, V, N, L, CTg H, and Ps.-J.) make in this verse explains why the Lord should have to say "fear not" to Abram after his victory over the kings. See *Gen. R.* 44,4.

[2]Lond. and *ed. pr.* have "they had killed."

[3]The belief that Abraham observed the Torah was common in Judaism; cf. Ginzberg, *Legends,* 5, 259, n. 275; Bowker, 1969, 235–236.

[4]Lit.: "was with."

[5]Omitted in Lond. and *ed. pr.*

[6]On the Targumists' conviction that the Lord rewards good deeds and on their belief in the world to come, see above, Gen 3:24 (Ps.-J.), and n. 58 to that verse.

what benefit do I have, *since I pass from the world* childless,[7] and Eliezer, the *manager* of my house,[8] *at whose hands miracles have been performed for me*[9] *in* Damascus, *expects to* be my heir?" 3. And Abram said, "Behold you have not given me a *son,* and behold the *manager* of my house will be my heir." 4. And behold, a word *from before* the Lord (came) to him saying, "This one will not be your heir, but *a son whom you will beget*[10] will be your heir." 5. Then he took him outside and said, "Look toward the heavens and count the stars, if you are able to count them." And he said to him, "So shall your *children* be." 6. *He had faith in the Memra of* the Lord, and he reckoned it to him as *merit*[11] *because he did not speak rebelliously against him.*[12] 7. He said to him, "I am the Lord who brought you out of *the fiery furnace*[13] of the Chaldeans to give you this land to inherit." 8. He said, "Lord *God,* how shall I know that I shall inherit it?" 9. He said to him, "Fetch me *offerings, and offer before*[14] *me* a heifer three years old,[15] a *he-goat*[16] three years old, a she-goat three years old, a turtledove, and a young pigeon."[17] 10. He *offered* all these *before* him, divided them in the middle, and *arranged* each part opposite the other; but he did not divide the birds. 11. *The nations,*[18] *that are like unclean birds,* came down *to plunder the property of Israel;* but *the merit of* Abram *protected them.*[19] 12. When the sun was *about* to set, a *deep* sleep *was cast* upon Abram, and behold *four kingdoms were rising to enslave his children:* "Dread"—*that is Babylon;* "Dark"—*that is Media;* "Great"—*that is Greece;* "Fell"—*that is Edom,*[20] *which is destined to fall*

Notes, Chapter 15

[7]The idiom "pass from the world" occurs again in Ps.-J. Deut 30:19.

[8]Onq.: "this manager who is in my house." See Theodotion: "the son of him who is over my house"; Vulg.: *filius procuratoris domus meae iste; Gen. R.* 44,9: "the son of my household." The Heb. idiom *bn mšq,* "heir" (RSV), is obscure. See further, Komlosh, 1973, 141; Grossfeld, 1988, 69, n. 3.

[9]*Gen. R.* 44,9: "for whose sake I pursued the kings … and God helped me."

[10]= Onq. HT reads literally: "the one who will issue from your bowels." This phrase must have seemed too crude for Onq. and Ps.-J. See also Gen 35:11, where Onq. and Ps.-J. avoid the phrase "come forth from your loins," whereas Nf translates it literally. But see Gen 46:26 and Exod 1:5, where Onq., Ps.-J., and Nf translate a similar idiom ("go forth from one's thigh") literally.

[11]Cf. *Mekilta* to Exod 14:15 (1, 220); *ibid.* to 14:31 (1, 253). On the meaning of *zkw(th),* see Bowker, 1969, 202.

[12]Ps.-J.'s phrase is a Hebraism. See the corresponding Heb. idiom in *b. Ta'an.* 25a (131): "to address oneself in a reproachful manner against God"; cf. Cook, 1986, 239.

[13]See above, n. 17 to 11:28 (Ps.-J.).

[14]Ps.-J. gives a double translation of Heb. *qḥḥ ly,* "bring me," first translating it as *sb ly,* "fetch me" (cf. Nfmg), and then using *qrb qdmy,* "offer before me," which corresponds to the readings in Nf and Onq.

[15]Onq. lists the animals as "three heifers, three she-goats, and three rams."

[16]Ps.-J. translates Heb. *'yl,* "ram," by *brḥ,* "he-goat." Ps.-J. changes the order of HT, which lists the ram after the she-goat.

[17]Lit.: "a *tasil,* the young of a dove." According to Jastrow (1682), a *tasil* is "a species of small doves." In Deut 32:11 Ps.-J. uses *tasil* to translate Heb. *gwzl* "the young (of an eagle)."

[18]*Ed. pr.* has "idolatrous nations," lit.: "nations (that are) adorers of idols."

[19]The Pal. Tgs. (including Ps.-J.) explain the different elements of the biblical verse: the birds of prey are the nations that attack Israel; the carcasses represent threatened Israel; Abram can drive off the enemies by his merits. See *Gen. R.* 44,16 and Tg. Jer 12:9. Explaining the words "Abram drove them away" Jerome (*Quaest. hebr. in Gen* 15:11) says *Illius enim merito saepe de angustiis liberatus est Israel.* See further, Böhl, 1987, 120–122.

[20]*Ed. pr.* reads "Persia" for fear of the censor. See also Nf Lev 26:44. In the literature of Judaism, Edom was often taken to refer to Rome, and later, to the Christians. For this reason the censor often erased the word Edom and Rome from Jewish texts (see, e.g., our present verse in Nf and Nfmg; Nf Num 20:14; Ps.-J. (Lond.) Num 24:18 (Idumaeans) and 19 (Constantinople), or the copyist prudently omitted these names (cf. Nf Num 24:19,24). The midrashim frequently find a reference to four kingdoms (cf. Dan 2:36-40) in Gen 15:12; see *Mekilta* to Exod 20:18 (2, 268); *Gen. R.* 44,17; *Exod. R.* 51,7; *Lev. R.* 13,5; *PRE* 28 (201). See also Tg. Lev 26:44 (P, V, N, Ps.-J.; cf. Nf); Deut 32:24 (Nf, P, V, N, L, Ps.-J.).

*and for which there will be no rising; from there the people of the house of Israel will
come up.* 13. He said to Abram, "Know for certain that your *children* will be
residents[21] *in a land that is not theirs, because you did not believe;*[22] *and they will
be enslaved and afflicted four hundred years.* 14. But the people whom they shall
serve I will judge *with two hundred and fifty plagues;*[23] *and after that they will go
forth to freedom* with great wealth. 15. As for yourself, you shall *be gathered*[24] to
your fathers; *your soul shall rest* in peace; you shall be buried at a good old age. 16.
And the fourth generation *of your children* shall return here *to take possession of
(the land),*[25] for the guilt of the Amorites is not yet complete." 17. When the sun
had set and it was dark, behold, *Abram saw Gehenna sending up* smoke and coals of
fire, *and sending forth*[26] *sparks of fire with which to judge the wicked. And behold* it
passed between these parts. 18. On that day the Lord made a covenant with Abram,
(promising) that he would not judge his children by it,[27] *and that he would deliver
them from the kingdoms,* (and) saying, "To your *children* I will give this land, from
the *Nile* of Egypt to the Great River, the river Euphrates, 19. the *Shalmaites,*[28] the
Kenizzites, the Kadmonites, 20. the Hittites, the Perizzites, the *Giants,*[29] 21. the
Amorites, the Canaanites, the Girgashites, and the Jebusites."

Notes, Chapter 15

[21] = Onq. M. Ohana, (1974, 317–332) has shown that Onq. translates Heb. *gr* by *gywr* only when it refers to one who has
formally converted to Judaism, and that it uses other words like *dyr,* "resident," as in our present verse, or *'rl,* "uncircumcised," when it does not have this technical meaning. Ps.-J. usually follows Onq. in this matter.

[22] Ps.-J. is the only Targum to express this view, but the idea that the slavery in Egypt was a punishment for Abraham's
lack of faith (cf. Gen 15:8) is found in *b. Ned.* 32a (97). It is to be noted that what Ps.-J. says in our present verse about the
consequences of Abram's disbelief does not fully harmonize with what that Targum says in v. 11 about Abram's merit.

[23] This is the opinion of R. Akiba in *Mekilta* to Exod 14:31 (Friedmann's edition, 33b; compare Lauterbach, 1, 251); cf.
Midrash Psalms 78,15 (2, 36–37); *Exod. R.* 23,9.

[24] Onq., Nf, and Ps.-J. translate the phrase "you shall go" by "you shall be gathered," which is the usual idiom used with
reference to the death of the patriarchs (cf. Gen 25:8; 35:29; 49:33). In our present verse Nfmg translates HT literally.

[25] Lit.: "of it."

[26] Lit.: "causing to pass." Midrashic literature tells of different things, including Gehenna, that were revealed to
Abraham when the Lord passed between the pieces (cf. Gen 15:17); see, e.g., *Mekilta* to Exod 20:18 (2, 268); *Gen. R.*
44,21; *Exod. R.* 51,7; *PRK* 5,2 (92); *PRE* 28 (202); *4 Ezra* 3,14; *2 (Syriac) Baruch* 4,4. See further, Ginzberg, *Legends*
1,236–237; 5, 229, n. 114. Prompted by the reference to "a smoking fire pot" and "a flaming torch" in HT, the Pal. Tgs.
(Nf, Nfmg, P, V, N, L) add a description of Gehenna in their versions of Gen 15:17. Ps.-J. offers an abbreviated version of
that tradition. The Pal. Tgs., including Ps.-J., explain the seeming redundancy in the reference to "a fire pot" and "a
torch." They take the fire pot to refer to Gehenna, and the torch to refer to the sparks of fire coming from Gehenna. See
further, Böhl, 1987, 122–124.

[27] The fire of Gehenna will have no power over the children of Israel; cf., e.g., *b. Erub.* 19a (129).

[28] = Onq.; cf. Grossfeld, 1988, 71, n. 17. Cf. also Pliny, *Natural History* 6,26,30. Josephus implicitly identifies the
Kenites with the Shalmaites; cf. Rappaport, 1930, XXIII. See the Targums of Num 24:21-22.

[29] On the translation of "Rephaim" as "Giants," see above, 14:5 (Ps.-J.), and n. 18 to that verse.

CHAPTER 16

1. Sarai, Abram's wife, bore him no children; but she had an Egyptian maid, whose name was Hagar, a *daughter of Pharaoh, whom he gave to her as maid when he took her*[1] *and was smitten*[2] *by a word from before the Lord.* 2. Sarai said to Abram, "Behold, I pray, the Lord has prevented me from bearing children. Now, go in to my maid, *and I will set her free.*[3] Perhaps I may have children[4] through her." And Abram listened to the word of Sarai. 3. Sarai, Abram's wife, took Hagar the Egyptian, her maid—after Abram had dwelt in the land of Canaan for ten years— *set her free* and gave her to Abram her husband as wife.[5] 4. He went in to Hagar, and she conceived; and when she saw that she had conceived, *the honor of* her mistress was of little value in her eyes. 5. Sarai said to Abram, "*All* my humiliation *(comes) from you,*[6] *because I trusted that you would do me justice, (seeing) that I left my country and my father's house and went with you into a foreign land. And now, because I have not borne children, I set* my maid *free* and gave her *(to you)* to lie in your bosom.[7] *But when she saw that she was with child, my honor was despised* in her sight. *Now let my humiliation be manifest*[8] *before the Lord, and let him spread his peace* between me and you, *and let the earth be filled from us, so that we will not need the children of Hagar, the daughter of Pharaoh, the son of Nimrod, who threw you into the furnace of fire.*"[9] 6. Abram said to Sarai, "Behold, your maid is in your *power;* do to her what seems right in your eyes." And Sarai treated her harshly, and she fled from her. 7. The angel of the Lord found her at the spring of water in the

Notes, Chapter 16

[1]The view that Hagar was Pharaoh's daughter was well known in Jewish tradition; cf., e.g., *Gen. R.* 45,1; *PRE* 26 (190). This tradition seems to be implied in 1 *QGenApoc* 20, 31-32. See further Ginzberg, *Legends,* 1, 223 and 237; 5, 221, n. 74, and 231, n. 119. Hagar is identified with Keturah in Tg. Gen 25:1 (P, V, N, L, Ps.-J., Nfmg 1 and 2).

[2]*'ytktš*. In Gen 12:17 the Targums (Onq., Nf, Nfmg, Ps.-J.) use the same root when saying that the Lord sent plagues (*mktšyn*) against Pharaoh. Ps.-J. uses the verb *'ytktš* in Exod 2:23 to say that the king of Egypt was smitten with leprosy. According to *Sefer Ha-Yashar* (15 [42–43]), an angel smote the king when he approached Sarai (cf. Gen 12:15).

[3]Ps.-J. states explicitly in vv. 2, 3, and 5 that the maid was set free. It would be unbecoming for the patriarch to have children by a slave. See *Gen. R.* 45, 3 and 6. See also Ps.-J. Gen 30:4, 9. Compare *b. Pesah.* 113a (582); Tg. 1 Chron 2:35.

[4]Lit.: "I may be built up." The Targums translate the Hebrew literally. See also the Targums of Gen 30:3.

[5]Gen 16:3 was understood to sanction divorce on the grounds of the wife's childlessness after ten years of marriage. See *Gen. R.* 45, 3; *b. Yeb.* 64a (428).

[6]The detailed account of Sarah's emotional outburst which the Pal. Tgs. insert into this verse has no parallel in the midrashic literature. *Gen. R.* 45, 5 simply records that Sarah accused Abraham of failing to defend her when Hagar insulted her. Onq. softens Sarah's words "May the wrong done to me be on you" to "I have cause for a legal complaint against you."

[7]HT: "I gave my maid into your bosom." Nf and P, V, N, L avoid a direct translation of this expression, which they regarded as indelicate. So also does Onq., which reads, "I gave my maid to you." Ps.-J. on the other hand strengthens the biblical image. See also Ps.-J. Deut 13:7; 28:54, 56, where the phrase "the wife (husband) of your (his, her) bosom" becomes "the wife (husband) *who sleeps (dmk['])* in your (his, her) bosom."

[8]=*Ed. pr.;* Lond.: "has been made manifest."

[9]On the tradition that Nimrod threw Abraham into the fiery furnace, see above n. 17 to Gen 11:28. The strange assertion that Pharaoh was the son of Nimrod, which we find in Ps.-J.'s version of our present verse (see also Nf, P, V, N, L), is known from no other source; cf. Brayer, 1964, 221.

wilderness, at the spring on the way to *Hagra.* [10] 8. He said, "Hagar, maid of Sarai, where are you coming from, and where are you going?" She said, "I have fled from Sarai my mistress." 9. The [11] angel of the Lord said to her, "Return to your mistress, and submit to her oppressive treatment." [12] 10. The angel of the Lord said to her, "I will greatly multiply your *children* and they will be too numerous to count." [13] 11. The angel of the Lord [14] said to her, "Behold you are with child, and you shall bear a son. You shall call his name Ishmael, because your affliction *has been revealed before* the Lord. 12. He shall be *like* a wild ass *among the children of men;* his hands will *take revenge on his enemies,* and the hands *of his enemies will be stretched forth to harm him.* He shall dwell alongside all his kinsmen *and he shall be mixed (with them)."* [15] 13. She *gave thanks* [16] *before* the Lord *whose Memra* had spoken to her, *and she spoke thus,* "You are *the Living and Enduring One, who sees but is not seen";* [17] for she said, *"Behold, here indeed the Glory of the Shekinah of the Lord was revealed, vision* [18] *after vision."* 14. Therefore the well was called "The well *at which the Living and Enduring One was revealed": and* behold *it is situated* between *Reqem* [19] and *Haluzah.* [20] 15. Hagar bore Abram a son; and Abram called the name of his son, whom Hagar bore, Ishmael. 16. Abram was eighty-six years old when Hagar bore Ishmael to Abram.

Notes, Chapter 16

[10] Onq. translates the Heb. place-name Shur as Hagra; cf. Gen 16:7; 20:1; 25:18; Exod 15:22. In all these texts Nf renders Shur as Haluzah, as do the Frg. Tgs. of Gen 16:7 (P, V, N, L); 25:18 (V, N, L); Exod 15:22 (P, V, N). Ps.-J. is inconsistent, reading Hagra in Gen 16:7 and 20:1, but Haluzah in Gen 25:18 and Exod 15:22. Like Onq., Tg. Jon. translates Shur as Hagra (cf. 1 Sam 15:7; 27:8). *Gen. R.* 45, 7 identifies Shur with Halizah. See further Neubauer, 1868, 410; Aberbach-Grossfeld, 1982, 97, n. 5.

[11] V. 9 is omitted in Lond.

[12] Lit.: "and be oppressed beneath her hands."

[13] Lit.: "they will not be counted for multitude."

[14] "Of the Lord" is omitted in Lond.

[15] We follow Schmerler (1932, 142) in taking Ps.-J. to mean that Ishmael will dwell among the nations and be mixed with them. Le-Déaut (1978, *Genèse,* 177, n. 10) suggests that Ps.-J's verb *yt'rbb* may be a play on the word "Arabs," the Arabs being the reputed descendants of Ishmael.

[16] Onq.: "she prayed." The Targums take the phrase "she called the name of the Lord" to mean that Hagar "prayed (or gave thanks)." However, no midrashic text associates Gen 16:13 with prayer. The *meturgemanim* may have been influenced by their translations of such texts as Gen 12:8; 13:4; 21:33, where the Targums understand the phrase "call on the name of the Lord" to refer to prayer. Cf. Shinan, 1979, 2, 330–331; idem, 1975, 90–91; Maher, 1990, 241.

[17] Ps.-J's interpretation (see also the Frg. Tgs.) of *'l r'y,* "a God of seeing," in this verse is based on the fact that he takes the words *lhy r'y,* lahai-roi (v. 14; RSV) to be derived from *hy,* "living," and *r'h,* "see." The divine title "the Living and Enduring One" is found again in Ps.-J. in v. 14 and in 24:62; 25:11; Num 23:19. A very similar title is found in the Koran (cf. Le Déaut, *Genèse,* 1978, 177, n. 12). The description of God as "He who sees but is not seen," which occurs again in Ps.-J. Gen 24:6 and 25:11, is also found in the Koran, as well as in rabbinic literature (cf., e.g., *j. Peah* 9, 21b; *b. Hag.* 5b [24]). See Ginzberg, *Legends,* 5, 213, n. 34.

[18] "Vision" is omitted in *ed. pr.* We follow the reading of Lond., since rabbinic tradition held that Hagar was accustomed to divine revelations (cf. *Gen. R.* 45, 7).

[19] See above, 14:7, and n. 22 to that verse.

[20] Onq., which usually translates Shur as Hagra, now translates Bered as Hagra, and Nf, which translates Shur as Haluzah, now uses that name to translate Bered. Ps.-J., which can use either Hagra or Haluzah to translate Shur, now renders Bered by Haluzah; see above, n. 10 to v. 7.

CHAPTER 17

1. When Abram was ninety-nine years old, the Lord revealed himself to Abram and said to him, "I am El Shaddai. *Worship* before me and be perfect *in your flesh.*[1] 2. I will establish my covenant between *my Memra* and you, and I will multiply you exceedingly." 3. *But because* Abram *was not circumcised he was not able to stand,*[2] and he bent down upon his face, and *the Lord* spoke with him saying, 4. "As for me, behold I *am making*[3] my covenant with you: you shall be the father of a multitude of peoples. 5. You shall no longer be called by the name Abram, but your name shall be Abraham, for I have made[4] you the father of a *great* multitude of peoples. 6. I will make you increase exceedingly, and I will make *assemblies*[5] of you; kings *(who) will rule over the nations*[6] shall come forth from you. 7. I will establish my covenant between *my Memra* and you and your *children* after you, throughout their generations, as an everlasting covenant, to be God to you and to your *children* after you. 8. I will give to you and to your *children* after you the land you sojourn in, all the land of Canaan, as an everlasting possession. And I will be their God." 9. And *the Lord* said to Abraham, "As for you, you shall keep my covenant, you and your *children* after you throughout their generations. 10. This is my covenant between *my Memra* and you and your children after you which you shall keep: to circumcise every male, *if he has no father to circumcise him.*[7] 11. You shall circumcise the flesh of your foreskin, and it shall be a sign of the covenant between *my Memra* and you. 12. He that is eight days old among you shall be circumcised, every male throughout your generations, *those who have been brought up in your* houses, and those who have been bought with your money from any gentile[8] who is not of your *children.* 13. *He who is circumcised* shall circumcise[9] *those who have been brought up in* your houses or bought with your money. Thus my covenant shall be in your flesh as an everlasting covenant. 14. An uncircumcised male who does not circumcise the flesh of his foreskin *when he has no one to circumcise him,*[10] that *man* shall be blotted out from his[11] people; he has *changed*[12] my covenant." 15. And *the Lord*

Notes, Chapter 17

[1]The reference is to circumcision. See *m. Ned.* 3,11; *b. Ned.* 32a (95); *Gen. R.* 46,1 and 4; *PRE* 29 (203).
[2]*PRE* 29 (205).
[3]= Onq.
[4]Lit.: "appointed."
[5]= Onq. Heb. *gwym,* which is used in HT, usually refers to gentiles in rabbinic literature. Onq. and Ps.-J. avoid a literal translation of this term, which cannot be applied to the descendants of Abraham.
[6]= Onq. See below, v. 16.
[7]Cf. *b. Qidd.* 29a (138), which states that the Beth Din is to circumcise a boy if his father did not do so. Ps.-J. seems to refer to a case where the boy's father is dead.
[8]= Onq. The Targums make it clear that Heb. *bn nkr* means gentile. According to *b. Yebam.* 48b (318), a slave bought from an idolater must be circumcised. See further Aberbach-Grossfeld, 1982, 102, n. 8; Grossfeld, 1988, 75, n. 7.
[9]*Gen. R.* 46,12; *b. Abod. Zar.* 27a (134); *Menah.* 42a (254). Heb. *himmol yimmol,* "shall be circumcised," is read as *hammul yamul,* "he who is circumcised shall circumcise."
[10]According to *b. Qidd.* 29a (138), one who has no one to circumcise him must circumcise himself.
[11]= *Ed. pr.;* Lond.: "my people."
[12]= Onq. See also, e.g., Ps.-J. and Onq. Deut 31:16, 20; Tg. Isa 24:5; 33:8; Jer 11:10

said to Abraham, "As for Sarai your wife, you shall not call her name Sarai, but Sarah shall be her name. 16. I will bless her *in her body*, [13] and I will also give you a son from her. I will bless *him*, [14] and she shall become *assemblies*, and kings *(who) will rule* over the nations shall come from her." 17. Abraham fell upon his face and *was amazed*, [15] and said to himself, "Can a child be born to a man who is a hundred years old? Can Sarah bear a child at ninety?" 18. And Abraham said *before the Lord*, "O that Ishmael might survive [16] *and serve* before you." 19. *The Lord* said, "*In truth* [16] Sarah your wife shall bear you a son, and you shall call his name Isaac; and I will establish my covenant with him as an everlasting covenant for his *children* after him. 20. As for Ishmael, I have *accepted your prayer.* [16] Behold I have blessed him, and I will increase him and multiply him exceedingly. He will beget twelve princes and I will make him a great nation. 21. But I will establish my covenant with Isaac, whom Sarah will bear to you at this time next year." 22. When he had finished speaking with him, the *Glory of the Lord* [16] went up from Abraham. 23. Then Abraham took his son Ishmael and all those *who had been brought up in* his house and all those bought with his money, every male among the members of Abraham's household, and he circumcised the flesh of their foreskin that same day, as *the Lord* had spoken to him. 24. Abraham was ninety-nine years old when he circumcised the flesh of his foreskin. 25. And his son Ishmael was thirteen years old when he circumcised the flesh of his foreskin. [17] 26. That very day, *on the fourteenth of <Nisan>* [18] Abraham and his son Ishmael were circumcised. 27. All the men of his house, *those who had been brought up in* the house and those bought with money from a gentile, were circumcised with him.

Notes, Chapter 17

[13]Ps.-J. echoes the view, expressed in *Gen. R.* 47,2, that the biblical phrase "I will bless her" teaches that God restored Sarah to her youth and gave her a son. See also Ps.-J. Exod 2:1, which tells us that the 130-year-old Jochebed had her youth restored to her. Among the Targums, only Ps.-J., in accordance with his fondness for the miraculous, refers to these miracles that were performed on behalf of Sarah and Jochebed.

[14]= Pesh., LXX, Vulg.; HT: "I will bless her."

[15]Onq.: "and rejoiced." See *Jubilees* 15:17: "he rejoiced and pondered in his heart." In Gen 21:6 Onq. twice translates "laugh" as "rejoice" (cf. also Nf, Nfmg), and Ps.-J. twice uses "be amazed." In our present verse the *meturgemanim* considered it disrespectful to say that Abraham laughed in God's presence. Ephraem, explaining the Peshitta's "laughed," says "that is, was astounded." Cf. Brock, 1979, 220. See below, 18:12 and n. 18 to that verse.

[16]= Onq.

[17]V. 25 is omitted in *ed. pr.*

[18]Omitted in Lond. *Ed. pr.* reads "years," which, in the light of vv. 24-25, cannot be correct. See also Ps.-J. 22:1, where Ishmael asserts that he was circumcised at the age of thirteen. It seems that we should read "Nisan" rather than "years" in our present verse. See S. Speier, "The Date of the Circumcision of Abraham and Ishmael according to Targum Pseudo-Jonathan" (in Hebrew), *Proceedings of the American Academy for Jewish Research*, 29 (1960–61) 69–73. According to PRE 29 (203–204), Abraham was circumcised on the Day of Atonement.

CHAPTER 18

1. *The Glory of* the Lord *was revealed* to him at the *Vision* of Mamre;[1] he was *suffering from the pain of circumcision,*[2] seated at the door of the tent at the *strength* of the day. 2. He lifted up[3] his eyes and saw, and behold, three *angels in the form of* men[4] were standing before him. *They had been sent for three things. For it is not possible for a ministering angel to be sent for more than one thing. One came to announce to him that Sarah would bear a male child; one came to rescue Lot; and one came to destroy Sodom and Gomorrah.*[5] When he saw *them* he ran from the door of the tent to meet them and bowed to the ground. 3. He said, *"I beseech you by the mercies from before you, O Lord,*[6] if now I have found favor *before* you, let not *the Glory of your Shekinah go up* from your servant *until I have received these travelers."*[7] 4. *Abraham again said to these men,* "Let a little water be brought, and wash your feet, and recline under the tree.[8] 5. And I will bring a morsel[9] of bread. Refresh your hearts *and give thanks to the Name of the Memra of the Lord,*[10] and after that you may go on. Because it was for this reason that *you chanced to come at mealtime,* and to pass by your servant, *so that you might refresh yourselves."* They said, *"You have spoken well.* Do according to your *word."* 6. Abraham hastened into the tent to Sarah and said, "Quick, three *seahs* of fine flour! Knead it and make cakes." 7. Abraham ran to the cattleyard and took a calf, tender and *fat,* and gave it to the servant, who hurried to prepare *dishes.* 8. He took *thick* cream[11] and milk, as well as the calf *from which the servant* had prepared *dishes,* and set (them) before

Notes, Chapter 18

[1]See above, n. 13 to 13:18 (Ps.-J.).

[2]According to *b. B. Mez.* 86b (499), the Lord visited Abraham on the third day after his circumcision. *PRE* 29 (205) also says that it was the third day and adds that Abraham was very sore. See also *Gen. R.* 48,8, which says that Abraham was in pain.

[3]= Onq. See above, n. 4 to 13:10.

[4]This solves the problem raised by the fact that the visitors are called "men" in 18:2, 16, 22, but "angels" in 19:1; cf. *Gen. R.* 50,2.

[5]This expansion, which Ps.-J. and Nfmg add to this verse, is placed in a slightly longer form in v. 1 by Nf and the Frg. Tgs. This Targumic expansion has parallels in *Gen. R.* 50,2; *b. B. Mez.* 86b (500). Josephus (*Ant.* 1 § 196) says that Abraham saw three angels and took them for strangers. R. Weiss claims that this tradition is also found in a fragment from cave 4 of Qumran; cf. R. Weiss, "Fragments of a Midrash on Genesis from Qumran Cave 4," *Textus* 7 (1969) 132–134. The angels mentioned in the Targums of Gen 18:1-2 are referred to by Ps.-J., and by Ps.-J. alone, in 18:10, 16, 22; 19:17; Ps.-J.'s additions in our present verse and in these latter verses form a complete story about the angels and their roles; cf. Shinan, 1979, 1, 121–122; idem, 1985, 78.

[6]The Targums take *'dny,* "my lord," of HT to refer to God. See the debate on this point in *b. Shebu.* 35b (205). See also Gen 19:18, where the Targums also take *'dny* to refer to God.

[7]*b. Shabb.* 127a (632).

[8]Apart from the words "under the tree," this verse is omitted in *ed. pr.*

[9]Lit.: "a sustenance."

[10]Ps.-J. is referring to "grace after meals." See also Gen 21:33 (Ps.-J., Nfmg) and Num 11:33 (Ps.-J.).

[11]Ps.-J. has a conflate reading, combining *lwwy,* "cream, curds," which is used in Nfmg, and in a slightly different form (*lyb'*) in Nf, with *šm(y)n,* "cream;" (= Onq.). Ps.-J., and Ps.-J. alone, uses the word *lww'y* in Deut 32:14.

them *according to the manner (and) custom of human beings.*[12] He *ministered*[13] before them *as they sat* <under the tree>[14] *and it seemed to him that they were eating.*[15] 9. They said to him, "Where is Sarah your wife?." And he said, "Behold, she is in the tent." 10. *One of them* said, "I will surely return to you *in the coming year, and you will (still) be alive,*[16] and behold, Sarah your wife shall have a son." Sarah was listening at the door of the tent, and *Ishmael was standing* behind *her*[17] *listening to what the angel said.* 11. Now Abraham and Sarah were old; they had advanced in age, and Sarah had ceased having the periods *of impurity* of women. 12. Sarah *wondered*[18] in her *heart,*[19] saying, "After I have grown old shall I become *pregnant*[20]—and my master *Abraham* so old?" 13. The Lord said to Abraham, "Why did Sarah laugh, saying, 'Shall I in truth bear a child, now that I am old? 14. *Is it possible* for anything to be *hidden* from *before* the Lord? At the time *of the feast*[21] I shall return to you, at this time, *and you shall (still) be alive,*[22] and Sarah shall have a son." 15. Sarah denied (it) saying, "I did not *wonder*";[23] for she was afraid.[24] *The angel*[25] said, "*Do not be afraid*; but in truth you did laugh." 16. The *angels who had the form of* men arose from there; *the one who had brought good news to Sarah went up to the heavens on high,*[26] *and two of them* looked towards Sodom. Abraham went with them to *accompany* them. 17. The Lord said in *his Memra,* "*I cannot* hide from Abraham what I am about to do. *By right I should not act until I have informed him.*[27] 18. Abraham is destined to become a great and mighty nation, and on account of him, *by his merits*[28] all the nations of the earth

Notes, Chapter 18

[12]Lit.: "the creatures of the world."

[13]= Onq. Cf. *Mekilta* to Exod 18:12 (2, 177–178); *b. Qidd.* 32b (158).

[14]Omitted in Lond. and *ed. pr.*

[15]Since it was believed that angels do not eat (cf. Tobit 12:19; *Gen. R.* 48,11, *Tanh., Wa-Yera* 11 [71]), Nf and Ps.-J. (but not Onq.) avoid saying that the angels actually ate. See *Gen. R.* 48,14; *b. B. Mez.* 86b (498); Josephus, *Ant.* 1 § 197; Philo, *De Abrahamo* § 118. *Jubilees* 16 omits the account of the meal. See also Tg. Gen 19:3 (P, V, N, L, Ps.-J.).

[16]Or perhaps: "in the coming year when you are well." Cf. Bowker, 1969, 208, 211.

[17]Onq.: "behind him." HT could be translated as "behind it" (the door), or "behind him" (the angel). Nf, V, N, L and Ps.-J. translate it as "behind her" (Sarah).

[18]Onq.: "laughed." The Pal. Tgs. regard it as disrespectful to say that Sarah laughed on hearing the angel's message (cf. v. 10). See above, n. 15 to 17:17, and see below, n. 23 to v. 15, and n. 4 to 21:6.

[19]Onq. translates HT literally and reads "in her bowels (or belly)."

[20]Lit.: "shall I have pregnancies?" or "shall I have periods?" See Jastrow, 1067, and *Gen. R.* 48,17. Onq.: "shall I have youth?" The Targums do not translate the biblical phrase "shall I have pleasure?" literally. They felt that this phrase had sexual connotations and that it was unworthy of Sarah.

[21]According to tradition, Isaac was born at Passover; cf. *b. Rosh Hash.* 11a (41). The visit described in Gen 18 is also said to have taken place at Passover; cf. *Gen. R.* 48,12.

[22]Or perhaps "and you shall be well." Onq.: "at the time when you are alive." See above, n. 16 to v. 10.

[23]Onq.: "I did not laugh." See above, n. 18 to v. 12.

[24]Thus *ed. pr.;* Lond.: "I was afraid."

[25]*Gen. R.* 48,20.

[26]*Gen. R.* 50,2. This resolves the contradiction between Gen 18:2 (three men) and 19:1 (two angels).

[27]Ps.-J. abbreviates the midrash, which is also found in Nf and Frg. Tgs. Compare the *Königsgleichnis* found in *Tanh., Wa-Yera,* 5 (66).

[28]Ps.-J. combines the reading of Onq. ("on account of him") with that of Nf and Nfmg ("by his merits").

shall be blessed. 19. For *his piety is manifest before me,* so that he will command his children and the *members of* his household after him to observe ways *that are right before* the Lord, doing what is just and right, so that the Lord may bring upon Abraham *the good things*[29] he has promised him." 20. The Lord said *to the ministering angels,* "The cry[30] of Sodom and Gomorrah—*because they oppress the poor and decree that whoever gives a morsel of bread to the needy shall be burned by fire*[31]—is indeed great, and their sin has indeed increased greatly. 21. I will now *be revealed,* and I will see whether they have (really) done according to complaint of *the maiden Peletith*[32] which has come before me.[33] (If so) *they deserve* total destruction,[34] *but if they do penance, shall they not be righteous before me as (if)* I *did not know, and I will not take revenge.*[35] 22. The two[36] angels *who were like* men turned from there and went to Sodom. Abraham was still *beseeching mercy for Lot, and ministering in prayer* before the Lord. 23. Abraham *prayed* and said, "Shall *your anger* wipe out the innocent with the guilty? 24. What if there are fifty innocent people within the city *who pray before you, ten for each city of the five cities of Sodom, Gomorrah, Admah, Zeboiim, and Zoar?*[37] Will *your anger*[38] wipe (them) out and not forgive the place for the sake of *the merits of* the fifty innocent people who are in it? 25. *It would be a profanation*[39] for you to do such a thing, to kill the innocent with the guilty, so that the innocent would be as the guilty; *that would be a profanation*[39] for you. *Is it possible that he who* judges the whole earth should not do justice?" 26. And the Lord said, "If in Sodom I find fifty innocent people within the city *who pray before me,* I will forgive the whole place[40] for their sake." 27. Abraham replied and said, "*I beseech, by (your) mercy!* Behold, I have begun to speak *before the Lord,* I who am *like* dust and ashes. 28. What if five of the fifty innocent are lacking? Will you destroy the whole city because of five *who are lacking in Zoar?*" He said, "I will not destroy if I find forty-five there." 29. He spoke again *before* him and said, "What if forty are found there, *ten for each of the four cities?*

Notes, Chapter 18

[29]Omitted in *ed. pr.*

[30]Or: "the outcry against."

[31]Ps.-J. gives an abbreviated version of a midrash that is found in *Gen. R.* 49,6; *b. Sanh.* 109b (752); *PRE* 25 (182–183).

[32]The text from *PRE* mentioned in the previous note names Peletith, daughter of Lot, as the one who was burned for coming to the assistance of a poor man. This midrash is based on the fact that the Hebrew text of the phrase "according to the outcry" (RSV) in v. 21 reads literally: "according to *her* outcry." See also the *Gen. R.* text mentioned in the preceding note, where Heb. *rabbah,* "great," in v. 20 is read as *ribah,* "maiden." Ps.-J.'s reference to Peletith makes no sense without a knowledge of the tradition recorded in *PRE.* See further J. Mulder, *Het Meisje van Sodom* (Kampen: J.H. Kok, 1970).

[33]Lond. and *ed. pr.* read "before him."

[34]Onq.: "I shall make an end of them." Heb. *klh,* "altogether," can also mean "destruction" (cf., e.g., Jer 4:27; 5:10), and the Targums understand it in that sense in our present verse.

[35]*Gen. R.* 49,6 also states that God gave the cities an opportunity to repent.

[36]"Two" is omitted in *ed. pr.*

[37]Ps.-J. adds special details about the numbers of people mentioned in Gen 18:24-32. In v. 24 the fifty people are those who pray, and they are divided in *minyanim* among the five cities. See vv. 28-32. See further, Shinan, 1979, 2, 331.

[38]The Targums (Nf, Ps.-J., Onq.) read Heb. *'p,* "also, even," as "anger"; cf. *Gen. R.* 49,8.

[39]*b. Abod. Zar.* 4a (14); *Gen. R.* 49,9. The word *hllh* in the Heb. idiom *hllh lk,* "far be it from thee" (RSV), is etymologically linked with *hll,* "profane."

[40]*Ed. pr.:* "the whole earth."

As for Zoar, whose guilt is light,[41] *forgive it, for the sake of your mercy."* He said, "I will not make *an end,* for the sake of the merits of forty." 30. He said, "Let not the anger of the Master *of all the worlds, the Lord,* be enkindled, and I will speak. What if thirty *who pray* are found there, *ten for each of the three cities? As for Zeboiim and Zoar, forgive them for the sake of your mercy."* He said, "I will not make *an end* if I find thirty there." 31. He said, "*I beseech, by (your) mercy!* Behold, I have begun to speak *before* the Master *of all the worlds,*[42] *the Lord.* What if twenty *who pray* are found, *ten for each of the two cities? As for the (other) three, forgive them for the sake of your mercy."* And he said, "I will not destroy, for the sake of *the merits of* twenty." 32. He said, "*I beseech by the mercy before you,* let not the anger of the Master *of all the worlds, the Lord,* be enkindled, and I will speak this last time.[43] What if ten are found there, *and they and I beseech mercy for the whole place and you forgive them?"* And he said, "I will not destroy, for the sake of the merits of ten." 33. *And the Glory of the Shekinah of* the Lord[44] *went up* when he *finished* speaking with Abraham. And Abraham returned to his place.

CHAPTER 19

1. The two angels came to Sodom in the evening as Lot was seated at the gate of Sodom. When Lot saw (them) he rose *from the door of the tent* to meet them, and bowed, with his face to the ground. 2. He said, "I pray, my lords, turn aside *hither*[1] and *come into* your servant's house to spend the night, and wash your feet; then you may rise early and go on your way." But they said, "No, for we will spend the night in the marketplace." 3. But he urged them strongly, and they turned aside to him and went into his house. He prepared a feast for them and baked unleavened bread *for them,*[2] *and it seemed to him that* they were eating.[3] 4. Before they lay down,

Notes, Chapter 18 (Cont.)

[41] According to Gen 19:20, 22, Zoar was a little place, and because of that its sins were few; cf. *b. Shabb.* 10b (38).

[42] *rbwn kl 'lmy'.* This title is not unusual in the Targums; see, e.g., vv. 31 and 32; 30:22 (Nf, V, N); 37:33 (CTg D); 38:25 (V, N, L, CTg D); Exod 17:16 (Nf, P, V, N); 32:31 (Ps.-J.); Num 23:19 (Ps.-J.); Deut 32:4 (V, N, Ps.-J.). There are variations of this title, e.g., "Master of the whole world," Gen 30:22 (P); 37:33 (P); Exod 17:16 (Nf); Num 21:15 (Nf, P, V, N); Deut 32:4 (P, L); "Master of the world," e.g., Gen 32:25 (Ps.-J.); Exod 23:17 and 34:23 (Onq.); Lev 1:1 (P); "God of the world," Gen 35:9 (P, V, N, L). Cf. also 1 *QGenApoc* 21,2-3; and see further D. Barthélemy and J. T. Milik, *Discoveries in the Judaean Desert I. Qumran Cave I* (Oxford: Clarendon, 1955; reprint 1964) 87.

[43] Lit.: "but this time." The word for this is omitted in Lond.

[44] *Ed. pr.* omits "Shekinah," so that, like Onq., it reads "the Glory of the Lord."

Notes, Chapter 19

[1] Lit.: "from here."

[2] = Onq.

[3] See above, 18:8 and n. 15 to that verse.

wicked men *who were in* the city, the men of Sodom, both young and old, all the people to the last man, surrounded the house. 5. They called to Lot and said to him, "Where are the men who went in to you tonight? Bring them out to us, that we may *have sexual relations with*[4] them." 6. So Lot went out to them to the entrance, shut the door[5] behind him, 7. and said, "*I beseech you,* my brothers,[6] do not, I pray, act wickedly. 8. Behold, I have two daughters who have never *had intercourse* with a man. Let me bring them out to you, and do to them what seems right to[7] you; but do no *evil* to these men, because they have come in *to pass the night and they have taken refuge*[8] under the shelter of *this*[9] roof of mine." 9. But they said, "Stand back!" And they said, "Did not this fellow come alone to sojourn *among us? And behold, he has made himself judge* and is judging *all of us.*[10] And now we will do worse to you than to them." And they pressed very hard against the man, against Lot, and drew near to break the door. 10. And the men stretched out their hands and brought Lot to them into the house, and shut the door. 11. The men who were at the door of the house, both *young and old,* they struck with blindness, so that they wearied themselves (trying) to find the door. 12. Then the men said to Lot, "Who else do you have here *in the city? A relative or a brother? Your* son-in-law, your sons, your daughters?[11] Take (them) out of the place; 13. for we are about to destroy this place, because the outcry (against it) has become great before the Lord, and the Lord has sent us to destroy it." 14. So Lot went out and spoke with his sons-in-law, who had married[12] his daughters, and he said, "Arise, get out of this place, for the Lord is about to destroy the city." But in the eyes of his sons-in-law *the idea* seemed *fantastic,*[13] like (that of) *a man* who jests. 15. At *the time of* the rising of the dawn[14] the angels pressed Lot saying, "Arise, take your wife and your two daughters who are *with you,*[15] lest you be blotted out because of the sins of *the inhabitants of* the city." 16. But he delayed. So the men seized his hand, and the hands of his wife and his two daughters, *because*[16] mercy *from before* the Lord was upon him. And they brought him out and placed him outside the city. 17. As they

Notes, Chapter 19

[4]Cf. *Gen. R.* 26,5; 50,5; *Lev. R.* 23,9; *PRE* 25 (185); Clement of Alexandria, *Paedagogus* 3,8.

[5]The word *dš'* used here and in vv. 9-10 by Onq. and Ps.-J., and by Ps.-J. in Deut 29:16 in an addition to the biblical text, is, it seems, not found in Nf or in other genuine Palestinian texts; cf. Kaufman, review of *Le Targum de Job de la grotte XI de Qumrân,* ed. and trans. J. P. M. van der Ploeg, *et al., JAOS* 93 (1973) 326, n. 58.

[6]Lond. and *ed. pr.* have "his brothers."

[7]Lit.: "before."

[8]Lit.: "hidden themselves." Omitted in *ed. pr.*

[9]Lond. and *ed. pr.* read *ḥd',* "one," for *hd',* "this."

[10]*Gen. R.* 50,3.

[11]Lond. and *ed. pr.* do not translate the words "or anyone you have in the city" (RSV).

[12]Nf, Onq., and Pesh., like the HT, use the participial form of the verb, which could, in the context, be translated as a perfect or as a future. Ps.-J. and LXX use the perfect. Cf. *Gen. R.* 50,9, and see further Ginzberg, *Legends,* 5, 241, n. 177.

[13]Lit.: "the word (or the matter) was like a wonder." See Josephus, *Ant.* 1 § 202; *Gen. R.* 50,9.

[14]Lond. and *ed. pr.* add "it was about to rise."

[15]Lit.: "who are found *with you.*" According to *Gen. R.* 50,9, Lot had two other daughters who were married and, presumably, living with their husbands rather than with Lot.

[16]*Ed. pr.:* "while"; cf. Nfmg.

were bringing them outside, *one of them returned to Sodom to destroy it. The other remained with Lot,* [17] and said *to him,* "Have consideration for[18] your life; do not look behind you, and do not stop anywhere in the plain; escape to the mountain lest you be wiped out." 18. And Lot said to *him,* "I beg of you, wait for me a little moment until I beg for mercy from before the Lord." [19] 19. Behold now, your servant has found *mercy before you,* and great is the kindness you have shown me in saving my life; but I cannot escape to the mountains lest misfortune overtake me and I die. 20. Behold now, *I pray,* this city *whose dwellings* are near. *It is (a) suitable (place)* to flee to. It is small, *and its sins are light.* [20] Let me escape there—is it not a little (place)?—and my life will be saved." 21. And he said to him, "Behold, I grant you this favor also, that I will not overthrow the city to which you have said *you will escape.* 22. Make haste, escape thither, for I cannot do anything until you have entered there." Therefore the name of the city was called Zoar. 23. The sun *had crossed the sea,* and risen upon the earth after *three hours,* [21] when Lot entered into Zoar. 24. And *the Memra of* the Lord *sent down favorable rains*[22] upon Sodom and Gomorrah, *so that they might repent;*[23] *but they did not do so, for they said, "Evil deeds are not manifest before the Lord." Therefore* sulphur and fire *came down upon them from before the Memra of* the Lord out of heaven. 25. He overthrew those cities, and the whole plain, and all the inhabitants of the cities and the vegetation of the ground. 26. His wife looked behind *the angel to know what would be the end of her father's house. She was one of the daughters of the Sodomites, and because she had sinned through salt by publicizing (the presence) of the afflicted ones,* [24] *behold she was made* into a pillar of salt. 27. Abraham went early in the morning to the place where he had *ministered in prayer* before the Lord. 28. And he looked carefully towards Sodom and Gomorrah and towards all the land of the plain; and he saw that the smoke of the land went up like the smoke of a furnace. 29. When *the Lord* destroyed the cities of the plain, *the Lord* remembered *the merit of* Abraham, and he sent Lot away from the midst of the upheaval when he overthrew the cities in which Lot dwelt. 30. Lot went up from Zoar and dwelt in the mountain with his

Notes, Chapter 19

[17]HT: "and when *they* had brought them forth, *he* said. . . ." Ps.-J. explains that the singular "he said" of HT refers to the angel who stayed with Lot. *Gen. R.* 50,2 says that Gabriel was sent to overthrow Sodom while Raphael saved Lot; cf. also *Gen. R.* 50,11.

[18]= Onq. See Grossfeld, 1988, 81, n. 7.

[19]*b. Shebu.* 35b (205–206). See above, n. 6 to 18:3, and cf. Churgin, 1943, 104; Díez Macho, *Neophyti 1,* III, 1971, 47*. Shinan (1979, 2, 331) notes that only the Targums (Nf, Frg. Tgs., Ps.-J.; and cf. Onq.: "I beg you, O Lord") interpret this verse to refer to prayer. This interpretation is not found in midrashic texts.

[20]See above 18:29 and n. 41 to that verse.

[21]Lit.: "at the end of three hours." *Gen. R.* 50,10 and *j. Berak.* 1,2c use Gen 19:15, 23 to show that one can walk eight miles between dawn and the time the sun begins to shine. The author of Ps.-J. may have concluded that this would have taken three hours; cf. Brayer, 1964, 224.

[22]Lit.: "rains of favor." The corresponding Heb. idiom occurs in *m. Ta'an.* 3,8. The midrash (*Mekilta* to Exod 15:6 [2, 40]) and the Targums (Frg. Tgs., Ps.-J.) of our present verse take the biblical words "he rained down" to refer to favorable rains, and they take "brimstone and fire" to refer to a divine punishment.

[23]Cf. *Mekilta* to Exod 15:6 (2, 40). See above, 6:3 and n. 9 to that verse.

[24]*Gen. R.* 51,5.

two daughters, for he was afraid to dwell in Zoar; and he dwelt in a cave, he and his two daughters. 31. The older said to the younger, "Our father is old, and there is not a man on earth to come in to us after the manner of all the earth. 32. Come, let us make our father drink wine, and *when he is drunk* we will have intercourse with him, that we may raise up *children* from our father." 33. That night they made their father drink wine, *and he got drunk.* And the elder *arose* and had intercourse with her father; and he did not know when she lay down, *but he knew* when she rose. [25] 34. The next day the elder said to the younger, "Behold I have *already* had intercourse with my father last evening. Let us make him drink wine tonight also *that he may get drunk* and let you go in and have intercourse with him, that we may raise up *children* from our father." 35. So that night also they made their father drink wine, *and he got drunk.* And the younger arose and had intercourse with him; and he did not know when she lay down or when she rose. 36. Thus the two daughters of Lot became pregnant by their father. 37. The elder bore a son and called his name Moab *because she had become pregnant by her father;* [26] he is the father of *the Moabites* to this day. 38. The younger also bore a son, and called his name "*His-son,*" [27] *for he was the son of her father;* he is the father of *the people of* the Ammonites [28] to this *very* day.

CHAPTER 20

1. Abraham set out from there to the land of the South, and dwelt between *Reqem* [1] and *Hagra,* [2] and sojourned in Gerar. 2. And Abraham said *of* his wife Sarah, "She is my sister." And Abimelech, king of Gerar, sent and took Sarah. 3. But *a word from before* God [3] came to Abimelech in a dream of the night and said to him, "Behold, you are to die on account of the woman whom you have *taken by force,* for she is married to a man." 4. Now Abimelech had not approached her *to*

Notes, Chapter 19 (Cont.)

[25] *Ed. pr.:* "he did not know when she lay down or when she rose." The reading in Lond. ("... *but he knew* ...") follows the midrashic tradition which took the dot over the second *waw* in the word *wbqwmh,* "or when she rose," in HT to mean that Lot noticed his daughter when she arose; cf., e.g., *Sifre* to Num 9:10 (edition Horovitz, 64–65); *Gen. R.* 51,8; *b. Nazir* 23a (82–83).

[26] Cf. *Gen. R.* 51,11; *b. Nazir* 23b (85).

[27] Lit.: "A-son-with-him" (*br 'ymyh*); cf. *Gen. R.* 51:11. *Ed. pr.,* like Nf and Onq., reads "son of my people" (*br 'my*). See also *b. Nazir* 23b (85).

[28] Lond. and *ed. pr.:* "the Moabites."

Notes, Chapter 20

[1] See above, n. 22 to 14:7.

[2] See above, n. 10 to 16:7.

[3] Onq.: "*a word from before the Lord.*"

defile her, and he said, "*O Lord, a gentile who has not sinned, who is* even *worthy of being declared innocent in judgment, shall he be put to death?*[4] 5. Did he not say to me *that* she is (his) sister? And she herself also said, 'He is my brother.' In the uprightness of my heart and in the innocence of my hands I have done this." 6. *The Memra of* God said to him in a dream, "*Before me, too, it was revealed* that you did this in the uprightness of your heart, and it was I also who kept you from sinning *before me.* Therefore I did not let you approach her. 7. And now restore the man's wife; for he is a prophet and he will pray for you, and you shall live. But if you do not restore her, know that you shall surely die, you and all that are yours." 8. Abimelech rose early in the morning, and called all his servants, and said all these things *in* their *presence;* and the men feared greatly. 9. Abimelech called Abraham and said <to him>,[5] "What have you done to us? And how have I sinned against you that you have brought such great guilt on me and on my kingdom? You have done to me deeds that *should not* be done."[6] 10. Abimelech said to Abraham, "What were you thinking of that you did this thing"? 11. Abraham said, "Because I said *to myself,*[7] Surely, there is no fear of God in this place, and they will kill me on account of my wife. 12. Besides, she is, in truth my sister, the daughter of my father's *brother,* but not *of the family* of my mother;[8] and she became my wife. 13. When *those who worship idols tried* to lead me astray,[9] I *went forth* from my father's house, and I said to her,[10] '<This>[5] is the favor you shall do me: whatever place we go to, say of me: He is my brother.' " 14. Abimelech took sheep and oxen, <menservants>[5] and maidservants, and gave (them) to Abraham; and he restored Sarah his wife to him. 15. Abimelech said, "Behold, my land is before you, *and* dwell wherever seems right in your eyes." 16. And to Sarah he said, "Behold, I have given a thousand silver *selas*[11] to your brother; behold, they will serve as a veil (over) your eyes[12] *in exchange for your having been hidden from your husband for*

Notes, Chapter 20

[4] HT ("wilt thou slay an innocent people?") is difficult. Onq. translates it directly, while Nf and Ps.-J. clarify the text. Cf. also *Gen. R.* 52,6.

[5] Omitted in Lond. and *ed. pr.*

[6] Lit.: "deeds that *are improper to be done.*" HT reads, literally, "deeds that are not done." The Targums (Nf, Onq., Ps.-J.) add "improper, not fit," although the meaning of the Heb. idiom is clear. The same addition is made in 34:7; Lev 4:2, 13, 22, 27; 5:17; see also Ps.-J. Deut 23:24.

[7] Lit.: "I said *in my heart.*"

[8] See above, 11:29 and n. 20 to that verse. See also *Gen. R.* 18,5; 52,11; *b. Sanh.* 58b (396).

[9] HT raised two problems for the *meturgeman:* first, the verb accompanying the name Elohim is in the plural, which might be taken to indicate that there is a plurality of gods; second, the verb means "cause to err," which might lead one to conclude that God actually led Abraham astray (cf. Bowker, 1969, 218–219). *Gen. R.* 52,11 proposes different solutions to these problems; see also *j. Meg.* 1,71d. Onq. avoids the difficulties by translating as follows: "*So when the nations erred after the works of their hands and* God *brought me near to revering him* from the house of my father. . . .*"

[10] Lond.: "him."

[11] The Targums usually translate Heb. "shekel" by *sela;* cf., e.g., 23:15, 16; Exod 21:32; 30:13. See vol. 1A, Introduction, pp. 32–33.

[12] The Heb. idiom translated here is, literally, "a covering of the eyes" (*kswt 'ynym*). Ps.-J. faithfully renders this idiom. Onq. has "*a garment of honor*"; cf. Levy, 1, 375. See *Gen. R.* 52,12. Ps.-J. goes on to give a second rendering of *kswt 'ynym* and reads "(for your) having been hidden (*'tksyt*) . . . while I saw . . . (cf. HT *'ynym,* eyes)." Onq. also gives a second rendering of *'ynym,* reading "in exchange for my . . . *having seen you.*" Cf. Beer, 1859, 166–167.

one night, while I saw your body. Even if I were to give you all that I have, I would not be worthy." [13] *Thus matters were clarified, and Abraham knew that Abimelech had not approached Sarah his wife.* 17. Abraham prayed *before* God, and God healed Abimelech and his wife and his *concubines,* and they were *able to bear children;* [14] 18. for *the Memra of* the Lord had firmly closed all *the openings* of the wombs of *the women who were in* the house of Abimelech on account of Sarah, the wife of Abraham.

CHAPTER 21

1. The Lord *remembered* Sarah as he had said *to him,* [1] and the Lord worked *a sign* for Sarah, like (that of which) *Abraham* had spoken *in his prayer on behalf of Abimelech.* [2] 2. Sarah became pregnant and bore Abraham in his old age a son *who was like him,* [3] at the time of which *the Lord* had spoken. 3. Abraham called the name of the son who was born to him, whom Sarah had borne to him, Isaac. 4. When his son Isaac was eight days old, Abraham circumcised him, as *the Lord* had commanded him. 5. Abraham was a hundred years old when Isaac his son was born to him. 6. And Sarah said, "*The Lord* has done *an amazing thing* [4] for me; anyone who hears (of it) will *be amazed at* [4] me." 7. And she said, "*How trustworthy was the messenger who made an announcement* to Abraham, saying 'Sarah *is destined to* suckle (children).' [5] For *she has* borne *him* a son *at the time of* <his old age>." [6] 8.

Notes, Chapter 20 (Cont.)

[13]Or: "able" (*kmyst*). This whole sentence ("even if . . . worthy"), which is paralleled in Nf and Frg. Tgs., may be based on a word-play on *kswt* (see preceding note). Cf. Beer, ibid.; see preceding note.

[14]= Onq. We follow Levy's translation (2, 411). Jastrow (1457) translates the verb in question (*rwwḥ,* Ithpa.) as "to be blessed with issue." Ps.-J. uses the same verb in Gen 22:20; 25:21; 26:31 in additions to the biblical text.

Notes, Chapter 21

[1]The reference is to the promise made to Abraham in Gen 18:14; cf. *Gen. R.* 53,1.

[2]Cf. *b. B. Qam.* 92a (533), based on *m. B. Qam.* 8,7. The actual prayer of Abraham on behalf of Abimelech is given in *PRE* 26 (192). See further Bowker, 1969, 220.

[3]The words "who was like him" are added to refute those who would say that the aged Abraham and Sarah could not have begotten a child; cf. *b. B. Mez.* 87a (502); *b. Sanh.* 107b (737); *Gen. R.* 53,9. According to *Gen. R.* 53,6, the phrase "a son in his old age" in Gen 21:2 teaches that Isaac's features were like Abraham's. See further Bowker, 1969, 220–221. The phrase "who was like him" (or some similar phrase) used by Ps.-J. in our present verse is found in this same Targum in Gen 5:3 (cf. Nf, Onq.); 25:19; 37:3.

[4]The *meturgemanim* consider it unbecoming to say that God caused Sarah to laugh or that others laughed over her; see above, n. 18 to 18:12.

[5]Ps.-J. turns Sarah's exclamation of surprise ("Who would have said to Abraham. . . ?") into a proclamation of the fidelity of God, who had promised that Sarah would bear a son (cf. Gen 17:19). See Onq.: "*Faithful* is He that promised Abraham *and fulfilled it, that* Sarah would nurse children."

[6]Omitted in Lond. and *ed. pr.*

The child grew and was weaned; and Abraham made a great feast the day he weaned Isaac. 9. Sarah saw the son of Hagar the Egyptian, whom she bore to Abraham, sporting *with an idol[7] and bowing down to it.[8]* 10. And she said to Abraham, "Cast out this maidservant and her son; for *it is not possible that* the son of this maidservant should inherit with my son *and (then) make war[9]* with Isaac." 11. But the matter was very distressing in Abraham's eyes on account of his son *Ishmael, who had practiced idolatry.[10]* 12. But the *Lord* said to Abraham, "Do not be distressed[11] about the boy *who has abandoned the training you have given him,* or about your maidservant whom you are *banishing. Pay heed to* all that Sarah will say to you—*for she is a prophetess[12]*—because through Isaac shall your children be named; *but this son of the maidservant shall not be recorded (in the genealogies) after you.[13]* 13. And I will make a nations *of robbers[14]* of the son of the maidservant also, because he is your *son."* 14. Abraham rose early in the morning, took some bread and a skin of water, and gave (them) to Hagar. He placed (them) on her shoulder—*tying (them) to her loins to show that she was a maidservant[15]*—along with the child.[16] He sent her away *with a bill of divorce.[17]* She went off and strayed *from the way,* to the desert *which is near* Beer-sheba. 15. *When they arrived at the entrance to the desert, they reverted to going astray after idolatry.[18]* Ishmael was

Notes, Chapter 21

[7]Lit.: "idolatry." Ps.-J., Nf, and Frg. Tgs. follow the traditional rabbinic interpretation (cf., e.g., *t. Sotah* 6,6 [Zuckermandel, 304]; *Sifre Deut* 31 to 6:4 [edition Finkelstein, 50]; *Gen. R.* 53,11) and take *mṣḥq* of HT to mean practicing idolatry. See also Jerome, *Quaest. hebr.* in Gen 21:9: "*quod idola ludo fecerit.*" In Exod 32:6 Nf, Frg. Tg., and Ps.-J. also take the verb *ṣḥq* to refer to idolatry. Further on in our present chapter (v. 11) Ps.-J. again refers to the idolatrous practices of Ishmael, and in vv. 15-16 the same Targum associates Ishmael and Hagar with idolatry. On the polemical nature of these verses, see Ohana, 1975, 367–387.

[8]*Ed. pr.:* "bowing down to the Lord (*lyy*)," which is clearly a mistake.

[9]*Gen. R.* 53:11 and *PRE* 30 (215) record that Ishmael tried to kill Isaac.

[10]Or: "who would practice idolatry." *Exod. R.* 1,1 says that Abraham was distressed because Ishmael had become depraved (*'l šyṣ' ltrbwt r'h*). The same idiom occurs in *Tanḥ., Shemoth* 1 (159).

[11]Lit.: "let it not be distressing in your eyes."

[12]See *Exod. R.* 1,1; *Tanḥ., Shemoth* 1 (159).

[13]I.e., he will not be called by your name; cf. Levy 1, 332.

[14]Ps.-J. uses the Greek word *lēstês,* "robber." This is the only place where this word occurs in Ps.-J. The same word is applied to Esau in Gen 25:27 (Nfmg). A Hebraized form of the same word, in verbal form, is used in *Exod. R.* 1,1 and in *Tanḥ., Shemoth* 1 (159), where it is said that Ishmael used to sit at the crossroads robbing passersby. By describing the descendants of Ishmael—that is, the Arabs—as a nation of robbers, Ps.-J. in our present verse betrays an anti-Moslem mentality; cf. Ohana, 1975, 369.

[15]Ps.-J. is obscure at this point, as is *PRE* 30 (216), with which Ps.-J.'s version of this verse has marked similarities. *PRE* reads: "he took the veil (other versions: a water-barrel, or a chain), and he bound it around her waist, so that it would drag behind her to disclose (the fact) that she was a bondwoman." See also *Gen. R.* 53,13. We may note the contradiction between our present verse, where Hagar is said to be a servant, and Ps.-J. Gen 16:2, where Sarah is said to have set Hagar free. By introducing the tradition from *PRE* into our present verse, Ps.-J. created the contradiction; cf. Shinan, 1979, 1, 139, n. 86.

[16]Lond. and *ed. pr.* have "the girl" (*ryb'*); read *rby',* "boy, child."

[17]*PRE* 30 (216). This tradition is not known from any source that is earlier than *PRE* and Ps.-J. (cf. Brayer, 1964, 227). It fits in with Gen 16:3, which says that Sarah gave Hagar to Abraham as wife.

[18]Lit.: "they remembered to go astray. . . ." Cf. *PRE* 30 (217): ". . . she (Hagar) began to go astray after the idolatry of her father's house." Note that *PRE* accuses only Hagar of idolatry. The idea that Hagar engaged in idolatry is not found in sources that are earlier than *PRE* and Ps.-J. (Shinan, 1979, 2, 349, n. 235).

stricken with a burning fever, [19] *and he drank all the water until all* the water in the skin was finished. And *his flesh became parched and thin.* [20] *So she carried him, and (when) she was exhausted she called to the god of her father,* [21] *but he did not answer her. And immediately* she threw the child under one of the *trees.* 16. She went and sat down *to one side, threw away the idol* [22] *and withdrew from her son,* about *the distance of* a bowshot; for she said, "I am not *able* to look upon the death of the child." So she sat opposite *her son* and lifted up her voice and wept. 17. The voice of the child *was* heard *before the Lord because of the merit of Abraham.* [23] And the angel of *the Lord* called to Hagar from heaven and said to her, "What is the matter, Hagar? Fear not, for the voice of the child *has been* heard *before the Lord, and he has not judged him according to the evil deeds he is destined to do.* [24] *Because of the merit of Abraham he has shown mercy to him in the place* where he is. 18. Arise, take the boy and hold him by the hand, for I will make a great nation of him." 19. *The Lord* uncovered her eyes, and a well of water *was revealed to her,* [25] and she went and filled the water-skin with water, and gave the boy a drink. 20. *The Memra of the Lord was at the assistance of* the boy, [26] and he grew up. He dwelt in the wilderness and became a *skilled* bowman. 21. He dwelt in the desert of Paran *and took as wife Adisha. But he divorced her,* and his mother took *Fatima* [27] as wife for him from the land of Egypt. 22. At that time Abimelech and Phicol, the commander of his army, said to Abraham, saying, "The *Memra of the Lord is at your assistance* in everything you do. 23. And now, swear to me here by *the Memra of the Lord* that you will not deal falsely with me or with my *son* or my *grandson;* according to the kindness I have done to you, you shall do to me and to the land in which you have resided." 24. And Abraham said, "I swear." 25. Abraham remonstrated with Abimelech on account of the well of water which the servants of Abimelech had taken *from him* by force. 26. Abimelech said, "I do not know who did this; you yourself did not tell me, and I did not hear (of it) from *others* except *from you*

Notes, Chapter 21

[19] Cf. *Gen. R.* 53,13.

[20] The verb *qlš*, which Ps.-J. uses here, occurs again in Ps.-J. Num 7:13, 19. Otherwise it is attested only in the Babylonian Talmud and in Tg. Job (cf. Cook, 1986, 258).

[21] Lit: "the fear of her father." According to Ps.-J. Gen 16:1, Pharaoh was Hagar's father.

[22] We know of no source for this addition. It seems to be an interpretation of the phrase *mngd hrḥq*, "over against him a good way off" (RSV); cf. Brayer, 1964, 227.

[23] Cf. *Gen. R.* 53,14.

[24] b. *Rosh Hash.* 16b (61); *Gen. R.* 53,14; *Tanḥ., Wa-Yeze* 5 (100). Ps.-J.'s hostile attitude to the Moslems, the descendants of Ishmael, is implicit in this addition. See also above, nn. 7 and 14.

[25] *PRE* 30 (218) states explicitly that "the well which was created at twilight" on the eve of the first Sabbath (cf., e.g., *m. Aboth* 5,6; Ps.-J. Num 22:28) was opened for Hagar and Ishmael. See *Gen. R.* 53,14, where the angels appeal to God not to "bring up a well" for Ishmael.

[26] On the translation of the biblical phrase "I/he (i.e., God), God, was/is/will be with . . ." in Ps.-J. see Muñoz León, 1974A, 718, 723, 725. See also Klein, 1982, 121–124; Hayward, 1981, 21.

[27] This mention of the names Adisha and Fatima, the wife and daughter of Mohammad, is often used as proof of the contention that Ps.-J., at least in its final form, cannot be dated earlier than the seventh century C.E.; cf., e.g., Seligsohn-Traub, 1857, 110; Splansky, 1981, 89. H. Z. Hirschberg, ("The Place of the Aramaic Targumim in the Life of the People" [in Hebrew], *Bar Ilan,* 1 [1963] 21) maintains that this midrash dates from the second half of the tenth century. The names Adisha (Ayisha) and Fatima are not mentioned in any Targum except Ps.-J. Ayisha was, in fact, Mohammad's favorite wife, while Fatima was his daughter. The tradition recorded here by Ps.-J. is preserved at greater length in *PRE* 30 (218-219).

today." 27. Abraham took sheep and oxen and gave (them) to Abimelech, and the two of them made a covenant. 28. Abraham set aside seven ewe lambs by themselves, *and separated them from the oxen.*[28] 29. Abimelech said to Abraham, "What is the meaning of these seven ewe lambs that you have set aside by themselves?" 30. He said, "You are to accept the seven ewe lambs from my hand, that they may serve as a witness that I dug this well." 31. Therefore he called that *well* "The Well-of-the-Seven-*Ewe-Lambs,*" because there the two of them swore an oath. 32. So they made a covenant at "The Well-of-the-*Ewe-Lambs,*" and Abimelech and Phicol, the commander of his army, arose and returned to the land of the Philistines. 33. (Abraham) planted *an orchard*[29] at "The Well-of-the-Seven-*Ewe-Lambs,*" *and in it he prepared food and drink for those who went and came.*[30] And *he used to proclaim to them* there, "*Give thanks, and believe*[31] in the name of *the Memra of* the Lord, the God of the world."[32]

CHAPTER 22

1. After these events,[1] *after Isaac and Ishmael had quarreled, Ishmael said,*[2] "*It is right that I should be my father's heir, since I am his first-born son." But Isaac said,*

Notes, Chapter 21 (Cont.)

[28]The significance of this addition is not clear. There is no reference to the separation of the ewe-lambs from the oxen in the other Targums or in the midrashim; cf. Brayer, 1964, 228.

[29]*prdys'* (= Gr. *paradeisos*) = Nf, Frg. Tgs. (with orthographical variations). *Gen. R.* 54,6 (Theodor-Albeck, 583), and *b. Sotah* 10a (47) also use the word *prds* in this context. The precise meaning of the underlying Heb. *'sl,* which is usually translated "tamarisk," is uncertain. See Aberbach-Grossfeld, 1982, 127, n. 8.

[30]Lit.: "those who passed by and returned." The corresponding Heb. idiom (*'wbrym wsbym*) occurs in the same context in *Gen. R.* 54,6 (Theodor-Albeck, 584) and in *Tanh., Lek-leka,* 12 (56). The Aramaic idiom occurs in Tg. Gen 25:27 (Nfmg). Compare *hoi erchomenoi kai hoi hypagontes,* "those who were coming and going," in Mark 6:31. In our present verse the *meturgemanim* (apart from Onq.) were prompted by the word *'sl,* "tamarisk," the consonants of which stand for *'kylh,* "food," *styh,* "drink," *lwyh,* "escort," to portray Abraham as a model of hospitality. In this the *meturgemanim* follow the midrashic tradition; cf., e.g., ARN A 7; *Gen. R.* 54,6; *b. Sotah* 10a-b (47-48); see further Ginzberg, *Legends,* 1, 270-271; 5, 248, nn. 223-225; Beer, 1859, 56; Bowker, 1969, 222-223.

[31]Abraham's instructions to those who enjoyed his hospitality are recorded in several sources; cf., e.g., *Gen. R.* 54,6; *b. Sotah* 10b (48); *Tanh., Lek-Leka* 12 (56).

[32]V. 34 is omitted in Lond. and *ed. pr.*

Notes, Chapter 22

[1]The *Aqedah,* or the "Binding (of Isaac)," which is described in Gen 22, has always had an important place in Jewish thought. On the traditional Jewish understanding of the *Aqedah,* see S. Spiegel, 1967; Vermes, 1961, 193-229; Le Déaut, 1963, 131-212; S. Sandmel, 1955, 151-332; G. Stemberger, 1974, 50-76; P.R. Davies and B.D. Chilton, "The Aqedah: A Revised Tradition History," *CBQ* 40 (1978) 514-546. On the Targumic account of the Aqedah, see, e.g., R. Hayward, "The Present State of Research into the Targumic Account of the Sacrifice of Isaac," *JJS* 32 (1981) 127-150.

[2]The long addition which Ps.-J., alone among the Targums, makes to this verse explains why God should have "tested Abraham," as the biblical text states. According to Ps.-J., Isaac's declaration of his readiness to offer his whole body to the Lord led to God's commanding Abraham to offer Isaac as a sacrifice (v. 2). *Gen. R.* 55,4; *b. Sanh.* 89b (596); *Tanh.* B., *Wa-Yera* 42 (1,109) and *Tanh., Wa-Yera* 18 (74) have partial parallels to the dialogue between Ishmael and Isaac which we find in Ps.-J., but none of them contains all the ideas that are expressed in this Targum. R. Le Déaut (*Biblica* 42 [1961] 37-43), followed by F. Lentzen-Deis (1970, 202), claims that Gal 4:29-30 may be understood against the background of the haggadah which is found in Ps.-J.'s addition to our present verse. However, there is no similarity between the wording of Ps.-J. Gen 22:1 and the text from Galatians.

"It is right that I should be my father's heir, because I am the son of Sarah his wife, while you are the son of Hagar, my mother's maidservant."[3] Ishmael answered and said, *"I am more worthy than you, because I was circumcised at the age of thirteen. And if I had wished to refuse, I would not have handed myself over to be circumcised. But you were circumcised at the age of eight days. If you had been aware, perhaps you would not have handed yourself over to be circumcised."* Isaac answered and said, *"Behold, today I am thirty seven years old,*[4] *and if the Holy One, blessed be He, were to ask all my members I would not refuse."*[5] These words were immediately heard before the Lord of the world, and at once the Memra of the Lord tested Abraham and said to him, "Abraham!" And he said *to him,* "Here I am." 2. He said, "Take your son, your only one, Isaac whom you love, and go to the land *of worship,*[6] and offer him there as a burnt offering on one of the mountains of which I will tell you." 3. Abraham rose early in the morning and saddled his ass and took with him his two servant boys *Eleazer and Ishmael*[7] and his son Isaac. He cut wood *of the olive tree,*[8] *the fig tree, and the palm tree, which are suitable for* the burnt offering,[9] and he rose and went to the place of which *the Lord* had told him. 4. On the third day Abraham lifted up his eyes and saw *the Cloud of Glory enveloping*[10] the mountain, and he *recognized it* from afar. 5. And Abraham said to his servants, *"Wait* here with the ass, while the lad and I betake ourselves over there to *find out if that which was an-*

Notes, Chapter 22

[3]Isaac bases his claim to the birthright on the fact that he is the son of Abraham's wife. This particular idea is found in no other source. The claims and counterclaims of Isaac and Ishmael to the birthright may reflect a polemic between Jews and Moslems, who could both claim to be authentic heirs of Abraham, their common father; cf. A. Shapira, "Traces of an Anti-Moslem Polemic in Targum Pseudo-Jonathan of Parasah 'Aqedah' " (in Hebrew), *Tarbiz* 54 (1985) 293–296.

[4]*Ed. pr.* "thirty-six." Like Lond. in our present verse, Tg. Exod 12:42 (Nf, V, N) and 15:18 (P) say that Isaac was offered on the altar at the age of thirty-seven. Ps.-J. is the only Targum of our present verse to mention Isaac's age. Thirty-seven is also the figure given in the midrashic literature; cf., e.g., *Gen. R.* 55,4; *Tanḥ.* B. *Wa-Yera* 42 (1,109); *PRE* 31 (225).

[5]Cf. *Gen. R.* 55,4; *b. Sanh.* 89b (596). On Isaac's readiness to offer himself at the moment of the Aqedah, see v. 10 below.

[6]= Onq. Ps.-J., Onq., and Nfmg identify Moriah with the mountain in Jerusalem where the Temple was built. See the Targums of v. 14, and Tg. Song 3:6. See also 2 Chron 3:1; *Jubilees* 18:13; Josephus, *Ant.* 1 § 224-226; *Gen. R.* 55,7; Jerome, *Quaest. hebr.* in Gen 22:2. On this whole question see further Komlosh, 1973, 225–226; Grossfeld, 1988, 87, n. 1.

[7]*Lev. R.* 20,2; 26,7; *PRE* 31 (224). On Ps.-J.'s tendency to give names to the nameless, see above, Gen 6:4 and n. 10 to that verse.

[8]= Lond. *Ed. pr.: dqyt'*, "finely (cut)." Jastrow, 319, proposes that we read "boughs of fig trees" with *b. Tamid* 29b (16).

[9]The kinds of wood that were suitable for the fire on the Altar are discussed in *m. Tamid* 2,3 and *b. Tamid* 29b (16). Both sources exclude the wood of the olive tree, which Ps.-J. in our present verse declares suitable. However, the olive tree is permitted by *Jubilees* 21,12 and by the Aramaic fragment of the *Testament of Levi* 23-24 (cf. R. H. Charles, *Apocrypha and Pseudepigrapha of the Old Testament* [Oxford: Clarendon, 1963] 2, 364). Thus, in our present verse Ps.-J. retains an ancient *halakah* which contradicts the mishnaic and talmudic rulings.

[10]*Gen. R.* 56,1; *Tanḥ., Wa-Yera* 23 (77); *Tanḥ.* B., *Wa-Yera* 46 (1, 113); *PRK* 26,3. Several midrashic texts give us to understand, as does Ps.-J., that the cloud enabled Abraham to recognize the mountain which the Lord had chosen. See, e.g., the *Gen. R.* text just referred to and *Lev. R.* 20,2. On the whole question of the cloud that was seen by Abraham (and Isaac), see J. Luzarraga, 1973, 76–82.

nounced to me—'so shall your children be'—will be fulfilled. [11] We will bow down [12] *to the Lord of the world,* and we will return to you." 6. Abraham took the wood for the burnt offering and placed (it) on Isaac his son, and he took the fire and the knife in his own hand; and the two of them went together. 7. Isaac spoke to his father Abraham, and said, "Father!" And he said, "Here I am <my son>." [13] He said, "Behold the fire and the wood; but where is the lamb for the burnt offering?" 8. Abraham said, "*The Lord* will *choose* [14] for himself the lamb for the burnt offering, my son." [15] And the two of them went together *with a perfect heart.* [16] 9. They came to the place of which *the Lord* had told him, and there Abraham (re)built the altar [17] *which Adam had built* [18] *and (which) had been demolished by the waters of the Flood. Noah rebuilt it, but it was demolished in the generation of the Division.* He arranged the wood *upon it,* and tied Isaac his son and placed him on the altar, on top of the wood. 10. Abraham put forth his hand and took the knife to slaughter his son. *Isaac spoke up* [19] *and said to his father: "Tie* [20] *me well lest I struggle* [21] *because of the anguish of my soul, with the result that a blemish will be found in your offering, and I will be thrust into the pit of destruction."* [22] The eyes of Abraham were

Notes, Chapter 22

[11] This interpretation links the Heb. words *'d kh,* "yonder," in our present verse with *kh,* "thus," in Gen 15:5, the text which Ps.-J. quotes in the addition we are now discussing. We find the same tradition in midrashic literature; cf., e.g., *Gen. R.* 56,2; *b. M. Qat.* 18a (113); *Tanḥ., Wa-Yera* 23 (77–78). *Tanḥ.* B., *Wa-Yera* 46 (1,113). Ephraem, John Chrysostom, and other Fathers described the words "and we will come again to you" as a prophecy; cf. Brock (see next note), 255.

[12] = Onq.; compare Nf, Nfmg: "we will pray." The anonymous Syriac homily published by Brock has Abraham say to the servants: ". . . I and the child will *go up to pray* and then return to you"; cf. S. P. Brock, "An Anonymous Syriac Homily on Abraham (Gen 22)," *Orientalia Lovaniensia Periodica* 12 (1981) 225–260; the words quoted are on p. 249.

[13] Omitted in Lond. and *ed. pr.*

[14] In using the verb "choose," Ps.-J. distinguishes itself from all the Targums of this verse. But see the Targum Tosefta to v. 5 (CTg K), where it is said that Abraham "knew that Isaac had been chosen."

[15] *Ed. pr.* omits "my son."

[16] Ps.-J. and other Pal. Tgs. of this verse translate Heb. *yḥdw,* "together," literally, and then add the explanatory words "with a perfect heart" (Nf, P, Ps.-J.), or "with a quiet heart" (V, N, L, Nfmg). The same happens in v. 6 (Nf and Nfmg). These texts make it clear that both Abraham and Isaac were ready to do God's will. See also the Targum Tosefta to v. 8 (CTg K); *Gen. R.* 56,3 and 4; *Tanḥ., Wa-Yera* 23 (78); *Tanḥ.* B., *Wa-Yera* 46 (1, 114); Philo, *De Abrahamo* § 172; Josephus, *Ant.* 1 § 225-232. All these texts give us to understand that Abraham and Isaac shared the same dispositions, and that Isaac was not merely a passive victim.

[17] The following midrash, which is peculiar to Ps.-J., is prompted by the fact that HT tells us that Abraham "built *the* altar."

[18] See above, Ps.-J. Gen 8:20 and n. 16 to that verse. According to *PRE* 31 (227), the altar on which Isaac was bound was the one on which Adam (according to some versions), Cain and Abel, and Noah and his sons had sacrificed.

[19] Lit.: "answered."

[20] Ps.-J., Nf, P, V, N and L all use the verb *kpt,* which Ps.-J. also uses in vv. 9, 14 and 20; 27:1. Ps.-J. and Nfmg use *kpt* in the same context in Gen 25:21. See below, v. 14 and n. 30 to that verse. Isaac's request to his father to tie him well indicates his willingness to become the victim (see above n. 16). See also *Gen. R.* 56,8.

[21] Jastrow (1229–1230) gives "move convulsively, struggle, kick" as meanings of the verb *prks,* the verb used here by Ps.-J., Nfmg, P, V, N and L. The corresponding Heb. verb is used of animals that move convulsively when their heads have been cut off; cf. *m. Ohol.* 1,6.

[22] Lond. and *ed. pr.* read: ". . . the anguish of my soul, and be thrust into the pit of destruction, and a blemish be found in your sacrifice." Following Ginsburger's edition (p. 37), we invert the order of the phrases and follow the order of Nf and the Frg. Tgs. *Gen. R.* 56,8; *Tanḥ., Wa-Yera* 23 (78) and *PRE* 31 (227) record the tradition that Isaac requested to be tied firmly lest he render the sacrifice unfit. See Le Déaut, 1963, 160.

looking at the eyes of Isaac, and the eyes of Isaac were looking at the angels on high.[23] *Isaac saw them but Abraham did not see them. The angels on high exclaimed: "Come, see two unique ones*[24] *who are in the world; one is slaughtering, and one is being slaughtered; the one who slaughters does not hesitate, and the one who is being slaughtered stretches forth his neck."* 11. But the angel of the Lord called to him from heaven and said *to him*: "Abraham, Abraham!" And he said "Here I am." 12. And he said, "Do not put forth your hand against the boy, and do not do him any *harm,* for *it is* now *manifest before me* that you fear *the Lord,*[25] since you have not withheld your son, your only one, from me." 13. Abraham lifted up his eyes and saw *one*[26] ram—*(the one) that had been created at twilight when the world was completed*[27]—caught by its horns in *the dense branches of a tree.* Abraham went and took *it* and offered it as a burnt offering instead of his son. 14. Abraham *gave thanks and prayed*[28] *there in* that place, *and said: "I beseech, by the mercy from before you, O Lord! It is manifest before you that there was no deviousness*[29] *in my heart, and that I sought to perform your decree with joy. Therefore, when the children of Isaac my son enter into a time of distress, remember them, and answer them, and redeem them. All these generations to come will say, 'On this mountain Abraham tied*[30] *his son Isaac, and there the Shekinah of the Lord was revealed to him!'*[31] 15. The angel of the Lord called to Abraham a second time from heaven 16. and said, "By *my Memra* I have sworn, says the Lord, because you have done this thing and have not refused your son, your only one, 17. I will bless you

Notes, Chapter 22

[23]Cf. *Gen. R.* 56,5 and 65,10. Ps.-J. Gen 27:1 says that Isaac saw the Throne of Glory at the moment of the Aqedah. See below, n. 1 to that verse.

[24]Abraham and Isaac are called "unique" because they are totally dedicated to doing the will of God. On the meaning of "unique," see above n. 49 to 3:22.

[25]= Onq.; lit.: "that you are a fearer of *the Lord."*

[26]Lit.: "and saw, and behold *one* ram." The word translated "one" here is "after" (*'ḥr*) in the HT. Ps.-J., like many Heb. MSS, as well as several ancient versions (e.g., LXX, Pesh.) reads *'ḥd*, "one," rather than *'ḥr*.

[27]Lit.: "at the twilight of the completion of the world," i.e., on the eve of the first Sabbath. The ram of the *Aqedah* is sometimes mentioned among the ten things which, according to tradition (see above 2:2 [Ps.-J.] and n. 4 to that verse), were created at the eve of the first Sabbath; cf., e.g., *m. Aboth* 5,6; *ARN B* 37 (217); *PRE* 18 (124–125). *Tanḥ., Wa-Yera* 23 (79) and *PRE* 31 (228) say that the ram seen by Abraham had been created at the twilight of the first Sabbath.

[28]Onq.: "And Abraham *worshiped and prayed."* Ps.-J.'s version of Abraham's prayer is somewhat shorter than that which is recorded in the other Pal. Tgs. Versions of this prayer appear in several midrashic texts; cf., e.g., *Gen. R.* 56,10; *Lev. R.* 29,9; *j. Ta'an.* 2,65d; *Tanḥ., Wa-Yera* 23 (78-79); *Tanḥ.* B., *Wa-Yera* 46 (1, 115); *PRK* 23,9. On this prayer of Abraham, see R. Hayward, 1981, 142–144; R. Le Déaut, 1963, 163–170; E. E. Urbach, 1975, 1, 502–506; Vermes, 1961, 206–208; Chester, 1986, 67–73.

[29]Reading *'wqm'* (with Lond.) to which Levy (2, 237) gives the meanings "perfidy, perversity," or *'wmq'* (with *ed. pr.*), to which Jastrow (1053) gives the meaning "cunning, reservation."

[30]Ps.-J. alone uses the verb "tie" (*kpt*) in this sentence. Nf, Nfmg, P, V, N, and L all read "offered." See above v. 10 and n. 20 to that verse. The *Aqedah,* or the binding of Isaac, is frequently referred to in the Targums; cf. Gen 27:1 (Ps.-J.); Exod 12:42 (Nf, V, N); 15:18 (P); Lev 9:2-3 (Ps.-J.); 22:27 (Nf, Nfmg, P, V, N, CTg F, Ps.-J.); 26:42 (Nf, P, V, N, Ps.-J.); Tg. Micah 7:20; Tg. Song 1:13; 2:17; 3:6; Tg. 1 Chron 21:15; 2 Chron 3:1; Tg. Sheni Esther 5:1.

[31]The Pal. Tgs. take the verb *yr'h* in the obscure Heb. phrase *bhr yhwh yr'h,* "on the mount of the Lord it shall be provided" (RSV), as a passive of *r'h,* "see." Onq. links *yr'h* with the root *yr',* "fear, revere," and translates the Heb. phrase just quoted as "on *this* mountain did *Abraham worship before* the Lord."

abundantly and multiply your *children* as the stars of heaven and as the sand that is on the seashore, and your *children* shall inherit *the cities*[32] of those who hate them. 18. All the peoples of the earth shall be blessed *because of the merits of your children,*[33] because you *obeyed my word.*" 19. *The angels on high took Isaac and brought him to the schoolhouse of Shem*[34] *the Great, and he was there three years.*[35] *On that day* Abraham returned to his servants, and they arose and went together to Beer-sheba. And Abraham dwelt in Beer-sheba.[36] 20. After these things, *after Abraham had tied Isaac, Satan went and told Sarah that Abraham had slaughtered Isaac. And Sarah arose and cried out and was choked and died of anguish.*[37] Abraham came and passed the night on the way, and Abraham was told: "Behold, Milcah also has given birth; *by the merit of her sister she was able to bear* children[38] to your brother Nahor: 21. Uz, his first-born, Buz his brother, Kemuel, *master of the Aramean magicians,*[39] 22. Chesed, Hazo, Pildash, Jidlaph, and Bethuel." 23. Bethuel begot Rebekah. These eight Milcah bore to Nahor, Abraham's brother. 24. His concubine, whose name was Reumah, also bore children: Tebah, Gaham, Tahash, and Maacah.

Notes, Chapter 22

[32]= Onq. *Ed. pr.:* "*the cities before* (those who hate them)."

[33]Onq.: "*because of your children.*" Ps.-J. explains the preposition *b* in the Heb. *bzr'k,* "by your descendants," to mean "because of the merits of." Onq. is similar.

[34]The "schoolhouse" (Beth ha-Midrash) is mentioned frequently in the Targums; see Gen 9:27 (Nfmg, Ps.-J., and see above, n. 23 to that verse); 22:19 (Ps.-J.); 24:62 (Nf, P, V, N, L, Ps.-J.); 25:22 (Nf, Nfmg, P, V, N, L, Ps.-J.); 25:27 (Nf, Nfmg, Ps.-J.); 30:13 (CTg E); 33:17 (Ps.-J.); 34:31 (Nf, P, V, N, L); 37:2 (Ps.-J.); 47:27 (Ps.-J.); Num 24:2 (Ps.-J.); 24:5 (Nf, Nfmg, Ps.-J.); 26:6 (Ps.-J.); Deut 28:6 (Nf, Nfmg, P, V, N, L, Ps.-J.); 29:5 (Ps.-J.); 30:14 (Ps.-J.); 33:18 (Nf, P, V, N, L, Ps.-J.). Such references indicate that the Targums may have had a role to play in the Jewish school system; cf. A. D. York, 1979, 74–86.

[35]The fact that the biblical verse says that "Abraham returned to his young men" gave rise to the question "What happened to Isaac?" *Gen. R.* 56,11 answers that "He (Abraham) sent him to Shem to study Torah." Neither Onq. nor Nf incorporates this tradition into their versions of our present verse. We know of no source other than Ps.-J. which says that it was the angels who took Isaac to the schoolhouse of Shem (cf. Brayer, 1964, 229). One can conclude that Isaac spent three years with Shem because he was thirty-seven years old at the time of the Aqedah (see above, v. 1 and n. 4) and forty when he returned from the School of Shem and married Rebekah. See the Targums (Nf, P, V, N, L, Ps.-J.) of Gen 24:62, and the biblical text of 25:20.

[36]Ps.-J. renders Heb. *b'r šb'* as *byr' dšb'* in Gen 22:19 (twice); 26:23; 28:10. In Gen 26:33 and 46:1, however, we find *byr/b'r šb'*. In Gen 21:31, 32, 33 Ps.-J. gives a special interpretation to that place-name.

[37]*Gen. R.* 58,5; (Theodor-Albeck, 623, with the apparatus) asserts that "Sarah died of grief." The text does not state explicitly that her grief was caused by her belief that Isaac was sacrificed, but this is understood. *PRE* 32 (233-234) is even more dramatic than Ps.-J. in telling that Sarah's death was caused by *Sammael's* announcement that Abraham had slain Isaac. See another version in *Lev. R.* 20,2 and *PRK* 26,3.

[38]We know of no source earlier than Ps.-J. which claims that Milcah's fertility was due to the merits of Sarah; cf. Brayer, 1964, 230; Shinan, 1979, 2, 322. We know from Ps.-J. Gen 11:29 that Milcah was Sarah's sister.

[39]According to *Gen. R.* 57,4, Kemuel was Laban, and Laban is Balaam (cf. Ps.-J. Num 22:5; 31:8), who was associated with divination and omens; cf. Num 22:7; 24:1; *b. Sanh.* 105a (717); Ps.-J. Num 31:8.

CHAPTER 23

1. Sarah's lifetime was a hundred and twenty-seven years—the years of Sarah's life—2. and Sarah died at Kiriath-arba, that is Hebron, in the land of Canaan. And Abraham came *from the mountain of worship* [1] *and found that she had died; and he sat down* to mourn for Sarah and to weep for her. 3. Then Abraham, *having paid his respects to* his dead, [2] spoke with the sons of *the Hittite,* saying, 4. "I am a stranger and a sojourner among you; *sell* me, *I pray,* [3] a burial site among you, that I may bury my dead *there.*" 5. And the sons of *the Hittite* replied to Abraham, saying to him, 6. "Listen to us, *our* master. You are a prince *before the Lord* among us; bury your dead in the best of our graves; none of us would withhold his grave from you, so as to prevent you from burying your dead." 7. Abraham arose and bowed to the people of the land, to the sons of *the Hittite,* 8. and he spoke with them, saying, "If it *pleases* you that I should bury my dead out of my *sight,* listen to me, and intercede for me *before* Ephron, son of Zohar, 9. that he may *sell* me the double cave [4] which belongs to him, which *is built* at the edge of his field. Let him give it to me for the full price, as a burial site among you." 10. Ephron was sitting among the sons of *the Hittite;* and Ephron the Hittite replied to Abraham in the presence of the sons of *the Hittite,* in (the presence of) all who entered the gate of his city, saying, 11. "*I beseech you,* my lord, listen to me; I have given you the field, and the cave that is in it I have given to you *as a gift;* I have given it to you in the presence of the sons of my people. Go! Bury your dead!" 12. Abraham bowed to him in the presence of the *sons of the Hittite,* [5] 13. and spoke with Ephron in *the presence* of the people of the land, saying, "If you really *wish to do me a favor,* [6] listen to me: I will give the *value* of the field in silver. Take (it) from me, that I may bury my dead there." 14. Ephron replied to Abraham, saying to him, 15. "My lord, listen to me: land, *the value of which is* four hundred *selas* of silver, what is that between you and me? Bury your dead!" 16. Abraham listened to Ephron, and Abraham weighed for Ephron the money of which he had spoken in the presence of the sons of *the Hittite:* four hundred *selas* of *good* silver current *at every table (of exchange) and ac-*

Notes, Chapter 23

[1] *Gen. R.* 58,5 and *PRE* 32 (234) state that Abraham came from Mount Moriah, which, according to Ps.-J., is the mountain of worship (see Ps.-J. Gen 22:2). Notice that Ps.-J.'s statement that Abraham came from the mountain of worship (Moriah) does not fit in with Gen 22:19, which says that Abraham had settled in Beer-sheba.

[2] Lit.: "Then Abraham arose *from seeing* the face of his dead." Ps.-J., alone among the Targums, explains what the biblical phrase "from before" (RSV) means in this context.

[3] Ps.-J.'s use of "sell" rather than "give" of HT precludes the idea that Abraham was requesting a free gift. See also v. 9. The addition of "I pray" gives a more polite tone to the request.

[4] *b. Erub.* 53a (368). The midrash and the *meturgeman* associate the place-name Machpelah with the root *kpl,* "to double." Cf. Vulg.: "*speluncam duplicem.*"

[5] "Sons of the Hittite" in both Lond. and *ed. pr.,* instead of "the people of the land," a mistake due to the influence of v. 7.

[6] Onq.: "If you would only *do me a favor.*"

ceptable in every business transaction.[7] 17. *The sale of* the field of Ephron which is in *Kapheltah,*[8] facing Mamre—the field and the cave that is in it, and all the trees that are in the field, anywhere within its limits—was ratified 18. for Abraham as his *purchase*[9] in the presence of the sons of *the Hittite,* of all who entered the gate of his city. 19. After this Abraham buried Sarah his wife in the cave of the field of *Kapheltah* which is facing Mamre, that is Hebron, in the land of Canaan. 20. Thus the field and the cave that was in it were made over to Abraham as a burial site by the sons of *the Hittite.*

CHAPTER 24

1. And Abraham was old, advanced in days, and *the Memra* of the Lord had blessed Abraham with *all kinds of blessings.*[1] 2. And Abraham said to *Eliezer*[2] his servant, the oldest of his house, who was in charge of all *his treasures,*[3] "Place, I pray, your hand *on the cut of my circumcision,*[4] 3. and I will make you swear by *the name of the Memra of* the Lord, the God *whose dwelling is in* the heavens *on high*—He is the God *whose dominion is over the earth*—*that you will not take a wife for my son from the daughters of the Canaanites, among whom I dwell,* 4. *but you will go to my land, to my kindred and to my family,* and take a wife for my son Isaac." 5. The servant said to him, "What if it is not the woman's wish to follow me to this land? Shall I then take your son back to the land from which you came?" 6. Abraham said to him, "See to it that you do not take my son back there. 7. The Lord the God *whose dwelling is in* the heavens *on high,* who took me from my father's house and from the land of my birth, and who spoke to me and swore to me

Notes, Chapter 23 (Cont.)

[7]*prqmty';* = Nf, P, V, N (with variations in spelling); = Gr. *pragmateia,* "the prosecution of a business, business." The same word is used in *Gen. R.* 58,7 (Theodor-Albeck, 627) in this context. Ps.-J. uses this word again (with variations in spelling) in Gen 34:10, 21; 37:28; 42:34; Deut 24:7; 25:16; 26:8; 28:19; 33:18.

[8]We take Aramaic *kpylt'* to be a place-name (comp. Nf) rather than translate it as "double (cave)" as in v. 9, since in v. 17 one can hardly say that the field was in the "double cave."

[9]Lit.: "purchases"; = Onq. Ps.-J.'s addition of "the sale" in v. 17 makes the transition to v. 18 awkward. One cannot really say that "a sale" becomes a purchase or a possession.

Notes, Chapter 24

[1]*Gen. R.* 59,7 names several blessings which Abraham received.

[2]Many sources identify Abraham's servant as Eliezer; cf., e.g., *b. Ta'an.* 4a (10); *Yoma* 28b (133); *B. Bat.* 58 a (233); *Gen. R.* 44,9; 68,2; PRE 16 (111).

[3]*'pwtyqy,* = Gr. *apothêkê.* Klein (1980, 2, 17 and 104) prefers to link this word, which occurs also in Ps.-J., P, V, N, and L in v. 10, with Gr. *hypothêkê,* "title deeds."

[4]Cf. *Gen. R.* 59,8; *Tanḥ.* B., *Hayye Sarah* 6 (1, 120). The phrase "the cut of my circumcision" is used again by Ps.-J. (and by Ps.-J. alone) in v. 9; 45:4; 47:29; Exod 4:25, 12:13; Deut 34:6.

saying, 'To your *children* I will give this land'—he will *appoint* his angel (who will go) before you, and you will take a wife for my son from there. 8. And if it is not the woman's wish to follow you, you shall then be released from this oath to me. But do not take my son back there." 9. So the servant put his hand *on the cut of the circumcision* of Abraham his master and swore to him about this matter. 10. And the servant took ten of his master's camels and went, (taking) with him all the choicest *treasures*[3] of his master; and he arose and went to Aram, *which is on the Euphrates,*[5] to the city of Nahor. 11. He made the camels kneel by the well of water outside the city, at evening time, the time when women go out to draw water. 12. And he said, "O Lord, God of my master Abraham, prepare, I pray, *a worthy*[6] *woman* before me today, and deal favorably with my master Abraham. 13. Here I am standing by the spring of water as the daughters of the men of the city come out to draw water. 14. Let the maiden to whom I say, 'Tilt, I pray, your jar, that I may drink,' and who will say, 'Drink, and I will also water your camels'—let her be the one you have ordained *by destiny* for your servant Isaac. Thus I shall know that you have dealt favorably with my master." 15. *Very soon afterwards,*[7] before he had finished speaking, Rebekah, who was born to Bethuel the son of Milcah, the wife of Nahor, Abraham's brother, came out with her jar upon her shoulder. 16. The maiden was very beautiful to see, a virgin, and no man had known her *through lying with her.*[8] She went down to the spring, filled her jar, and came up. 17. The servant ran to meet her and said, "Let me, I pray, *taste* a little water from your jar." 18. And she said, "Drink, my lord." She hastened and lowered her jar upon her hand and let him drink. 19. When she had finished giving him to drink, she said, "I will draw for your camels also, until they have drunk enough." 20. So she hurried and emptied her jar into the *troughs of* the drinking place,[9] and ran again to the well to draw, and she drew for all his camels. 21. The man was *waiting for her and* was silent, wondering[10] whether the Lord had made his journey successful or not. 22. When the camels had <drunk>[11] enough, the man took a gold ring weighing a *daric*[12]—*corresponding to the daric per head*—*which her children would be prepared to give*[13] *for the making of the Tabernacle,*[14] *and he put* two bracelets weighing ten *selas* of gold on her hands, *the sum of their weights corresponding to the two tables*

Notes, Chapter 24

[5]= Onq. See Aberbach-Grossfeld, 1982, 138–139, n. 1; Grossfeld, 1988, 91, n. 3.

[6]*mhgn'*. This word, which occurs again in v. 26 and in Ps.-J. Num 12:1; 22:32, is a Hebraism; see Cook, 1986, 235.

[7]Lit.: "and it happened in a short time."

[8]*Gen. R.* 60,5.

[9]Ps.-J. has a conflate rendering of Heb. *šqt*, "trough," combining *mwrkywwt* (see Nf: *mwrkywn*), "troughs," with *byt šqty,* (see Onq.: *byt šqy'*), "drinking place."

[10]Lit.: "to know."

[11]Lond. and *ed. pr.* have "drawn."

[12]A Persian gold or silver coin worth half a shekel; see Jastrow, 324; Levy 1, 188. Onq.: "a shekel." The Heb. word *bq',* which Ps.-J. translates as "daric," occurs only here and in Exod 38:26. Ps.-J. uses the same translation in both places.

[13]Lond. and *ed. pr.: lmytb;* read: *lymhb.*

[14]Cf. Exod 38:26.

on which the Ten Words would be written. [15] 23. And he said, "Whose daughter are you? Tell me, I pray, is there a *suitable* [16] place in your father's house for us to spend the night?" 24. She said to him, "I am the daughter of Bethuel the son [17] of Milcah, whom she bore to Nahor." 25. And she *told him,* saying, "We have both straw and fodder in plenty, and also a *suitable* [16] place to spend the night." 26. And the man bent down and bowed down *before* the Lord *who had prepared a worthy* [6] *woman before him.* 27. And he said, "Blessed be *the Name of* the Lord the God of my master Abraham, who has not withheld his favor and his faithfulness from my master. As for me, *by his merit,* the Lord has led me in the *right* [18] way to the house of my master's kinsmen." 28. [19] 29. Now Rebekah had a brother whose name was Laban; and Laban ran out to the man at the spring. 30. When he saw the ring and the bracelets on his sister's hands, and when he heard the words of his sister Rebekah, who said, "Thus the man spoke to me," he came to the man, and behold, he was standing beside the camels at the spring. 31. *Now Laban thought that he was Abraham,* [20] and he said, "Come in, O blessed of the Lord. Why are you standing outside? For I have cleared the house of *idolatry* [21] and I have prepared a place for the camels." 32. So the man entered the house and loosed the *muzzles* [22] *of the* camels. Laban gave straw and fodder to the camels, and he brought water to wash his feet and the feet of the men who were with him. 33. And they set before him a *dish* to eat *in which there was a deadly poison;* [23] *but he noticed it* and said, "I shall not eat until I have said what I have to say." And he said, "Speak". 34. So he said, "I am Abraham's servant. 35. The Lord has blessed my master greatly, and he has prospered. He has given him sheep and oxen, silver and gold, menservants and maidservants, camels and asses. 36. And Sarah, my master's wife, bore a son to my master when she had grown old, and he has given him all that he owns. 37. Now my master made me swear, saying, 'You shall not take a wife for my son from the daughters of the Canaanites, in whose land I dwell; 38. but you shall go to my father's house and to my family, and get a wife for my son.' 39. And I said to my master, 'What if the woman does not follow me?' 40. But he said to me, 'The Lord before whom *I worship* [24] will appoint his angel (who will go) with you and make your journey suc-

Notes, Chapter 24

[15] *Gen. R.* 60,6 states that the two bracelets corresponded to the two tables of stone, and the ten shekels in weight to the Ten Commandments.

[16] *kšr* = Onq. In this verse *kosher* probably means free of idols. *ARN* A 8 says that even the camels of Abraham would not enter the house of Laban until all idols were removed from their sight; see below, v. 31.

[17] = *Ed. pr.;* Lond.: "daughter."

[18] = Onq.

[19] V. 28 is omitted in Lond. and *ed. pr.,* but both note the omission by leaving a blank space.

[20] *Gen. R.* 60,7.

[21] *Gen. R.* 60,7. See above, v. 23 and n. 16.

[22] *Gen. R.* 60,8. The camels were muzzled lest they graze on other people's property. See above 13:7 (Ps.-J., Nf, P, V, N, L).

[23] This addition is probably based on HT *wyyśm,* "(food) was set," which the Targumist linked with *sm,* "poison." See below, v. 55, where Ps.-J. refers to the attempted poisoning mentioned in our present verse.

[24] = Onq. See also above 5:22 and n. 6 to that verse.

cessful, and you shall take a wife for my son from my kindred and from *the family of* my father's house. 41. Then you will be released from (your) oath to me when you come to *the house of* my family; if they do not give (her) to you, you will be released from (your) oath to me.' 42. I came to the spring today, and I said, 'O Lord, God of my master Abraham, if you will indeed make the journey on which I am going successful, 43. behold, as I am standing by the spring of water, let the girl who comes out to draw, and to whom I shall say, "Pray give me a little water to drink from your jar," 44. and who will say to me, "Drink, <and> [25] I will draw for your camels also," (let her be) the wife whom the Lord has ordained *by destiny* for my master's son.' 45. I had not yet finished these reflections in [26] *the thoughts of* my heart when, behold, Rebekah came out with her jar on her shoulder, and went down to the spring and drew. And I said to her, 'Give me a drink, I pray.' 46. She quickly lowered her jar and said, 'Drink, and I will also water your camels.' So I drank, and she also watered the camels. 47. Then I asked her and said, 'Whose daughter are you?' And she said, 'The daughter of Bethuel the son of Nahor, whom Milcah bore to him.' And I put the ring on her nose [27] and the bracelets on her hand. 48. And I bent down and bowed down *before* the Lord, and I blessed the Lord, the God of my master Abraham who led me by the right way to take the daughter of my master's brother for his son. 49. And now, if you will deal kindly and faithfully with my master, tell me; and if not, tell me, that I may turn to the *south* or to the *north*." [28] 50. Then Laban and Bethuel answered and said, "The matter comes from *before* the Lord—*that Rebekah has been given to Isaac;* [29] we cannot speak to you bad or good. 51. Behold, Rebekah is before you; take (her) and go, and let her become the wife of your master's son, as the Lord has spoken." 52. When Abraham's servant heard their words, he bowed down to the ground *before* the Lord. 53. Then the servant brought out vessels of silver and vessels of gold, and garments, and gave (them) to Rebekah; and he gave *gifts* [30] to her brother and to her mother. 54. And they ate and drank, he and the men who were with him, and they spent the night. When they arose in the morning he said, "Send me back to my master." 55. But *while they were* [31] *speaking in the evening, Bethuel ate of that dish, and in the early morning they found that he was dead.* [32] And her brother and mother said, "Let the

Notes, Chapter 24

[25] Omitted in Lond. and *ed. pr.*

[26] Lit.: "speaking with."

[27] Lit.: "face." See Levy, 1, 52. The word *qdš'* here and in vv. 22 and 30 above can refer to rings for the nose or the ear; cf. S. Lieberman, *Greek in Jewish Palestine,* (2nd ed.; New York, 1965) 49.

[28] Onq.: "to the right or to the left." See above, Gen 13:9, where "right" and "left" of HT are also translated in the Targums (Nf, Onq., Ps.-J.) as "south" and "north."

[29] From the words "the thing comes from the Lord" (RSV) in this verse the rabbis concluded that marriages are made in heaven; cf. *b. M. Qat.* 18b (118–119).

[30] = LXX.

[31] Reading *w'd dhww* for *w'l dhww* of *ed. pr.* Lond. has *w'mr w'l dhww,* i.e., it translates the first word of the biblical verse, "and (he) said," (which it translates again after the haggadic addition) and then begins the midrashic addition.

[32] "That dish" referred to in this verse is the poisoned dish mentioned in v. 33 (Ps.-J.). The rabbis wished to explain why Bethuel, who was mentioned in v. 50, is not mentioned in vv. 53 and 55, as one might expect. See *Gen. R.* 60,12; Josephus, *Ant.* 1 § 248. See further Rappaport, 1930, p. 20, no. 88, and pp. 108–109, n. 107. The folkloristic account of Bethuel's death which Ps.-J. incorporates into vv. 33 and 55 of our present chapter has parallels only in sources that are much later than Ps.-J.; cf. Shinan, 1979, 1, 51,128 and 2, 286, n. 208; idem, 1983A, 154.

girl dwell with us for a period of *one year* or ten *months,* [33] and after that she may go." 56. And he said to them, "Do not delay me, since the Lord has made my journey successful. *Accompany* [34] me, and I will go to my master." 57. And they said, "Let us call the maiden and *hear what she says.*" 58. And they called Rebekah and said to her, "Will you go with this man?" And she said, "I will." 59. They *accompanied* [34] *Rebekah their sister and her governess,* [35] along with Abraham's servant and his men. 60. And they blessed Rebekah and they said to her, "*Until now you have been our sister; and now you are going to be married to the righteous one; may it be the will (of heaven) that* thousands of myriads *go forth from you,* and may your *children* inherit the *cities* [36] of those who hate them." 61. Then Rebekah and her maids arose, mounted the camels and followed the man. And the servant took Rebekah *with him* and went his way. *And as the way was shortened for him when he was going to Paddan-aram, so was it shortened for him when he returned; for in one day he went (there) and in one day he returned.* [37] 62. Isaac was coming from the *schoolhouse of Shem the Great,* [38] by the way that leads to [39] the well *where the Living and Enduring One, who sees but is not seen,* [40] *was revealed to him.* And he was dwelling in the land of the south. 63. Isaac went out *to pray* [41] in the open country at evening *time,* and lifting up his eyes saw camels approaching. 64. And Rebekah lifted up her eyes, and seeing Isaac she *slipped down* from the camel 65. and said to the servant, "Who is the man, (so) *majestic and handsome,* [42] who is walking in the field to meet us?" And the servant said, "He is my master." And she took the veil and wrapped herself *in it.* 66. And the servant told Isaac all the things that he had done. 67. And Isaac brought her into the tent of Sarah, his mother. *And immediately the light that had gone out at the death of Sarah* shone (again). [43] And he took Rebekah, and she became his wife, and he loved her *because he saw that her deeds were upright like the deeds of his mother.* [44] And Isaac was consoled after his mother had died.

Notes, Chapter 24

[33] Lit.: "for the days of one year or ten months." Onq.: "for *a year* (lit.: for a time in time) or ten *months.*" Cf. *b. Ketub.* 57b (338); *Gen. R.* 60,12.

[34] In vv. 56 and 59, Ps.-J. translates Heb. *šlḥ,* "send," by *lwy,* "accompany, escort." See also Gen 12:20; 18:16; and 26:31, where the same thing occurs.

[35] *pdgwgth;* Gr.: *paidagôgos* = Nfmg. See 35:8 and n. 9 to that verse.

[36] = Onq. See also 22:17 (Onq., Ps.-J.).

[37] Several sources state that the way was shortened for the servant when he was going to Paddan-Aram; cf. *Gen. R.* 59,11; 60,6; *b. Sanh.* 95a (642); *PRE* 16 (108). *PRE* 16 (109–110) says that it was also contracted for him on his return.

[38] Ps.-J., and Ps.-J. alone among the Targums, has told us earlier (22:19) when and how Isaac arrived at the schoolhouse of Shem. See notes 34 and 35 to that verse.

[39] Lit.: "(by) the entrance to"; cf. Vulg.: *per viam quae ducit ad.* On the translation of the underlying Heb. word, see Geiger, 1928, 459.

[40] See above 16:13, 14.

[41] The Targums (Nf, Onq., Ps.-J.) take the obscure Heb. *lśwḥ* (RSV: "to meditate") to mean "to pray." This is in accord with rabbinic tradition; see, e.g., *Mekilta* to Exod 14:10 (1, 206); *j. Berak.* 4, 7a; *b. Berak.* 26b (160); *PRE* 16 (110).

[42] HT reads *h'yš hlzh,* "that man." The word *hlzh* is also used in Gen 37:19 with reference to Joseph, who was very handsome (cf. 39:6). Therefore, the *meturgeman* concludes that Isaac was also handsome. Cf. *Gen. R.* 60,15.

[43] *Gen. R.* 60,16.

[44] *Gen. R.* 60:16; *PRE* 16 (111).

CHAPTER 25

1. Abraham took another wife, whose name was Keturah; *she is Hagar, who was bound to him from the beginning.*[1] 2. She bore him Zimran, Jokshan, Medan, Midian, Ishbak, and Shuah. 3. Jokshan begot Sheba and Dedan. The sons of Dedan were *merchants, traders and heads of peoples.*[2] 4. The sons of Midian were Ephah, Epher, Hanoch, Abida, and Eldaah. All these were the children of Keturah. 5. Abraham gave all that he had *as a gift*[3] to Isaac. 6. And to the sons of Abraham's concubines Abraham gave *movable goods*[4] as gifts, and while he was still living he *drove* them away from his son Isaac. *And they went* to the east *to dwell,* to the land of the Orient. 7. This is the *total* of the days of the life of Abraham, who lived a hundred and seventy-five years. 8. Abraham expired[5] and died in a good old age, old and satisfied *with every good; even Ishmael had repented in his days;*[6] and *then* he was gathered to his people. 9. His sons Isaac and Ishmael buried him in the cave *of Kapheltah,*[7] in the field of Ephron son of Zohar the Hittite, which is facing Mamre, 10. the field that Abraham bought from the sons of *the Hittite.* There Abraham was buried, and Sarah his wife. 11. *Because Abraham had not wished to bless Ishmael, he had not blessed Isaac either; for if he had blessed Isaac and had not blessed Ishmael, the latter would have hated him.*[8] But after Abraham had died *the Lord* blessed Isaac his son. And Isaac dwelt *near* the well *where the Glory of the Living and Enduring One, who sees but is not seen, was revealed to him.*[9] 12. These are the generations of Ishmael the son of Abraham, whom Hagar the Egyptian, the maidservant of Sarah, bore to Abraham. 13. And these are the names of the sons of Ishmael, by their names, according to their generations: *Nebath,*[10] the first-born of

---

Notes, Chapter 25

[1]See above, 16:1-3. Ps.-J. and Nfmg 2 (see also Nfmg 1) play on the name Keturah, linking it with the Aram. verb *qṭr,* "bind." They can say that Hagar was bound (*qṭyr'*) to Abraham from the beginning, i.e., from the time of the events described in Gen 16:1-3. *Gen. R.* 61,4 identifies Keturah with Hagar. Cf. Jerome, *Quaest. hebr.* in Gen 25:1. *PRE* 30 (219) says that Abraham had divorced Hagar and now takes her back.

[2]The names given to Dedan's sons have a masc. plur. termination (*-im*). This prompted the targumists (Nf, V, N, L, Ps.-J.) to treat these names as designations of occupations. See *Gen. R.* 61,5; Jerome, *Quaest. hebr.* in Gen 25:3; *Liber Interpretationis Hebraicorum nominum* (Genesis), sub "Latusim." See Cashdan, 1967, 38; McNamara, 1966A, 54–56; idem, 1966, 8–9; Shinan, 1979, 1, 10–11.

[3]*Gen. R.* 61,6.

[4]= Lond.; *ed. pr.:* "property and movable goods."

[5]Lit.: "extended, stretched himself"; = Onq. The same verb (*ngd;* Ithpe.) is used with the same general meaning in our present chapter in vv. 8 and 17 (Ps.-J., Onq.) and in Gen 5:24 (Nf, V, N, L, Ps.-J.); 6:17 (Ps.-J.); 35:29 (Ps.-J.); 49:33 (Ps.-J., Onq.).

[6]*b. B. Bat.* 16b (85); *Gen. R.* 59,7; see below v. 17. Ps.-J. refers to the conversion of Ishmael both when he records the death of Abraham (in our present verse) and the death of Ishmael (v. 17). The tendency to repeat traditions is characteristic of Ps.-J. See above, Introduction, p. 6.

[7]See above, 23:17 (Ps.-J.) and n. 8 to that verse.

[8]Lit.: "would have retained hatred for him." See *Gen. R.* 61,6; *Num. R.* 11,2; *Tanḥ.* B., *Naso* 17 (33). These texts, however, do not mention the possibility that Ishmael might hate Isaac. Ps.-J.'s addition of this element may be regarded as a polemic against the Moslems, the descendants of Ishmael; cf. Splansky, 1981, 92–93; Shinan, 1979, 1, 52.

[9]See above, 16:13, 14; 24:62.

[10]*Ed. pr.* by mistake reads *nbwy.* Ps.-J. took the biblical Nebaioth to refer to the Nabateans; cf. also Tg. 1 Chron 1:29.

Ishmael, Arab,[11] Adbeel, Mibsam, 14. *Tsayetha,*[12] *Shetuka, Sobara,* 15. *Haripha,* Tema, Jetur, Naphish, and Kedmah. 16. These are the sons of Ishmael, and these are their names by their villages and by their encampments:[13] twelve chieftains according to their peoples. 17. These are the years of the life of Ishmael: a hundred and thirty-seven years. He *repented*[14] and expired <and died>,[15] and was gathered to his people. 18. They dwelt from *India*[16] to *Haluzah,*[17] which is opposite Egypt, as you go to Assyria. He *dwelt*[18] opposite all his brothers *in his inheritance.* 19. These are the generations of Isaac, the son of Abraham. *Because Isaac's features*[19] *were like the features of Abraham, the sons of men said, "In truth Abraham begot Isaac."* 20. Isaac was forty years old when he took as wife Rebekah, the daughter of Bethuel the Aramean *who* was from Paddan-Aram, the sister of Laban the Aramean. 21. Isaac *went to the mountain of worship, the place where his father had tied him.*[20] *And by his prayer Isaac changed the intention of the Holy One, blessed be He,*[21] *from what he had decreed* concerning his wife,[22] *because she, like him,*[23] was barren *for twenty-two years;*[24] *and because of him the intention of the Holy One, blessed be He, was changed from what he had decreed concerning him, for he also was childless. He was able to beget children,* and Rebekah his wife became pregnant. 22. The children pushed one another in her womb *like men doing battle.*[25] And she said, "If such is *the distress of one who gives birth,* why then *do I*

Notes, Chapter 25

[11]Ps.-J. takes biblical Kedar to refer to the Arabs; see also Tg. Isa 21:16, 17; 42:11; 60:7; Tg. Ps 120:5; Tg. 1 Chron 1:29. See also Jerome, *In Hieremiam,* 1, 21.

[12]Reading *ṣyyt'* with Tg. 1 Chron 1:30 rather than *ṣ'yt'* of Lond. or *ṣmyt'* of *ed. pr.;* cf. Levy, 2, 330. Ps.-J. translates the names Mishma, Dumah, and Massa in our present verse, and Hadad in the following verse, as if they were common nouns. Thus Mishma becomes *Tsayetha,* "Listening," as if it were derived from *šm'* "hear"; Dumah becomes *Shetuka,* "Silence," as if it were the Heb. noun *dwmh,* which has that meaning; Massa becomes *Sobara,* "Endurance, Patience," as if it were from the verb *ns',* "carry"; Hadad becomes *Haripha,* "Sharpness," as if it were derived from *ḥdd,* "be sharp." These names are treated in the same way in Tg. 1 Chron 1:30. Cf. Cashdan, 1967, 38–39. On the translation of proper names in the Targums in general, see Díez Macho, *Neophyti 1,* III, 50*.

[13]*qsṭrwwthwn* = Nfmg, N, L; see also V; = Latin *castra.* The same word is used in Tg. 1 Chron 4:32, 33 to translate Heb. *ḥṣr,* "village," which is translated by *kwprn'* in our present verse (Nf, V, N, L, Ps.-J.).

[14]*hdr btywwb';* lit.: "turned in repentance." The same idiom is used by Ps.-J. in Exod 33:7 and 40:7 in additions that are special to this Targum. See also Gen 4:24 (Ps.-J.), where the idiom *tb btywb',* lit., "(Cain) returned in repentance," occurs. On the repentance of Ishmael which is in question in our present verse, see above v. 8.

[15]Lond. and *ed. pr.* omit this phrase.

[16]See above, 2:11, where Nf and Ps.-J. also translate Havilah as *India.*

[17]See above, 16:7 and n. 10 to that verse, as well as 16:14 and n. 20 to that verse.

[18]= Onq. See Aberbach-Grossfeld, 1982, 149, n. 6; Grossfeld, 1988, 95, n. 4.

[19]*'yqwnyn.* Gr. *eikonion.* See above 5:3 and n. 3 to that verse. On the midrash about Isaac's features being like those of Abraham, see above, 21:2 and n. 3 to that verse.

[20]PRE 32 (235); *Sefer Ha-Yashar* 26 (74).

[21]The title "the Holy One, blessed be He," is used, e.g., in Tg. Gen 22:1 (Ps.-J.); 25:21 (Ps.-J.); 38:25 (P, Ps.-J.); see further Shinan, 1979, 2, 339, n. 192; Díez Macho, *Neophyti 1,* IV, 40*.

[22]Gen. R. 63,5; *b. Yeb.* 64a (429) and *b. Sukkah* 14a (58) use our present verse (Gen 25:21) to prove that the prayers of the righteous changed the intention of God.

[23]Lit.: "with him." *b. Yeb.* 64a (428-429) affirms that Isaac was barren.

[24]Read "twenty years" with PRE 32 (235). Compare vv. 20 and 26.

[25]Gen. R. 63,6: "Each ran to slay the other." PRE 32 (235): "the children were contending with one another within her womb like mighty warriors."

have children?" [26] And she went *to the schoolhouse of Shem the Great* [27] to beseech *mercy from before* the Lord. [28] 23. And the Lord said to her, "Two peoples are in your womb, and two *kingdoms* (issued) from your womb shall be separated; and one *kingdom* shall be stronger than the other, [29] and the older shall *be subjected* to the younger *if the children of the younger keep the commandments of the Law.* [30] 24. When *the two hundred and seventy* days *of her pregnancy* [31] for giving birth were completed, behold, there were twins in her womb. 25. The first came red, like a hairy cloak all over, and they called his name Esau, *because he was born fully completed,* [32] *with hair of the head, beard, teeth, and molars.* 26. Then his brother came forth, his hand holding on to Esau's heel; so they called his name [33] Jacob. Isaac was sixty years old when she bore them. 27. When the boys grew, Esau became a skilled hunter [34] *(able) to hunt birds and wild beasts,* a man *who would go out into* the field *to kill people. It was he who killed Nimrod and his son Henoch.* [35] But Jacob became a man *(who was) perfect in his works, ministering in the schoolhouse of Eber,* [36] *seeking instruction from before the Lord.* 28. Isaac loved Esau, because there were *deceptive words* [37] in his mouth; but Rebekah loved Jacob. 29. *The day Abraham died,* [38] Jacob boiled *dishes of lentils and went to comfort his father.* Esau came from the country, and he was exhausted *because he had committed five transgressions that day: he had practiced idolatry; he had shed innocent blood; he had gone in to a betrothed maiden; he had denied the life of the world to come, and had despised the birthright.* [39] 30. And Esau said to Jacob, "Let me *taste,* I pray, of that red dish, for I am exhausted." Therefore they called him Edom. 31. Jacob said,

Notes, Chapter 25

[26] *Gen. R.* 63,6.

[27] The mention of the *beth midrash* is prompted by the verb *drš,* "inquire," in HT. On the schoolhouse of Shem, see above 9:27, with n. 23 to that verse, and 22:19, with n. 34 to that verse.

[28] The Targums (Nf, Nfmg, P, V, N, L, Ps.-J.) take the verb *drš,* "inquire," of HT to refer to prayer, as does *PRE* 32 (235). Rabbinic tradition, on the other hand, understood *drš* in its ordinary meaning of seeking an answer from God or from a Sage; see Shinan, 1975, 90; idem, 1979, 2, 330.

[29] Reading *mlkw mmlkw* with *ed. pr.* (= Nf, Onq.); Lond.: *mlkn mmlkn.*

[30] *Gen. R.* 63,7. See above 3:15 with n. 27 to that verse, and 3,24 with nn. 58 and 60 to that verse.

[31] *Gen. R.* 63,8.

[32] The name Esau (*'św*) is taken to be the past participle (*'śwy*) of the verb *'śh,* "make." *Sefer Ha-Yashar* 26 (75): ". . . this one (Esau) was made complete from the womb." See further Ginzberg, *Legends,* 5, 274, n. 28.

[33] Lit.: "he called his name."

[34] *gbr nhšyrkn* = Onq. See Le Déaut, 1978, *Genèse,* 247, n. 19.

[35] *PRE* 24 (177–178) says that Esau slew Nimrod because he coveted his garments. See *Gen. R.* 63,13, which says that Nimrod was seeking to kill Esau. According to *Sefer Ha-Yashar* 27 (77), Esau killed Nimrod and two of his men; cf. Ginzberg, *Legends,* 1, 318; 5, 276, n. 38. Ps.-J. does not explain why Esau killed Nimrod and his son.

[36] Onq.: "Jacob was a perfect man *who attended the house of study.*" *Gen. R.* 63,10 mentions the schoolhouse of Shem and Eber in this context. The word "tents" of HT is taken to refer to the schoolhouse rather than to a shepherd's tent; cf. Aberbach-Grossfeld, 1982, 152, n. 18. See above 9:27 and n. 23 to that verse.

[37] *Gen. R.* 63,10 and *Tanh., Toledoth* 8 (91) say that Esau was a deceiver in that he pretended to be scrupulous about the laws of tithing. See further Ginzberg, *Legends,* 1, 316; 5, 274, n. 31. Ps.-J. simply hints at this tradition.

[38] *Gen. R.* 63,11; *b. B. Bat.* 16b (84). Abraham's death is recorded in Gen 25:8, but the haggadist can ignore chronology; cf. Le Déaut, *Genèse,* 1978, 247, n. 23. See, e.g., below, 27:29 (Ps.-J.) with n. 19 to that verse; 31:21 with n. 15 to that verse; 37:35 with n. 33 to that verse.

[39] For similar lists of Esau's crimes cf., e.g., *Gen. R.* 63,12; *Exod. R.* 1,1; *b. B. Bat.* 16b (84); *Tanh., Toledoth* 8 (91) and *Shemoth* 1 (160).

"Sell me your birthright *today as on the day you are to inherit*." [40] 32. And Esau said, "Behold, I am about to die, *and I shall not live again in another world;* so of what use is the birthright to me *or a portion in the world <to come>*?" [41] 33. But Jacob said, "Swear to me as on *that* day." [42] So he swore to him and sold his birthright to Jacob. 34. Jacob then gave bread and a dish of lentils to Esau; he ate and drank, and he rose and went away. Thus Esau despised the birthright *and the portion of the world to come.*

CHAPTER 26

1. There was a *great* famine in the land *of Canaan,* besides the former famine that had occurred in the days of Abraham, and Isaac went to Abimelech, the king of the Philistines at Gerar. 2. *And it had been Isaac's intention*[1] *to go down to Egypt.* But the Lord *revealed himself* to him and said, "Do not go down to Egypt; dwell in the land of which I shall tell you. 3. Reside in this land and *my Memra* will be *at your assistance*[2] and I will bless you; for to you and to your *children* I will give all these lands, and I will fulfill the oath which I swore to your father Abraham. 4. And I will multiply your *children* as the stars of the heavens, and I will give all these lands to your *children,* and *because of* your *children* all the peoples of the earth shall be blessed, 5. because Abraham *obeyed my Memra* and faithfully observed *my word,*[3] my commandments, my statutes, and my laws." 6. So Isaac dwelt in Gerar. 7. The men of the place asked about his wife, and he said, "She is my sister," for he was afraid to say *to her:* "My wife." *For he thought in his heart:* "Perhaps the men of the place will kill me on account of Rebekah, because she is beautiful in appearance." 8. Now, when he *had dwelt* there for some time, Abimelech, king of the Phil-

Notes, Chapter 25 (Cont.)

[40]Ps.-J.'s peculiar phrase may have been influenced by the legal principle that "a man cannot transfer to another possession of something that does not exist" (*b. B. Bat.* 63a [255]); cf. Aberbach-Grossfeld, 1982, 153, n. 21; Grossfeld, 1988, 95, n. 10.
[41]Reading *d'ty* rather than *d't 'mr* of both Lond. and *ed. pr.* This latter reading may be due to a combination of Aram. *'ty* with *'mr* of the Heb. lemma of the following verse.
[42]Onq. also has "as on *that* day," probably referring to the day when Isaac would die and Esau would inherit the birthright. See the references to Aberbach-Grossfeld and to Grossfeld in n. 40 above.

Notes, Chapter 26

[1]Lit.: "it had been in Isaac's heart." *Tanḥ.* B., *Toledoth* 6 (1, 128): "Isaac wanted to go down to Egypt." *Sefer Ha-Yashar* 28 (78): "Isaac rose to go down to Egypt." The midrash wishes to explain why the Lord appeared to Isaac.
[2]= Onq. See also vv. 24 and 28, where Onq., Nfmg, and Ps.-J. use the same idiom. When the biblical text says that God "is with" someone, the Targums often translate this as God "is at someone's assistance"; see, e.g., below, Gen 28:15; 31:3, 5. See above, n. 26 to 21:20.
[3]= Onq.; lit. "observed the observance of my word." The rabbinic tradition that Abraham observed the Torah was based on this verse; cf., e.g., *m. Qidd.* 4,14; Philo, *De Abrahamo* 46, § 275-276. See further Bowker, 1969, 235-236.

istines, looked out of the window and saw Isaac fondling[4] Rebekah his wife. 9. And Abimelech called Isaac and said: "Behold, she is your wife! How then did you say: 'She is my sister'?" Isaac said to him, "Because I said *to myself:*[5] 'Perhaps I may *be killed*[6] because of her' " 10. Abimelech said, "What is this you have done to us? *The king, who is distinguished among* the people,[7] might easily have lain with your wife, and you would have brought guilt upon us." 11. Abimelech then commanded all the people, saying, "Whoever approaches this man or his wife *with evil intent*[8] shall surely *be killed.*" 12. Isaac sowed in that land *for the sake of almsgiving,*[9] and he reaped in that year a hundred times *as much as he had estimated.*[10] And the Lord blessed him. 13. The man grew rich, and went on growing richer until he became very rich. 14. He had flocks of sheep and herds of cattle and many servants,[11] and the Philistines were jealous of him. 15. Now the Philistines stopped up all the wells which his father's servants had dug in the days of Abraham his father, and they filled them with earth. 16. And Abimelech said to Isaac, "Go away from us, for you have become much mightier than us *in possessions.*"[12] 17. So Isaac departed from there and encamped in the valley of Gerar and dwelt there. 18. Isaac dug anew the wells of water which *his father's servants*[13] had dug in the days of Abraham his father, and which the Philistines had stopped up when Abraham had died; and he gave them the names his father had given them. 19. Isaac's servants dug at *the edge of* the valley and found there a well of spring water. 20. And the shepherds of Gerar quarreled with Isaac's shepherds saying, "The water is ours." *Now, it was the will of heaven that (the well) should dry up. So they returned it to Isaac and it began to flow (again).*[14] And he called the name of the well Esek,[15] because they contended with him *about it.* 21. They dug another well, and they quarreled about it also. *And it dried up and did not flow again.* And he called its name Sitnah.[16] 22. And he withdrew from there and dug another well, and they did not

Notes, Chapter 26

[4]Lit.: "jesting with"; = Onq.

[5]Lit.: "in my heart."

[6]= Onq., Nfmg. On the possible reasons for changing HT "(lest) I die" to "(Perhaps I may) be killed," see Aberbach-Grossfeld, 1982, 155, n. 5; Grossfeld, 1988, 97, n. 6.

[7]Onq.: "the one *who is unique* (or: *distinguished*) *among* the people." Onq., like Ps.-J., is referring to the king. HT "one of the people" might be taken to mean that any commoner might have lain with Rebekah. Onq. and Ps.-J. considered this idea beneath the dignity of the matriarch. According to *Num. R.* 3,6, "one" in the phrase "one of the people" in our present verse indicates greatness. See Komlosh, 1973, 213; Aberbach-Grossfeld, 1982, 155, n. 6; Grossfeld, 1988, 97, n. 7.

[8]Lit.: "for evil"; see also v. 29. Onq. in our present verse reads: "Anyone who *injures* this man or his wife."

[9]*PRE* 33 (239; Luria 74a) says that Isaac sowed so as to have charity for the poor (*zr' ṣdqh l'nyym*).

[10]= Onq.; lit.: ". . . as much as his estimates;" cf. Jerome, *Quaest. hebr.* in Gen 26:12: (*aestimationes*). Ps.-J. and Onq. link *š'rym* in the Heb. *m'h š'rym,* "a hundredfold," with the *š'r* (Piel), "to estimate." Cf. also *Gen. R.* 64,6.

[11]Lit.: "and much service." Onq. is the same, except that it uses the Heb. *'bwdh* rather than *pwlḥn'* (Ps.-J.).

[12]See *Gen. R.* 64,7.

[13]= Pesh., LXX, Vulg.; Ps.-J. and these versions may have been influenced by v. 15; cf. Geiger, 1928, 459; Peters, 1935, 35.

[14]There is no known source for this addition. See Schmerler, 1932, 206. But compare the fourth miracle mentioned in 28:10 below (Ps.-J.).

[15]= "Contention."

[16]= "Opponent, hostility."

quarrel about it *as (they did) about the first ones.* So he called its name *"Wide Spaces,"*[17] and said, "Now the Lord had made room for us, and he will make us *increase* in the land." 23. From there he went up to Beer-sheba. 24. And the Lord *revealed himself* to him that night and said, "I am the God of your father Abraham. Do not be afraid, for *my Memra will be at your assistance,* and I will bless you, and multiply your *children* for the sake of *the merits of* Abraham my servant." 25. So he built an altar there and *prayed*[18] in the name of the Lord. He pitched his tent there, and Isaac's servants dug a well there. 26. *When Isaac went from Gerar, their wells dried up and their trees produced no fruit; and they realized that all this had happened to them because they had driven him away.*[19] So Abimelech went to him from Gerar, and he *took*[20] *his friends,* as well as Phicol, the commander of his army, *to go with him.* 27. Isaac said to them, "Why have you come to me *so that I might pray for you,* seeing that you have hated me and have driven me away from you?" 28. And they said, "We have seen plainly that *the Memra of* the Lord *was at your assistance, for through your merits all good was ours. But now that you have departed from our land, our wells have dried up and our trees have produced no fruit. So we said, 'Let us bring him back to us,'* and let the oath *that existed* between us *be confirmed, and from now on let it be* between us and you,[21] and let us make a covenant with you, 29. that you do us no evil, just as we have not approached you *with evil intent,*[22] and just as we have done nothing but good to you, and we have sent you away in peace; you are now the blessed one of the Lord." 30. ....[23] 31. They rose early in the morning and swore to each other; *and he divided the bridle of his ass and gave one part to them as a testimony.*[24] *And Isaac prayed for them and they became productive.*[25] Isaac *accompanied* them, and they departed from him in peace.

Notes, Chapter 26

[17]Aramaic: *rwwḥt'* (Rewawheta). Ps.-J. gives the Aramaic form of Heb. Rehoboth, which Nf and Onq. take over directly. To preserve the play on the place-name, Ps.-J. uses the verb *rwḥ* (Af.) "make room," whereas Nf and Onq. lose that word-play by using the verb *pty* (Af.), "to widen, give space to."

[18]See above, 12:8 and n. 9 to that verse.

[19]Schmerler (1932, 207) says there is no parallel to this haggadah in traditional rabbinic literature. See also Ginsburger, *Pseudo-Jonathan,* XX–XXI. However, Shinan (1979, 1, 54 and 2, 329, n. 160) points out that there is a parallel account in *The Chronicles of Moses;* see M. Gaster, *The Chronicles of Jerahmeel,* 1899; reprint with Prolegomenon by H. Schwarzbaum (New York: Ktav, 1971) 117. Shinan notes further (ibid., 1, 54) that the addition in our present verse forms a unit with Ps.-J.'s additions to vv. 27, 28 and with Ps.-J.'s statement in v. 31 about Isaac's effective prayer. The concept of "the merits of the Fathers" is implicit in Ps.-J.'s version of our present verse. See also the Pal. Tgs. of Gen 29:22 and 31:22.

[20]Lit.: "seized." In the biblical phrase "Ahuzzath his adviser" (*'ḥzt mr'hw*), *'ḥzt* is interpreted as if it were derived from *'ḥz,* "seize, hold," and *mr'hw* is treated as if it meant "friend" (*r'*). Onq. has the same interpretation as Nf (with orthographical variations). See *Gen. R.* 64,9; Jerome, *Quaest. hebr.* in Gen 26:26: *collegium amicorum.*

[21]Onq.: "Let the oath *that existed* between *our fathers* be confirmed now between us and you." Cf. *Gen. R.* 64,10. Because of the repetition involved in the phrase "between our two parties, between you and us," Onq. and Ps.-J. saw in that phrase a reference to the covenant between Abraham and Abimelech (cf. Gen 21:31–32) and to the covenant which Abimelech now proposes to make; cf. Komlosh, 1973, 174.

[22]Lit.: "for evil"; see v. 11 and n. 8.

[23]V. 30 is omitted in Lond. and *ed. pr.*

[24]PRE 36 (278–279); see also Ginzberg, *Legends,* 4, 93–94.

[25]On the verb (*rwwḥ*) used here, see above, 20:17 and n. 14 to that verse. The productiveness mentioned in our present verse refers to the wells and fruit trees which we heard of in v. 28; cf. Schmerler, 1932, 208.

32. That same day Isaac's servants came and told him about the well they had dug, and said to him, "We have found water." 33. He called it Shibah; therefore the name of the city is Beer-sheba to this day. 34. When Esau was forty years old, he took to wife Judith, the daughter of Beeri the Hittite, and Basemath, the daughter of Elon the Hittite. 35. And they *bent down in idolatry,*[26] *and they deliberately rebelled*[27] against Isaac and Rebekah *with their evil deeds.*

CHAPTER 27

1. When Isaac had grown old, his eyes were too dim to see. *For when his father tied him, he looked upon the Throne of Glory, and from that time on his eyes began to grow dim.*[1] He called Esau, his older son, *on the fourteenth of Nisan* and said to him, "My son, *behold, tonight the heavenly beings praise the Lord of the world, and the storehouses of (the) dews are opened.*"[2] And he said to him, "Here I am." 2. And he said, "Behold, I am old; I do not know the day of my death. 3. So now, take your weapons, your quiver, and your bow, and go out to the field and hunt game for me. 4. Then prepare dishes such as I love, and bring (them) to me that I may eat, so that my soul may bless you before I die." 5. And Rebekah heard *through the Holy Spirit*[3] while Isaac spoke with Esau his son. And Esau went out to the field to hunt game to bring (back). 6. And Rebekah said to her son Jacob, saying, *Behold, tonight the heavenly beings praise the Lord of the world, and the storehouses of (the) dews are opened;*[4] *and I heard your father speaking with your brother Esau, saying, 7. 'Bring me game and prepare a dish for me to eat, so that I may bless you before the Lord before I die.' 8. And now, my son, *obey me* (and do) what I command you: 9.

Notes, Chapter 26 (Cont.)

[26] *Gen. R.* 65,4; *Tanḥ., Toledoth* 8 (91).

[27] Lit.: "they intended to rebel." Ps.-J interprets the word *mrt* in the phrase *wthyyn mrt rwḥ,* "and they were a source of bitterness," as if it were derived from *mrh,* "rebel." See Schmerler, 1932, 208.

Notes, Chapter 27

[1] See Exod 12:42 (Nf, V, N, CTg FF); cf. also 15:18 (P). See above, 22:10 and n. 23 to that verse. Cf. *Gen. R.* 65, 10; *Deut. R.* 11,3; *PRE* 32 (236).

[2] See also v. 6. Cf. *PRE* 32 (236). *2 Enoch* 6,1 uses the phrase "the treasuries of the dew"; see *1 Enoch* 60,20. b. *Ta'an* 4b (12) associates prayer for rain with Passover. The Targums associate various events with Passover; see v. 9 below and 17:26 above. The praises of the angels are mentioned in several Targumic passages; besides Gen 27:1 (Ps.-J.), see v. 6 (Ps.-J.); 32:27(26) (Nf, P, V, N, CTg C, Ps.-J.); Exod 14:20 (Nfmg); 14:24 (Ps.-J.); Deut 32:3 (Nf, P, V, N, L; cf. Ps.-J.).

[3] *Tanḥ., Toledoth* 10 (93); according to *Gen. R.* 67,9, Rebekah knew what Isaac had said because she was a prophetess. By saying that Rebekah knew in the Holy Spirit or through prophecy, the midrash shows that Rebekah was not spying. In v. 42 below, Ps.-J. says that in another context Rebekah again received knowledge from the Holy Spirit. See also v. 13 (Onq.): "To me (Rebekah) it was said in a prophecy that no curses will come upon you." See Schäfer, 1970, 304–314; idem, 1972, 55.

[4] *PRE* 32 (236-237); see above, v. 1.

Go now to the sheep shed, and bring me from there two *fat* kids, *one for the Pass-over and one for the festival offerings,*[5] and I will make of them dishes for your father, such as he loves. 10. Then bring (them) to your father to eat, so that he may bless you before his death." 11. *Because* Jacob *feared sin, he was afraid that his father might curse him;*[6] and he said,[7] "Behold, my brother Esau is a hairy man, and I am a smooth(-skinned) man. 12. What if my father touches me and I *appear* in his eyes as one who laughs at *him,* and I bring upon myself *curses* and not *blessings?"*[8] 13. But his mother said to him, *"If he blesses you with blessings, let them come upon you and upon your children; but if he curses you with curses,*[8] *let them come* upon me *and upon my soul;*[9] only *obey me,* and go and bring (them) to me." 14. So he went and took (them) and brought (them) to his mother, and his mother prepared dishes such as his father loved. 15. Rebekah then took the precious[10] garments of her older son Esau, *which had (come down) from the first man.*[11] *That day Esau had not put them on, so that they remained* with her in the house, and she put them on Jacob, her younger son; 16. and the skins of the kids she put on his hands and on the smooth part of his neck. 17. She arranged in the hands of her son Jacob the dishes and the bread that she had prepared. 18. He went in to his father and said, "My father." And he said, "Here I am. Who are you, my son?" 19. Jacob said to his father, "I am Esau, your first-born; I have done as you said to me. Sit up, I pray; *be seated,*[12] and eat of my game, that your soul may bless me." 20. And Isaac said to his son, "How did you find it so quickly, my son?" And he said, "Because the Lord your God prepared (it) for me." 21. And Isaac said to Jacob, "Come closer, I pray, that I may touch you my son, (to find out) whether you are really my son Esau or not." 22. So Jacob drew closer to Isaac his father, who touched him and said, "This voice is the voice of Jacob, but *the touch of* his hands is *like the touch of* the hands of Esau." 23. And he did not recognize him, because his hands were hairy like the hands of Esau his brother; and he blessed him. 24. Then he said, "Are you really

Notes, Chapter 27

[5]*PRE* 32 (237): "... he brought one as a Paschal offering, and with the other he prepared the savory meat. ..." On the festival offering, see *m. Pesah.* 6,3; *b. Pesah.* 69b–70a (356–357); 114b (589). The midrash explains why two kids were needed for Isaac's meal. On the association of this episode with the Passover, see above, v. 1.

[6]*PRE* 32 (237): "Jacob was skilled in Torah, and his heart dreaded the curse of his father." Ps.-J.'s reference to a curse in this verse may be due to the influence of the following verse.

[7]Lond. and *ed. pr.* omit "to Rebekah his mother."

[8]= Onq. Onq. and Ps.-J. take "a curse" and "a blessing" of HT as collective nouns, since Jacob gave several blessings (cf. vv. 28–29) and curses (cf. v. 40).

[9]*PRE* 32 (237; Luria 73b): "(If he gives you) blessings, let them be upon you and upon your children; but if curses, let them be upon me and upon my soul (*'l npšy*)." Notice that *PRE,* like Ps.-J., has "blessings" and "curses" in the plural, and that, like Ps.-J., it uses the phrase "upon me and upon my soul."

[10]Or: "desirable." Onq.: "clean." See Aberbach-Grossfeld, 1982, 163, n. 5; Grossfeld, 1988, 101, n. 7.

[11]*Tanḥ.* B., *Toledoth* 12 (1, 133); *Num. R.* 4,8. Ps.-J. here refers to a tradition which is recorded at greater length by Nf, Nfmg, P, V, N, and CTg Z in Gen 48:22. On the garments of Adam, see above, 3:21. Jerome, *Quaest. hebr.* in Gen 27:15, records a Jewish tradition which says the choicest garments (cf. Gen 27:15) were those worn by the first-born who acted as priests before Aaron's time. See Ginzberg, *Legends,* 5, 283, n. 89.

[12]= Onq. The verb *sḥr* (Ithpa.), which also has the basic meaning of "turn around," also has the meaning "be seated at table." This verb occurs again in Ps.-J. in Exod 32:6 (= Onq.); Num 22:8, 19 as a translation of *yšb,* as is the case in our present verse, and in Gen 50:15, 20 in additions that are special to Ps.-J.

my son Esau?" And he said, "I am." 25. And he said, "Serve me [13] that I may eat of my son's game, so that my soul may bless you." And he served him [14] and he ate. *Since he had no wine with him, an angel provided (some) for him, and brought of* the wine *that had been stored up in its grapes since the days of the beginning of the world. And he gave it into Jacob's hand,* [15] *and Jacob handed it to his father,* and he drank. 26. And his father Isaac said to him, "Come closer, I pray, and kiss me, my son." 27. And he went closer and kissed him. And he smelled the smell of his clothes and blessed him and said, "See, the smell of my son is like the smell of *the fragrant incense that will be offered on the mountain of the Sanctuary,* [16] *which has been called* 'Field which the Lord blessed, *and where it has pleased him to make his Shekinah dwell.*' 28. May *the Memra of the Lord* give you of *the goodness of* the dews *that come down from* heaven, and of *the goodness of the springs that come up and make the vegetation of* the earth *grow from below,* and abundance of grain and wine. 29. Let nations—*all the sons of Esau*—be subjected to you; and let *kingdoms—all the sons of Keturah* [17]—bend down *before* you. You will be *master and ruler* [18] over your brothers, and let your mother's sons *come forward to salute you.* Those who curse you, *my son,* will be cursed, *like Balaam son of Beor,* and those who bless you will be blessed, *like Moses* [19] *the prophet, the scribe of Israel.*" [20] 30. When Isaac had finished blessing Jacob, and Jacob had just gone out *about two steps* [21] from the presence of Isaac his father, his brother Esau came in from his hunting. 31. *Now, the Memra of the Lord withheld clean game from him; but he found a dog and killed him.* [22] And he also made dishes *of him* and brought (them) to his father. And he said to his father, "Let my father arise and eat of his son's game, that your soul may bless me." 32. Isaac his father said to him, "Who are you?" And he said, "I am your son, Esau, your first-born." 33. Isaac trembled with a <very> great trembling *when he heard the voice of Esau and (when) the smell of*

Notes, Chapter 27

[13]Lit.: "bring to me."

[14]Lit.: "he brought to him."

[15]*Tanḥ.* B., *Toledoth* 16 (1, 135): "(Since his mother had not given Jacob wine [cf. v. 17] we conclude that) Michael brought him wine from the Garden of Eden." Cf. *b. Berak.* 34b (215); *Sanh.* 99a (671) and Tg. Song 8:2, which tell of wine which had been preserved in its grapes from the time of creation for the righteous in the world to come.

[16]*Tanḥ.* B., *Toledoth* 22 (1, 141) records a tradition which says that God breathed into Jacob's clothes the fragrance of incense that would be offered up in the Temple. See *Gen. R.* 65,23.

[17]*Gen. R.* 66,4; *Tanḥ.* B., *Toledoth* 16 (1, 136).

[18]Onq.: "be master."

[19]Tg. Num 24:9 (Nfmg, P, V, N, Ps.-J.); *Tanḥ.* B., *Toledoth* 16 (1, 136); cf. *Gen. R.* 66,4. The reference to Balaam and Moses in our present verse anticipates events. See above, 25:29 and n. 38 to that verse.

[20]Moses is given the title "scribe of Israel" in the Targums in Gen 27:29 (Nf, P, V, N, L, Ps.-J.); Num 11:26 (Nfmg, P, V, N, L); 21:18 (Nf, Nfmg, Nfi, P, V, N, Ps.-J.); 24:9 (Nfmg, P, V, N, Ps.-J.); Deut 33:21 (Nf, P, V, N, L, Ps.-J., Onq.); Tg. Ps. 62:12; Tg. Song 1:2; 2:4; 3:3. Moses is also given this title in the Talmud; cf., e.g., *b. Sotah* 13b (71–72). See also *b. B. Bat.* 14b-15a (71–73), where Moses' part in the writing of the Scriptures is discussed.

[21]Conjectural translation; Lond.: *typwzyn* = "jumps" (?); see Levy 1, 314–315; *ed. pr.: tpwḥyn,* "handbreadth, step" (Levy, 1, 315) or "rapping (at the door)" (Jastrow, 545).

[22]See, e.g., *Gen. R.* 67,2, and *Tanḥ., Toledoth* 11 (93), which record that God did not allow Esau to catch game. The haggadah about the dog has no parallel (cf. Schmerler, 1932, 212; Zunz, 1892, 76; Shinan, 1979, 1,55). This haggadah finds an echo in v. 33 (Ps.-J.).

his dish came into his nostrils like the smell of the fire of Gehenna.[23] And he said, "Who was this that hunted game and brought (it) to me? I ate of all *that he brought me* before you came in, and I blessed him. And *even so,* he will be blessed." 34. When Esau heard his father's words, he cried out with an exceedingly great and bitter cry, and he said to his father, "Father, bless me, me also!" 35. He said, "Your brother came in with *wisdom*[24] and *received*[25] your blessing *from me.*" 36. He said, "His name has *rightly* been called Jacob; he has *deceived* me twice. He took away my birthright, and behold, now he has *received* my blessing." And he said, "Have you not kept a blessing for me?" 37. Isaac answered and said to Esau, "Behold, I have appointed him ruler over you, and I have placed all his brothers before him as servants, <and I have sustained him with wheat and wine>.[26] *So go and leave me;*[27] for what can I do for you, my son?" 38. Esau said to his father, "Have you but one blessing, father? Father, bless me, me also!" And Esau raised his voice and wept. 39. Isaac answered and said *to Esau,*[28] "Behold, *in the goodness of the fruits* of the earth shall your dwelling be, and far from the dew of heaven above.[29] 40. You shall *put your trust* in your sword, *entering into every place and causing alarm as you go.*[30] But you shall be subjected to your brother; but if you *go astray*[31] *and cause his children to abandon the observance of*[32] *the commandments of the law,* you shall break the yoke *of his slavery* from your neck."[33] 41. And Esau *harbored* hatred *in his heart* against *his brother* Jacob because of *the order of* blessings with which his father had blessed him. And Esau said to himself, "*I will not do as Cain did, who killed Abel while his father was alive; but his father then begot Seth. Rather, I will restrain myself until the time when* the days of mourning *for the death* of my father *come,* and then I will kill my brother Jacob,[34] *and I will be murderer and heir.*"[35] 42. The words of Esau, her older son who *was planning*[36] *to kill Jacob,* were told to Rebekah *by the Holy Spirit.*[37] So she sent and called her younger son Jacob and said to him, "Behold, your brother Esau is *lying in wait for*[38] you and *plots*

Notes, Chapter 27

[23] *Gen. R.* 65,22 and 67,2 say that when Esau went in to Isaac Gehenna went in with him; cf. also *Tanḥ., Toledoth* 11 (93).

[24] = Onq. See Aberbach-Grossfeld, 1982, 165, n. 11; Grossfeld, 1988, 101, n. 12.

[25] = Onq. See Aberbach-Grossfeld, ibid., n. 12; Grossfeld, ibid., n. 13.

[26] Omitted in Lond. and *ed. pr.*

[27] Lit.: "Go and be banished from me."

[28] Thus Lond. and *ed. pr.,* probably under the influence of v. 37.

[29] Ps.-J.'s translation is self-contradictory. Isaac's words contain a favorable ("in the goodness . . .") and an unfavorable ("far from the dew . . .") promise.

[30] The Aramaic is obscure; the translation "and causing alarm as you go" is based on Levy, 2, 424 (*rkk*; Pa.), 525 (*t'*).

[31] Reading *tṭ'y* with Lond. *Ed. pr.: rš'y,* "(if) they are wicked."

[32] Lit.: "and cause his sons to go down from observing." Ps.-J. understands HT *tryd,* ("when) you break loose" (RSV), as *twryd,* "(when) you cause to go down." Cf. Geiger, 1928, 459; Shinan, 1979, 2, 219.

[33] Onq.: ". . . *when his descendants will transgress the words of the Law* you will remove his yoke . . ."; cf. *Gen. R.* 67,7. See above, 3:15 with n. 27 to that verse, and 3:24 with nn. 58 and 60 to that verse.

[34] *Tanḥ., Emor* 13 (460); *Gen. R.* 67,8; *Sefer Ha-Yashar* 29 (82).

[35] Cf. 1 Kings 21:19: "Have you killed, and also taken possession?"

[36] Lit.: "who was thinking in his heart."

[37] *Gen. R.* 67,9. See above v. 5 and n. 3 to that verse.

[38] = Onq. Cf. *Gen. R.* 67,9; see Grossfeld, 1988, 103, n. 18.

against you to kill you. 43. And now, my son, *obey me:* Arise, flee *for your life, and go*[39] to Laban my brother, to Haran. 44. Dwell with him a few days until your brother's wrath has quieted, 45. until your brother's anger towards you *subsides*[40] and he forgets what you did to him; then I will send (for you) and bring you (back) from there. Why should I also be bereft of both of you on one day *when you are killed and he driven away, as Eve was bereft of Abel whom Cain killed, and both were driven away from the presence of Adam and Eve all the days of the lives of Adam and Eve?"*[41] 46. And Rebekah said to Isaac, "I am greatly distressed[42] because of *the annoyance (caused by)* the daughters of Heth. If Jacob takes a *wicked*[43] wife from among the daughters of Heth like these from among the daughters of *the people of the land,* what good will life be to me?"

CHAPTER 28

1. Isaac called Jacob and blessed him. Then he commanded him and said to him, "Do not take a wife from among the daughters of the Canaanites. 2. Arise, go to Paddan *of* Aram[1] to the house of Bethuel, your mother's father, and from there take a wife for yourself from among the daughters of Laban, your mother's brother. 3. And may El Shaddai bless you *with great possessions,* may he increase you and multiply you *into twelve tribes,* and may you *be worthy of* the assembly *of the masters*[2] *of the Sanhedrin, the sum of which is seventy, like the number of*[3] the peoples. 4. May he give you the blessing of Abraham, to you and your *children* with you, *and may he bring you back* to inherit the land where you are sojourning, which *the Lord* gave to Abraham." 5. Then Isaac sent Jacob away, and he went to Paddan *of* Aram to Laban, the son of Bethuel the Aramean, the brother of Rebekah, the mother of Jacob and Esau. 6. Now Esau saw that Isaac had blessed Jacob and sent him to Paddan *of* Aram to take a wife for himself from there, blessing him and commanding him, saying, "Do not take a wife from among the daughters of the Canaanites,"

Notes, Chapter 27 (Cont.)

[39]Onq.: "Arise and go." Ps.-J. translates Heb. *brḥ,* "flee," literally, and then adds "and go." This latter verb is used by Onq. and Nf out of deference to Jacob; cf. Aberbach-Grossfeld, 1982, n. 18; Grossfeld, 1988, 103, n. 19.

[40]Lit.: "until your brother's anger rests from you."

[41]The source of this addition is unknown; cf. Schmerler, 1932, 216.

[42]Lit.: "I am distressed in my life." The same idiom occurs in Exod 1:12 (Ps.-J.) and Num 22:3 (Ps.-J.; cf. Nfmg).

[43]Cf. *Gen. R.* 67,11, which says that when referring to the Hittite women, Rebekah expressed herself with gestures of abhorrence. In this context *Jubilees* 27,8 remarked that the daughters of Canaan were evil.

Notes, Chapter 28

[1]Ps.-J. usually writes the place-name Paddan-Aram as *pdn d'rm;* cf. Gen 28:2, 5, 6, 7; 31:18; 33:18; 35:9, 26; 46:15. In Gen 24:61, where that place-name occurs in an addition to the biblical text, and in 25:20, it is written as *pdn 'rm.* In Gen 48:7 the place-name is omitted in Ps.-J. In this latter text and in 35:26 it also occurs as *pdn d'rm* in Nf.

[2]Reading *rbny* with Lond., rather than *dbny,* "of the sons of," of *ed. pr.* This latter form (*dbny*) is grammatically incorrect, since it follows a construct.

[3]"The assembly ... *the number of*"; the source of Ps.-J.'s addition is unknown; cf. Schmerler, 1932, 216.

7. and that Jacob had obeyed *the word of* his father and *the word of* his mother and had gone to Paddan *of* Aram. 8. Esau saw that the daughters of the Canaanites were displeasing to Isaac his father. 9. So Esau went to Ishmael, and took as wife, besides the wives he had, Mahalath, the daughter of Ishmael, Abraham's son—*she is Basemath*[4]—the sister of Nebaioth *by his mother.*[5] 10. *Five miracles*[6] *were performed for Jacob at the time that he went forth from Beer-sheba. The first miracle: the hours of the day were shortened and the sun set before*[7] *its time, because the Debbira*[8] *desired to speak with him.*[9] *The second miracle: the four stones which he had placed as a pillow, he found in the morning (joined) into one stone.*[10] *The third miracle: the stone which they rolled from the mouth of the well, when all the flocks were gathered, he rolled it with one of his arms.*[11] *The fourth miracle: that the well flowed, and the waters came up before him and continued to flow all the days that he was in Haran.*[12] *The fifth miracle: the earth shrank before him, and on the very day*[13] *that* he went forth he arrived at Haran. 11. And he *prayed*[14] in the place *of the Sanctuary*[15] and passed the night there because the sun had set. And he took *four*[16] of the stones of the *holy* place and placed (them as) his pillow and lay down in that place. 12. He had a dream, and behold, a ladder was fixed in the earth with its top reaching towards the heavens. And behold, the *two* angels *who had gone to Sodom and who had been banished from their apartment because they had revealed the secrets of the Lord of the world, went about when they were banished until the time that Jacob went forth from his father's house.*[17] *Then, as an act of kindness,*

Notes, Chapter 28

[4]Cf. Gen 36:3; *j. Bikkurim* 3,65d; *Gen. R.* 67,13.

[5]Since Ishmael had two wives (cf. Ps.-J. Gen 21:21), this specification is required.

[6]This "pre-translation haggadah" (see above, Introduction, p. 5) at the beginning of the *seder* occurs in Nf, P, V, N, L, and Ps.-J. The content of all these Targums is basically the same, although the order of the miracles is not the same in all the targumic traditions. Ps.-J.'s version of the haggadah is shorter than that of the other Targums; (cf. Clarke, 1974–75, 367–377. See also Ginzberg, *Legends,* 1, 349–350; 5, 289–290, nn. 130–133.

[7]Lit.: "not in, not at (*bl'*)."

[8]*dbyr'* = Nf. P, V, N, L use the form *d(y)bwr'.*

[9]*Gen. R.* 68,10. *PRE* 35 (264) tells that the sun set before its time, but it does not state that God wanted to speak to Jacob. Cf. also *b. Hul.* 91b (512).

[10]*Gen. R.* 68,11; *b. Hul.* 91b(512); *PRE* 35 (264); *Midrash Psalms* 91,6(2, 104). Ps.-J. is the only Targum of this verse to mention that Jacob placed *four* stones under his head. But see v. 11 (Ps.-J., Nfmg). The midrashim and the Targums wish to explain the fact that v. 11 refers to "the stones," whereas v. 18 mentions "the stone."

[11]*PRE* 36 (268); cf. *Gen. R.* 70, 12; *Qoh. R.* 9,11.1; *Tanḥ., Wa-Yishlah* 4 (107). See also Ps.-J. Gen 29:10 and 13.

[12]*PRE* 36 (268); cf. *Gen. R.* 70,19. See Gen 29:10, 13 (Ps.-J.) and 31:22 (Nf, Nfmg, P, N, CTg E).

[13]*b. Sanh.* 95b (642); *Hul.* 91b (512); *Gen. R.* 68,8.

[14]Nf, P, and Ps.-J. take *wypg',* "and he came" (RSV), to refer to prayer. In this they follow traditional rabbinic interpretation, which uses this verse to prove that Jacob instituted evening prayer; cf., e.g., *Mekilta* to Exod 14:10 (1, 206–207); *Gen. R.* 68,9; *j. Berak.* 4,7a-b; *b. Berak.* 26b (160); *Sanh.* 95b (642). See Maher, 1990, 237–238.

[15]*Gen. R.* 68,9; *PRE* 35 (263) identifies "a certain place" (RSV) with Mount Moriah, on which see above, 22:2 and n. 6 to that verse. See below, v. 17 (Ps.-J., Nf, Nfmg 1 and 2).

[16]= Nfmg. See v. 10 and n. 10 to that verse.

[17]*Gen. R.* 50,9; 68,12. Both of these texts use the word *mhyṣh* (cf. Theodor-Albeck, 524, 789), which occurs in Ps.-J. and which we translate as "apartment." The reference is, of course, to the heavenly precincts. Both texts also use the word *m(y)styryn,* which is the Gr. *mystêria,* which we also find in Ps.-J. and which we translate as "secrets." According to *Gen. R.* 68,12, the secret revealed by the angels was God's intention to destroy Sodom (cf. Gen 19:13). Ps.-J. mentions *two* angels; cf. *b. Hul.* 91b (512). On the possible relation of this verse to the N.T., see McNamara, 1972, 146–147.

they accompanied him to Bethel, and on that day they ascended *to the heavens on high, and said,*[18] *"Come and see Jacob the pious, whose image is fixed in the Throne of Glory,*[19] *and whom you have desired to see." Then the rest of the holy* angels of *the Lord* came down *to look at him.* 13. And, behold, *the Glory of*[20] the Lord stood beside him and said *to him,* "I am the Lord, the God of your father Abraham and the God of Isaac. The land on which you are lying I will give to you and to your *children.* 14. Your *children* shall be *as numerous*[20] as the dust of the earth, and you shall *have power* to the west and to the east, to the north and to the south; and all the families of the earth shall be blessed because of *your merits* and because of *the merits of* your children.[21] 15. And behold, my *Memra* is *at your assistance,*[22] and I will protect you wherever you go, and I will bring you back to this land; for I will not forsake you until I have done[23] what I have promised[24] to you." 16. And Jacob awoke from his sleep and said, *"In truth the Glory of the Shekinah of*[25] the Lord *dwells* in this place, and I did not know it." 17. He was afraid and said, "How awesome *and glorious* is this place! This is not *a profane place,* but *a sanctuary to the name of the Lord; and this is* (*a place*) *suitable*[26] *for prayer, corresponding to* the gate of heaven,[27] *founded beneath the Throne of Glory."* 18. Jacob rose early in the morning and took the stone,[28] the one which he had placed as his pillow, and placed it as a pillar, and poured oil on the top of it. 19. And he called the name of that place Bethel; but Luz was the name of the city *before that.* 20. And Jacob swore[29] saying, "If *the Memra of the Lord comes to my assistance*[22] and keeps me *from shedding innocent blood,* (*from*) *idol worship, and* (*from*) *sexual immorality*[30] on this journey on which I am going, and (if) he gives me bread to eat and clothing to wear, 21. and (if) I return in peace to my father's house, the Lord shall be my God, 22. and this stone which I have placed as a pillar shall be *arranged* as *a sanctuary of the Lord,*[31] *and the generations shall worship upon it to the Name of the Lord;* and of all that you give me I will *set aside* a tithe *before you."*

Notes, Chapter 28

[18]Lit.: "answering and saying."

[19]*Gen. R.* 68,12; 78,3; *Num. R.* 4,1; *Lam. R.* 2,1.2; *b. Hul.* 91b (512); *PRE* 35 (265); Tg. 1 Chron 21:15. As the text from *Gen. R.* 68,12 shows, the idea that Jacob's image was inscribed in heaven is based on Isa 49:3 ("Israel in whom I will be glorified"), where "Israel" is taken to be the patriarch Jacob.

[20]= Onq.

[21]See above, 22:18 (Ps.-J.).

[22]= Onq. See above 26:3 and n. 2 to that verse.

[23]Lit.: "until the time that I do."

[24]Lit.: "spoken"; = Nf, Onq.

[25]Onq.: *"the Glory of* the Lord." Cf. *Gen. R.* 69,7: "Where dwells the *Shekinah?* In this place, . . ."

[26]*kšr;* see the use of this word in 24:23 above, and see n. 16 to that verse.

[27]See *Mekilta* to Exod 15:17 (2, 78); *j. Berak.* 4,8c; *PRE* 35 (265–266). Cf. Ginzberg, *Legends,* 5, 292, n. 141; 6,74, n. 381; A. Aptowitzer, 1930–1931, 137–153, 257–287.

[28]Note that Ps.-J. had said (above vv. 10–11) that Jacob took four stones.

[29]= Onq.

[30]Lit.: "revealing of nakedness." On the triad of sins mentioned in our present verse, see above, 13:13 and n. 9 to that verse. In a parallel passage to our present verse (*Tanḥ., Wa-Yishlah* 8 [110-111]), the same three sins are mentioned. In the corresponding passage in *Gen. R.* (70,4), slander is added to these three.

[31]According to *PRE* 35 (266), the Sanctuary stands on the stone which Jacob erected as a pillar; cf. also *Midrash Psalms* 91,7 (2, 106)

CHAPTER 29

1. Jacob set out *on his journey at a sprightly pace*[1] and went to the land of the children of the East. 2. And he looked, and behold, there was a well in the field, and there were three flocks of sheep lying beside it, because they used to water the flocks from that well. And a large stone *was laid* on the mouth of the well. 3. When all the flocks were gathered there, they used to roll the stone from the mouth to the well and water the sheep; then they used to put the stone back in its place on the mouth of the well. 4. Jacob said to them, "My brothers, where are you from?" And they said, "We are from Haran." 5. He said to them, "Do you know Laban, the son of Nahor?" And they said, "We know (him)." 6. And he said <to them>, "Is he well?" And they said: "He is well. And behold, Rachel his daughter is coming with the flock." 7. And he said, "Behold, it is (still) high day*time;*[2] it is not time to gather the animals; water the flock and go, pasture (them)." 8. And they said, "We cannot until all the flocks are gathered; then they will roll the stone from the mouth of the well, and we will water the flock." 9. While he was still speaking with them, Rachel came with her father's flock, because she was a shepherdess *at that time. For there had been a plague of the Lord on Laban's flock, and only a few of them remained. So he dismissed his shepherds and placed what remained in the care of his daughter Rachel.*[3] 10. And when Jacob saw Rachel, the daughter of Laban, his mother's brother, <and the flock of Laban, his mother's brother>,[4] Jacob drew near and, *with one of his arms,* rolled the stone from the mouth of the well; *and the well began to flow, and the waters came up before him,* and he watered the flock of Laban, his mother's brother; *and it continued to flow for twenty years.* 11. Then Jacob kissed Rachel, and raised his voice and wept. 12. Jacob told Rachel that *he had come to dwell*[5] with her father *and to take one of his daughters. Rachel answered and said, "It is not possible for you to dwell with him, for he is a deceitful man." Jacob said to her, "I am more deceitful and more clever than he,*[6] *and he has no power to harm me, because the Memra of the Lord is at my assistance." And when she knew that* he was Rebekah's son, she ran and told her father. 13. And when

Notes, Chapter 29

[1]Lit.: "Jacob lifted up his feet *lightly to travel.*" Ps.-J. is the only Targum to add the words "lightly" and "to travel" to a literal translation of the unusual Heb. idiom that is being translated. Compare *Gen. R.* 70:8: "Since he (Jacob) had been given these good tidings, his heart carried his feet."

[2]Lit.: "(there is) much day*time.*" Ps.-J. translates Heb. *'wd,* "still," by *'dn,* "time." The same word (*'ydn*) follows almost immediately as a translation of Heb. *'t,* "time."

[3]According to *PRE* 36 (269), God sent the plague on Laban's sheep so that when Jacob arrived he would find Rachel sheperding the few sheep that remained.

[4]Omitted in Lond. and *ed. pr.* In this verse Ps.-J., and Ps.-J. alone, records the third and fourth (Ps.-J.) or the fourth and fifth (Nf, P, V, N, L) miracles which are enumerated in the Pal. Tgs. of Gen 28:10. See above, nn. 11-12 on that verse. Ps.-J., and Ps.-J. alone, mentions these miracles again in v. 13 below. See also *PRE* 36 (268); *Gen. R.* 70,12.

[5]*Ed. pr.:* "to approach."

[6]*b. Meg.* 13b (77); *B. Bat.* 123a (511). Cf. *Gen. R.* 70,13. The association of Laban with deceit is based on a play on the words *'rmy,* "Aramean" (in the name "Laban the Aramean"; cf., e.g., Gen 25:20) and *rm'y,* "deceiver." See, e.g., *Gen. R.* 70,19 and Tg. Gen 31:24 (Ps.-J.).

Laban heard the report of *the strength and piety* of Jacob, his sister's son, *how he had taken the birthright and the order of blessings*[7] *from his brother,*[8] *and how the Lord had revealed himself to him at Bethel, how he had rolled the stone, and how the well flowed and came up before him,*[9] he ran to meet him, embraced him and kissed him, and brought him into his house. And he told Laban all these things. 14. Laban said to him, "You are indeed my *relative*[10] and my *blood";*[11] and he dwelt with him a whole month.[12] 15. Laban said to Jacob, "*Just* because you are *considered* my kinsman,[13] should you serve me for nothing? Tell me, what your wages should be." 16. Now Laban *had* two daughters; the name of the older was Leah, and the name of the younger was Rachel. 17. Leah's eyes were *running,*[14] *because she used to weep and pray before the Lord that he would not destine her for Esau the wicked.*[15] Rachel was lovely in figure and beautiful in appearance.[16] 18. Jacob loved Rachel; and he said, "I will serve you seven years for your younger daughter Rachel." 19. Laban said *with deceit,*[17] "It is better that I give her to you than that I should give her to another man; dwell with me." 20. So Jacob served seven years for Rachel; and in his eyes they *seemed* like a few days, because he loved her. 21. Then Jacob said to Laban, "Give (me) my wife, for the days *of my service*[18] are completed, and I will go in unto her." 22. Laban gathered all the men of the place and made *them* a feast. *He spoke up and said*[19] *to them, "Behold, it is seven years since Jacob came among us; our wells have not failed, and our watering places have multiplied.*[20] *So now, come, let us plan a plan of deceit so that he may remain among us." And they gave him a counsel of deceit, to have him take Leah instead of Rachel.*[21] 23. So in the evening he took his daughter Leah and brought her in to him; and he went in unto her.

Notes, Chapter 29

[7]The same words ("order of blessings") occur in 27:41 (Ps.-J.).

[8]Lit.: "from his brother's hand."

[9]*PRE* 36 (270): "When Laban heard the tidings of Jacob, the son of his sister, and the power of his might which he had displayed at the well, he ran to meet him, . . ." Ps.-J. is the only Targum of this verse to list the marvelous things that happened to Jacob and the great things he did. On the rolling away of the stone and the miraculous waters, see above 28:10 and 29:10.

[10]= Onq.

[11]*dmy*; Le Déaut (1978, *Genèse*, 277) prefers the translation "like me."

[12]Lit.: "a month of days."

[13]Or "my brother." *PRE* 36 (270): ". . . the son of a man's sister is like his son."

[14]Or "discharging pus"; cf. Jastrow, 1281. Onq.: "lovely." HT describes Leah's eyes as "weak." Rabbinic tradition considered this a disparaging remark (see the texts referred to in the next note). Ps.-J.'s choice of the word "running" is not complimentary, but his explanation of Leah's defect is the same as that of Nfmg, P, V, N, L, and CTg E. See also LXX, which translates the Heb. word directly as *astheneis*, "weak," and Vulg.: *lippis oculis*, "blear-eyed." See Churgin, 1933–1934, 63; McNamara, 1966A, 54; Aberbach, 1969, 20.

[15]*Gen. R.* 70,16; *b. B. Bat.* 123a (510); *Tanh., Wa-Yeze* 4 (99).

[16]Onq.: "beautiful in figure and lovely in appearance." For a synoptic view of the different translations of "beautiful and lovely" (RSV) in the Targums and in Pesh., cf. Peters, 1935, 4.

[17]See v. 22.

[18]= Onq.

[19]Lit.: "He answered and said."

[20]The theme of the "merits of the Fathers" is implicit here. See also 26:26 above.

[21]*Gen. R.* 70,19 offers a close parallel to Ps.-J.'s addition to this verse.

24. And Laban gave *him*[22] Zilpah *his daughter, whom his concubine had borne to him, and he gave her*[23] to his daughter Leah as a maidservant. 25. At morning *time he looked at her,* and behold it was Leah! *During the whole night he had thought that she was Rachel, because Rachel had entrusted to her all the things that Jacob had entrusted to her.*[24] *When he saw this,* he said to Laban, "What is this you have done to me? Did I not serve you for Rachel? And why did you trick me?" 26. And Laban said, "Such is not done in our place[25]—to marry off[26] the younger before the elder. 27. Complete *then* the seven *days of* this one's *(marriage-)feast,* and we will give you that one also for the service you will render me for yet another seven years." 28. Jacob did so, and completed the seven *days of Leah's (marriage-)feast;* and (Laban) gave him Rachel his daughter as wife. 29. Laban gave Bilhah, *his daughter whom his concubine had borne to him,* to his daughter Rachel, *and he gave her* to her as a maidservant.[27] 30. And he went in unto Rachel also, and he loved Rachel more than Leah. And he served him for her yet another seven years. 31. *It was manifest before* the Lord that Leah was *not loved by*[28] *Jacob, and he decided through his Memra to give her children;* but Rachel was barren. 32. And Leah conceived and bore a son and called his name Reuben; for she said:[29] "Because my humiliation *was manifest before* the Lord, surely now my husband will love me. *And as my humiliation was manifest before the Lord, so shall the humiliation of my children be manifest before him when they shall be enslaved in the land of the Egyptians."*[30] 33. She conceived again and bore a son, and said, "Because *it was heard before* the Lord that I was hated, he gave me this one also. *And similarly, the voice of my children will be heard before him when they will be enslaved in Egypt."* And she called his name Simeon.[31] 34. And she conceived again and bore a son, and said, "This time my husband will be *united* to me because I have borne him three sons. *And*

Notes, Chapter 29

[22]In HT the feminine suffix (*lh,* "to her") refers to Leah. Pesh. and LXX change the word order of the sentence; cf. Geiger, 1928, 460.

[23]*PRE* 36 (271–272). See also below, v. 29 (Ps.-J.). The tradition that Bilhah and Zilpah were Laban's daughters by a concubine occurs in *Gen. R.* 74, 13. The tradition that Zilpah and Bilhah were sisters is recorded in *Jubilees* 28, 9.

[24]Ps.-J.'s explanation of how Jacob could have taken Leah for Rachel is taken from the Talmud. In *b. B. Bat.* 123a (511) we are told how Rachel suspected that Laban would try to marry off her older sister before her. Hearing this, Jacob gave certain identification signs to Rachel by which he would recognize her even in the dark. Rachel, however, feeling sympathy for Leah, gave the identification signs to the latter. Thus, when Leah presented Jacob with these signs in the bedroom, he was misled into believing that he was with Rachel. See also *b. Meg.* 13b (77-78). Ps.-J. gives an abbreviated version of this tradition, a version which is not at all clear unless one is familiar with the Talmudic tradition. See Shinan, 1979, 1, 166.

[25]Reading *b'trn* with Nfmg and CTg E rather than *b'tryn,* "in places," which is the reading in Lond. and *ed. pr.*

[26]Lit.: "to give."

[27]See v. 24 above and n. 23 to that verse.

[28]Lit.: "not loved in the face of"; = Nfmg, CTg E. Onq.: "hated." Cf. *b. B. Bat.* 123a (510–511); in v. 33 below, Nfmg and CTg E again avoid saying that Leah was hated.

[29]"For she said" is omitted in *ed. pr.*

[30]*Tanḥ., Shemoth* 3 (163): "All the tribes were named with reference to the (future) redemption of Israel; Reuben because of 'I have seen (*r'h r'yty*) the affliction (*'ny*) of my people' (Exod 3:7)." See also *Exod. R.* 1,5.

[31]*Tanḥ., Shemoth* 3 (163): "All the tribes were named with reference to the (future) redemption of Israel: . . . Simeon because of 'And God heard (*wyšm'*) their groaning' (Exod 2:24)." See also *Exod. R.* 1,5.

similarly, his children will be united to serve before the Lord." [32] Therefore his name was called Levi. [33] 35. And she conceived again and bore a son, and said, "This time I will give thanks *before* the Lord: *because from this my son there will come forth kings, and from him will come forth David the king who will give thanks before the Lord."* [34] Therefore she called his name Judah. And she ceased bearing.

CHAPTER 30

1. Rachel saw that she bore no children to Jacob, and Rachel became jealous of her sister. So she said to Jacob, *"Pray before the Lord* [1] *that he may* give me children; and if not, I shall be *reckoned as* dead." [2] 2. And Jacob became very angry [3] at Rachel, and he said, *"For how long will you beseech me? Beseech from before the Lord, for it is from before him that children (come), and it is he* who has withheld from you the fruit of the womb." 3. She said, "Behold my maidservant Bilhah; go in unto her; she will bear (a child whom) *I will rear* [4] and I too will have children [5] through her." 4. So *she set her maidservant* Bilhah *free* [6] for him and *handed her over* to him as wife, and Jacob went in unto her. 5. And Bilhah conceived and bore a son to Jacob. 6. Rachel said, *"The Lord* has done me justice *in his good mercies, and he has also heard the voice of my prayer* [7] and has given me a son. *Similarly, he is destined to judge through Samson, son of Manoah, who shall be (one) of his descendants, and to deliver into his hand the people of the Philistines."* [8] Therefore she

Notes, Chapter 29 (Cont.)

[32] *Gen. R.* 71,4 (Theodor-Albeck, 826): "He will escort (*'tyd llwt*) the children to their Father in Heaven." See also the texts from *Tanḥuma* and *Exod. R* referred to in the preceding note, and *Jubilees* 31,16.

[33] Lit.: "he called his name Levi"; = Nf, Onq.; CTg E: "she called."

[34] *Gen. R.* 71, 5.

Notes, Chapter 30

[1] Ps.-J. is the only Targum that introduces the theme of prayer into this verse. But see v. 2 (Nf, Nfmg, CTg E, Ps.-J.). The mention of prayer in this context is, without doubt, due to the influence of Gen 25:21. See *Gen. R.* 71,7 ("Did he [Isaac] not gird up his loins by her [Rebekah]?"), which links Gen 30:2 with 25:21.

[2] *Gen. R.* 71,6: "Four are regarded as dead: the leper, the blind, he who is childless, and he who has become impoverished"; cf. also *b. Ned.* 64b (206); *Abod. Zar.* 5a (21).

[3] Lit.: "Jacob's anger grew strong."

[4] = Onq. In Gen 50:23, where the same idiom—"(bear) on someone's knees"—occurs, Onq. interprets it as it does in our present verse. Compare Ps.-J.

[5] Lit.: "will be built up." See above 16:2 and n. 4 to that verse.

[6] See above 16:2, 3, 5 (Ps.-J.).

[7] Onq.: "accepted my prayer." Onq. and Ps.-J. take the biblical phrase "heard my voice" to refer to prayer. See also Gen 21:17b (Nf); Num 20:16 (Nf, Ps.-J., Onq.); 21:3 (Nf, Ps.-J., Onq.); Deut 1:45 (Ps.-J., Onq.); 26:7 (Nf, Nfmg, Ps.-J., Onq.); 33:7 (Nf, V, N, L, CTg DD, Ps.-J., Onq.)

[8] See below 49:16-17 (Nf, P, V, N, CTg Z, Ps.-J., Onq.).

called his name Dan. 7. Bilhah, Rachel's maidservant, conceived again and bore a second son to Jacob. 8. And Rachel said, *"I strove insistently[9] before the Lord in prayer*; but he accepted *my plea that I might have a son like* my sister. *He has even given me two. Similarly, his children will be redeemed from the hand of their enemies when they strive in prayer before the Lord."*[10] And she called his name Naphtali. 9. When Leah saw that she had ceased bearing children, she *set* her maidservant Zilpah *free*[11] and gave her to Jacob as wife. 10. Leah's maidservant Zilpah bore Jacob a son. 11. Leah said, *"Good* fortune[12] *has come; surely his sons will take possession of their inheritance in the east, beyond the Jordan."*[13] And she called his name Gad. 12. Leah's maidservant Zilpah bore Jacob a second son. 13. And Leah said, *"This has brought me praise,*[14] for the daughters *of Israel (will) praise*[15] me. *Similarly, his sons will praise before the Lord for the goodness of the fruit of their land."*[16] And she called his name Asher. 14. In the days of *Sivan,*[17] *at the time of* the wheat harvest, Reuben went and found mandrakes in the field, and brought them to his mother Leah. And Rachel said to Leah, "Give me, I pray, some of your son's mandrakes." 15. And she said to her, "Is it a small matter that you have taken my husband; and *you wish to* take my son's mandrakes also?" Rachel said, "Then let him lie with you tonight in exchange for your son's mandrakes." 16. When Jacob came in from the field in the evening, *Leah heard the sound of the braying of the donkey, and she knew that Jacob had come.*[18] Leah went out to meet him and said, "You are to come in unto me, for I have hired you from *my sister Rachel* with my son's mandrakes." And he lay with her that night. 17. *The Lord accepted* Leah's *prayer,* and she conceived and bore a fifth son to Jacob. 18. And Leah said, *"The Lord* gave (me) my reward, because I gave my maidservant to my husband. *Similarly, his sons are destined to receive a good reward, because they will be occupied in (the study of) the Law."*[19] And she called his name Issachar. 19. And Leah conceived again and bore a sixth son to Jacob. 20. And Leah said, *"The Lord* has pre-

---

Notes, Chapter 30

[9]Or: "pressed insistently." The Targums (Nf, CTg E, Ps.-J., Onq.) associate the Heb. phrase *nptwly 'lhym nptlty,* "with mighty wrestlings I have wrestled," with *tephillah,* "prayer." By using the verb *dḥq,* "press, push," Ps.-J. retains something of the idea of wrestling which we find in the original Hebrew. All the Targumic renderings of this verse avoid saying that Rachel and her sister engaged in unseemly rivalry.

[10]"Similarly . . . before the Lord": the redemption referred to may be the victory of Deborah (cf. Judg 4–5), who was regarded as a descendant of Naphtali; cf. *Gen. R.* 98,17. There is no source in rabbinic literature for Ps.-J.'s haggadic addition; cf. Schmerler, 1932, 227–228.

[11]See v. 4 (Ps.-J.).

[12]*mzl'* = Nfmg. By using this word to translate HT "good fortune" (RSV), these Targums lose the play on the name Gad. See further Grossfeld, 1988, 109, n. 5.

[13]See the Targums of Gen 49:19.

[14]Lit.: "I have had praise"; = Onq.

[15]The Targums associate Heb. *b'šry . . . 'šrwny,* "Happy am I . . . will call me happy" (RSV), with "praise"; cf. Aberbach-Grossfeld, 1982, 179, n. 5; Grossfeld, 1988, 109, n. 6.

[16]See below, 49:20.

[17]Only Ps.-J. adds the name *Sivan,* the post-exilic name for the month in which the Harvest Feast (cf. Exod 23:16) took place. See also above, Gen 8:22, where Ps.-J. names the seasons.

[18]*Gen. R.* 99,10; cf. *b. Nid.* 31a (216).

[19]See below 49:14 (Ps.-J.). Cf. *Gen. R.* 72:5.

sented me with good presents *in (my) children*. This time my husband will cohabit with me, [20] because I have borne him six sons. *Similarly, his children are destined to receive a good portion.*" [21] And she called his name Zebulun. 21. And afterwards she bore a daughter, and called her name Dinah; *for she said, "It was decreed from before the Lord that half the tribes would be from me. But from my sister Rachel two tribes shall go forth, just as (two tribes) went forth from each of the maidservants." And Leah's prayer was heard before the Lord, and the embryos were exchanged in their wombs; Joseph was placed in Rachel's womb, and Dinah in the womb of Leah.* [22] 22. Now the remembrance of Rachel came *before the Lord, and the voice of her prayer was heard before him, and he decided through his Memra to give her children.* [23] 23. She conceived and bore a son, and said, "*The Lord* has taken away my disgrace. *Similarly, Joshua the son of Joseph is destined to take away the disgrace of Egypt from the children of Israel, and to circumcise them beyond the Jordan.*" [24] 24. And she called his name Joseph, saying, "May the Lord add another son *to this one* for me. 25. When Rachel had borne Joseph, Jacob said *in the Holy Spirit: "Those of the house of Joseph are destined to be like a flame to destroy those of the house of Esau." He said, "From now on I will not be afraid of Esau and his legions.*" [25] *And he said* to Laban, "Send me away that I may go to my place and to my country. 26. Give *me* my wives and my children for whom I have served you, and I will go; for you know the service I have rendered you." 27. But Laban said to him, "If, I pray, I have found *mercy* in your eyes, behold I have learned by divination that [26] the Lord has blessed me because of you." 28. And he said, "Designate your wages to me, and I will give (them to you)." 29. He said to him, "You know how I have served you, and how your livestock has been *kept* with me. 30. For the little *flock* you had before I came [27] has increased greatly, and the Lord has blessed you wherever I went, [28] *because I have brought you profit since I came into your house. And now, when shall I too do (my) work, since I am obliged to provide for the*

Notes, Chapter 30

[20]Lit.: "the habitation of my husband will be with me"; = Onq. Cf. Aberbach-Grossfeld, 1982, 181, n. 9; Grossfeld, 1988, 109, n. 7.

[21]See *Exod. R.* 1,5.

[22]*b. Berak.* 60a (374); *j. Berak.* 9, 14a–b; *Gen. R.* 72,6. This bizarre miracle was performed because Leah wanted Rachel to have two sons so that she would not be inferior to the two maidservants, who had two sons each.

[23]See above, 29:31, where the same biblical idiom ("he opened her womb") is translated in the same way. The long midrash on the "four keys" which Nf, Nfmg, P, V, and N insert at the beginning of this verse is placed at the beginning of Deut 28:12 by Ps.-J.

[24]Cf. Josh 5:2-9, where the word "disgrace" or "reproach" occurs in v. 9.

[25]*b. B. Bat.* 123b (512); *Gen. R.* 73,7; 75,5. This tradition is based on Obad 18, a text which is quoted in the passage from *B. Bat.* just referred to. That this is an old tradition is indicated by the fact that the two texts from *Gen. R.* just referred to introduce it with the words "It is a tradition." Cf. Ginzberg, *Legends,* 1,369; 5, 300, n. 203.

[26]Lit.: "I have observed divinations, and, . . ." Nf and Onq. use the verb *nsy,* which has the basic meaning of "test." These latter Targums thus avoid saying that Laban practiced divination. Cf. Churgin, 1933–34, 63; Díez Macho, *Neophyti 1,* III, 47*–48*.

[27]Lit.: "before me."

[28]Lit.: "at my foot (*brygly,*" which is almost a direct rendering of Heb. *lrgly.* Onq.: "on my account."

members of my household?"[29] 31. And he said, "What shall I give you?" And Jacob said, "Give me nothing *else*! If you do this thing for me, I will again pasture your flock and keep (it): 32. I will go through your whole flock today, and I will remove from there every speckled and spotted lamb, and every reddish lamb among the lambs, and the spotted and the speckled among the goats, and (they) shall be my wages. 33. Let my *merit* testify for me in future when you come[30] concerning my wages: whatever is not speckled and spotted among the goats, and reddish among the lambs, will be (considered) stolen by me.[31] 34. And Laban said, "Good! *Would that* it may be according to your word!"[32] 35. That day he separated the he-goats *that had a mark on their legs,* or were spotted, and all the speckled and spotted she-goats, every one that had a white *spot* on it, and every one that was reddish among the lambs, and he gave them into his sons' hands. 36. Then he put a three days' journey between *his flock* and Jacob; and Jacob was pasturing Laban's flock, *the old and the sick* that were left.[33] 37. Jacob took rods[34] of white poplar,[35] of almond, and of *laurel,* and peeled white stripes in them to expose the white of the rods. 38. He stuck the rods which he had peeled in the troughs, in the watering places, *(at)* the place where the flocks used to come to drink. *He placed them* in front of the flocks; and they used to mate when they came to drink. 39. And the flocks mated in front of the rods; and the flocks brought forth young (that were) streaked,[36] *that had a mark on their legs,* (that were) spotted, and *had white backs.* 40. And Jacob set the lambs[37] apart, and put at the head of the flock, *as leaders of the flock,*[38] all that were streaked, and all that were reddish in Laban's flock. Thus he produced flocks for himself alone, and he did not mix them with Laban's flock. 41. And whenever the *early-breeding* flock mated, Jacob would place the rods in the troughs before the eyes of the flock, so that they would mate *facing* the rods. 42. But for the

Notes, Chapter 30

[29]*Gen. R.* 73,8.

[30]Lit.: "when you are."

[31]Lit.: "to be mine."

[32]Cf. *Gen. R.* 73,9. The midrash took it that Laban, who was a deceiver, suspected Jacob of trying to deceive him; cf. Ginzberg, *Legends,* 1, 370; 5, 300, n. 208.

[33]*Gen. R.* 73,9. Since the Heb. plural *nwtrt,* lit., "that remained," is written *defective,* the midrash concludes that the animals were defective.

[34]Lit.: "the rod."

[35]Jastrow, 690 and 1223. We might also render the Aramaic phrase as "a rod that was blooming white"; cf. Levy, 1, 401.

[36]The word used here (*rgwl*) means "streaked at the leg" (Jastrow, 1447); cf. Levy (2, 406): "was am Fusse (oder am Schenkel) gefleckt, gezeichnet ist." It occurs in Onq. in vv. 35, 39, 40 and 31:8. Ps.-J. adds "that had a mark on their legs," which seems to be a second translation of the underlying Hebrew *'qdym,* "striped" (RSV). See v. 40, where Ps.-J. translates the same Heb. word by *rgwl,* "streaked," and in 31:8 it is twice rendered by "(that which) has a spot on its legs"; see also 31:10,12.

[37]This is one of the rare places where *tly'* is used with the meaning "lamb." It usually means "boy" or "servant"; cf. Le Déaut, *Genèse,* 1978, 290, n. 15; Cook, 1986, 239.

[38]The word used here (*mškwkyt'*) is explained in *b. B. Qam.* 52a (301) as "the goat that leads the herd." Ps.-J. may have read the Heb. preposition *'l* as *'yl,* "ram"; cf. Levy, 2, 77.

late-breeding[39] flock he did not place them; and the *late-breeding* ones became Laban's, and the *early-breeding* ones Jacob's. 43. And the man grew exceedingly powerful, and had numerous flocks, and maidservants and menservants, and camels and asses.

CHAPTER 31

1. He heard the words of Laban's sons, *who* were saying, "Jacob has taken all that was our father's; and from what was our father's he has made for himself all this mass *of possessions.*" 2. And Jacob saw *the expression of*[1] Laban's face, and behold, it was not *friendly* towards him as it had been yesterday *and before that.* 3. The Lord said to Jacob, "Return to the land of your fathers and to your native country, and *my Memra will be at your assistance.*"[2] 4. And Jacob sent *Naphtali, who was a swift messenger,*[3] to call Rachel and Leah, *and they came* to the field to his flock. 5. And he said to them, "I see *the expression of* your father's face, and behold, it is not friendly towards me as it had been yesterday *and before that.* But *the Memra* of the God of my father has been *at my assistance.*[2] 6. You know that I served your father with all my strength. 7. But your father deceived me and changed my wages ten *parts,*[4] but *the Lord* did not give him *power* to harm me. 8. If he said thus: 'The spotted shall be your wages,' then all the flock bore spotted (young). And if he said thus: 'Those that *have a spot on their legs* shall be your wages,' then all the flock bore (young) *that had a spot on their legs.* 9. Thus *the Lord* has taken away[5] your father's livestock and given (it) to me. 10. And when the flocks mated, I lifted up my eyes and saw in a dream that the he-goats mounting the flock had *a spot on their*

Notes, Chapter 30 (Cont.)

[39]The word used (*lqyš*) means "late," and in the context might mean either "late-breeding" or "late-born." Nf, Nfmg, CTg E, Onq., and Pesh. use the same word (in different forms). *Gen. R.* 73,10 (Theodor-Albeck, 855), in a comment on our present verse, employs the same word, as well as the contrasting word *bkyr,* "early-breeding," which occurs later in our present verse in Ps.-J.

Notes, Chapter 31

[1]On this idiom, which also occurs in Onq., see Grossfeld, 1988, 111, n. 2.

[2]See above, 26:2 and n. 2 to that verse.

[3]See Gen 49:21 (Nf, P, V, N, Ps.-J.); cf. 50:13 (Ps.-J.). In Gen 49:21, where the biblical text mentions Naphtali and compares him to a hind, all the Pal. Tgs. refer to him as a swift messenger. Ps.-J. is alone in taking up this theme in our present verse and in 50:13. There is no source in rabbinic tradition for Ps.-J.'s assertion in our present verse that Naphtali was the one who was sent to call Rachel and Leah; cf. Schmerler, 1932, 236.

[4]Nf, CTg E, Onq., Pesh., and Vulg., like modern translators, take the unusual *mnym* (*mônim*) to mean "times"; cf. also v. 41. Ps.-J. seems to have taken *mnym* to be the plural of *mnh,* "share, portion," although the plural of that word would really be *mnwt.* Cf. Geiger, 1928, 460.

[5]Lit.: "emptied"; = Nf, P, V, N, CTg E; Onq.: "set aside." See also v. 16 (CTg E, Ps.-J.) and Exod 3:22; 12:36 (Nf, Ps.-J., Onq.); 33:6 (Nfmg 1 and 2, P, Ps.-J.), where the same Heb. verb (*nṣl*) is translated by the same Aramaic verb (*rwqn*).

legs, were spotted, and *had white backs.* 11. And the angel of *the Lord* said to me in a dream, 'Jacob!' And I said, 'Here I am.' 12. And he said, 'Lift up your eyes, I pray, and see: All the he-goats mounting the flock have *a spot on their legs,* are spotted, and have *white backs,* because all the (*acts of*) *robbery* that Laban has committed against you *are manifest before me.* 13. I am the God *who was revealed to you at* Bethel,[6] where you anointed a pillar, where you *swore an oath before* me. Now arise, go forth from this land and return to the land of your birth.' " 14. And Rachel answered *with the consent of Leah,*[7] and they said to him, "*Is it possible that* we still have a portion and an inheritance in our father's house? 15. Have we not been considered strangers by him, for he has sold us and has even consumed our money? 16. All the wealth which *the Lord* has taken away[8] from our father belongs to us and to our children: and now do all that *the Lord* has told you." 17. Then Jacob arose and put[9] his children and his wives upon the camels. 18. He drove off all the cattle and all the riches he had acquired—the livestock *and* the riches he had acquired in Paddan *of* Aram to go to his father Isaac, to the land of Canaan. 19. When Laban had gone to shear his flock, Rachel stole[10] the *images. For they would slay a man a first-born, cut off his head and sprinkle it with salt and spices. They would write magical formulas on a plate of gold and put it under its tongue. Then they would set it up on the wall, and it would speak to them.*[11] *And it was to these* (idols) *that* her father bent down. 20. Jacob deceived[12] Laban the Aramean by not telling him that he was *going away.*[13] 21. And he *went* with all he had. He arose and crossed *the Euphrates,*[14] and set his face to *go up* to the mountain of Gilead; *for he saw in the Holy Spirit that his children would experience liberation there in the days of Jephthah, who was from Gilead.*[15] 22. *When Jacob had gone, the shepherds stood by*

Notes, Chapter 31

[6]= Onq.; cf. LXX. The Hebrew might be read as "I am the God Bethel," which would be intolerable for the *meturgeman.* Furthermore, the syntax of HT is awkward without the addition of a phrase like that which we find in the Targums and in LXX. Cf. Aberbach-Grossfeld, 1982, 186, n. 9; Grossfeld, 1988, 111, n. 9.

[7]HT has the verb in the singular even though Rachel and Leah are in question. Ps.-J. explains this by saying that Leah agreed with what Rachel said. See also Num 32:25, where Ps.-J. adds a similar idiom, "in agreement," "with one accord," in the same kind of situation. In our present verse Ps.-J. also gives us to understand that since Rachel spoke with the consent of Leah, she did not act improperly by speaking before the latter, who was her older sister (cf. Gen 29:16). See *Gen. R.* 74,4.

[8]Lit.: "emptied"; = CTg E. See above, v. 9 and n. 5 to that verse.

[9]Lit.: "carried."

[10]Onq.: "took." Cf. Aberbach-Grossfeld, 1982, 187, n. 12; Grossfeld, 1988, 112, n. 12. Although Ps.-J. states that Rachel stole the images, he goes on to explain that by doing so she was saving her father from a particularly crude form of idolatry.

[11]*Tanh., Wa-Yeze* 12 (104); *PRE* 36 (273–274); *Sefer Ha-Yashar* 31 (88).

[12]Lit.: "stole the mind of"; = Nf, CTg E. Onq.: "concealed from." See also below, vv. 26 and 27. Cf. Grossfeld, 1988, 113, n. 14.

[13]= Onq. Onq. and Ps.-J. (cf. Nfmg, CTg E), out of respect for the ancestors, avoid saying bluntly that Jacob fled; cf. also vv. 21 and 27, and see above 27:43.

[14]= Onq. See above, 24:10.

[15]The mention of Gilead in HT prompts Ps.-J. to anticipate events and to refer to the future liberation that would be effected by Jephtah the Gileadite (see Judg 11). See above, 25:29 and n. 38 to that verse. There is no known source for Ps.-J.'s addition to our present verse; cf. Schmerler, 1932, 239.

the well but found no water. And they waited three days (to see) if perhaps it might flow. But it did not flow. Therefore Laban was told on the third day, *and he knew that* Jacob had fled, *because it was through his merits that it had flowed for twenty years.*[16] 23. He took his *relatives* with him and pursued him a distance of seven days. And he overtook him *while he camped* on the mountain of Gilead, *giving thanks and praying before his God.*[17] 24. *An angel* came *by a decree from before the Lord and drew the sword*[18] *against* Laban *the deceitful*[19] in a dream of the night. And he said to him, "Take care lest you speak to Jacob either good or bad." 25. Laban overtook Jacob. Jacob had pitched his tent on the mountain, and Laban made his kinsmen encamp[20] at *that same* mountain of Gilead. 26. And Laban said to Jacob. "What have you done? You have deceived me and led away my daughters like captives of the sword. 27. Why did you *go away*[21] secretly and deceive me, and not tell me? *For if you had told me,* I would *surely* have sent you away with rejoicing, with (songs of) praise,[22] with timbrels and with lyres. 28. You did not wait for me to kiss my *daughter's* children and my daughters. Now, you have acted foolishly (in doing) what you have done. 29. I have the means[23] to do you harm; but yesterday evening the God of your father spoke to me, saying, 'Take heed that you speak to Jacob neither good nor bad.' 30. And now, you have gone away because you greatly desired your father's house. (But) why did you steal the *images of my idols?*"[24] 31. Jacob replied and said to Laban, "Because I was afraid and said that you might take your daughters from me by force. 32. *Anyone* with[25] whom you find *the images of your idols shall die before his time.*[26] In the presence of all your brothers, identify what I have *that belongs to you,* and take (it)." Now Jacob did not know that Rachel had stolen them. 33. And Laban went into Jacob's tent and into Leah's tent and into the tents of the two *concubines*; but he did not find (them). So he came out of Leah's tent and entered Rachel's tent. 34. Now Rachel had taken the *images* and placed them in the camel's saddle and sat on them. And <Laban>[27] searched about the tent but did not find (them). 35. And she said <to her

Notes, Chapter 31

[16]On the tradition about the well that flowed up during Jacob's stay in Paddan Aram, see above, 28:10 and n. 12 to that verse. The haggadah in our present verse is known only from the Targums of this verse; cf. Schmerler, 1932, 239; Shinan, 1979, 1, 68. This haggadah explains how it came about that Laban did not get to know about Jacob's flight for three days.

[17]Ps.-J. seems to presume that Laban overtook Jacob in the evening, and that Jacob, the one who instituted evening prayer (see above 28:11 [Ps.-J.] and n. 14 to that verse), would have prayed in the evening; cf. Schmerler, 1932, 239–240.

[18]PRE 36 (273). PRE calls the angel Michael.

[19]See above, 29:12 and n. 6 to that verse. Gen. R. 75,5 calls Laban "the prince of all cheats."

[20]= Onq.

[21]= Onq. See above v. 20 and n. 13 to that verse.

[22]= Onq.; cf. Aberbach-Grossfeld, 1982, 189, n. 23; Grossfeld, 1988, 113, n. 19.

[23]Onq.: "I have power (lit.: "strength in my hands"). Onq. uses this same idiom in Deut 28:32, where the same Heb. formula (yš ['yn] l'l yd) is used. The Heb. idiom occurs also in Neh 5:5; Prov 3:27; Micah 2:1, and we also find it in the Talmud; cf., e.g., b. Qidd. 30b (148) and 35a (170).

[24]Onq.: "my deities (dḥlty)." When Heb. 'lhym (elohim) refers to idols or pagan gods, the Targums usually translate it as "deities" (dḥln) or "idols" (t'wwt'). In our present verse and in v. 32, where the reference is to Laban's gods, Onq. uses the term "deities." The other Targums differ somewhat in their translations. Cf. Grossfeld, 1988, 113, n. 20.

[25]In Lond. the word for "with" occurs as a lemma, but it is omitted in the translation of the verse.

[26]PRE 36 (274).

[27]Omitted in Lond. and ed. pr.

father>:[27] "Let not my lord be angry that *it is* not *possible* (for me) to rise before you, because I have the period of women." And he searched but did not find the *images*. 36. Jacob became very angry and argued with Laban. And Jacob replied and said to Laban, "What is my sin, *and* what is my offense, that you *were in such a hurry to come* after me? 37. Although you have searched through all my things, what have you found[28] of all your household things? *Now* present *your case* before my kinsmen and your kinsmen, and let them judge *justly* between the two of us. 38. These twenty years I have been with you; your ewes and your she-goats have not miscarried, nor have I eaten *the price* of the rams of your flock. 39. What was torn *by the beasts of the field*[29] I did not bring to you; *for if I had sinned in this,*[30] you would have demanded it of me. What[31] was stolen in the daytime *by men I had to make good;* and what was stolen at night *by the beasts of the field I had to make good.* 40. I was *in the field* by day and the heat consumed me, and the frost at night; and sleep fled from *me.* 41. These twenty years I have been in your house; I have served you fourteen years because of your two daughters, and six years because of your flock, and you have changed my wages ten *parts.*[32] 42. If the God of my father, the God of Abraham, and *he whom* Isaac *fears*[33] had not been *at my assistance,* you would now have sent me away empty-handed. My misery and the labor of my hands *were manifest before the Lord; therefore* he rebuked (you) yesterday evening." 43. And Laban replied and said to Jacob, "The daughters *whom you took as wives* are my daughters, and the children *they have borne are regarded as* my children,[34] and the flock *comes from* my flocks, and all that you see *comes from* what is mine. But what *can* I do to these daughters of mine today, or to the children they have borne? 44. So come now, let us make a covenant, you and I, and let it be a witness between me and you." 45. So Jacob took a stone and set it up as a pillar. 46. And Jacob said to *his sons whom he used to call* his brothers,[35] "Gather stones." And they *gathered* stones and made a heap; and they ate there upon the heap. 47. And Laban called it *Ogar Sahid;*[36] and Jacob called it *in the language of the Sanctuary*[37] Galeed.[38] 48.[39] And Laban said, "This heap is a witness between you and me this

Notes, Chapter 31

[28]Omitted in Lond.

[29]*Gen. R.* 74,11 explains that Heb. *ṭrph,* "that which was torn," means "killed (by wild beasts)."

[30]Ps.-J. renders Heb. *'ḥṭnh,* "I bore the loss of it" (RSV), as if it were derived from the root *ḥṭ',* "sin."

[31]The rest of this verse reads as follows in Onq.: "*I was on guard* by day and *I was on guard* by night." The Targums make it clear that Jacob was extremely diligent in his duties as a shepherd; cf. Geiger, 1928, 460-462; Aberbach-Grossfeld, 1982, 190-191, nn. 30-31; Grossfeld, 1988, 115, nn. 26-27.

[32]See above, v. 7 and n. 4.

[33]= Onq. The Targums avoid a direct translation of the obscure title "the Fear of Isaac." They make it clear that Isaac was a worshiper of the true God. See also v. 53.

[34]*b. Yeb.* 62b (416); *PRE* 36 (270–271).

[35]*Gen. R.* 74,13; *PRE* 36 (279); *Tanḥ., Wa-Yishlaḥ* 4 (107).

[36]= "Stone-heap of Witness."

[37]*j. Soṭah* 7,21c. On the idiom "the language of the Sanctuary," see above 11:1 and n. 2 to that verse.

[38]= *Ed. pr.;* Lond.: *gyl'd,* "Gilead." Heb. Galeed has the same meaning as the Aramaic Ogar Sahid, which occurs earlier in the verse (see n. 36). Since Laban is identified with Balaam (see Ps.-J. Num 22:5; 31:8), it is not surprising that the covenant described in vv. 44ff. in our present chapter is referred to in Ps.-J. Num 22:24.

[39]V. 48 is omitted in *ed. pr.*

day." Therefore he called its name Galeed. 49. And *it was called Sakutha,* [40] because he said, "May the Lord watch between me and you, when we are hidden from each other. 50. If you afflict my daughters *and humiliate them,* and if you take <wives> besides my daughters, (although) there is no one *to judge* us, see, *the Memra of the Lord* is a witness between me and you." 51. And Laban said to Jacob, "Behold this heap, and behold the pillar which I have erected between me and you. 52. This heap is a witness, and the pillar is a witness, that I will not pass beyond this heap to you, and that you will not pass beyond this heap and this pillar to me, to do evil. 53. May the God of Abraham and the God [41] of Nahor judge between us [42]—the God of their father." And Jacob swore by *the God whom* his father Isaac *feared.* [43] 54. Then Jacob offered a sacrifice on the mountain and invited his *relatives who had come with Laban* to share a meal; and they shared a meal [44] and passed the night on the mountain.

CHAPTER 32

1. Laban rose early in the morning and kissed *Jacob's* children and his *own* daughters, and blessed them. Then Laban departed and returned home. 2. Jacob went on his way, and the angels of *the Lord* met him. 3. When Jacob saw them he said, "*These are not the camps* [1] *of Esau that are coming to meet me, and neither are they the camps of Laban that are pursuing me again;* [2] but they are the camps of *the holy angels who have been sent from before the Lord.*" [3] Therefore he called the name of that place, *in the language of the Sanctuary,* [4] Mahanaim. 4. Jacob sent messengers before him to Esau his brother to the land of *Gabla,* [5] to the territory of

Notes, Chapter 31 (Cont.)

[40] = "Watchpost." Aramaic *Sakutha* has the same meaning as the underlying Heb. *Mizpah.*

[41] Although the reference is to a pagan deity (cf. *Gen. R.* 74,16), the Targums translate Heb. *'lhy* literally; see above v. 30 and n. 24 to that verse.

[42] "Between us" is written twice in Lond., first in the form *bynn* (cf. Nf, CTg E: *bynynn*), and then in the form *bynn'* (*ed. pr.*), which is the reading in Onq.

[43] Onq.: "by *him whom his father feared.*" See above, v. 42 and n. 33 to that verse.

[44] Lit.: "to eat bread; and they ate bread" (*lms'wd lḥm' ws'dw lḥm'*). Nf and Onq. use the verb *'kl* rather than *s'd.* See also 43:25, where Ps.-J. again uses the idiom *s'd lḥm.* In this latter verse Nf, CTg E, and Onq. employ *'kl lḥm.* See also above, 18:5, where Ps.-J. uses the idiom *s'yd dlḥym,* which we translated as "a morsel of bread."

Notes, Chapter 32

[1] The plural "camps" (see also Nf, P, V, N) is based on the fact that the place-name Mahanaim in HT is dual in form and means "two camps."

[2] We know of no source for this addition; cf. Shinan, 1979, 1, 154. We may note that we have not been told how Esau would have known of Jacob's return (see vv. 4-6).

[3] *Gen. R.* 74,17; *Tanḥ.* B., *Wa-Yishlaḥ* 3 (1, 163).

[4] On this phrase see above, 11:1 and n. 2 to that verse.

[5] See above, 14:6 and n. 19 to that verse.

the Edomites. 5. And he commanded them, saying, "Thus shall you say to my master Esau: 'Thus says your servant Jacob: I have sojourned with Laban, and I have tarried until now. 6. *And of all those things with which my father blessed me I have nothing;*[6] I have *but a few* oxen and asses, sheep and menservants and maidservants, and I have sent to tell my master *that that blessing has not profited me,* and so that I might find mercy in your eyes, *that you might not bear a grudge against me because of it.*' " 7. The messengers returned to Jacob, saying, "We came to your brother Esau. He himself is coming to meet you, and there are four hundred *warriors*[7] with him." 8. And Jacob was greatly afraid, *because for twenty years he had not been concerned with the honor of his father;*[8] and he was distressed; and he divided the people who were with him and the sheep and oxen and camels into two camps, *as a present for Leah and as a present for Rachel.*[9] 9. And he said, "If Esau comes to the camp *of one of them* and smites it, the camp that remains will escape." 10. And Jacob said, "O God of my father Abraham, You *who are*[10] (also) the God of my father Isaac, O Lord, who said to me, 'Return to your land and to your native country, and I will do you good.' 11. *I am not worthy,*[11] and I am too little for all the benefits and all the fidelity which you have shown your servant. For with my staff *alone* I crossed this Jordan, and now I have become two camps. 12. Deliver me now from the hand of my *older* brother, from the hand of Esau, for I am afraid of him—*for he has been concerned with the honor of his father*[12]—lest he come and smite us,[13] the mother with the children. 13. But you have *assured me,* 'I will surely do you good, and I will make your *children* as numerous as the sand of the sea that cannot be numbered for multitude.' " 14. He passed that night there, and from *what happened to be* at hand he took a gift for his brother Esau: 15. Two hundred she-goats and twenty he-goats, two hundred ewes and twenty rams; 16. the *female* camels with their young *were* thirty; forty cows and ten bulls, twenty she-asses and ten *Libyan asses.*[14] 17. He *arranged* (them) in the hands of his servants, each herd separately, and he said to his servants, "Pass on ahead of me, and leave a distance between one herd and the other." 18. Then he commanded the first, saying, "When my brother Esau meets you and asks you, saying, 'To whom do you belong? Where are you traveling to? And whose (herds) are these before you?' 19. you shall say, 'To

Notes, Chapter 32

[6]*Tanḥ.* B., *Wa-Yishlaḥ* 5 (1, 164). It is to be noted that Ps.-J.'s additions to this verse change the meaning of the biblical text completely.

[7]Or: "commanders," *gwbryn pwlwmrkyn*; Gr.: *polemarchos.* Cf. *Gen. R.* 75,12.

[8]*Gen. R.* 76,2; cf. *b. Meg.* 16b–17a (101–102). Jacob was afraid that Esau, who had acquired merit by serving his father, might now prevail over his returning brother; cf. v. 12 (Ps.-J.), and Deut 2:5 (Ps.-J.). See also Gen 15:1 (Nf, Nfmg, P, V, N, L, CTg H, Ps.-J.), where the question of the merits acquired through good deeds is raised in a similar manner.

[9]We know of no source in traditional rabbinic literature for this addition. But see the late (12th century) midrashic commentary *Sekel Tob* on Genesis, in a commentary on our present verse.

[10]Lit.: "he is."

[11]Lit.: "I am not enough" (*lyt 'n' kmyst*); cf. *Gen. R.* 76:5.

[12]See above v. 8 and n. 8.

[13]Lit.: "me"; = HT.

[14]Or perhaps simply "asses." The reference is to the kind of ass (*lwbdqym, lwbdqys*) discussed in *m. Kilayim* 8,4; *Shabb.* 5,1; cf. Jastrow, 705; Le Déaut, *Genèse,* 1978, 306, n. 5.

your servant Jacob; it a gift that has been sent to my master Esau; and behold he too *is coming* after us.' " 20. He also commanded the second and the third and all who were following the herds, saying, "Thus shall you speak with Esau when you reach him. 21. And you shall say, 'Moreover, behold, your servant Jacob is *coming* behind us.' " For he said, "I will appease him with the present that goes before me, and afterwards I will see his face. Oh that he would show me favor!" 22. So the gift passed on ahead of him, but he himself passed that night in the camp. 23. He arose that night and took his two wives, his two *concubines,* and his eleven children and crossed the ford of the Jabbok. 24. He took them and sent them across the stream, and he sent what belonged to him across. 25. Jacob was left alone *beyond the Jabbok.* And *an angel in the form of* a man wrestled with him. [15] *And he said, "Did you not promise to tithe all that would be yours?[16] Now behold, you have twelve sons and one daughter, and you have not tithed them." Immediately he set aside the four first-born of the four mothers,[17] and there remained eight. And he began to count from Simeon, and Levi happened to be the tenth. Michael[18] spoke up and said, "Master of the world, this one is your lot." It was on account of these things that he tarried beyond the stream* until *the column of* the dawn rose. 26. When he saw that he had no power to *harm him,* he touched the socket of his hip, and he *dislocated*[19] the socket of Jacob's hip when he wrestled with him. 27. And he said, "Let me go, for *the column of* the dawn has risen, *and the hour has come when the angels on high praise the Lord of the world,[20] and I am one of the angels who praise; but from the day that the world was created my time to praise did not come until this time.*[21] And he said, "I will not let you go unless you bless me." 28. And he said to him, "What is your name?" And he said,[22] "Jacob." 29. He said, "Your name shall no longer be called[23] Jacob but Israel, because you have *gained superiority* over *the angels of the Lord*[24] and over men, and you have prevailed *against them."* 30. Jacob asked and said, "Tell me your name, I pray. And he said, "Why do you ask my name?" And *Jacob*[25] blessed him there. 31. Jacob called the name of the place

Notes, Chapter 32

[15]*Gen. R.* 77,3; 78,3; cf. vv. 27 (Nf, P, V, N, CTg C, Ps.-J.) and 33 (Ps.-J.), where we learn that it was an angel that struggled with Jacob.

[16]Gen 28:22. Cf. *Gen. R.* 70,7; *PRE* 37 (283); *Jubilees* 32:1-3. Splansky (1981, 46–47) believes that Ps.-J.'s midrashic addition to our present verse depends on *PRE.*

[17]Since the first-born are already consecrated, they are not considered in the reckoning of the tithe; cf. *Gen. R.* 70,7; *b. Bek.* 53b (366–367).

[18]*PRE* 37 (284) also mentions Michael in the context of the choice of Levi. The angel Michael is mentioned again in Tg. Gen 38:25 (Nf, P, V, N, L, CTg D); Exod 24:1 (Ps.-J.); Deut 32:9 (Ps.-J.); 34:3, 6 (Ps.-J.).

[19]Lit.: "moved, shook." Ps.-J. and Onq. use different forms of the same verb, *zw'*, "shake, move."

[20]*Gen. R.* 78,2; *b. Hul.* 91b (513); *PRE* 37 (281–282); *LAB* 18,6. The praises of the angels are mentioned in several Targumic passages; see above, 27:1 and n. 2 to that verse. On the title "Lord of the world," see above, 14:13 and n. 28 to that verse.

[21]*b. Hul.* 91b (513).

[22]Lond. adds "to him."

[23]Lit.: "said;" = Nfmg, Onq., HT.

[24]*Gen. R.* 78,3. Onq.: "for you are a prince before the Lord." All the Targums avoid the anthropomorphic idea that Jacob actually strove with God.

[25]By adding the name Jacob, Ps.-J. reverses the meaning of the final clause of this verse.

Peniel, because *he said,* "I have seen *the angels of the Lord* face to face, and my life has been saved." 32. The sun, *which had set before its time for his sake when he was going out from Beer-sheba,*[26] rose for him *before its time*[27] as he passed Penuel. And *he began to walk,* and he was limping on his hip. 33. Therefore, to this day the children of Israel do not eat the sinew of the hip that is on the socket of the hip *of cattle and of wild animals,*[28] because the *angel* touched *and held* the socket of Jacob's *right*[29] hip, in the place of the sinew of the hip.

CHAPTER 33

1. Jacob lifted up his eyes and saw, and behold, Esau was coming, and four hundred *warriors*[1] with him. So he divided the children between Leah, Rachel, and the two *concubines.*[2] 2. He placed the *concubines* in front, *they* and their children. *For he said, "If Esau comes to slaughter the young men and to abuse the women, he will do it with these, and meanwhile I will arise and make war against him."*[3] Then (he placed) Leah and her young men next, and Rachel and Joseph last. 3. He himself went on ahead of them, *praying and beseeching mercy from before the Lord;*[4] and he bent down to the ground seven times until he was near his brother. 4. Esau ran to meet him and embraced him and *inclined* upon his neck and *bit* him; and they wept. *Esau wept because of the pain of his teeth that were loosened; and Jacob wept because of the pain of his neck.*[5] 5. He lifted up his eyes and saw the women and the boys and said, "Who are these with you?" And he said, "They are my children *who were given to me* your servant *as a favor from before the Lord."*[6] 6. The *concubines,* they and their children, approached and bent down. 7. Leah and her children also approached and bent down. And afterwards Joseph approached and *placed himself*

Notes, Chapter 32 (Cont.)

[26]See above, the second (V, N, L), third (Nf, P) or fifth (Ps.-J.) miracle mentioned in the Targums of 28:10.
[27]*b. Hul.* 91b (512); *Sanh.* 95b (643): ". . . the sun which had set for his sake now rose for his sake." Cf. *Gen. R.* 68, 10.
[28]*m. Hul.* 7,1.
[29]*Gen. R.* 78,6; *b. Hul.* 91a (509).

Notes, Chapter 33

[1]*gwbryn pwlmrkyn;* see above, 32:7 and n. 7 to that verse.
[2]= Onq. According to Ps.-J. (see above 30:3-4, 9), Bilhah and Zilpah were wives of Jacob.
[3]The source of this addition is unknown; but see Gen 32:9(8); cf. Schmerler, 1932, 252.
[4]cf. *Gen. R.* 78, 8 which understands that Jacob bowed not to Esau but to God.
[5]In HT the word *wyšqhw,* "and he kissed him," has a dot over each letter. *Gen. R.* 78, 9 says that this means that Esau wished to bite Jacob, but that Jacob's neck turned to marble so that Esau's teeth were loosened. Hence, Esau wept because his neck was sore; cf. *Song R.* 7, 5.1; *Tanh., Wa- Yishlah* 4 (108); *PRE* 37 (285); see also *ARN* A 34. By reading *nšyk* (a Hebraism), "bit," in the early part of the verse rather than *nšyq,* "kissed," which we find in *ed. pr.,* Lond. prepares for the midrash which is added in the second part of the verse.
[6]"The Lord" is omitted in Lond.

before Rachel and *hid her with his stature;*[7] and they bent down. 8. And he said, "What do you mean by[8] all this camp that I have met?" And he said, *"It is a gift I sent* so that I might find mercy in the eyes of my master." 9. And Esau said, "I have great *possessions,* my brother; let what is yours remain yours." 10. And Jacob said, *"Do not speak thus,* I pray; if now I have found *mercy* in your eyes, you must accept my gift from my hand; because it is for this I have seen your countenance, *and it seems to me like* seeing the face of *your angel;*[9] and *behold,* you have received me favorably. 11. *Accept,* I pray, the gift[10] which was brought to you, for *it has been given to me as a favor from before the Lord,* and because I have *great possessions."* And he pressed him, and he accepted. 12. And he said, "Let us set out and go, and I will go alongside you *until you reach your dwelling place."* 13. And he said to him, "My master knows that the children are frail, and the flocks and herds that are giving suck are a care to me, and if *I* press them for a single day all the flock will die. 14. I pray, let my master pass on *and go* ahead of his servant, and I *on my part* will lead on quietly according to the pace of the cattle that are before me, and according to the *usual* pace of the children, until I come to my master at *Gabla."*[11] 15. Esau said, "Let me, I pray, leave with you some of the *soldiers*[12] who are with me." But he said, "Why that? Let me (only) find *mercy* before my master." 16. *Now, a miracle was performed for Jacob,*[13] and Esau returned that day on his way to *Gabla.*[11] 17. Jacob journeyed to Succoth *and tarried there for a period of twelve months.*[14] He built himself a *school*house[15] and for his livestock he made booths; therefore he called the name of the place Succoth. 18. Jacob arrived safely *with all that he had*[16] in the city of Shechem, which is in the land of Canaan, when he came from Paddan *of* Aram, and he camped opposite the city. 19. The *possession*[17] of the field where he pitched his tent he purchased from the children of Hamor, the father of

Notes, Chapter 33

[7]*Gen. R.* 78, 10 says that Joseph stood before Rachel in order to hide her from the lustful gaze of Esau. This explains why Joseph is mentioned before Rachel, his mother, in our present verse. The author presumes that the person named first went first.

[8]Lit.: "Who to you?" We take *mn* of the Aramaic text to correspond to *my,* "who?" of HT.

[9]Onq.: "as the sight of the face of the *great ones.*" The Targums avoid the anthropomorphic idea of seeing face of the Lord.

[10]*dwrwn;* = Gr. *dôron.* Onq.: "my offering."

[11]See above, 14:6 and n. 19 to that verse.

[12]*pwlmwsyn* = ed. pr.; Lond.: *pwlymwsyn;* cf. Gr. *polemistês.*

[13]Ps.-J. does not tell us what the miracle was. It may be that the men who accompanied Esau (cf. v. 15) abandoned him (cf. *Gen. R.* 78, 15), so that he had to return alone to Seir. Or the miracle may be the fact that Esau left Jacob so quickly. Cf. Schmerler, 1932, 255; Shinan, 1979, 1, 56.

[14]According to *b. Meg.* 17a (102), Jacob remained eighteen months in Sukkoth and six months in Bethel. According to *Gen. R.* 78, 16, he spent eighteen months in Bethel.

[15]There is no source in rabbinic literature for Ps.-J.'s assertion that Jacob built a schoolhouse at Sukkoth; cf. Schmerler, 1932, 255.

[16]Cf. *b. Shabb.* 33b (158): "bodily whole, financially whole (*šlm bmmwnw;* compare Ps.-J.: *šlym bkl dlyh*), and whole in his learning." See also *Gen. R.* 79, 1, where Gen 31:18 is quoted to prove that Jacob would come "with everything to the grave, full and lacking nought."

[17]= Onq.; see Aberbach-Grossfeld, 1982, 201, n. 7; Grossfeld, 1988, 119, n. 10.

Shechem, for a hundred *pearls.*[18] 20. And he erected an altar there, and there *he gave tithes which he had set aside from all that he had, before* El,[19] the God of Israel.

CHAPTER 34

1. Dinah, the daughter of Leah, whom she had borne to Jacob, went out to see *the customs of*[1] the daughters of *the people of* the land. 2. Shechem, son of Hamor the Hivite, the chief of the land, saw her and took her *by force*[2] and lay with her and afflicted her. 3. And he took delight in Dinah, the daughter of Jacob, and he loved the maiden and spoke *soothing words*[3] to the maiden's heart. 4. Shechem said to his father Hamor, saying, "Take this girl for me as wife." 5. And Jacob heard that he had defiled his daughter Dinah; his sons were with his livestock in the field, and Jacob was silent until they came. 6. Hamor, Shechem's father, went out to Jacob to speak to him. 7. Jacob's sons came in from the field when they heard of (it); and the men were distressed and very angry because *Shechem* had done a disgraceful deed in Israel in lying with Jacob's daughter, since it was not *proper*[4] that such a thing be done. 8. And Hamor spoke with them, saying, "The soul of Shechem my son takes delight in your daughter; give her to him, I pray, as wife. 9. *Intermingle* with us *through marriage;* give your daughters to us, and take our daughters for yourselves. 10. And you shall dwell with us, and the land shall be before you; dwell *where you will be at ease, and do business*[5] *there,* and take possession of it." 11. Shechem said to her father and to her brothers, "Let me find mercy in your eyes, and whatever you say to me I will give. 12. Demand of me a great bride price and a present, and I will give according as you say to me; but give me the maiden as wife." 13. The sons of Jacob answered Shechem and his father Hamor *with*

Notes, Chapter 33 (Cont.)

[18]*mrglyyn,* = P, V, N; = Gr. *margaritês.* Onq., LXX, Vulg.: "lambs." The value of the biblical *kesitah* is unknown. According to *Gen. R.* 79, 7, Jacob paid a hundred precious stones, a hundred sheep, and a hundred *selas* for the field. See further Aberbach-Grossfeld, 1982, 200, n. 6; Grossfeld, 1988, 119, n. 9.

[19]There is no source in rabbinic literature for Ps.-J.'s addition to this verse; but see the mention of tithing in 32:25 (Ps.-J.). Cf. Schmerler, 1932, 256.

Notes, Chapter 34

[1]*PRE* 38 (287): "Shechem . . . brought dancing girls who were (also) playing on the pipes in the streets. Dinah went forth to see those girls."

[2]*PRE* 38 (287; Luria 87b): "he seized her (*wsllh*)": HT says that Shechem "took" Dinah. Ps.-J. makes it clear that she did not consent to go with him.

[3]*Gen. R.* 80,7: "Can then a man speak to the heart? But it means with words that comfort the heart." Cf. *Qoh. R.* 1:16,1.

[4]= Onq. See above 20:9 and n. 6 to that verse.

[5]*prqmṭyy';* = Gr. *pragmateia;* see above, 23:16 and n. 7 to that verse. Onq.: "trade in it." In our present verse the Targums (see also Pesh. and LXX) translate Heb. *shr,* "trade" (RSV), according to the meaning it had in late Hebrew and in Aramaic (cf. Speiser, 1964, 264–265). See also v. 21 (Nf, CTg C, Ps.-J., Onq.); 42:34 (CTg E, Ps.-J., Onq.).

wisdom,[6] and they spoke (thus), because he had defiled their sister Dinah. 14. And they said to them, "We cannot do this thing, to give our sister to man who is uncircumcised, for that is a shame for us. 15. Only on this (condition) will we agree with you: if you become like us by circumcising every male among you. 16. Then we will give our daughters to you, and we will take your daughter for ourselves; and we will dwell with you, and we will become one people. 17. But if you will not listen to us and be circumcised, we will take our daughter *by force* and go." 18. Their words were pleasing to Hamor and to Shechem, Hamor's son. 19. The young man did not delay in doing the thing, for he delighted in Jacob's daughter. Now he was the most honored in all his father's house. 20. Hamor and his son Shechem came to the gate of their city and spoke with the men of *the gate of* their city, saying, 21. "These men are peaceful toward us; let them dwell in the land and *do business*[5] in it, for, behold, the land is broad in its boundaries before them. Let us take their daughters to us as wives, and let us give them our daughters. 22. But (only) on this (condition) will the men agree with us to dwell among us so that we may become one people: that we circumcise every male among us, just as they are circumcised. 23. Will not their livestock and their possessions and all their cattle be ours? Only let us agree with them, so that they may dwell with us." 24. All who went out of the gate of his city listened to Hamor and to his son Shechem; and they circumcised every male, all who went out of the gate of his city. 25. And on the third day, when they were *weakened by* the pain *of their circumcision,* two *of the* sons of Jacob, Simeon and Levi, Dinah's brothers, took each man his sword, entered the city which *was dwelling* in security,[7] and killed every male. 26. And they killed Hamor and his son Shechem with the edge of the sword, took Dinah out of Shechem's house, and went away. 27. *The rest of* the sons of Jacob went in *to strip*[8] the slain, and they plundered the city because they had defiled their sister *within it.* 28. They *plundered*[8] their sheep, their oxen, and their asses, whatever was in the city and whatever was in the field. 29. All their possessions, all their little ones, <their wives>,[9] and all that was in the house they took captive and plundered. 30. And Jacob said to Simeon and Levi, "You have brought trouble upon me, *spreading a bad reputation*[10] *about me* among the inhabitants of the land, among the Canaanites and among the Perizzites. I have few men, and (if) they unite against me and smite

Notes, Chapter 34

[6] = Onq. See also above 27:35 (Ps.-J.) and n. 24 to that verse. In our present verse Nf, Ps.-J., and Onq., but not CTg C, avoid the biblical statement that the sons of Jacob spoke deceitfully or with guile. *Gen. R.* 80,8 says that Jacob's sons were not guilty of deceit, because the fact that Shechem had defiled their sister justified their proposal. *Jubilees* 30, 3, on the other hand, stresses the brothers' treacherous intentions.

[7] = Onq.; Ps.-J. and Onq. take Heb. *bṭḥ,* lit. "in security," (RSV: "unawares") to refer to the city of Shechem rather than to Simeon and Levi.

[8] = Onq.

[9] Omitted in Lond. and *ed. pr.*

[10] Lit.: "causing a bad reputation to go forth." The same phrase is used in Num 13:32 (Ps.-J.; Nfmg; cf. Nf); 14:36, 37 (Ps.-J.; cf. Nf, Nfmg) to translate a different Heb. idiom. See also Gen 37:2 (Ps.-J.; Nf), where the verb *'t* rather than *npq* is used. See similar idioms in Exod 5:21 (CTg D); 32:25 (Ps.-J.; cf. Nf, P). M. Black (1967, 136) compares the phrase we are considering with Luke 6:22; see also Luke 4:14.

me, I will be wiped out, I and *the members of* my house." 31. *Simeon and Levi answered, "It is not fitting that it should be said in the congregation of the children of Israel:*[11] *'(The) uncircumcised defiled the virgin, and the worshipers of idols polluted the daughter of Jacob.' But this is what it is fitting to say: '(The) uncircumcised were killed on account of the virgin, and the worshipers of idols on account of the daughters of Jacob.' And Shechem, Hamor's son, will not boast against us with his words;* he would have treated our sister like a prostitute, *a harlot who has no avenger,*[12] *if we had not done this thing."*[13]

CHAPTER 35

1. *The Lord* said to Jacob, "Arise, go up to Bethel and dwell there; and make an altar there to the God who *revealed himself* to you when you were fleeing from before your brother Esau." 2. Jacob said to *the members of* his house and to all who (were) with him, "Take away the *idols of the nations*[1] that are among you, *which you took from the house of idols of Shechem,*[2] and purify yourselves *from the defilement of the slain whom you have touched,*[3] and change your clothes. 3. And let us arise and go up to Bethel, and I will make an altar there to the God who *accepted my prayer*[4] in the day of my distress, and whose *Memra* was *at my assistance*[5] on the journey on which I went." 4. They *delivered into the hand of* Jacob all the *idols of the nations* that were in their hands, *that they had taken from the house of*[6] idols of *Shechem,* and the rings that were on the ears *of the inhabitants of the city of Shechem, on which the likeness of his idol was designed;*[7] and Jacob hid them under the terebinth that was *near the city of* Shechem. 5. As they set out *from there giving thanks and praying before the Lord,*[8] there was a terror *from before the Lord* upon

Notes, Chapter 34 (Cont.)

[11]*Ed. pr.*: "in the congregation of Israel."

[12]Compare Nf, Nfmg, P, V, N, L. Ps.-J. uses the same verb (*tb'*, lit.: "seek, demand") as these Targums, but it does not have a direct object ("blood, shame") for this verb.

[13]There are no parallels in rabbinic literature to the long addition which the Pal. Tgs. and Ps.-J. make to this verse; cf. Ginsburger, *Pseudo-Jonathan*, XX–XXI; Gottlieb, 1944, 33, n. 30.

Notes, Chapter 35

[1]= Onq. The Targums avoid using the term "god" to refer to pagan deities; see above 31:30 and n. 24 to that verse.

[2]We know of no source for this addition. See the corresponding addition in v. 4 (Ps.-J.); cf. Brayer, 1950, 51.

[3]Cf. Num 31:19 and *b. Yeb.* 61a (405).

[4]= Onq. Ps.-J. and Onq. take the statement that God answered to mean that he heard Jacob's prayer. See also, e.g., Tg. 1 Sam 7:9; 8:18; 14:37; Isa 41:17. See Maher, 1990, 236.

[5]See above 26:3 and n. 2 to that verse.

[6]"House of" is omitted in *ed. pr.*

[7]Cf. *Gen. R.* 81,3.

[8]We know of no rabbinic source for this addition.

the peoples who were in the cities round about them, so that they did not pursue the sons of Jacob. 6. And Jacob came to Luz—that is Bethel—which is in the land of Canaan, he and all the people who were with him. 7. He built an altar there and called the place "El *who caused his Shekinah to dwell in* Bethel," because there *the angels of the Lord* had been revealed to him when he was fleeing from before *Esau* his brother. 8. And Deborah, Rebekah's *governess,*[9] died, and was buried below Bethel, *at the bottom of the plain.*[10] *Besides, it was there that Jacob was told about the death of Rebekah his mother;* and he called its name *"Another Weeping."*[11] 9. *The Lord was revealed* again to Jacob when he came from Paddan *of* Aram, and he blessed him[12] *in the name of his Memra after his mother had died.*[13] 10. And *the Lord* said to him, "*Until now* your name *was* Jacob; your name shall no longer be called Jacob, but Israel shall be your name." So he called his name Israel. 11. Then *the Lord* said to him, "I am El Shaddai; increase and multiply; a *holy*[14] people and an assembly *of prophets and priests*[15] shall come *from the sons you have begotten,* and *two*[16] kings shall *also* issue from *you.*[17] 12. The land that I gave to Abraham and to Isaac I will give to you; and to your *children* after you I will give the land." 13. And the *Glory of*[18] *the Shekinah of the Lord* ascended from upon him at the place where it had spoken to him. 14. And *he* erected a pillar *there,* at the place where it had spoken to him, a pillar of stone; and he offered a libation *of wine and a libation of water* on it—*for thus would his children do on the Feast of Tabernacles*[19]—and he poured *olive* oil upon it. 15. Jacob called the name of the place where *the Lord* had spoken to him, Bethel. 16. They set out from Bethel, and it was still *the height of the harvest season*[20] of the land when he came to Ephrath.

Notes, Chapter 35

[9] *pydgwgt'* = Gr. *paidagôgos.* The same word (with spelling variations) is used in 24:59 (Nfmg, Ps.-J.) and in Num 11:12 (Nf, Ps.-J., P, V, N, L). In our present verse (Gen 35:8) the variant *rbywt',* "nurse," is written on the margin of Lond.; compare *mrbyth,* which is used (with variations in spelling) in Nfmg, V, N, L, CTg C.

[10] Or: "at the edge of the plain"; = Onq. Onq. and Ps.-J. avoid saying that Deborah was buried "under the oak," in order to remove any suspicion that Jacob was associated with a tree that might have been connected with idolatrous worship.

[11] This midrash ("Besides . . . 'Another Weeping' ") is well known (cf., e.g., *Gen. R.* 81,5; *Qoh. R.* 7,2.3; *Tanḥ., Teze* 4 [662]; *PRK* 3,1), and it is based on a play on the word *'lwn,* "oak," which is taken to be the Gr. *allos,* "another."

[12] With Ginsburger (*Pseudo-Jonathan,* 65) we read *ytyh* rather than *yyy/yy* (the Lord), which we have in Lond. and *ed. pr.*

[13] Ps.-J. (Nf, Nfmg, P, V, N, CTg C) portrays God as reciting the mourner's Benediction; cf. *Gen. R.* 81,5; 82,3. The pious Jew must imitate God in this matter; cf. *b. Sotah* 14a (73). See also Ps.-J. Exod 18:20. The long tradition which Nf, Nfmg, P, V, N, L, and CTg C add in this verse is inserted in Deut 34:6 by Ps.-J.

[14] Cf. Exod 19:6.

[15] There is no source in rabbinic literature for this addition; cf. Schmerler, 1932, 262.

[16] The source of this addition, *Gen. R.* 82,4, identifies the *two* kings as Jeroboam and Jehu, or Saul and Ishbosheth.

[17] = Onq. HT: "from your loins." Compare 15:4 and see n. 10 to that verse. See also Grossfeld, 1988, 123, n. 9.

[18] Omitted in *ed. pr.*

[19] According to *Jubilees* 32,3-6, Jacob made offerings and libations in Bethel each day from the fifteenth to the twenty-second of the seventh month, i.e., during the feast of Tabernacles. When *Gen. R.* 78,16 says that Jacob poured many libations in Bethel, the reference is probably to the water-libations that were offered at the feast of Tabernacles. Only Ps.-J. specifies that the libations were to be of wine and water. See Ginzberg, *Legends,* 5, 317, n. 299. On the water-libations at the feast of Tabernacles, see *m. Sukkah* 4,9.

[20] Lit.: "there was still much time of the harvest of the land." See *Gen. R.* 82,7.

And Rachel was in childbirth, and she had difficulty in giving birth. 17. And as she was giving birth with difficulty, the midwife said to her, "Fear not; for this is also a *male* child for you." 18. As her soul departed—for *death came upon her*—she called his name "Son of my Agony"; but his father called him Benjamin. 19. And Rachel died and was buried on the way to Ephrath, that is Bethlehem. 20. Jacob erected a pillar over her grave; it is the pillar of Rachel's grave to this day. 21. *Jacob journeyed on and pitched his tent beyond the Tower of the Flock, the place from which the King Messiah will reveal himself at the end of days.* [21] 22. While Israel dwelt in that land, Reuben went and *disarranged the couch of Bilhah, his father's cuncubine, which had been arranged opposite the couch of Leah his mother; and it was reckoned to him as if he had lain with her.* [22] *When Israel heard (this) he was distressed, and he said, "Woe! Perhaps an unworthy* [23] *person has gone forth from me, as Ishmael went forth from Abraham and Esau went forth from my father." The Holy Spirit replied and said thus to him, "Fear not, for they are all righteous, and there is no unworthy person among them."* [24] Now, *after the birth of Benjamin* the sons of Jacob were twelve. 23. The sons of Leah: Reuben, the first-born of Jacob, Simeon, Levi, Judah, Issachar, and Zebulun. 24. The sons of Rachel: Joseph and Benjamin. 25. The sons of Bilhah, Rachel's maidservant: Dan and Naphtali. 26. The sons of Zilpah, Leah's maidservant: Gad and Asher. These are the sons of Jacob who were born to him in Paddan *of* Aram. 27. And Jacob came to his father Isaac at [25] Mamre, at Kiriath-Arba, that is Hebron, where Abraham and Isaac had sojourned. 28. The days of Isaac were a hundred and eighty years. 29. And Isaac expired and died, and was gathered to his people, old and full of days; and his sons Esau and Jacob buried him.

Notes, Chapter 35

[21]Tg. Micah 4:8. Migdal-eder is mentioned only in Gen 35:21 and Micah 4:8, and it is to be located south of the Jerusalem. Tg. Micah 4:8 and Gen 35:21 (Ps.-J.) associate this place with the Messiah, probably because it is near Bethlehem, from which, according to Micah 5:1, the expected ruler was to come. See Le Déaut, 1963, 276–277; Pérez Fernández, 1981, 207–209; Levey, 1974, 4.

[22]Gen 35:22 was one of those verses which, for the sake of the honor of the patriarchs, were to be read but not translated; cf. *m. Meg.* 4,10; *t. Meg.* (3)4,35 (Zuckermandel, 228). Cf. McNamara, 1966A, 46–47; Alexander, 1976; Le Déaut, 1978, *Genèse*, 328, n. 14; Shinan, 1979, 1, 12–14. Ps.-J. softens the biblical statement by saying that Reuben "disarranged" Bilhah's couch; cf. *b. Shabb.* 55b (256); *Gen. R.* 98,4. Ps.-J. mentions this tradition not only in our present verse, which tells of Reuben's sin, and in Gen 49:4 (see also Nf, V, N, CTg Z), where the biblical text refers to that deed, but also in 37:29, where the biblical verse makes no reference to Reuben's sin. On Ps.-J.'s tendency to repeat haggadic traditions, see above, Introduction, p. 6.

[23]*pswl'*. On the meaning of this word, see Le Déaut, 1978, *Genèse*, 328, n. 15.

[24]*Sifre* to Deut 6:4 (edition Finkelstein, 52); *Lev. R.* 36,5; *b. Pesaḥ.* 56a (279). See also the Targums of Gen 49:2 (Nf, P, V, N, and the Tosefta Targum [CTg Z]), and Deut 6:4 (Nf, V, N, Ps.-J.).

[25]Lit.: "to"; = Onq.

CHAPTER 36

1. These are the genealogies of Esau, he *who is called* Edom. 2. Esau took his wives from the daughters of Canaan; Adah, daughter of Elon the Hittite, and Oholibamah, daughter of Anah, daughter of Zibeon the Hivite, 3. and Basemath, the daughter of Ishmael, *whom* Nebaioth *her brother gave him in marriage.*[1] 4. And Adah bore to Esau Eliphaz; and Basemath bore Reuel. 5. And Oholibamah bore Jeush, Jalam, and Korah. These are the sons of Esau who were born to him in the land of Canaan. 6. And Esau took his wives, his sons, his daughters, and all the members of his household, his livestock, <all>[2] his cattle, and all the possessions he had acquired in the land of Canaan and journeyed to *another* land, because *fear* of his brother Jacob *lay upon him.*[3] 7. For their possessions were too many for them to dwell together, and the land where they sojourned could not support them because of their livestock. 8. So Esau dwelt in the mountain of *Gabla;*[4] Esau is *the chief of the Edomites.* 9. And these are the genealogies of Esau, *chief of the Edomites, whose dwelling-place was* in the mountain of *Gabla.*[4] 10. These are the names of the sons of Esau: Eliphaz, the son of Adah, the wife of Esau; Reuel, the son of Basemath, the wife of Esau. 11. The sons of Eliphaz were Teman, Omar, Zepho, Gatam, and Kenaz. 12. Timna was a concubine of Eliphaz, son of Esau, and she bore Amalek to Eliphaz. *Eliphaz is the friend of Job.*[5] These were the sons of Adah, Esau's wife. 13. These were the sons of Reuel: Nahath, Zerah, Shammah, and Mizzah. These were the sons of Basemath, Esau's wife. 14. These were the sons of Oholibamah, daughter of Anah, daughter of Zibeon, wife of Esau: she bore to Esau Jeush, Jalam, and Korah. 15. These were the chieftains of the children of Esau. The sons of Eliphaz, the first-born of Esau: the chief Teman, the chief Omar, the chief Zepho, the chief Kenaz, 16. the chief Korah, the chief Gatam, the chief Amalek. These were the chieftains of Eliphaz, *whose dwelling* (was) in the land of Edom. These are the sons of Adah. 17. These were the sons of Reuel, son of Esau: the chief Nahath, the chief Zerah, the chief Shammah, the chief Mizzah. These are the chieftains of Reuel, *whose dwelling (was)* in the land of Edom. These are the sons of Basemath, Esau's wife. 18. These were the sons of Oholibamah, Esau's wife: the chief Jeush, the chief Jalam, the chief Korah. These were the chieftains of Oholibamah, the daughter of Anah, Esau's wife. 19. These were the sons of Esau, and these were their princes. He is *the father of the Edomites.* 20. These were the sons of *Gebal,*[6] *the nobles*[7] *who had formerly* been the inhabitants of *that* land:

Notes, Chapter 36

[1] *b. Meg.* 17a (101). See above, 28:9 (Ps.-J.).
[2] Omitted in Lond. and *ed. pr.*
[3] *Gen. R.* 82, 13 gives other reasons for Esau's departure.
[4] See above, 14:6 and n. 19 to that verse.
[5] *Tanḥ. B., Wa-Yera* 30 (1, 104).
[6] Since the locality Seir (HT) is called *Gabla* (see above vv. 8 and 9 [Nf, Ps.-J.]), it is not surprising that the personal name Seir (HT) becomes *Gebal* in our present verse (Ps.-J.) and in v. 21 (Ps.-J.; Nfmg).
[7] *gnwsy';* Gr.: *gennaios*; cf. Deut 2:12 (Ps.-J.). See Levy, 1, 149.

Lotan, Shobal, Zibeon, Anah, 21. Dishon, Ezer, and Dishan; these are the chieftains of *the nobles*[7] *of* the children of *Gebal,*[6] *whose dwelling (was) since long ago* in the land of *the Edomites.* 22. The sons of Lotan were Hori and Heman; and Lotan's sister was Timna. 23. These were the sons of Shobal: Alvan, Manahath, Ebal, Shepho, and Onam. 24. These are the sons of Zibeon: Aiah and Anah; that was the Anah who *crossed wild asses with she-asses, and in due time* found *the mules that had come forth from them,*[8] while he was pasturing the asses of Zibeon his father. 25. These were the children of Anah: Dishon, and Oholibamah, the daughter of Anah. 26. These were the sons of Dishon: Hemdan, *Yeshban,* Ithran, and Cheran. 27. These were the sons of Ezer: Bilhan, Zaavan, and Akan. 28. These were the sons of Dishan: Uz and *Aram.* 29. These were the chieftains of the *nobles:* chief Lotan, chief Shobal, chief Zibeon, chief Anah, 30. chief Dishon, chief Ezer, chief Dishan; these were, according to their *princes,* the chieftains of the *nobles whose dwelling had formerly been* in the land of *Gabla.*[4] 31. These are the kings who reigned in the land of Edom, before any king reigned over the children of Israel. 32. *Balaam,*[9] son of Beor, reigned in Edom; and the name of his *royal* city[10] was Dinhabah. 33. Bela died, and Jobab, son of Zerah, from Bozrah, reigned in his stead. 34. Jobab died, and Husham, from the land of the *south,*[11] reigned in his stead. 35. Husham died, and Hadad, son of Bedad, who *slew the Midianites when he waged war with them* in the fields of Moab, reigned in his stead; and the name of his *royal* city[10] was Abith. 36. Hadad died, and Samlah, from Masrekah, reigned in his stead. 37. Samlah died, and Shaul, who was from Rehoboth on the *Euphrates,* reigned in his stead. 38. Shaul died, and Baal-hanan, son of Achbor, reigned in his stead. 39. Baal-hanan, the son of Achbor, died, and Hadar reigned in his stead; and the name of his *royal* city was Pau; and his wife's name was Mehetabel, daughter of Matred. *He is the man who toiled in trade*[12] *and with the (gold-) sieve,*[13] *and (who), when he had become wealthy and acquired possessions, became proud in his heart saying "What is silver, and what is gold"?*[14] 40. And these are the names of the chieftains of Esau in their generations, according to their *dwelling-places,* by their names: the chief Timna, the chief Alvah, the chief Jetheth, 41. the chief Oholibamah, the chief Elah,

Notes, Chapter 36

[8]*Gen. R.* 82, 14; *j. Berak.* 8, 12b; *b. Pesah.* 54a (266-267); *B. Bat.* 115b (475). The midrashim take HT *hymm,* "hot springs," to mean "mules." For other interpretations of the obscure Heb. *hymm,* see Ginzberg, *Legends,* 5, 322, n. 322.

[9]Cf. Tg. 1 Chron 1, 43. The identification of Bela (*bl'*) with Balaam is based on a popular etymology which derives the name Balaam from *bl' 'm,* "he swallowed the people." See, e.g., Num 22:5 (Ps.-J.).

[10]Lit.: "the city of his royal house."

[11]= Onq. HT: "the land of the Temanites." HT *tymn* can be a place-name, or it can mean "south." The Targums give it this latter meaning.

[12]*mtrd';* in translating this word as "trade," we follow Levy (2, 30) rather than Jastrow (769), who translates it as "hunter's spear." In the present context *mtrd'* is a play on the name Matred.

[13]In translating *srdyt'* as "sieve," we follow Levy (2, 188; see also 2, 30 under *mtrd'*). Jastrow (1023) translates it as "hunter's net."

[14]The phrase "what is gold?" is a play on the name Mezahab of HT. The meaning of the Targumic addition which we find in our present verse (Nf, P, V, N, L, Ps.-J.) and which is paralleled in Tg. 1 Chron 1, 50 (see also *Gen. R.* 83, 4), is obscure, and it has baffled the commentators of the Targums and the Midrash; cf. Shinan, 1979, 1, 101–102. On the *Gen. R.* text just referred to, see Kutscher, 1976, 37–38.

the chief Pinon, 42. the chief Kenaz, the chief Temam, the chief Mibzar, 43. the chief Magdiel—*he was called Magdiel because of the name of his city, "Mighty Tower," that is Rome the guilty*[15]—the chief Iram. These are the chieftains of Edom—that is Esau, the father of *the Edomites,* according to their settlements in the land which they possessed.

CHAPTER 37

1. And Jacob dwelt *securely*[1] in the land where his father had sojourned, in the land of Canaan. 2. These are the descendants of Jacob. Joseph was seventeen years old[2] *when he went forth from the schoolhouse.*[3] He was a youth *brought up* with the sons of Bilhah and with the sons of Zilpah, his father's wives. And Joseph brought an evil report[4] about them, *for he had seen them eating flesh that had been torn from a living animal,*[5] *the ears and the tails.*[6] *And he came and told* their father. 3. Now Israel loved Joseph more than all his children because *Joseph's features were like his own features;*[7] and he made him an *embroidered* cloak.[8] 4. His brothers saw that their father loved him more than all his brothers, and *they harbored enmity against him, and they did not wish* to speak peaceably with him. 5. And Joseph dreamed a dream and related (it) to his brothers, and *they harbored* still greater *enmity* against him. 6. He said to them, "Hear, I pray, this dream which I have dreamed. 7. Behold we were binding sheaves in the field, and behold my sheaf arose and stood upright; and behold your sheaves came around and bent down to my sheaf." 8. His brothers said to him, "Do *you imagine* that you are to reign over

Notes, Chapter 36 (Cont.)

[15]"Rome the guilty" is omitted in *ed. pr.* Compare Num 24:19 (Nf, P, V, N, Ps.-J.). Compare Ps.-J.'s interpretation of the name Magdiel with *Gen. R.* 83, 4; *PRE* 38 (290).

Notes, Chapter 37

[1]*PRE* 38 (290); cf. *Gen. R.* 84, 1 and 5.

[2]The phrase "was shepherding the flock with his brothers" is omitted in Lond. and *ed. pr.*

[3]In a comment on v. 3 ("Now Israel loved Joseph . . . because he was the son of his old age"), *Gen. R.* 84, 8 says that Jacob handed on to Joseph all the laws that he had learned from Shem and Eber; see above 25:27 (Nf, Nfmg, Ps.-J., Onq.). See also *Gen. R.* 95,3.

[4]On the idiom "bring (or spread) an evil report (or reputation)" see above, 34:30 (Nf, Ps.-J.) and n. 10 to that verse.

[5]*Gen. R.* 84,7; *j. Peah.* 1,15d; *Tanḥ.* B., *Wa-Yeshev* 6 (1,180); *PRE* 38 (291).

[6]We know of no source for Ps.-J.'s reference to the ears and tails.

[7]*Gen. R.* 84, 8; *Tanḥ.* B., *Wa-Yeshev* 5 (1,179); cf. *Testament of Joseph* 18,4. The problem for the authors of the midrash was that, like Joseph (Gen 37:3), Benjamin was a son of Jacob's old age (cf. Gen 44:20). Therefore, this could not be the reason why Jacob loved Joseph more than all his other children. In our present verse Onq. translates "because he was the son of his old age" as "for he was a wise son to him." On this translation, see Aberbach-Grossfeld, 1982, 215, n. 1; Grossfeld, 1988, 127, n. 2; Komlosh, 1973, 175; Y. Yaeger, "Dialectical Expressions in Targum Onkelos to Genesis" (in Hebrew), *Beth Miqra* 22 (1977) 381.

[8]*prgwd* = Nf, P, V, N, L; = Latin *paragauda,* "a border, lace, worked on a garment"; hence, "bordered cloak"; cf. Levy, 2, 286. On the ancient translations of the obscure underlying Hebrew, cf. Bowker, 1969, 237.

us? Or do you *think* that you are to have dominion over us?" And they *harbored* still greater *enmity* against him because of his dreams and because of his words. 9. And he dreamed yet another dream and related it to his brothers, and said, "Behold, I have again dreamed a dream. And behold the sun and the moon and eleven stars were bending down to me." 10. When he told (it) to his father and to his brothers, his father rebuked him and said to him, "What is this dream you have dreamed? Are we to come, your mother, and your brothers and I, to bend down to you to the ground?" 11. His brothers were jealous of him, but his father kept the matter *in his heart.*[9] 12. His brothers went to pasture their father's flock at Shechem. 13. *After some time*[10] Israel said to Joseph, "Are not your brothers pasturing in Shechem? *I am afraid lest the Hivites come and smite them for having smitten Hamor and Shechem and the inhabitants of the city.*[11] Come, *then*, and I will send you to them." And he said to him, "Here I am." 14. He said to him, "Go, then, see how your brothers are and how the flocks are, and bring me back word." And he sent him *for the sake of the deep design which had been communicated*[12] *to Abraham in* Hebron;[13] *and on that day the exile of Egypt began.*[14] *So Joseph arose* and came to Shechem. 15. *Gabriel,*[15] *in the likeness of* a man, found him, and behold, he was wandering in the field. And the man asked him saying, "What are you looking for?" 16. And he said, "I am looking for my brothers. Tell me, I pray, where they are pasturing." 17. The man said, "They have gone from here, for I heard *from behind the veil*[16] *that from this day the servitude to the Egyptians has begun. And it was said to them in prophecy that the Hivites sought to engage in battle with them. Therefore* they said, 'Let us go to Dothan.' " So Joseph went after his brothers and found them in Dothan. 18. They saw him afar off, and before he came close to them, they took counsel against him to kill him. 19. *Simeon and Levi, who were brothers in counsel,*[17] said one to another, "Behold, this master of dreams is com-

Notes, Chapter 37

[9]Jacob knew that dreams could not be ignored. According to *Gen. R.* 84, 12, Jacob wrote down the dream so that he could verify its fulfillment. According to Josephus (*Ant.* 2 § 14-15), Jacob was delighted with the dream and with the great things it foretold. Compare Ps.-J.'s statement that Jacob "kept the matter in his heart" with Luke 2:51.

[10]It is clear from the scriptural text that some time must have elapsed between v. 12 and v. 13. Ps.-J. makes this explicit by inserting "after some time." Compare Jacob's words in *PRE* 38 (292): "Verily, I have (waited) many days without hearing of the welfare of thy brethren. . . ."

[11]Josephus (*Ant.* 2 § 18-19) says that Jacob's sons went to pasture the flocks without telling their father. Not knowing where they were, Jacob "conceived the gloomiest of forebodings concerning them," and sent Joseph to see what had happened. *Sefer Ha-Yashar* 41 (126–127) says that the brothers were late in returning from the flocks, and their father feared that the people of Shechem might have attacked them. See below, 45:28 and n. 26 to that verse.

[12]Lond. and *ed. pr.* have "that will be communicated (lit.: spoken)."

[13]*Gen. R.* 84,13; *b. Sotah* 11a (51). The midrash understands HT *'mq,* "valley," as *'mwq,* "deep (designs)."

[14]Joseph's departure for Shechem marked the beginning of the train of events that led to the exile in Egypt. It can therefore be said that on the day of that departure the prophecy about the exile that had been made to Abraham (cf. Gen 15:13) was fulfilled. See below, v. 17 (Ps.-J.).

[15]*PRE* 38 (292); *Tanḥ., Wa-Yeshev* 2 (115). *Tanḥ.* B., *Wa-Yeshev* 13 (1, 183) says that "an angel" found Joseph. According to *Gen. R.* 84, 14, Joseph was met by three angels. See further Ginzberg, *Legends,* 5, 327–328, n. 29. On Ps.-J.'s tendency to name persons who are nameless in the Bible, see above, 6:4 and n. 10 to that verse.

[16]The curtain that veils the divine throne; cf. Ginzberg, *Legends,* 2, 10.

[17]Cf. Tg. Gen 49:5–6 (Nf, V, N, CTg Z, Ps.-J.). See Gen 34:25-31 and especially the Targums (Nf, P, V, N, L, Ps.-J.) of v. 31 in that passage. *Gen. R.* 98, 5 calls Simeon and Levi "brothers of Dinah, but not of Joseph," because they avenged Dinah (cf. Gen 34:25-31) but plotted against Joseph. Cf. also *Gen. R.* 97; *Tanḥ.* B., *Wa-Yeshev* 13 (1, 183).

ing! 20. Come now, let us kill him and throw him in one of the pits, and we will say, 'A savage beast has devoured him,' and we will see what will be *the interpretation of his dreams."* 21. Reuben heard (this), and he saved him from their hands, and said, "Let us not *kill* him, *lest we become guilty of his blood."* 22. And Reuben said to them, "Do not shed *innocent* blood. Throw him into this pit in the wilderness, but do not extend a *murderous* hand against him." (His intention was) to save him from their hands so as to restore him to his father. 23. When Joseph came to his brothers, they stripped Joseph of his cloak, the *embroidered* cloak he had on, 24. and they took him and threw him into the pit. And the pit was empty; there was no water in it, *but there were serpents and scorpions in it.*[18] 25. They *returned* to eat bread, and lifting up their eyes, they saw a company of *Arabs*[19] coming from Gilead, with their camels laden with *wax, gum,* balm, and resin, traveling on the way to bring (them) down to Egypt. 26. Judah said to his brothers, "What *monetary* profit *shall we have* if we kill our brother and cover his blood? 27. Come, let us sell him to the *Arabs,* and let our hand not be upon him to kill him, for he is our brother, our flesh." And his brothers agreed.[20] 28. Now, Midianite men, merchants,[21] passed by, and pulling Joseph they raised him up out of the pit. They sold Joseph to the *Arabs* for twenty silver *meah, and they bought sandals from them.*[22] And they brought Joseph to Egypt. 29. Reuben returned to the pit, *for he had not been with them to eat when they sold him, since he was sitting (and) fasting because he had disarranged his father's couch.*[23] *And he had gone and sat in the mountains (intending) to return to the pit to raise him up*[24] *(and restore him) to his father, hoping that he might win his favor. But when he returned and looked,* behold, Joseph was not in the pit; he rent his clothes. 30. He returned to his brothers and said, "The boy is not there! And I, where shall I go? *And how can we see my father's countenance?"*[25] 31. They[26] took Joseph's cloak, slaughtered a young male goat— *because its blood is like that of a man*[27]—and they dipped the cloak in the blood. 32. And they had the *embroidered* cloak taken *by the sons of Zilpah and the sons of Bilhah,*[28] who brought it to their father and said, "We have found this. Identify, we

Notes, Chapter 37

[18]*Gen. R.* 84, 16; *b. Shabb.* 22a (94); *Hag.* 3a (8); *Tanḥ., Wa-Yeshev* 2 (116). HT states that "the pit was empty" and that "there was no water in it." The midrash explains that this redundancy teaches that there was no water in the pit, but there were serpents and scorpions in it.

[19]= Onq. See also vv. 27, 28, and 39:1, where Ps.-J. agrees with Onq. in translating "Ishmaelites" as "Arabs." See Splansky, 1981, 88–89.

[20]Lit.: "accepted." Onq.: lit. "accepted from him," i.e., they agreed to his proposal.

[21]Lit.: "*masters of* business," *mry prqmṭy'*. On the word *prqmṭy'* see above n. 7 to 23:16.

[22]*Tanḥ., Wa-Yeshev* 2 (115); *PRE* 38 (292-293); *Testament of Zebulun* 3,2.

[23]Ps.-J. is the only Targum to refer to this tradition in our present verse. See above, 35:22 and n. 22 to that verse. The author of Ps.-J. takes *wyšb,* "returned," in our present verse to mean "repented," and he sees in it a reference to Reuben's conversion. Cf. *Gen. R.* 84, 19; *PRK* 24,9.

[24]*PRE* 38 (292).

[25]On the idiom *sbr 'pyn,* "countenance," see Grossfeld, 1988, 111, n. 2.

[26]V. 31 is omitted in Lond.

[27]*Gen. R.* 84,19.

[28]This tradition is found, apart from Ps.-J., only in the late (twelfth century) midrashic work *Sekel Tob* in a commentary on Gen 37:32. This contradicts the tradition that Judah was the one who brought the bloodstained cloak to Jacob; cf. Tg. Gen 38:25 (Nf, Ps.-J.), 26 (P, V, N, L, CTg D, X, FF); *Gen. R.* 84, 8 and 18.

pray, whether it is your son's tunic or not." 33. He identified it and said, "*It is* my son's cloak. *It was not a wild* beast that devoured him; *and he was not killed by men.*[29] *But I see by the Holy Spirit that an evil woman is standing before him.*"[30] 34. Jacob rent his clothes, *bound* sackcloth on his loins, and mourned for his son many days. 35. All his sons and all *his sons' wives*[31] arose *and went* to console him, but he refused to *accept consolation,*[32] and said, "No, I will go down mourning to my son in *the grave.*" And his father *Isaac*[33] *also* wept for him. 36. The Midianites sold him in Egypt to Potiphar, an *official* of Pharaoh, the chief *executioner.*[34]

CHAPTER 38

1. It[1] happened at that time that Judah *lost his possessions*[2] and *parted* from his brothers, and turned aside to an Adullamite man whose name was Hirah. 2. There Judah saw the daughter of a *merchant*[3] whose name was Shua; and he *proselytized*[4] *her* and went in unto her. 3. And she conceived and bore a son, and *she* called his name Er, *because he was destined to die childless.*[5] 4. And she conceived again and

Notes, Chapter 37 (Cont.)

[29]P, V, N, L, CTg D, (see also the addition by a later hand in E), and Ps.-J. all say the direct opposite to the biblical text which has Jacob declare that a wild beast had devoured Joseph. The Targumic statements that Jacob knew that Joseph was alive do not fit in with vv. 34-35, which say that the patriarch mourned. They are, however, related to the midrash which says that Jacob refused to be comforted (Gen 37:35) because one cannot be comforted for the living; cf. *Gen. R.* 84,21. See Klein, 1976, 522–523; Shinan, 1979, 1, 150–151; Böhl, 1987, 131–134.

[30]*Gen. R.* 84,19.

[31]*Gen. R.* 84,21. See also *PRE* 39 (303–304). HT has "daughters." Aware that Jacob had only one daughter, the midrash and Ps.-J. interpret the text.

[32] = Onq. "To accept consolation" is a rabbinic idiom for the formal acceptance of condolence. See Aberbach-Grossfeld, 1982, 220, n. 10; Grossfeld, 1988, 129, n. 11.

[33]*Gen. R.* 84, 22. Despite Gen 35:29, which says that "Isaac breathed his last," Isaac was still thought to be alive. The haggadist can ignore chronology; see above 25:29 and n. 38 to that verse.

[34]*spwqltwry'* = Nf, V, N, L (with orthographical variations); Latin: *spiculator;* cf. Gr. *spekoulatôr,* Mark 6:27; see also 39:1 (Nf, CTg E, Ps.-J.); 40:3, 4 (Nf, Nfmg, Ps.-J.); 41:10, 12 (Nf, CTg E, Ps.-J.).

Notes, Chapter 38

[1]For a study of the Targums of Gen 38, see Bloch, 1955B, 5–35; idem, 1957, 381–389.

[2]Lit.: "went down from his possessions." The same idiom occurs in Ps.-J. Exod 4:19 (also Nfmg) and 10:29. In our present verse Ps.-J. takes Heb. *yrd,* "went down," to mean "to go down from one's possessions." See *b. Sotah* 13b (69), where *yrd* in our present verse is understood as "go down (or be deposed) from one's greatness." Cf. also *Gen. R.* 85,1. According to tradition, Judah was deprived of his dignity for his failure to rescue Joseph (cf. Gen 38:26) and for his part in the sale of his brother (v. 27).

[3]Most versions of Onq. also read "merchant." These versions and Ps.-J. wish to avoid saying that Judah married a Canaanite woman; *cf. b. Pesah.* 50a (241). See further Aberbach-Grossfeld, 1982, 221, n. 1; Grossfeld, 1988, 129, n. 1; Komlosh, 1973, 209. See Num 12:1, where all the Targums (Nf, P, V, N, L, Ps.-J., Onq.) solve the problem raised by the biblical statement that Moses had a Cushite wife. See also below, 41:45 with n. 22 to that verse.

[4]By using the word "merchant," Ps.-J. had avoided the problem raised by the biblical statement that Judah married a Canaanite (see preceding note). Now Ps.-J. says that Judah converted the woman, a statement which makes no sense if she was not in fact a Canaanite. It seems that Ps.-J. has placed side by side two mutually exclusive solutions to the problem raised by HT; cf. Shinan, 1979, 1, 175–176.

[5]Cf. *Gen. R.* 85,4. Ps.-J. links the name Er with Heb. *'ryry,* "lonely, childless."

bore a son, and she called his name Onan, *because his father was indeed destined to grieve because of him.*[6] 5. Yet again she bore a son, and she called his name Shelah, *because her husband had forgotten her.*[7] He was in *Paskath*[8] when she bore him. 6. Judah took a wife for Er his first-born, *the daughter of Shem the Great,*[9] whose name was Tamar. 7. But Er, the first-born of Judah, was evil *before* the Lord, *because he did not have intercourse with his wife according to the manner of all the earth.*[10] *And the anger of the Lord blazed forth against him,* and the Lord *killed* him. 8. And Judah said to Onan, "Go in unto your brother's wife and take her in levirate marriage, and raise up offspring to your brother*'s name."* 9. But Onan knew that *the children would not be called by his name;* and when he went in unto his brother's wife, he destroyed his *deed* upon the ground, so as not to *raise up*[11] *children* to his brother*'s name.* 10. And what he did was displeasing *before* the Lord, and he *cut short his days* also. 11. Then Judah said to his daughter-in-law Tamar, "Remain a widow in your father's house until my son Shelah grows up"; for he thought, "Perhaps he too may die like his brothers." So Tamar went and dwelt in her father's house. 12. Many days went by, and Shua's daughter, the wife of Judah, died. When Judah was comforted, he went up to Timnah to his sheepshearers, he and his friend Hirah the Adullamite. 13. Tamar was told, saying, "Behold, your father-in-law is going up to Timnah to shear his flock." 14. So she took off the garments of her widowhood, covered herself with a veil, wrapped herself up, and sat at the *crossroads* on the way to Timnah, *where all eyes look.*[12] For she saw that Shelah had grown up, and she had not been given to him as wife. 15. Judah saw her, and *in his eyes he compared* her to a harlot, *because she was of sullen* appearance[13] *in the house of Judah, and Judah did not love her.* 16. He turned aside to her by the road and said, "Come now, let me go in unto you," for he did not know that she was his daughter-in-law. And she said, "What will you give me that you may come in unto me?" 17. He said, "I will send a kid from the flock." And she said, "Will you give me a pledge until you send (it)?" 18. And he said, "What pledge shall I give you?"

Notes, Chapter 38

[6]Cf. *Gen. R.* 85,4, which, like Ps.-J., links the name Onan with the word *'nh*, "be afflicted."

[7]Ps.-J. plays on the name Shelah, linking it with the Aramaic verb *šly*, "neglect, forget."

[8]Nf, P, V, N, L, and Ps.-J. play on the place-name Chezib, linking it with the Heb. verb *kzb*, which can mean "fail, cease" (cf. Isa 58:11). See also *Gen. R.* 85,4. The Targums just mentioned use the Aramaic verb *psq*, "cease," in their translations. However, Ps.-J. is alone in constructing a place-name from this root.

[9]*Gen. R.* 85,10; *Tanh.* B., *Wa-Yeshev* 17 (1, 187). Shem was regarded as a priest (cf. Ginzberg, *Legends,* 5, 225, n. 102), and it is therefore logical that Tamar—his daughter, according to the midrash—was condemned to be burned for prostitution (cf. Lev 21:9); see below v. 24. Ps.-J. alone mentions in our present verse that Tamar was Shem's daughter, and this same Targum is again alone in v. 24 when it states that Tamar was the daughter of a priest. See further Ginzberg, *Legends,* 5, 333, n. 79.

[10]*Ed. pr.*: "because he did not give his seed to his wife." Cf. *Gen. R.* 85,4; *b. Yeb.* 34b (215).

[11]= Onq. The Targums replace the verb "give" of the biblical verse with "raise up," which is used in Deut 25:6-7 in the context of levirate marriage. The "deed" referred to is the emission of semen; see Levy, 2, 196.

[12]Ps.-J., Nf, and Onq. (cf. Pesh., Vulg., and Jerome, *Quaest. hebr.* in Gen 38:14) translate *petah* in the phrase *pth 'ynym*, "the entrance of Enaim," as "crossroads." Ps.-J. also interprets *pth 'ynym* as if *'ynym* had the meaning "eyes"; cf. *b. Sotah* 10a (47). See Ginzberg, *Legends,* 5, 334, n. 84; Le Déaut, 1978, 348, n. 8.

[13]Nf, V, N, L, and Onq. (cf. HT) say that Tamar had covered her face. Ps.-J. goes its own way in saying she was "of sullen appearance (*k'yst 'pyn*)"; cf. Jastrow, 656; Levy, 1, 378. This sullen appearance would explain why, as Ps.-J. goes on to say, Judah did not love her; cf. Schmerler, 1932; 276–277; Geiger, 1928, 462.

And she said, "Your signet-ring and your *fringes,*[14] and the staff that is in your hand." So he gave (them) to her and went in unto her, and she conceived by him. 19. Then she arose and went away, took off her veil, and put on the garments of her widowhood. 20. And Judah sent the kid by his friend the Adullamite, to receive the pledge from the hand of the woman. But he did not find her. 21. And he asked the men of the place, saying, "Where is the prostitute[15] who was at (the place) on the way *where eyes look?*[16] And they said, "There was no prostitute here." 22. So he returned to Judah and said, "I did not find her; the men of the place said, 'There was no prostitute here.'" 23. And Judah said, "Let her keep *the pledges,* lest we become a laughingstock; behold, I sent this kid but you did not find her." 24. Now, after *a period of* three months *it became known that she was pregnant;*[17] and Judah was told, as follows: "Your daughter-in-law Tamar has played the harlot; and moreover, behold, she is pregnant because of (her) harlotry." And Judah said, "*Is she not the daughter of a priest?*[18] Bring her out and let her be burned." 25. So *Tamar*[19] was brought out *to be burned, and she looked for the three pledges but did not find them.*[20] *She lifted up her eyes to the heavens on high*[21] *and said thus: "I beseech by the mercies before you, O Lord, answer me in this hour of my distress,*[22] *and enlighten my eyes that I may find my three witnesses. And I will raise up for you from my loins three holy ones who will sanctify your name by going down to the furnace of fire in the valley of Dura."*[23] *That hour, the Holy One, blessed be he,*[24] *beckoned to Michael,*[25] *and he enlightened her eyes so that she found them.*[26] *She took them and threw them at the feet of the judges and said,* "The man to whom these *pledges* belong, by him I am pregnant. *Yet even if I were burned I would not make him known.*[27] *But the Lord of the world will put it in his heart to recognize them, and he will deliver me from this great judgment."* And when Judah saw them he recognized

Notes, Chapter 38

[14] *Gen. R.* 85,9.

[15] *mṭ 'yt'*. Ps.-J. uses this word twice in our present verse, 38:21, and once in the following verse, to translate Heb. *qdš,* "cult prostitute, harlot." In Deut 23:19 Ps.-J. uses it to translate Heb. *zwnh,* "harlot." We also find it used by Ps.-J. in Gen 42:9, 12 and Num 24:14 in additions to the biblical verse. In Gen 34:31 Ps.-J. uses the form *mt'yy'*.

[16] I.e., at the crossroads, where one looks carefully to choose one's way; see Levy, 2, 162. See above, v. 14 (Ps.-J.).

[17] *Gen. R.* 85:10; *b. Nid.* 8b (54).

[18] See above, v. 6 and n. 9 to that verse.

[19] A long midrashic expansion has been added, with some variations, to all the Pal.Tgs. of vv. 25-26 (Nf, P, V, N, L, CTg D, E, FF, X). Other versions of this midrash are found in the *ed. pr.* of Ps.-J. after the text of Gen 50 and in Tosefta texts attached to Onqelos. See Epstein, 1895, 45; Sperber's edition of Onqelos, 1959, 354; Klein, 1986, 1, 90–93. For a synoptic view of the different versions of this midrash, see Díez Macho, *Neophyti 1,* I, 125*–127*. Only partial parallels to this targumic midrash are known; cf. Ginzberg, *Legends,* 2, 34–35; 5, 335, nn. 87-89.

[20] *Gen. R.* 85,11. According to the Tosefta preserved in the *ed. pr.* of Ps.-J. (see preceding note), it was Sammael who hid the pledges, and it was Gabriel who gave them back to Tamar; cf. *b. Sotah* 10 b (48-49).

[21] *Tanḥ.* B., *Wa-Yeshev* 17 (1,187).

[22] *'nnqy;* (Gr.: *anagkê*). The same word is used in Nf, P, V, N, L. It is vocalized in Lond. See above, Introduction, p. 12.

[23] *b. Sotah* 10b (50). Cf. Dan 3:19-23.

[24] "Blessed be he" is omitted in Lond. On the formula "The Holy One, blessed be He," see above, 25:21 and n. 21 to that verse.

[25] See above, 32:25 (Ps.-J.), and n. 18 to that verse.

[26] *Tanḥ.* B., *Wa-Yeshev* 17 (1, 187).

[27] *b. Sotah* 10b (49); *Ketub.* 67b (413); *B. Mez.* 59a (350).

them. Then he said in his heart, "It is better for me to be ashamed in this world, which is a passing world, than to be ashamed in the presence of my fathers, the righteous ones, in the world to come; it is better for me to be burned in this life in extinguishable fire than to burn in the world to come in inextinguishable fire. For this is measure for measure,[28] *according to what I said to my father Jacob: 'Identify, I pray, your son's cloak.'*[29] *Because of that I must hear in the courthouse: '(Identify, I pray), whose are these, the signet-ring, the* fringes, *and the staff?' "* 26. Then Judah acknowledged (them) and said, "*Tamar is* innocent; *she is pregnant* by me."[30] *Then a heavenly voice*[31] *came down from heaven and said, "The matter has come from before me." So both of them were delivered from the judgment.*[32] *And he (Judah) said,* "Because I did not give her to my son Shelah *this has happened to me.*" And he did not know her again *in sexual intercourse.* 27. When the time (came) for her to give birth, behold there were twins in her womb. 28. And when she was giving birth, *an infant* put forth its hand; and the midwife took a crimson thread and tied it on his hand saying, "This one came out first." 29. But when *the infant* drew back its hand, behold, his brother came forth, and she said, "*(With)* what *great power you have prevailed! And it is* you who are *to prevail, since you are destined to possess the kingship."*[33] And *she* called his name Perez. 30. Afterwards his brother who had the crimson thread *tied* to his hand came out; and *she* called his name Zerah.

CHAPTER 39

1. Joseph was taken down to Egypt, and Potiphar, an *official*[1] of Pharaoh, the chief *executioner,*[2] an Egyptian, bought him *with a surety*[3] from the *Arabs* who had taken him down there. *For he saw that he was handsome, and (he intended) to prac-*

Notes, Chapter 38 (Cont.)

[28]The principle "measure for measure" is expressed, e.g., in *m. Sotah* 1,7; *Mekilta* to Exod 13:21 (1, 184–185); ibid. to Exod 15:8 (2, 50); Tg. Lev 26:43 (Nf, P, V, N, Ps.-J.). See McNamara, 1966A, 138–142; H. P. Ruger, "Mit welchem Mass ihr messt, wird euch gemessen werden," *ZNW* 60 (1969) 174–182.

[29]This contradicts 37:32, which attributes these words to the sons of Zilpah and the sons of Bilhah; see above, n. 28 to that verse.

[30]= Onq. See Aberbach-Grossfeld, 1982, 225, n. 8; Grossfeld, 1988, 131, n. 10.

[31]Lit.: "a daughter of a voice." On the use of this term, see Bacher, 1899 (1965) 2, 206–207; Liebermann, 1962, 194–199. See also vol. 1A, p. 39.

[32]*b. Mak.* 23b (168); *Sotah* 10b (50); *Gen. R.* 85,12. The heavenly justification of Tamar helps us to understand how she could be included in the genealogy of Jesus (Matt 1:3); cf. Bloch, 1957, 388.

[33]*Gen. R.* 85,14.

Notes, Chapter 39

[1]= Onq.; see above, 37:36 (Ps.-J.).
[2]See above, 37:36 and n. 34 to that verse.
[3]I.e., with a guarantee that he was not stolen; cf. *Gen. R.* 86,3. See also *Testament of Joseph* 13.

tice sodomy with him; and immediately *a (divine) decree was issued against him, and his testicles dried up, and he became impotent.*[4] 2. But *the Memra of* the Lord was *at* Joseph's *assistance,* and he was a successful man; and he was in the house of his Egyptian master. 3. His master saw that *the Memra of* the Lord was *at* his *assistance,* and the Lord caused everything he did to prosper in his hand. 4. And Joseph found mercy in his eyes, and he waited upon him; and he appointed him *administrator*[5] over his house, and he put all that he owned in his hand. 5. And from the time that he appointed him *administrator* over his house and over all that he owned, the Lord blessed the Egyptian's house because of *the merit of* Joseph. And the blessing of the Lord was on all that he owned, in the house and in the field. 6. He left all that he owned in Joseph's hand, and with him (there) he concerned himself with nothing[6] except *his wife with whom he lay.*[7] And Joseph was handsome in figure and lovely in appearance. 7. After these events his master's wife set her eyes upon[8] Joseph and said, "Lie with me." 8. But he refused *to approach her,* and he said[9] to his master's wife, "Behold, with me (here), my master concerns himself with nothing in the house, and he has put all that he owns in my hand. 9. He is no greater in this house than I, and he has withheld nothing from me except yourself, since you are his wife. How, then, could I do this great evil and become guilty *before the Lord?*" 10. And when she spoke with Joseph each day,[10] he did not listen to her to lie with her, *(lest) he be declared guilty* with her *on the day of the great judgment in the world to come.*[11] 11. On a certain day he came into the house *to study his reckoning tablets,*[12] and there was not one of the members of the household there in the house. 12. And she caught him by his garment, saying, "Lie with me." But he left his garment in her hand and fled into the street. 13. And when she saw that he had left his garment in her hand and fled into the street, 14. *she threw the white of an egg on the bed,*[13] called the members of the household, and said, "See *the effusion of semen which this fellow has scattered*—the Hebrew man whom *your master* brought to jest with us. He came in to me to lie with me, and I cried out with a loud voice. 15. And when he heard that I raised my voice and cried out, he left his garment with me and fled into the street." 16. She *put* the garment *down* be-

---

Notes, Chapter 39

[4]*Gen. R.* 86,3; *b. Sotah* 13b (70); *Tanh.* B., *Wa-Yeshev* 14 (1, 185). The midrash gives Heb. *srys,* "officer" (RSV), its usual meaning of "eunuch," and it explains how Potiphar became a eunuch. See Ginzberg, *Legends,* 5, 337, n. 101; Ps.-J. is the only Targum of this verse to refer to sodomy, to Potiphar's testicles, and to his impotency. On Ps.-J.'s readiness to refer to indelicate matters, see above, Introduction, p. 7.

[5]*'pwtrwpws.* Gr.: *epitropos*; = Nf, V, N, L, CTg E (with variations in spelling).

[6]Lit.: "did not know anything."

[7]*Gen. R.* 86,6; *Exod. R.* 1,32; *Tanh., Shemoth* 11 (170). The biblical phrase "the food which he ate" is taken as a euphemism for his wife, with whom he had marital intercourse; see also *b. Ketub.* 13a (71).

[8]Lit.: "lifted up her eyes on." See above, 13:10 with n. 4 to that verse.

[9]Lond.: "and she said."

[10]Lit.: "today and tomorrow."

[11]*Gen. R.* 87,6; *b. Yoma* 35b (164); *Sotah* 3b (11); *Jubilees* 39,6.

[12]*pynqsy*; Gr. *pinakes.* Onq.: "to examine his accounts." Cf. *Gen. R.* 87,7. See Aberbach-Grossfeld, 1982, 227, n. 8; Grossfeld, 1988, 133, n. 6.

[13]*b. Git.* 57a (263) makes a similar statement about a man who wanted to divorce his wife.

side her until his master came home. 17. Then she spoke to him in these words, saying, "The Hebrew slave whom you brought to us came to me to jest with me. 18. But when I raised my voice and cried out, he left his garment with me and fled into the street." 19. And when his master heard the words his wife spoke to him, namely, "This is what your servant did to me," he became very angry. 20. Joseph's master took *counsel from the priests*[14] *who discovered*[15] *that it was the white (of an egg). So he did not put him to death,*[16] but he put him in prison, the place where the king's prisoners were imprisoned. And he remained there in the prison. 21. But *the Memra of* the Lord was *at the assistance of* Joseph, and he extended kindness to him and caused him to win favor in the eyes of the governor of the prison. 22. The governor of the prison placed all the prisoners who were in the prison in Joseph's charge, and whatever was done there, it was he *who ordered its doing.*[17] 23. *It was not necessary for* the governor of the prison *to guard Joseph as is the custom with all prisoners, because* he saw no *fault*[18] in him, because *the Memra of* the Lord was *at his assistance,* and whatever he did the Lord made successful.

CHAPTER 40

1. After these events *it was announced as follows:* "The *chief* cup-bearer of the king of Egypt and the *chief* baker gave offense; *they plotted to put a mortal poison into his food and drink to kill* their master,[1] the king of Egypt." 2. And Pharaoh was angry when he heard about his two officers, about the chief butler and the chief baker. 3. And he put them in custody in the house of the chief *executioner*[2] in the

Notes, Chapter 39 (Cont.)

[14]*kwmrny'*. The Targums use the word *kwmr'* or *kwmrn'* to refer to a pagan priest. See above, n. 44 to Gen 14:18 (Ps.-J.).

[15]Lit.: "examined." Cf. *b. Git.* 57a (263–264), where it is said that the white of an egg was tested in similar circumstances.

[16]This addition is understandable in the light of Ps.-J.'s expansion of v. 14, and fits in with Ps.-J.'s reference in 47:22 to the priests who saved Joseph's life. Ps.-J.'s addition to these three verses forms a literary unit on its own. On Ps.-J.'s tendency to attach elements of a tradition to different verses, see above, Introduction, p. 5. In our present verse Ps.-J.'s addition explains why Joseph, who deserved the death penalty (cf. Deut 22:22), was simply put in prison.

[17]Onq.: "*was done by his order* (lit.: word)." HT ("he was the doer of it") might be taken to mean that Joseph actually worked in the prison. Onq. and Ps.-J. make it clear that he supervised the work.

[18]= Onq. Onq. and Ps.-J. read Heb. *m'wmh*, "anything," as if it were *mwm*, "blemish, fault."

Notes, Chapter 40

[1]Ps.-J. explains how the cup-bearer and the baker "offended their lord" (RSV). In v. 21 Ps.-J. says that the chief butler was reinstated because he had not taken part in the plot to kill the king. In v. 22 the same Targum says that the chief baker was put to death because he took part in the plot. Thus Ps.-J. fits three elements that form a unit in themselves into three different verses; see above, Introduction, p. 5. The story in question has no parallel in rabbinic literature, and it may be that the story of Bigthan and Teresh (cf. *Gen. R.* 88,3; *b. Meg.* 13b [78]; Targum Sheni to Esther 2:21) was transferred to the Joseph story. Cf. Shinan, 1979, 1, 125–126; idem, 1985, 80.

[2]See above 37:36 and n. 34 to that verse.

prison, the place where Joseph was imprisoned. 4. The chief *executioner*[2] assigned Joseph to them, and he ministered to them; and they remained *in the house of* custody for some time. 5. And they both—the cup-bearer and the baker of the king of Egypt, who were imprisoned in the prison—dreamed a dream, each his own dream on the same night, each *his own dream* with the interpretation of *his companion's* dream.[3] 6. Joseph came to them in the morning and saw them, and behold, they were sad. 7. He asked the nobles of Pharaoh who were with him in custody in his master's house, saying, "Why is it that *the expression of* your faces is more downcast today than all the days *you have been here?*" 8. They said to him, "We have dreamed a dream, but there is no one to interpret it." And Joseph said to them, "Is not the interpretation *of dreams from before the Lord?* Tell me (your dreams), I pray." 9. Then the chief cup-bearer told his dream to Joseph and said to him, "*I saw* in my dream, and behold there was a vine before me. 10. And on the vine there were three stalks.[4] As soon as it had budded it brought forth blossoms, and *immediately* its clusters ripened *and became* grapes. 11. *I continued to look until they placed* Pharaoh's cup in my hand. Then I took the grapes, pressed them into Pharaoh's cup, and placed the cup in Pharaoh's hand." 12. Joseph said to him, "This is the *purpose* (and) the interpretation[5] *of the dream:*[6] The three stalks are the three *fathers of the world, namely, Abraham, Isaac and Jacob,*[7] *some of whose descendants are destined to be enslaved in Egypt in clay and brick, and in all (kinds of) work in the open field.*[8] *But afterwards they will be redeemed by three shepherds.*[9] *And (as regards) what you said, 'I took the grapes, pressed them into Pharaoh's cup, and placed the cup in Pharaoh's hand': this is the goblet*[10] *of anger which Pharaoh is destined to drink in the end.*[11] *But you, chief cup-bearer, you shall receive a good reward for the favorable dream you have dreamed.*[12] *And this is its interpretation for you:* The three stalks are the three days *until your release.* 13. *At the end of* three days *the remembrance of you will come before Pharaoh,*[13] and he will

---

Notes, Chapter 40

[3]*Gen. R.* 88,4; *b. Berak.* 55b (341). The midrash takes the words "they both dreamed" to mean that they (each) dreamed the dream of both. This would explain how in v. 16 the chief baker could say that Joseph's interpretation of the chief butler's dream was correct (*ṭwb*). See below v. 16 and n. 17.

[4]*mṣwgy'* (also used twice in v. 12). In the margin of Lond. (v. 10) we find *šrbyṭyn*, which is the reading of Nf and CTg E in vv. 10 and 12. Apparently the word *mṣwgy'* is known only from these two verses in Ps.-J.; cf. Cook, 1986, 241.

[5]Le Déaut (1978, *Genèse,* 363) translates the Aramaic phrase *swp pwšrn'* (lit.: "the end of the interpretation") as "l'interprétation *finale.*" It seems, however, that Ps.-J. gives a double translation of Heb. *ptrn,* "interpretation," rendering it first as *swp* in the sense of "end, purpose," and then translating it directly as *pwšrn'.* In vv. 5, 8, 18 and in 41:11, Ps.-J. translates *ptrn* directly by its Aramaic cognate. On the interpretation of our present verse in the Targums, see Böhl, 1987, 124–128.

[6]Pesh., Vulg. Cf. Peters, 1934, 52–53.

[7]*b. Hul.* 92a (515).

[8]Cf. Exod 1:14.

[9]Nf, P, and CTg E name the three who are to redeem the enslaved Israelites as Moses, Aaron, and Miriam. See also *Gen. R.* 88,5; *b. Hul.* 92a (515); cf. also *Ta'an.* 9a (38); Tg. Micah 6:4.

[10]*pyyl',* Gr. *phialê,* = Nfmg, P, CTg E (with variations in spelling). For the image "the goblet of anger," cf., e.g., Isa 51:17, 22; Jer 25:15.

[11]*b. Hul.* 92a (516); cf. *Gen. R.* 88,5.

[12]*Gen. R.* 88,5.

[13]Onq.: "Pharaoh will *remember you.*"

lift up your head *in honor*[14] and restore you to your ministry, and you will place Pharaoh's cup in his hand according to (your) former custom when you were his cup-bearer." 14. *Joseph abandoned his trust in heaven and put his trust in a human being,*[15] *and he said to the chief cup-bearer,* "But remember me when it will be well with you, and do me, I pray, the kindness of remembering me *before* Pharaoh and bring me out of this *prison.* 15. For I was indeed kidnapped from the land of the Hebrews; and here, too, I have done no *evil* that they should put me in *prison.*"[16] 16. The chief baker saw that he had interpreted correctly,[17] *because he had seen the interpretation of his companion's dream;*[18] *and he began to speak angrily*[19] and said to Joseph, "I too *saw* in my dream, and behold there were three baskets *of white bread*[20] on my head. 17. In the top basket there were all kinds of *delicious* food for Pharaoh, the work of a baker; and the birds were eating them out of the basket above my head." 18. Joseph replied and said, "This is its interpretation: The three baskets are the three *enslavements*[21] *in which the house of Israel is destined to be enslaved, and you, chief baker, you shall receive an evil reward for the unfavorable dream which you have dreamed."*[22] *And Joseph interpreted for him what seemed right in his eyes. And he said to him: "This is its interpretation for you:* the three baskets are the three days *until your execution.* 19. *At the end of* three days Pharaoh, *with the sword,* will *remove*[23] your head from *your body* and hang you upon a tree,[24] and the birds will eat the flesh off you." 20. And on the third day, the birthday of Pharaoh, he made a feast for all his servants, and he lifted up the head of the chief cup-bearer and the head of the chief baker among his servants. 21. He restored the chief cup-bearer to his cup-bearing—*because it had been discovered that he had not taken part in that plot*[25]—and he placed the cup in Pharaoh's hand. 22. But the

Notes, Chapter 40

[14]Ps.-J. clarifies the meaning of HT "lift up your head." See below, v. 19, where Ps.-J. again interprets the same Heb. phrase.

[15]Lit.: "Joseph abandoned the security of above, and held on to the security of a son of man." Cf. *Gen. R.* 89,2–3; *Tanh. B., Mikez* 2 (1, 189–190); *Tanh., Wa-Yeshev* 9 (124). Nf and CTg E, our only Pal. Tgs. of this verse (apart from Ps.-J.), do not take up this midrash in our present verse. But Nf, (cf. Nfmg), P, V, N, and L incorporate a longer version of the same midrash in v. 23. Ps.-J. has a short version of the midrash in this latter verse also. Cf. Shinan, 1979, 1, 58–59.

[16]= Onq. It would be beneath Joseph's dignity to say that he was thrown into a common dungeon (HT). See Aberbach-Grossfeld, 1982, 233, n. 8; Grossfeld, 1988, 135, n. 9.

[17]= Onq. The underlying Heb. *ṭwb* can mean "correctly" or "favorably." See Aberbach-Grossfeld, ibid., n. 9; Grossfeld, ibid., n. 10. On the translation of Heb. *ṭwb* in Onq., see I. Drazin, *Targum Onkelos to Deuteronomy* (New York: Ktav, 1982) 62, n. 14. In that note correct Num 3:6 to Num 36:6.

[18]See above, v. 5 and n. 3 to that verse.

[19]Lit.: "with an angry tongue." The *meturgeman* understands Heb. *'p,* which in the biblical verse means "also," according to its second meaning, "anger." Cf. *Gen. R.* 88,6.

[20]Reading *pyt' nqy'* with ed. pr. (= Nf, CTg E, with spelling variations) rather than *ṣbyt'* (?) *nqy'* of Lond.

[21]*Gen. R.* 88,6.

[22]*Gen. R.* 88,6.

[23]"will remove" = Onq. Onq. and Ps.-J. clarify the meaning of HT "lift up." See above, v. 13 and n. 14.

[24]The phrase translated as "and hang you upon a tree" might also be translated as "and impale you upon a pole." See Aberbach-Grossfeld, 1982, 233, n. 10: Grossfeld, 1988, 135, n. 12. On the question of crucifixion in Judaism, see L. Díez-Merino. 1976, 31–120.

[25]See above, v. 1 (Ps.-J.) and n. 1 to that verse.

chief baker he hanged[26]—*because he had plotted to kill him*—as Joseph had interpreted for them. 23. *Because Joseph had abandoned the favor that is above and had trusted in the chief cup-bearer, in flesh that passes,*[27] *therefore*[28] the chief cup-bearer did not remember Joseph but forgot him *until the time appointed from before the Lord (for him) to be released had come.*

CHAPTER 41

1. At the end of two years *the remembrance of Joseph came before the Memra of the Lord:* Pharaoh had a dream and behold, he was standing by the river. 2. And behold, seven cows, beautiful to look at and fat of flesh, came up from the river, and they were grazing among the reeds.[1] 3. And behold, seven other cows, ugly to look at and lean *in their* flesh, came up from the river <after them> and stood *opposite* the (other) cows on the bank of the river. 4. And the cows that were ugly to look at and lean *in their* flesh ate up the seven cows that were beautiful to look at and fat. And Pharaoh awoke *from his sleep,* 5. He fell asleep and *saw* a dream a second time, and behold, seven ears of grain, fat and good, grew on one stalk. 6. And behold, seven ears, *blighted,* and beaten by the east (wind), sprouted after them. 7. And the *blighted* ears swallowed up the seven fat and full ears. And Pharaoh awoke, and behold it was a dream. 8. In the morning his spirit was troubled, and he sent and called all the sorcerers of Egypt and all its wise men; and Pharaoh told them his dream. But no one *was able* to interpret it <for Pharaoh> *for it had been (so) arranged from before the Lord, since the time had come for Joseph to leave the prison.*[2] 9. And the chief cup-bearer spoke *before* Pharaoh, saying, "I remember my faults today. 10. *It was arranged from before the Lord*[3] that Pharaoh was angry with his servants, and he put me in custody in the house of the chief *executioner,* me and the chief baker. 11. And we dreamed a dream on the same night, he and I; each (of

Notes, Chapter 40 (Cont.)

[26]Or "impaled" or "crucified"; = Onq., Nf.

[27]Reading *'byr* with Lond. (= Nf, L; Nfmg, P: *'bwr*) rather than *'byd* of *ed. pr.* (= V, N).

[28]This midrashic addition explains why the chief cup-bearer forgot Joseph. See above, v. 14 (Ps.-J.) and n. 15. See Shinan, 1979, 1, 70–71; 2, 235–236; Böhl, 1987, 135–136.

Notes, Chapter 41

[1]*gwmyy'.* This word, which is used here to translate Heb. *'ḥw,* "reed grass," is used by Ps.-J. to translate *swp,* "reeds," in Exod 2:3,5. In our present verse Lond. has the marginal variant *'pr'y,* "meadow," which is the word (with variations in spelling) used to translate *swp* in Exod 2:3 (Nf, V, P) and 2:5 (Nf).

[2]Omitted in Lond. and *ed. pr.* For Ps.-J.'s addition to this verse, see *Gen. R.* 89,1.

[3]These words are surprising on the lips of the Egyptian cup-bearer, and we know of no parallel to them in rabbinic literature. Cf. Shinan, 1979, 1, 59–60, 173.

us) dreamed *his own dream* and the interpretation of *his companion's* dream.[4] 12. There with us was a Hebrew youth, a servant of the chief *executioner.* We told him our dream and he interpreted it for us, giving to each an *interpretation* corresponding to his dream. 13. And as he interpreted for us, so it came to pass; me he restored *by his word* to my *usual* ministry,[5] and him he hanged." 14. Pharaoh sent and called Joseph, who was quickly taken[6] from *the prison.* He cut his hair and changed his clothes, and came before Pharaoh. 15. And Pharaoh said to Joseph, "I have dreamed a dream, and there is no one to interpret it; and I have heard it said about you that *if you* hear a dream, *you* (can) interpret it." 16. Joseph replied to Pharaoh, saying, "Not I.[7] *There is no one who (can) interpret dreams; but from before the Lord* a reply will be given (concerning) the welfare of Pharaoh." 17. And Pharaoh spoke to Joseph, *saying, "I saw* in my dream, (and) behold, I was standing on the bank of the river; 18. and behold, seven cows, fat of flesh and beautiful to look at, came up from the river, and they were pasturing among the reeds. 19. And behold, seven other cows, wretched and very ugly to look at, and lean *in their* flesh, came up after them. I have never seen the likes of them for ugliness in all the land of Egypt. 20. The wretched and ugly cows ate up the first seven fat cows. 21. They entered their belly, but no one knew that they entered their belly, for their appearance was as ugly as before. And I awoke. 22. And I saw in my dream, and behold, seven ears of grain, full and good, grew on one stalk. 23. And behold, seven ears, shriveled, *blighted,* and beaten by the east (wind), sprouted after them. 24. And the *blighted* ears swallowed the seven good ears, and I told the sorcerers, but there was no one to explain[8] (it) to me." 25. Joseph said to Pharaoh, "The dream of Pharaoh is one. *The Lord* has told Pharaoh what he *is about* to do. 26. The seven good cows *announce* seven years, and the seven good ears *announce these* seven years; it is one dream. 27. The seven emaciated and ugly cows that came up after them *announce* seven *other* years, and the seven ears, blighted and beaten by the east (wind), *announce this:*[9] *that* there will be seven years of famine.[10] 28. It is just as I have spoken to Pharaoh: *the Lord* has shown Pharaoh what he is *about* to do. 29. Behold, seven years of great abundance are coming in all the land of Egypt. 30. But after them will arise seven years of famine, and all the abundance *that was* in the land of Egypt will be forgotten, and the famine will blot out *the inhabitants*[11] of the land.

Notes, Chapter 41

[4]Ps.-J. renders this verse in conformity with that Targum's rendering of 40:5.

[5]Lit.: "to the order of my ministry"; see above, 40:13.

[6]Lit.: "and they had him skip from the prison." Lond. uses the verb *dlg,* "leap, skip," while later printed editions use *dly* (= CTg E), "draw, raise."

[7]Onq.: "*Not through my wisdom.*" Cf. Jerome (*Quaest. hebr.* in Gen 41:16): In hebraeo aliter habet: *sine me deus respondebit pacem Pharaoni.*

[8]Lit.: "to tell."

[9]Lit.: "thus."

[10]In Gen 50:3 Ps.-J. says that God had decreed that there would be a famine of forty-two years, but that the famine was reduced to two years because of the merit of Jacob. See below 47:7 and n. 6 to that verse, and 50:3 with n. 7 to that verse. On contradictions in Ps.-J., see above, Introduction, pp. 5–6.

[11]Onq.: "the people."

31. The abundance *that was* in the land will be unknown because of that famine which *will come* afterwards, because it will be very severe. 32. The fact that the dream was communicated to Pharaoh twice (means) that the matter was determined from *before the Lord,* and *the Lord* hastens to do it. 33. And now, let Pharaoh seek out an intelligent and wise man, and *appoint*[12] him over the land of Egypt. 34. Let Pharaoh take action and appoint administrators over the land, and let them take a fifth *of all the corn of* the land[13] of Egypt during the seven years of abundance. 35. Let them gather all *the corn* of these good years that are coming, and let them store the corn under the authority of Pharaoh's *administrators, and let them put the corn* in the cities and keep it. 36. Let *the corn be reserved in the caves* in the land *to provide food* during the seven years of famine that will be in the land of Egypt, so that *the people of* the land may not be wiped out by the famine." 37. The proposal seemed good *before* Pharaoh and *before* all his servants. 38. And Pharaoh said to his servants, "Could we find a man like this in whom there is the spirit *of prophecy from before the Lord?*"[14] 39. Then Pharaoh said to Joseph, "Since *the Lord* has made all this known to you, there is no one as intelligent and as wise as you. 40. You shall be *administrator* over my house, and by *the decree of the word of* your mouth[15] shall all my people be fed; only with respect to the *royal* throne will I be greater than you." 41. Pharaoh said to Joseph, "See, I have appointed you *prince*[16] over all the land of Egypt." 42. Pharaoh took his signet ring from his hand and put it on Joseph's hand; and he had him clothed in garments of fine linen, and he placed a gold necklace around his neck. 43. He had him ride in Pharaoh's second chariot, and they cried out before him, "*This is the father of the king, great in wisdom, tender in years.*"[17] And he appointed him *prince* over all the land of Egypt. 44. Pharaoh said to Joseph, "I am Pharaoh the king, *and you are the vice-regent,*[18] and without your *command*[19] no man shall raise his hand *to gird on weapons,* or his foot *to ride a horse,*[20] in all the land of Egypt." 45. Pharaoh called Joseph's name

Notes, Chapter 41

[12] = Onq., CTg C.

[13] Onq.: "let them equip the land"; cf. Aberbach-Grossfeld, 1982, 239, n. 9; Grossfeld, 1988, 137, n. 13.

[14] = Onq. Cf. Grossfeld, 1988, 138, n. 15.

[15] Onq.: "by your word." Ps.-J. combines the reading of Nf with that of Onq., CTg C.

[16] *srkn.* This word, which according to Levy (2,191) is probably derived from Gr. *archôn,* occurs again in v. 43. None of the other Targums of these verses uses this word. Ps.-J. also uses it in Exod 24:1 in an addition that is special to this Targum.

[17] *Sifre* to Deut 1:1 (edition Finkelstein, 8); *Gen. R.* 90,3; *b. B. Bat.* 4a (12). The word *'brk* in the HT is an Egyptian word of uncertain meaning (see, e.g., Vermes, 1963B, 162; 1975, 130). The midrashim and the Targums (Nf, P, V, N, L, CTg E) render that obscure word as if it were a combination of two Heb. words, *'b,* "father," and *rk,* "tender." This tradition was known to Origen (cf. *Selecta in Genesim* in Gen 41:43 [*PG* 12,133]) and to Jerome (*Quaest. hebr.* in Gen 41:43). See also the Targums of Gen 49:22 (Nf, P, V, N), where our present verse is quoted. See further Geiger, 1928, 463–464; Bowker, 1969, 254; R. Kasher, 1986, 7–8.

[18] *'lqpṭ'.* The *Alkafta* was a high Persian dignitary, and he is mentioned in *b. Shebu.* 6b (20) as the official who is next in importance to the king. The title is probably of Persian origin. See Jastrow, 73; Levy 1, 34. Compare Tg. 2 Chron 28:7, where we find reference to *'rqbt' dmlk',* "the vice-regent of the king."

[19] Lit.: "word," = Onq.

[20] = Onq. *Gen. R.* 90,3.

"The man-who-uncovers-hidden-things." [21] And he gave him as wife Asenath, *whom Dinah had borne to Shechem, and whom the wife of* Potiphera, *chief of Tanis, had reared.* [22] And Joseph went forth *as ruler* over the land of Egypt. 46. Joseph was thirty years old when he stood before Pharaoh, king of Egypt. Joseph went forth from Pharaoh's presence and passed through all the land of Egypt *as chief and ruler.* 47. The earth *was so fertile* [23] during the seven years of plenty that *every ear* produced *two full* handfuls *until all the granaries were filled.* 48. He gathered all the *corn* of the seven years *of plenty* that were in the land of Egypt, and he put the *corn* in the cities; *the corn* of the fields around each city he *gathered* into it. 49. [24] 50. Before the year of famine came, two sons were born to Joseph, whom Asenath, *who had grown up in the house of* Potiphera, the *chief of Tanis,* [25] had borne to him. 51. And Joseph called the name of the first-born Manasseh, for *he said,* "The Lord caused me to forget all my trouble and all my father's house." 52. And he called the name of the second Ephraim, for *he said,* "The Lord has strengthened [26] me in the land of my misery; *and similarly my father's house is destined to become strong here in their misery."* 53. The seven years of plenty that were in the land of Egypt came to an end, 54. and the seven years of famine began to come as Joseph had said. There was a famine in all lands; but in all the land of Egypt there was bread. 55. All the land of Egypt was hungry, *because the seed did not produce;* and the people cried out *before* Pharaoh for bread. And Pharaoh said to all the Egyptians, "Go to Joseph; whatever he tells you, you shall do." 56. When the famine was upon all the face of the land, Joseph opened all the *granaries* where *the corn* (was stored) and *sold (it) to the Egyptians;* [27] and the famine was severe in the land of Egypt. 57. And all *the inhabitants of* the earth came to Egypt to purchase *corn from* Joseph, for the famine was severe in all the land.

Notes, Chapter 41

[21] *Gen. R.* 90,4. This text reads the name Zaphenath-paneah as *zefûnôth* ("hidden things") *môfi'a* ("he reveals") *nôhôth* ("easily").

[22] *PRE* 36 (272); 38 (287–288). Cf. *Gen. R.* 89,2. This midrash eliminates the difficulty raised by the biblical statement that Joseph married a pagan woman. (See also above, 38:2, with n. 3 to that verse.) Ps.-J. does not explain how Asenath got to Egypt. This is explained in *PRE* 38. Ps.-J. simply alludes to this tradition. See further V. Aptowitzer, 1924, 239–306; Burchard, 1970, 3–34.

[23] Lit.: "prospered." Cf. *Gen. R.* 90,5. Onq.: "the *inhabitants of* the land *gathered grain.*"

[24] V. 49 is omitted in Lond and *ed. pr.*

[25] See above, v. 45. The Targums (Nf, CTg E, Ps.-J., Onq.) deprive Potiphera of the title "priest." See above, 14:18 and n. 44 to that verse.

[26] Or "increased."

[27] = Onq.

CHAPTER 42

1. Jacob saw that *provisions were being bought and that* corn *was being brought* from Egypt. And Jacob said to his sons, "Why *then are you afraid*[1] *to go down to Egypt?*" 2. And he said, "Behold, I heard that there is corn *being sold*[2] in[3] Egypt. Go down there and purchase for us from there, that we may live and not die." 3. So ten of Joseph's brothers went down to purchase corn from Egypt. 4. But Jacob did not send Joseph's brother Benjamin with his brothers; for he said, "*Behold, he is (but) a boy, and I am afraid that death*[2] might befall him." 5. The sons of Israel came, *each one by a different gate,*[4] *lest the evil eye*[5] *should have power over them if they came together*[6] to purchase among *the Canaanites* who were coming *to purchase;* for there was a famine in the land of Canaan. 6. Joseph was ruler over the land, *and he knew that his brothers were coming to buy. He appointed guards at the city gates, to register everyone who entered that day—his name and his father's name.*[7] It was he who sold *corn*[2] to all the people of the land. And Joseph's brothers came *and searched in the streets and in the squares and in the brothels,*[8] *but they did not find him.* They entered his house and they bowed down to him *with*[9] their faces *to*[9] the ground. 7. Joseph saw his brothers and he recognized them; but *he acted like a stranger in their presence*[10] and spoke harsh words to them. He said to them, "Where do you come from?" And they said, "From the land of Canaan to purchase corn." 8. Joseph recognized his brothers, *because when he was separated from them they had the sign of a beard;* but they did not recognize him, *because he did not have the sign of a beard (then), but at that time he had it.*[11] 9. Joseph remembered the dreams he had dreamed about them, and he said to them, "You are spies; you have come to see the nakedness *of the prostitutes*[12] of the land.[13] 10. And

---

Notes, Chapter 42

[1]Ps.-J. (see also Pesh.) translates Heb. *r'h,* "see," as if it were *yr',* "fear."

[2]= Onq.

[3]Lond. and *ed. pr.* read "to."

[4]Lit.: "by one gate."

[5]On Ps.-J.'s belief in magical powers, see above, Introduction, p. 6.

[6]*Gen. R.* 91,2.6; *Tanh., Mikez* 8 (129). See further Ginzberg, *Legends* 2, 80 and 5, 347, n. 201; Rappaport, 1930, 111–112, n. 118.

[7]*Gen. R.* 91,6: *Tanh., Mikez* 8 (130).

[8]*Gen. R.* 91,6; *Tanh., Mikez* 8 (130). These texts say that the brothers feared that Joseph, who was a handsome man, might have been set up in a harlot's tent.

[9]Lit.: "upon"; = Onq.

[10]Onq.: "he considered what he should say to them." Onq. tones down the aloofness which the biblical text attributes to Joseph.

[11]*Gen. R.* 91,7; *b. Yeb.* 88a (599); *B. Mez.* 39b (237); *Ketub.* 27b (150); *Tanh., Wa-Yiggash* 5 (139). The Talmud texts and the text from *Tanhuma* use the Heb. idiom *htymt zqn,* "the mark or stamp of a beard," which corresponds to the idiom *rwšm dqn,* which Ps.-J. employs. Jastrow (512–513) translates the Heb. idiom as "the mature manly expression which the beard gives, full manhood."

[12]*Gen. R.* 91,6; *Tanh., Mikez* 8 (130). Ps.-J.'s interpretation of the words "the nakedness of the land" fits in with that Targum's addition to v. 6, where it is said that the brothers searched for Joseph in the brothels. In reality, the "nakedness of the land" (HT) refers to things that should be hidden from potential enemies. Onq. translates it in that sense: "the vulnerable part of the land." Vulg.: "*infirmiora terrae.*" See also v. 12.

[13]Lond. and *ed. pr.* add a second "to see" at the end of the verse. Following Ginsburger, (*Pseudo-Jonathan,* 79), we omit it.

they said to him, "No, my lord; your servants have come to *purchase corn*. 11. We are all the sons of one man; we are trustworthy men; your servants have not been spies." 12. And he said to them, "No! But you have come to see the nakedness *of the prostitutes* of the land." 13. And they said, "We, your servants were twelve brothers, sons of one man in the land of Canaan; behold, the youngest is with our father this day; one *left us, and we do not know what became of him in the end.*" [14] 14. Joseph said to them, "It is as I said to you, you are spies. 15. In this *manner* you shall be tested; by the life of Pharaoh, you shall not depart from here unless your youngest brother comes here. 16. Send one of you, and let him bring your brother; but you shall be imprisoned and your words shall be tested, (to see) if the truth is in you; and if not, by the life of Pharaoh, you are spies." 17. Then he put them all together in *the house of* custody for three days. 18. And on the third day Joseph said to them, "Do this and you shall live, (for) I fear *from before the Lord:* 19. if you are trustworthy men, let one of your brothers be imprisoned in your house of custody, and you go, bring *the corn you have bought for* your starving households. [15] 20. You shall bring your youngest brother to me, that your words may be verified and that you may not die." And they did so. 21. They said to one another, "*In truth* we are guilty concerning our brother, for we saw the anguish of his soul when he implored us, and we did not listen to him; that is why this distress has come upon us." 22. Reuben answered them and said, "Did I not say to you, 'Do not sin against the boy?' But you paid no heed *to me*. And so, behold, his blood is required *of us*." 23. They did not know that Joseph understood *the language of the sanctuary,* [16] because *Manasseh* [17] was between them *as* an interpreter. 24. He turned away from them and wept. Then he turned back to them and spoke with them; and he took from among them Simeon, *who had counseled to kill him,* [18] and he tied him before them. 25. Joseph commanded *his servants* to fill their receptacles with corn, and to replace each man's money *within* his sack, and to give them provisions for the journey. And this was done for them. 26. They loaded their corn on their asses and departed from there. 27. *Levi, who had been left alone without Simeon his companion,* [19] opened his sack to give fodder to his ass at the lodging place, and he saw his money, and behold it was in the mouth of his bag. 28. He said to his brothers, "My money has been returned, and behold it is in my bag." And *knowledge* failed (from) their heart, [20] and they looked anxiously at one another, saying, "What is this that *the Lord* has done, *even though* [21] *there is no guilt* on our part?" 29. They

Notes, Chapter 42

[14] = Nf, P. See the phrase "what has become of him" (RSV) in Exod 32:1 and in the Targums (Nf, Ps.-J., Onq.) of that verse. See Tg. Gen 5:24 (P); 42:32 (Ps.-J., Nf), 36 (Nf, P, V, N, L, CTg E).

[15] Lit.: "the starving of your households."

[16] See above, 11:1 and n. 2 to that verse.

[17] *Gen. R.* 91,8.

[18] *Gen. R.* 91,6. *Tanh., Wa-Yiggash* 4 (135).

[19] HT "one (*ha'eḥad*) of them" is taken to mean "the one who was left alone." This one is then taken to be Levi, whom Joseph had separated from Simeon lest the two of them plot against him. We know of no source earlier than Ps.-J. for this tradition. See Schmerler, 1932, 301.

[20] Lit.: "the knowledge of their heart departed"; = Onq.

[21] *b. Ta'an* 9a (37).

came to their father Jacob in the land of Canaan, and they related to him all that had happened to them, saying, 30. "The man (who is) lord of the land spoke harsh *words* to us and *despised* us as spies of the land. 31. But we said to him, 'We are trustworthy men; we are not spies. 32. We were twelve brothers, sons of our father;[22] (as regards) one, *we do not know what became of him in the end;*[23] and this day the youngest is with our father in the land of Canaan. 33. But the man (who is) lord of the land said to us, 'By this I shall know that you are trustworthy; leave one of your brothers with me, and take *what is necessary* for your starving households[24] and go. 34. And bring your youngest brother to me, and I shall know that you are not spies *but* trustworthy men. I will restore your brother to you, and you shall travel about the land *doing business.'* " 35. When they were emptying their *saddle-bags,*[25] behold each man's bundle of money was in his *saddle-bag.* When they and their father saw the bundles of money, they were afraid *for Simeon, whom they had left there.* 36. Their father Jacob said to them, "You have made me childless; (of) Joseph *you have said. 'A savage beast has devoured him';* and (of) Simeon, *you have said, 'The King of the land has bound him';*[26] and Benjamin *you wish to* take away; *the sufferings of* all of them have come upon me." 37. And Reuben said to his father, "You may kill my two sons *with the ban*[27] if I do not bring him back to you; put him in my hands, and I will bring him back to you." 38. But he said, "My son shall not go down with you, because his brother is dead, and he alone is left *of his mother.*[28] And should *death*[29] befall him on the way in which you are to go, you would bring my grey head in sorrow to *the grave."*[30]

Notes, Chapter 42

[22]Lond.: "of father."

[23]See v. 13 and n. 14 to that verse.

[24]See v. 19 and n. 15.

[25]= *ed. pr.*: *dysqyyhwn*; Lond.: *dysqyynwn*; Gr.: *duo sakkos*; cf. Levy, 1, 172.

[26]All the Pal. Tgs. make similar but not identical additions to this verse. These additions are based on biblical texts. For "a savage beast has devoured him" (cf. P, Ps.-J.), see Gen 37:20, 33; for "the king of the land has bound him" (cf. P, Ps.-J.), see Gen 42:24; for "from the time I sent Joseph to you (in Dothan)" (Nf, P, V, N, L, CTg E), see Gen 37:13–17; for "from the time Simeon descended with you to Egypt" (P, V, N, L, CTg E), see Gen 42:19, 24). See Klein, 1986, 2, 40.

[27]Ps.-J., and Ps.-J. alone, uses the same noun (*šmt'*), "ban," in similar idioms in Num 21:24 and Deut 7:2. The same root is used with the same meaning by Ps.-J., and by Ps.-J. alone, in Deut 7:26 (twice); 13:18. This root occurs with this meaning only in the Babylonian Talmud and in Mandaic; cf. Cook, 1986, 259. Ps.-J.'s version of our present verse and of Num 21:24 and Deut 7:2 expresses a belief in the magical power of the ban; cf. Shinan, 1979, 2, 253; idem, 1983B, 423.

[28]Joseph and Benjamin were Rachel's only sons; cf. Gen 35:24. Ps.-J., probably under the influence of Gen 44:20, clarifies the biblical verse.

[29]= Onq. See also v. 4 above.

[30]See also Gen 37:35 (Ps.-J.) and 44:29 (Ps.-J.).

CHAPTER 43

1. Now the famine was severe in the land. 2. And when they finished eating the corn which they had brought from Egypt, their father said to them, "Go back and purchase a little *corn* for us." 3. But Judah said to him, "The man warned us solemnly, saying, 'You shall not see my countenance if your *young* brother is not with you.' 4. If you send our brother with us, we will go down and purchase *corn* for you. 5. But if you do not send (him), we will not go down, because the man said to us, 'You shall not see my countenance if your brother is not with you!' "[1] 6. And Israel said, "Why did you do me harm by telling the man that you had another brother?" 7. They said, "The man questioned us carefully about ourselves and about our genealogy, saying, 'Is your father still alive? Have you (another) brother?' And we answered him accordingly.[2] Could we have known that he would say, 'Bring your brother down'?" 8. And Judah said to Israel his father, "Send the boy with me, and we will arise and go, that we may live and not die, both we and you and also our little ones. 9. I will be surety for him; you may require him from my hand. If I do not bring him back to you and set him before you, let me be considered guilty *before* you forever. 10. For if we had not delayed, we would have returned twice by now." 11. Israel their father said to them, "If it must be so, do this: take some of what is most *renowned*[3] in the land, *put it* in your receptacles, and bring it down to the man as a present—a little gum, balm, and a little honey, wax and resin, *oil of*[4] pistachios and *oil of* almonds. 12. And take double the money in your hands and bring back in your hands the money that was replaced in the mouth of your bags; perhaps it was (done) by mistake. 13. Take your brother too; arise and go back to the man. 14. And may El Shaddai grant you mercy before the man, and may he release to you your other brother, as well as Benjamin. And as for me, *behold, I have already been informed by the Holy Spirit that if* I have been bereaved *of Joseph,* I will be bereaved *of Simeon and of Benjamin.*"[5] 15. The men took that present, and they took double the money in their hands; they took Benjamin, and they arose and went down to Egypt, and presented themselves before Joseph. 16. When Joseph saw Benjamin with them, he said to *Manasseh, whom he had appointed administrator* over his house, "Bring the men into the house, and *let them see the mark of the slaughtering, and remove the sinew of the hip,*[6] and prepare *a dish in their presence,*

Notes, Chapter 43

[1]After v. 5 the scribe of Lond. began v. 7. Having written five words, he noticed his mistake, and having put lines around these words from v. 7, he began v. 6.

[2]Lit.: "we told him according to (*'l mymr,* = Onq.) these words."

[3]= Onq.; *Gen. R.* 91,11: "things about which people sing."

[4]*Gen. R.* 91,11.

[5]Apart from Ps.-J., the Pal. Tgs. (Nf, P, V, N, L, CTg D) give a converse translation of this verse. Cf. Schäfer, 1972, 35; Klein, 1974, 224–225; idem, 1976, 523–524; idem, 1986, 2, 43.

[6]Lit.: "uncover the place of the slaughtering, and take the sinew of the hip." Ps.-J. gives an Aramaic version of the Heb. words in his source, *b. Hul.* 91a (511). The midrash is intended to show that Jacob's sons could see that the slaughtering was done according to the ritual laws.

because the men will eat with me at *the time of* the midday *meal.*[7] 17. The man did as Joseph said, and the man brought the men into Joseph's house. 18. The men were afraid because they were brought into Joseph's house, and they said, "It is because of the money that (was) replaced in our bags the first time that we are brought in, to *dupe*[8] us and *seek a quarrel* with us, and to *acquire* us as slaves and to take our asses." 19. So they approached the man who *had been appointed administrator* over Joseph's house, and they spoke with him at the door of *his* house. 20. And they said, "If you please,[9] my master, we came down before to purchase *corn.* 21. But when we reached the lodging place and opened our bags, behold, each man's money was in the mouth of his bag, our money in (full) weight; and we have brought it back in our hands. 22. And we have brought other money down in our hands to purchase *corn.* We do not know who put our money in our bags." 23. He said, "Peace to you *from my master*; do not be afraid. Your God and the God of your father put treasure in your bags for you. Your money has come to me." And he brought Simeon out to them. 24. The man brought the men into Joseph's house; he gave (them) water, and they washed their feet, and he gave fodder to their asses. 25. They prepared the present while they waited for Joseph to come[10] to the midday *meal,*[7] for they had heard *from him* that they were to share a meal[11] there. 26. When Joseph came into the house, they presented to him the present they had in their hands in the house, and they bowed down to him to the ground. 27. He inquired about their welfare and said, "Is your father well,[12] the old man of whom you spoke *to me? Is* he still alive?" 28. They said, "Your servant our father is well;[12] he is still alive." And they bent down and bowed down. 29. He lifted up[13] his eyes and saw Benjamin his brother, his mother's son, and he said, "Is this your youngest brother of whom you spoke to me?" And he said, "Mercy *from before the Lord* be *upon* you my son." 30. Then Joseph hurried, for his love for his brother was aroused and he wanted to weep; so he went into the bedchamber[14] and wept there. 31. He washed *the tears* from his face and came forth; and he controlled himself and said, "Serve the meal." 32. They served him by himself, and them by themselves, and the Egyptians who ate with him by themselves; for Egyptians *are not permitted* to eat bread with the *Jews, because the Jews eat the cattle which the Egyptians worship.*[15] 33. And they sat around before him, the eldest according to *the*

Notes, Chapter 43

[7]Onq.: "the meal." See also v. 25.

[8]*lmt'qp'*; Cf. Levy, 2,237. Jastrow, 1107, gives the meaning "seek occasion against."

[9]The word *bmṭw* used here by Ps.-J. (see also Ps.-J. Gen 44:18 [twice]; 50:17; Exod 32:31; Num 12:11,12), is found in the Babylonian Talmud, in Tg. Psalms, and in Mandaic. See Cook, 1986, 256.

[10]"while . . . to come;" lit.: "until Joseph's coming."

[11]See above 31:54 and n. 44 to that verse.

[12]From "is your father well" in v. 27 to "he is still alive" in v. 28 is omitted in Lond. through haplography. Essentially the same section was deleted by the scribe of CTg E; cf. Klein, 1986, 1, 122–123.

[13]See above 13:10 and n. 4 to that verse.

[14]Ps.-J. has a double translation of Heb. *ḥdr*, "room," first using *qyṭwn'* (Gr.: *koitôn*), "bedchamber" (= Nf, V, N, L, CTg E), and then *(d)by mdmk'*, "bedroom" (cf. Onq.: *'ydrwn byt mškb'*, "the alcove of the bedroom"). The translation in Onq. is also a double rendering; cf. Bacher, 1874, 67, n. 2.

[15]= Onq. See also Tg. Exod 8:22 (Nf, Nfmg, Ps.-J., Onq.); *Sibylline Oracles* 3,30. See Grossfeld, 1988, 145, n. 12.

rank of his seniority, and the youngest according to *the rank of* his youth. *He took the silver cup in his hand, and striking (it) like a diviner,*[16] *he arranged the sons of Leah on one side, the sons of Zilpah on another side, the sons of Bilhah on another side, and he placed Rachel's son Benjamin beside himself.*[17] And the men looked at each other in amazement. 34. He took portions from *his table and had them sent* from him to them. But Benjamin's portion was five times bigger than any of their portions: *one portion was his own portion, another portion was his,*[18] *one portion was his wife's, and two portions were those of his two sons.* And they drank and got drunk with him *because from the day they were separated from him they had not drunk wine, neither he nor they, until that day.*

CHAPTER 44

1. Then he commanded *Manasseh,*[1] *who had been appointed administrator* over his house, saying, "Fill the men's *saddle-bags* with *corn,* as much as they can carry, and put each man's money in the mouth of his bag. 2. Put my goblet, the silver goblet, in the mouth of the bag of the youngest, as well as the money of his purchases." And he did as Joseph said. 3. When morning broke[2] the men were sent off, they[3] and their asses. 4. They had left the city, but had not gone far when Joseph said to *Manasseh, who had been appointed administrator* over his house, "Arise, pursue the men; and when you overtake them, say to them, 'Why have you repaid evil for good? 5. Is not this the one from which my master would drink and with which he would practice augury?[4] You have done evil (by doing) what you have done.' " 6. He overtook them and spoke *all* these words to them. 7. And they said to him, "Why does my master speak such words? Far be it from your servants to do such a thing. 8. Behold, the money that we found in the mouth of our bags we brought back to you from the land of Canaan. How *then* could we steal *vessels of*[5] silver or *vessels of*[5] gold from your master's house? 9. With whomsoever of your servants it

Notes, Chapter 43 (Cont.)

[16]Cf. *Gen. R.* 92,5; 91,6; 93,7. Note that Ps.-J. does not hesitate to say that Joseph pretended to practice divination.

[17]HT does not explain why Joseph's brothers should be amazed. Ps.-J. explains that it was the fact that Joseph knew which brothers were born of the different mothers that caused the amazement.

[18]That is, Joseph's. The phrase "another portion was his" is repeated in Lond. Cf. *Gen. R.* 92,5.

Notes, Chapter 44

[1]*Tanḥ., Mikez* 10 (132).

[2]Lit.: "shone."

[3]The word for "they" is omitted in Lond.

[4]Nfmg, V, N, L; Onq. uses the verb *bdq,* "examine, test," and thus avoids saying that Joseph practiced divination. See above, 30:27 and n. 26 to that verse, and below, v. 15 and n. 8.

[5]= Onq.

shall be found, he shall *incur the death penalty;*[6] and moreover, we shall be slaves to my master." 10. He said, "Very well, then; let it be according to your words; the one with whom it is found shall be my slave, but you shall be innocent." 11. So each man hurried and lowered his bag to the ground, and each man opened his bag. 12. He searched, beginning with *Reuben* and ending with *Benjamin;* and the goblet was found in Benjamin's bag. 13. They rent their garments; *but mighty strength was given to them*[7] and each man loaded his ass, and they returned to the city. 14. When Judah and his brothers entered the house of Joseph, he was still there, and they fell upon the ground before him. 15. Joseph said to them, "What is this deed that you have done? Did you not know that a man like me practices augury?"[8] 16. Judah said, "What shall we say to my master *about the first money?* And what shall we say *about the next money?* And how shall we be proved innocent *in respect of the goblet?*[9] *From before the Lord* guilt has been found in your servants. Behold, we are slaves to my master, both we and him in whose possession the cup was found." 17. But he said, "Far be it from me to do this. The man in whose hand the cup was found, he shall be my slave; but you go up in peace to your father." 18. Then Judah approached him and said, "Please, my master! Please let your servant speak a word in the hearing of my master, and let not your anger be enkindled against your servant; for *from the hour that we came to you, you said to us, 'I fear from before the Lord'; and now your judgments have turned out to be like the judgments of Pharaoh.*[10] 19. My master asked his servants, saying, 'Have you a father or a brother?' 20. We said to my master, 'We have an aged father, and a son of (his) old age, the youngest; his brother is dead, and he alone is left of his mother, and *therefore* his father loves him.' 21. Then you said to your servants, 'Bring him down to me, that I may set my eyes[11] on him *for good.'* 22. We said to my master, 'It is not possible for the boy to leave his father, *for if* he should leave him, his father would die.'[12] 23. You said to your servants, 'If your youngest brother does not come down with you, you shall not see my countenance again.' 24. When we went up to your servant my father, we reported my lord's words to him. 25. Our father said, 'Go

Notes, Chapter 44

[6]Ps.-J. uses the same idiom in Gen 2:17; Onq.: "let him be killed;" see Grossfeld, 1988, 147, n. 6.

[7]*Gen. R.* 92,8: "each man took his baggage in one hand. . . ." Cf. also *Tanḥ., Mikez* 10 (133). The phrase "mighty strength" (*kḥ gbwrt'*), which Ps.-J. alone uses in our present verse, occurs again in Ps.-J., and in Ps.-J. alone, in Exod 2:17 and 8:15.

[8]= Nfmg, P; Onq. uses the verb *bdq* as in v. 5 above. See n. 4 to that verse. Unlike Onq., Ps.-J. and the other Pal. Tgs. of our present verse (Nf, Nfmg, P, CTg D) and of v. 5 above (Nf, Nfmg, V, N, L, CTg D) do not hesitate to say that Joseph practiced divination. See Díez Macho, *Neophyti 1*, III, 47*–48*; Churgin, 1943, 104.

[9]*Gen. R.* 92,9.

[10]Ps.-J.'s addition to this verse is a truncated version of a long midrash which appears in other Targumic versions of the same verse (Nf, P, V, N, L, CTg D). Versions of the same midrash are found in several toseftas; cf. Díez-Macho, 1956, 319–324; Klein, 1986, 1, 134–143; Vermes, 1961, 11–25. See also Niehoff, 1988, 247–250. The biblical phrase "for you are like Pharaoh himself" is meant as a compliment, but the Targums, including Ps.-J., take it as a reproach; cf. *Gen R.* 93,6.

[11]Lond. and *ed. pr.* read "his eyes," as does Nfi. This may be a case of the third pers. suffix being used instead of the first pers., so that we need not correct the text. Cf. Díez-Macho, 1981, 70.

[12]Lit.: "for if he should leave his father, he would die."

back and purchase a little *corn* for us.' 26. We said, 'It is not possible for us to go down. If our youngest brother is with us, we will go down; for it is not possible for us to see the man's countenance if our youngest brother is not with us.' 27. Your servant my father said to us, 'You know that my wife bore me two sons. 28. One left me, and I said, Surely he has been *killed.* [13] And up to now I have not seen him. 29. Should you take this one from before me also, and should death befall him, you would bring my grey head in *sorrow* down to *the grave.'* [14] 30. . . . [15] 31. . . . [15] 32. For your servant became surety for the boy to my father saying, 'If I do not bring him back to you, let me be considered guilty *before* my father forever.' 33. And now, I beseech you, let your servant remain instead of the boy as a slave to my master, and let the boy go up with his brothers. 34. For how can I go up to my father if the boy is not with me? Let me not see the sorrow [16] that would *pierce* my father."

CHAPTER 45

1. Joseph could not bear *not being able to cry* [1] *on account of* all who were standing *before* him; and he said, "Make everyone go out from *before* me." So no one stayed with him when Joseph made himself known to his brothers. 2. He wept aloud, [2] so that the Egyptians heard (him), and *the members of* Pharaoh's household heard (him). 3. Joseph said to his brothers, "I am Joseph. Is my father still alive?" But his brothers could not answer him *a word,* because they were dumbfounded before him. 4. Joseph said to his brothers, "Come near to me, I pray, *and see the cut of my circumcision."* [3] And they came near. And he said, "I am Joseph your brother, whom you sold into Egypt. 5. And now do not be distressed, and do not be angry with yourselves because you sold me hither, for *the Lord* sent me before you to keep *you* alive. 6. For the famine has been in the land these two years; and there are still

Notes, Chapter 44 (Cont.)

[13] The words which are here attributed to Jacob do not agree with that patriarch's statement as recorded earlier in Ps.-J. 37:33; see above n. 29 to that verse.

[14] See 37:35; 42:38 (Ps.-J.).

[15] Verses 30-31 are omitted through homoioteleuton in Lond. and *ed. pr.* The scribe of Lond. was aware that there was an omission in the MS he was copying, and he left a space of several lines in his text.

[16] Lit.: "the evil."

Notes, Chapter 45

[1] Lit.: "could not bear that he would not cry."

[2] Lit.: "He raised (*'rym*; cf. Nfmg as corrected by Díez Macho: *'r'm*) his voice in weeping."

[3] *Gen. R.* 93,10; *Tanḥ., Wa-Yiggash* 5 (139). On the phrase "the cut of my circumcision," see above, 24:2 and n. 4 to that verse. There is a certain contradiction between Ps.-J.'s claim in our present verse that Joseph identified himself by showing the mark of his circumcision and the same Targum's statement (in agreement with Nf and Onq.) in v. 12 that he did so by speaking Hebrew. See Levine, 1968, 37; idem, 1969, 119; Shinan, 1979, 1, 134 and 142–143; idem, 1985, 85.

five years (to come) in which they will neither plough nor reap. 7. *The Lord* sent me before you to ensure your survival[4] in the land and to keep you alive for a great deliverance. 8. So it was not you who sent me here, *but the situation*[5] *came about from before the Lord;* and he placed me as *master*[6] to Pharaoh, and as master over all his house, and (as) ruler in all the land of Egypt. 9. Make haste and go up to my father and say to him, 'Thus says your son Joseph, *the Lord* has placed me as master to all *the Egyptians.* Come down to me; do not delay. 10. You shall dwell in the land of Goshen, and you shall be near me, you and your children, and your grandchildren, your flocks and herds, and all that is yours. 11. I will support you there— for there are still five years of famine (to come) lest you and *the members of* your household and all that is yours be reduced to poverty.' 12. Behold, your eyes see, as well as the eyes of my brother Benjamin, that my mouth speaks with you *in the language of the Sanctuary.*[7] 13. Tell my father of all the glory *I have* in Egypt and of all *my greatness* that you have seen; make haste <and bring> my father <down>[8] here." 14. Then he *inclined*[9] upon the *joint of* his brother Benjamin's neck[10] and wept, *because he saw*[11] *that the Sanctuary was to be built in the portion of Benjamin and was to be destroyed twice.* And Benjamin wept on *the joint of Joseph's* neck, *because he saw the Tabernacle of Shiloh that was to be in the portion of Joseph and (that) was to be destroyed.*[12] 15. And he kissed all his brothers and wept upon them, *because he saw that they would be enslaved to the children of the nations;*[13] then his brothers spoke with him. 16. The report was heard in Pharaoh's *royal* palace: "Joseph's brothers have come," and *the matter* was pleasing in the eyes of Pharaoh and in the eyes of his servants. 17. And Pharaoh said to Joseph, "Say to your brothers, 'Do this: Load your beasts and set out, and *bring*[14] (provisions) to the land of Canaan. 18. Take your father and *the members of* your households and come to me, and I will give you what is best *(and) most desirable*[15] in the land of Egypt, and you shall eat the fat of the land.' 19. And you, *Joseph,* are given responsibility for *the honor of your father. Therefore, say to your brothers,* 'Do this: Take from the land of

Notes, Chapter 45

[4]Lit.: "to give you a remnant"; = Onq.

[5]Lit.: "the thing."

[6]*rb; Gen. R.* 93,10; Theodor-Albeck, 1160: *ptrwn bsylyws* = Gr. *patrôn basileôs,* "king's protector."

[7]Onq.: "that I speak with you in your own language." See *Mekilta* to Exod 12:6 (1,36). *Gen. R.* 93,10; *Lev. R.* 32,5; *Tanh., Wa- Yiggash* 5 (139); *Jubilees* 43,15. See above, v. 4 (Ps.-J.) and n. 3 to that verse. On the idiom "the language of the Sanctuary," see above, 11:1 (Ps.-J.) and n. 2 to that verse.

[8]"And bring down" is omitted in Lond. and *ed. pr.*

[9]*'trk(y)n* = Nf; Onq.: "he fell."

[10]The idiom "the joint of the neck" occurs twice in our present verse (Ps.-J.), in 46:29 (Ps.-J.), and in Deut 33:29 (Nf, N, Ps.-J., Onq.).

[11]"He saw" is omitted in *ed. pr.*

[12]*Gen. R.* 93,10 and *b. Meg.* 16b (98) conclude from the fact that "neck" (HT) is in the plural that the biblical text refers to two sanctuaries, both of which would be destroyed.

[13]There is no known source for this addition.

[14]= Onq.; see Aberbach-Grossfeld, 1982, 263, n. 9; Grossfeld, 1988, 149, n. 9. Pesh.: "load your beasts *with corn* and go."

[15]*špr 'rg.* This idiom is used again in v. 20. These are the only places where it occurs in Ps.-J.; cf. Clarke, 1984, Concordance 68 and 587. It is used also in Tg. Psalms 45:14; cf. Jastrow, 114.

Egypt carriages[16] *drawn by oxen* so that *you may carry* your little ones and your wives in them; and take your father and come. 20. Do not be concerned about your belongings,[17] because what is best *(and) most desirable* in all the land of Egypt is yours.' " 21. The sons of Israel did so. And Joseph gave them carriages according to *the word*[18] of Pharaoh, and he gave them provisions for the journey. 22. To each of them he gave *a robe*[19] *and clothes;* but to Benjamin he gave three hundred *selas* of silver and five *suits of clothes.*[20] 23. And to his father he sent the following *present:* ten he-asses laden with *wine*[21] and (with) some of the best things of Egypt, and ten she-asses laden with corn, bread, and provisions for his father for the journey. 24. Then he sent his brothers away, and they set off. He said to them, "Do not quarrel *about my sale, lest those who make* the journey *(with you) become angry with you."*[22] 25. They went up from Egypt and came to the land of Canaan to their father Jacob. 26. And they told him, saying, "Joseph is still alive, and indeed he is ruler in all the land of Egypt." But his heart *was divided,*[23] because he did not believe them. 27. But they recounted to him all the words that Joseph had spoken with them, and when he saw the carriages that Joseph had sent to take him, the spirit *of prophecy which had departed from him when they sold Joseph returned and rested upon*[24] their father Jacob. 28. And Israel said, *"The Lord has done many good things for me;*[25] *he delivered me from the hands of Esau and from the hands of Laban, and from the hands of the Canaanites who pursued me;*[26] *and I have seen and expected to see many consolations. But this I did not expect: that* my son Joseph was still alive. I will go then, and see him before I die."

Notes, Chapter 45

[16]The word *sdn,* which Jastrow (957) tentatively links with Latin *essedum,* "traveling carriage," occurs in Ps.-J. in our present verse, in vv. 21,27, and in 46:5. Nfmg has this word as a variant in our present verse.

[17]Lit.: "Let your eyes not have consideration for your vessels"; = Onq., HT.

[18]Ps.-J., Nfmg, and Onq. use the word *memra.* HT: "mouth."

[19]*'stwly;* Gr.: *stolê;* Latin = *stola.*

[20]Lit.: "five robes (*'stwly;* see preceding note) of clothes." Ps.-J. is inconsistent in its translation of Heb. *ḥlpwt śmlt,* "change of clothing," which occurs twice in our present verse. Rendering that phrase first as "a robe and clothes," it agrees with Nf; reading (lit.) "robes of clothes" in the second part of the verse, it follows Onq.

[21]*b. Meg.* 16b (98).

[22]According to *b. Ta'an.* 10 b (46), Joseph told his brothers not to discuss words of Torah on the journey. We know of no text earlier than Ps.-J. which says that Joseph warned them not to discuss his sale.

[23]That is, he did not know whether to believe them or not. Compare Hos 10:2, where the corresponding Heb. phrase means "(their) heart is false." Onq.: "the words failed on his heart."

[24]*ARN* A 30; *PRE* 38 (294); *Tanḥ., Wa-Yeshev* 2 (116); *Midrash Psalms* 24,3 (1, 338–339). See Ginzberg, *Legends* 2,116; 5,356, n. 294. There might seem to be a contradiction between Ps.-J.'s statement in our present verse that the spirit of prophecy had departed from Jacob when Joseph was sold (cf. Gen 37:25-28) and 43:14 (Ps.-J.), where Jacob is said to have received a communication from the Holy Spirit. But if, as Schäfer (1970, 309–311) claims, the "Holy Spirit" and "the spirit of prophecy" are not to be identified in the Targums, there is no real contradiction in the texts; cf. Shinan, 1979, 1, 134.

[25]Onq.: "Great is my joy." The Targums (Nf, P, V, N, L, Ps.-J., Onq.) treat Heb. *rb,* "Enough!" as an adjective, "great, much," and explain what it means.

[26]See *Jubilees* 34,1-9; *Testament of Judah* 3-7. On Jacob's fear of attacks from the Canaanites, see above 37:13 (Ps.-J.) and n. 11 to that verse. See Ginzberg, *Legends* 1, 408–411; 5, 315, n. 292.

CHAPTER 46

1. Israel set out with all that was his, and came to Beer-sheba, and offered sacrifices to the God of his father Isaac. 2. *The Lord* spoke to Israel in a *prophecy*[1] of the night and said, "Jacob! Jacob!" He said, "Here I am." 3. And he said, "I am God, the God of your father. Do not be afraid to go down to Egypt *because of the slavery which I decreed with Abraham;*[2] for there I will make of you a great nation. 4. *It is* I who *in my Memra* will go down with you to Egypt. *I will look upon the misery of your children, but my Memra will exalt you there;* I will also bring *your children up from there.*[3] Besides, Joseph's hand shall close your eyes."[4] 5. So Jacob arose from Beer-sheba; and the sons of Israel carried their father Jacob, their little ones, and their wives in the carriages which Pharaoh had sent to carry him. 6. They took their cattle[5] and the possessions they had acquired in the land of Canaan, and they came to Egypt, Jacob and all his *children* with him. 7. He brought with him to Egypt his sons, and his sons' sons with him, his daughters and his sons' daughters, and all his offspring. 8. These are the names of the children of Israel, Jacob and his children who came to Egypt: Jacob's first-born, Reuben. 9. The sons of Reuben: Hanoch, Pallu, Hezron, and Carmi. 10. The sons of Simeon: Jemuel, Jamin, Ohad, Jachin, Zohar, and Shaul, *that is Zimri, who followed the practices*[6] *of the Canaanites in Shittim.*[7] 11. The sons of Levi: Gershon, Kohath, and Merari. 12. The sons of Judah: Er, Onan, Shelah, Perez, and Zerah; but Er and Onan died *because of their evil deeds*[8] in the land of Canaan, *and Shelah and Zerah did not beget children in the land of Canaan.*[9] And the sons of Perez *who went down to Egypt*[10] were Hezron and Hamul. 13. The sons of Issachar, *sages and masters of calculation,*[11] whose names were Tola, Puvah, Iob, and Shimron. 14. The sons of Zebulon, *merchants, masters of trade, providing for their brothers, the sons of*

Notes, Chapter 46

[1] Onq.: "vision." HT: "visions." See Gen 15:1, where the Targums (Nf, V, N, L, CTg H, Onq.) refer to a prophetic communication, while the biblical text speaks of "a vision."

[2] Cf. Gen 15:13. We know of no text other than Ps.-J. that links our present verse with the prophecy of Gen 15:13.

[3] *PRE* 39 (304) says that the Lord entered into the number of those who went down to Egypt and into the number who left Egypt. *j. Sotah* 1,17c takes the repetition of the verb *'lh* in the words *"lk gm 'lh,* "I will also bring you up," which are addressed to Jacob, to mean that the Lord would bring up not only Jacob himself but all the tribes as well.

[4] Lit.: "Joseph will lay his hand on your eyes"; = HT.

[5] Heb. *mqnh,* "possessions (especially cattle)" is translated by Nf and Ps.-J. as *qnyn,* which has the same meaning, while Onq. uses *gyt',* "herd, flock."

[6] Lit.: "did the deed." Ps.-J. uses the Aramaic equivalent of the Hebrew idiom used in his source (see next note).

[7] *b. Sanh.* 82b (548). See Num 25.

[8] Cf. Gen 38:7-10.

[9] The biblical text of our present verse does not mention the children of Shelah and Zerah, but their families are referred to in Num 26:20.

[10] *Seder Olam* 2; *Yalkut Shimoni, Genesis* 145 (1,90). See Brayer, 1950, 60; Rieder's edition of Pseudo-Jonathan (1984), Hebrew section, 91, n. 12.

[11] 1 Chron 12:33 and the Targum of that verse; *Gen. R.* 72,5; Tg. Gen 49:14 (Ps.-J.). See Ginzberg, *Legends* 5,368, n. 391.

Issachar, and receiving a reward like theirs; [12] *and their names were* Sered, Elon, and Jahleel. 15. These are the sons of Leah, whom she bore to Jacob in Paddan *of Aram, together with his daughter Dinah; all the persons, between sons and daughters, were thirty-three. 16. The sons of Gad: Ziphion, Haggi, Shuni, Ezbon, Eri, Arodi, and Areli. 17. The sons of Asher: Imnah, Ishvah, Ishvi, Beriah, and their sister Serah, *who was taken to the garden* <*of Eden*> [13] *while still alive* [14] *because she had announced to Jacob that Joseph was alive.* [15] *It was she who delivered the inhabitants of Abel from the judgment of death in the days of Joab.* [16] *And the sons of Beriah who went down to Egypt were Heber and Malchiel. 18. These were the children of Zilpah, whom Laban had given to Leah his daughter; these she bore to Jacob, sixteen persons. 19. The sons of Rachel, Jacob's wife, Joseph and Benjamin. 20. To Joseph were born *sons* in the land of Egypt, Manasseh and Ephraim, whom Asenath, daughter of *Dinah, who had grown up in the house of* Potiphera, *chief of Tanis,* [17] bore him. 21. The sons of Benjamin *were ten, and their names (were given) according to the wonders that befell Joseph his brother:* [18] Bela, *because he was swallowed up from him;* Becher, *because he was the first-born of his mother;* Ashbel, *because he went into captivity;* Gera, *because he sojourned in a foreign land;* Naaman, *because he was pleasant and honorable;* Ehi, *because he was his brother, his mother's son;* Rosh, *because he was at the head of his father's house;* Muppim, *because he was sold in Memphis;* [19] Huppim, *because at the time that he was separated from him he was eighteen years and ready for the wedding canopy;* [20] Ard, *because he went down to Egypt. 22. These were the children of Rachel who were born to Jacob, fourteen persons in all. 23. The sons of Dan, *alert men and traders,* [21] *whose number is beyond counting.* [22] 24. The sons of Naphtali: Jahzeel, Guni, Jezer, and Shillem. 25. These were the children of Bilhah, whom Laban had given to Rachel his daughter; these she bore to Jacob, seven persons in all. 26. All the persons who came into Egypt with Jacob—his direct descendants, [23] besides the wives of Jacob's sons—

Notes, Chapter 46

[12]*Gen. R.* 72,5; 98,12. Cf. *b. Ketub.* 111b (720): "Any man who . . . carries on a trade for scholars . . . is regarded by Scripture as if he had cleaved to the divine presence."

[13]"Of Eden" is not in either Lond. or *ed. pr.,* but it should be restored as in Ps.-J. Num 26:46.

[14]*Derek Erez Zuta* 1 (570). Cf. *b. Sotah* 13a (67).

[15]*Sefer Ha-Yashar* 54 (176–177). Ps.-J.'s statement in our present verse that Serah announced that Joseph was alive contradicts the Targums (Ps.-J., Nf, P, V, N) of Gen 49:21, which state that it was Naphtali who communicated that message. Cf. Levine, 1969, 119; idem, 1968, 37; Shinan, 1979, 1,143; idem, 1985, 86.

[16]*Gen. R.* 94,9.

[17]See above 41:45, 50 (Ps.-J.).

[18]For the midrashic explanations of the names in this verse, see *Gen. R.* 94,8; *b. Sotah* 36b (181); *Tanh., Wa-Yiggash* 4 (136); *Tanh. B., Wa-Yiggash* 7 (1,206–207).

[19]*mwp.* There is no source for this interpretation in rabbinic literature. Cf. Schmerler, 1932, 318; Brayer, 1950, 61.

[20]According to *Pirke Abot* 5,21, a man was ready for marriage at eighteen.

[21]Or possibly "wise"; cf. Levy 1,37 (under *'mpwryn*). HT reads "The sons of Dan: Hushim." The fact that the plural "sons" is followed by only one name, "Hushim," which is plural in form, attracted the attention of the rabbis; cf. *Gen. R.* 94,9; *b. B. Bat.* 143b (613). Ps.-J.'s interpretation of Hushim as "alert men and traders" is without parallel in rabbinic literature. The author links that name with *hws,* "hasten." Cf. Cashdan, 1967, 39.

[22]Or: "whose total number is not mentioned." Lit.: "there is no total to their numbers."

[23]Lit.: "those who came forth from his thigh (*npqy yrkyh*)"; = Onq. See also the Targums of Exod 1:5.

were sixty-six persons in all. 27. The sons of Joseph who were born to him in Egypt were two persons. *(Thus), with Joseph, who was already in Egypt, and Jochebed, the daughter of Levi, who was born between the walls*[24] *when they were going into Egypt,*[25] the sum total of the persons[26] in the household of Jacob who came into Egypt was seventy. 28. He sent Judah before him to Joseph *to point out*[27] *the way before him, to subdue the pillars of the land,*[28] *and to prepare a dwelling place before him in* Goshen.[29] And they came to the land of Goshen. 29. Joseph had his chariot made ready, and he went up to Goshen to meet his father Israel. *But before his father recognized him, he bowed down to him, and (Joseph) was condemned to have his years shortened.*[30] *But (Joseph) repented* and presented himself to him, and inclined upon *the joint of* his neck[31] and wept upon his neck very much *because (his father) had bowed down to him.* 30. Israel said to Joseph, *"If* I were to die now, I *would be consoled, for I would die the death that the righteous die,*[32] having seen your countenance, since you are still alive." 31. Joseph said to his brothers and to his father's household, "I will go up and tell Pharaoh, and I will say to him, 'My brothers and my father's household, who were in the land of Canaan, have come to me. 32. The men are shepherds, for they have been *owners* of livestock, and they have brought their sheep and their oxen and everything they possess.' 33. So when Pharaoh summons you and says, *'Tell me* what your occupation is,' 34. you shall say, 'Your servants were *owners* of livestock from our youth until now, <both we and our fathers>'[33] so that you may dwell in the land of Goshen; for the Egyptians abhor all shepherds."

Notes, Chapter 46

[24]Reading *šwry'* with Lond. rather than *ṭwry'*, "mountains," of *ed. pr.* The fact that *šwry'* is used in the parallel text in Num 26:59 (Ps.-J.) proves that this is the reading that is to be preserved in our present verse. See also the parallel texts mentioned in the next note.

[25]*Gen. R.* 94,9; *Num. R.* 13,20; *b. B. Bat.* 123b (512); *Sotah* 12a (60-61); *PRK* 11,13. The midrashim and Ps.-J. explain how v. 27b could say that seventy persons came to Egypt, whereas vv. 26-27a give us to understand that the total was sixty-nine persons, including Joseph and his sons. There is a certain inconsistency between Ps.-J.'s version of our present verse, where Jochebed is counted among the seventy who entered Egypt, and the same Targum's version of Exod 1:5, where that name is not mentioned.

[26]Lit.: "the sum of all the persons." The same idiom is used in the same context in Exod 1:5 (Ps.-J.).

[27]Ps.-J. interprets the obscure Heb. *lhwrt*, "to appear" (cf. RSV; see Grossfeld, 1988, 151, n. 4) in three different ways (to point out; to subdue; to prepare).

[28]That is, mighty ones of the land; cf. Levy, 2, 222. See Ps.-J. Gen 49:19; Exod 15:14, 15. See also Tg. Num 20:29 (Nfmg, P, V, N, Ps.-J.), where Aaron is called a "pillar of prayer." The word "pillar" is used as an image for an official in Ugaritic, and probably in Hebrew as well (see, e.g., Zech 3:7); cf. A. A. Wieder, "Three Philological Notes," *Bulletin of the Institute of Jewish Studies* 2 (1974) 103–106. See also A. Jaubert, 1963, 2, 101–108.

[29]= Nf, P, V, N, CTg D. See *Gen. R.* 95,3 and *Tanḥ., Wa-Yiggash* 11 (142): "to prepare an academy for him."

[30]Rabbinic sources give different reasons for the fact that Joseph died before his brothers; cf., e.g., *b. Berak.* 55a (335); *Sotah* 13b (69); *Gen. R.* 100,3; *PRE* 39 (304–305). Ps.-J.'s explanation in our present verse is unique, and it is not known in rabbinic sources.

[31]See above 45:14 (Ps.-J.) and n. 10 to that verse.

[32]Onq.: *"If* I were to die now. . . ." All the Targums turn Jacob's declaration into a conditional clause. Ps.-J. introduces the idea of dying the death of the righteous, i.e., physical death in this world and not a second death in the world to come; cf. *Tanḥ.* B., *Wa-Yiggash* 10, (1,209). See Klein, 1976, 524–525.

[33]Omitted in Lond. and *ed. pr.*

CHAPTER 47

1. Joseph came and announced to Pharaoh and said, "My father and my brothers with their flocks and herds and all that they possess have come from the land of Canaan; and behold they are in the land of Goshen." 2. And he took a few of his brothers, five men, *Zebulun, Dan, Naphtali, Gad, and Asher,*[1] and presented them before Pharaoh. 3. Pharaoh said to *Joseph's*[2] brothers, "What are your occupations?" And they said to Pharaoh, "Your servants *were* shepherds, both we and our fathers." 4. They said to Pharaoh, "We have come to sojourn in the land, because there are no pasturing *grounds*[3] for your servants' flocks, for the famine is severe in the land of Canaan, and now, we pray, let your servants dwell in the land of Goshen." 5. Pharaoh said to Joseph, saying, "Your father and your brothers have come to you. 6. The land of Egypt is before you; settle your father and your brothers in the best *part* of the land; let them dwell in the land of Goshen; and if you know that there are capable men among them, you shall put them in charge of the livestock, over what is mine." 7. And Joseph brought Jacob his father and presented him before Pharaoh. And Jacob blessed Pharaoh *and said, "May it be the will (of heaven)*[4] *that the waters of the Nile be full,*[5] *and that the famine may cease from the world in your days."*[6] 8. Pharaoh said to Jacob, "How many *are* the days of the years of your life?" 9. And Jacob said to Pharaoh, "The days of the years of my sojournings are one hundred and thirty years; few and evil have been the days of the years of my life; *for from my youth I fled from*[7] *my brother Esau and sojourned in a land that was not mine; and now, in my old age, I have come down to sojourn here.*[8] And *my days* have not reached the days of the years of the life of my fathers in the days of their sojourning." 10. Jacob blessed Pharaoh and went out from before Pharaoh. 11. Joseph settled his father and his brothers, and gave them a possession in the land of Egypt, in the best *part* of the land, in the land of *Pelusium,*[9]

Notes, Chapter 47

[1] *Sifre* to Deut 33:18, 19, 22, 23, 24 (Finkelstein, 415, 417, 419; *Gen. R.* 95,4; *b. B. Qam.* 92a (533). Ps.-J., alone among the Targums, follows these midrashic texts and names the "five" who are referred to in the biblical text.

[2] = Pesh., Sam., LXX. This reading may represent an ancient Palestinian textual tradition; cf. Isenberg, 1968, 91–92, 122–123.

[3] Lit.: "there is no place of pasturage."

[4] See above, 24:60, where Ps.-J. uses the same prayer formula. Compare the formula used by Nfmg in v. 10 of our present chapter and in Exod 39:43. See also Gen 48:16 (Ps.-J.).

[5] Nfmg v. 10; *Num. R.* 12,2; *Tanh., Naso* 26 (513); *Tanh.* B., *Naso* 26 (2,39); cf. Tg. Zech 14:18. See Ginzberg, *Legends* 2, 124; 5, 360, n. 329.

[6] Cf. Nfmg v. 10. See below 50:3 (Ps.-J.), where it is said that the famine in Egypt was shortened because of the merits of Jacob. See also *Sifre* to Deut 11:10 (Finkelstein, 75); *t. Sotah* 10,9 (Zuckermandel, 314).

[7] Lit.: "from before."

[8] Ps.-J. explains that *mgwry,* "my sojourning," of the HT refers to Jacob's stay in Paddan Aram (Gen 28–31) and to his present journey to Egypt.

[9] The biblical place-name Rameses is rendered in the Pal. Tgs., including Ps.-J., by Pelusium. Besides our present verse (Nfmg, V, N, L, Ps.-J.), see Exod 1:11 (Nf, V, Ps.-J.); 12:37 (Nf, Ps.-J.); Num 33:3 (Nf, P, V, N, Ps.-J.); 33:5 (Nf, [as corrected in Díez Macho's edition], Ps.-J.). Ps.-J. mentions Pelusium twice in Exod 19:4 in a midrashic addition that is special to this Targum.

as Pharaoh had commanded. 12. Joseph provided his father and his brothers and all his father's household with bread, according to *the needs of* the little ones.[10] 13. There was no bread in all the land, because the famine was very severe; and *the inhabitants of*[11] the land of Egypt and *the inhabitants of*[11] the land of Canaan languished because of the famine. 14. Joseph gathered in all the money that was found in the land of Egypt and in the land of Canaan in return for the corn which they bought; and Joseph brought the money into Pharaoh's *treasury.*[12] 15. When the money of the land of Egypt and of the land of Canaan was spent, <all>[13] the Egyptians came to Joseph, saying, "Give us bread; why should we die in your presence? For *all*[14] the money is spent." 16. And Joseph said, "Give your livestock, and I will give you *food* in return for your livestock if the money has come to an end."[15] 17. So they brought their livestock to Joseph, and Joseph gave them bread in return for horses, for flocks of sheep, and for herds of oxen, and for asses; and that year he *sustained* them with bread in return for all their livestock. 18. And when that year came to an end, *all the Egyptians* came to him the second year and said to him, "We will not hide from my master that since the money is spent and the herds of cattle belong to my master, there is nothing left *to us* before my master except our bodies and our land. 19. Why should we die *while* your eyes *see,* both we and our land? Take[16] us and our land in return for bread, and we and our land will be slaves to Pharaoh. Give (us) seed that we may live and not die, and that the land may not become desolate."[17] 20. Joseph acquired all the land of the Egyptians for Pharaoh, because every Egyptian sold his field, for the famine was severe upon them. And the land became *the property* of Pharaoh. 21. He transferred the people *of the provinces* to the towns, *and the people of the towns he transferred to the provinces, because of Joseph's brothers, that they might not be called exiles.*[18] *Therefore he removed them* from one end of the territory of Egypt to the other. 22. Only the land of the *priests*[19] he did not *buy, because they had seen his innocence at the time when his master wanted to kill him, and they had delivered him from the sentence of death.*[20] *Besides, he decreed* that a portion *was to be given to them* on behalf of Pharaoh. They lived on[21] the portion that Pharaoh gave them, and therefore they

Notes, Chapter 47

[10]Lit.: "according to what was necessary for the little ones." Ps.-J. explains the obscure Heb. *lpy ḥṭp,* "according to the little ones."

[11]Onq.: "people of." See above 41:30 and n. 11 to that verse.

[12]On the word *h(y)ptyq',* Gr. *apothêke,* "storehouse," which Ps.-J. uses here and in Deut 23:22, cf. Cook, 1986, 235–236, and see above 24:2 and 10 (Ps.-J.) with n. 3 to v. 2.

[13]Omitted in Lond. and *ed. pr.*

[14]= Lond.; not in *ed. pr.*

[15]Reading *psq* with Lond. rather than *psd,* "be diminished, scarce," of *ed. pr.*

[16]Lit.: "acquire."

[17]= HT; Onq., Nf: "lie fallow"; Cf. Aberbach-Grossfeld, 1982, 273, n.2; Grossfeld, 1988, 155, n. 2.

[18]Or: "wanderers." Ps.-J. uses a word *(glwwl'y)* that corresponds to the word *glwwt'* used in his source, *b. Ḥul.* 60b (334); see also *Tanḥ.* B., *Wa-Yeshev* 16 (1, 186).

[19]The Targums of our present verse (Nf, Nfmg, Ps.-J., Onq.) and of 26 (Nf, Ps.-J., Onq.) use the term *kwmr* or *kwmrn* to refer to the idolatrous priests of Egypt. See above, Gen 14:18 and n. 44 to that verse, and 39:20, with n. 14 to that verse.

[20]See above, 39:20 (Ps.-J.) and n. 16 to that verse.

[21]Lit.: "they ate"; = HT.

did not sell their land. 23. Joseph said to the people, "Behold, this day I have acquired you and your land for Pharaoh. Here is seed for you, that you may sow the land. 24. And *at the time of the ingathering of* the produce you shall give a fifth to Pharaoh, and four parts shall be yours as seed for the fields,[22] as your food, as the *sustenance of* your households, and as food for your little ones." 25. And they said, "You have kept us alive. Let us find *mercy*[23] in the eyes of my master, and we will be slaves to Pharaoh." 26. So Joseph established a decree concerning the land of Egypt unto this day, that Pharaoh *take* a fifth[24] *of the produce.* Only the land of the *priests,*[25] theirs alone, did not become Pharaoh's. 27. And Israel dwelt in the land of Egypt, *and they built for themselves schoolhouses and palaces*[26] in the land of Goshen. There they took *possession of fields and vineyards,* and they increased and multiplied greatly. 28. Jacob lived seventeen years in the land of Egypt, and the days of Jacob *the sum of the days* of his life, were a hundred and forty-seven years. 29. And when the days drew near for Israel to die, he called his son Joseph and said to him, "If, now, I have found mercy *before* you, put, I pray, your hand *on the cut of my circumcision,*[27] and perform for me, *I pray,* (an act of) *goodness* and fidelity. Do not bury me, I pray, in Egypt. 30. When I lie down with my fathers, take me from Egypt and bury me in their grave." *But because he was his son he did not put his hand, but*[28] he said, "I will do according to your word." 31. And he said, "Swear to me." And he swore to him. *Immediately the Glory of the Shekinah of the Lord was revealed to him.*[29] And Israel bowed down on the head of the bed.

CHAPTER 48

1. After these things Joseph was told,[1] "Behold, your father *is lying* ill." So he took with him his two sons, Manasseh and Ephraim. 2. Jacob was told *saying,* "Behold, your son Joseph is coming to you." And Israel summoned up his strength and

Notes, Chapter 47 (Cont.)

[22]*Ed. pr.* reads "for the land."

[23]= Onq.

[24]Onq.: "that *they should give* a fifth to Pharaoh."

[25]See above v. 22, and n. 19 to that verse.

[26]*Gen. R.* 95,3, in a comment on Gen 46:28, says that Jacob sent Judah before him to Egypt to prepare an academy where he would teach Torah. See above, 46:28 (Ps.-J.) and n. 29 to that verse. According to *b. Yoma* 28b (133), the Hebrews had the scholars' council in Egypt.

[27]*PRE* 39 (308): "Swear to me by the covenant of circumcision." See above 24:2 (Ps.-J.) and n. 4 to that verse.

[28]Ps.-J., who does not hesitate to mention indelicate matters (see above, Introduction, p. 7) informs us in our present verse that Joseph was too sensitive to carry out the command given in the preceding verse. None of the other Targums (Nf, CTg D, Onq.) of this verse shared Ps.-J.'s sensitivity. We know of no source for Ps.-J.'s addition.

[29]Lit.: "over him." Cf. *Tanh., Wa-Yehi* 3 (147): "Israel prostrated himself to the Shekinah that was standing over him." See Tg. Gen 49:1 (Ps.-J.).

Notes, Chapter 48

[1]Lit.: "it was said to Joseph; *ed. pr.* adds "saying."

sat up in bed. 3. And Jacob said to Joseph, "El Shaddai appeared to me at Luz in the land of Canaan, and he blessed me, 4. and he said to me, 'Behold, I will increase you and multiply you, and I will make of you an assembly of *tribes*,[2] and I will give this land to your *son* after you for an everlasting possession.' 5. And now, your two sons who were born to you in the land of Egypt before I came to you in Egypt shall be mine; Ephraim and Manasseh shall be *considered* mine, just like Reuben and Simeon. 6. But *the children* whom you beget after them shall be yours; they shall be called by the name of their brothers in their inheritance. 7. As for me, *what I asked of you is that you bury me with my fathers.* <When I was coming from Paddan>[3] Rachel died *suddenly,* to my sorrow,[4] on the way in the land of Canaan, while there was still *some* distance[5] (to go) before entering Ephrath. *Since I was not able to carry her to bury her in the double cave,*[6] I buried her there on the way to Ephrath, that is Bethlehem."[7] 8. When Israel saw the sons of Joseph, he said, "*From* whom *were* these *born to you*?" 9. And Joseph said to his father, "These are my sons, whom *the Memra of the Lord* has given to me *according to this marriage contract,*[8] *in accordance with which I took to wife Asenath, the daughter of Dinah, your daughter*."[9] And he said, "*Bring* them *near* to me, I pray, that I may bless them." 10. Now Israel's eyes were heavy with age, *and* he could not see. So he brought them near to him, and he kissed them and embraced them. 11. And Israel said to Joseph, "I had not counted on[10] seeing your countenance (again), and behold *the Lord* has let me see your *children* also." 12. Joseph removed them[11] from his knees,[12] and he bowed down with[13] his face to[13] the ground. 13. Joseph took the two of them, Ephraim *on his right side, which was* Israel's left, and Manasseh *on* his left *side, which was* Israel's right, and brought (them) near to him. 14. And Israel stretched out his right hand and laid (it) upon Ephraim's head, although he was the younger, and (he placed) his left hand upon Manasseh's head, exchanging his hands, for Manasseh was the first-born. 15. And he blessed Joseph and said, "*Lord,* before whom my fathers Abraham and Isaac worshiped; *Lord,* who *sustained* me[14]

Notes, Chapter 48

[2]= Onq.

[3]Omitted in Lond. and *ed. pr.*

[4]Lit.: "on me"; = HT.

[5]Lit.: "much country (or land)."

[6]See above 23:9 (Ps.-J.) and n. 4 to that verse.

[7]According to Ps.-J., Jacob explained why he had not buried Rachel in the ancestral grave.

[8]Ps.-J. takes Heb. *bzh,* "here," to refer to the marriage contract. By producing the marriage contract, Joseph allayed any fears Jacob might have had about the regularity of Joseph's marriage. Cf. Ginzberg, *Legends,* 2, 136. See also *Gen. R.* 97, which says that Joseph presented Asenath to show that the children were really his.

[9]See above, Ps.-J. 41:45, 50; 46:20. In these verses Ps.-J.'s statement about the identification of Asenath as the daughter of Dinah was occasioned by the mention of Asenath in the biblical text. This is not the case in our present verse.

[10]Ps.-J. uses the verb *ḥšb,* "consider, count," to translate Heb. *pll,* the basic meaning of which is "to estimate." Nf and CTg D use the verb *sky,* "look out, hope, expect," while Onq. and Pesh. employ *sbr,* "look for, be hopeful." Thus, Ps.-J. differs from all the other Targums.

[11]Lit.: "brought them out"; = HT.

[12]Onq.: "from before him." See Aberbach-Grossfeld, 1982, 276, n. 4; Grossfeld, 1988, 157, n. 10.

[13]Lit.: "upon." See above 42:6 (Ps.-J.), with n. 9 to that verse.

[14]= Onq. See *b. Pesaḥ.* 118a (606).

since (the beginning of) my existence to this day, 16. *may it be pleasing before you*[15] *that* the angel *whom you assigned to me to* redeem me from all evil, bless[16] the boys; and let my name be recalled in them, and the name of my fathers Abraham and Isaac. [16] *And as the fishes*[17] *of the sea multiply continually in the water,*[18] *so* may *the children of* Joseph grow into a multitude on the earth." 17. Joseph saw that his father was placing his right hand on Ephraim's head, and it was displeasing to him. [19] So he took[20] his father's hand to remove it from Ephraim's head *so as to lower it*[21] upon Manasseh's head. 18. Joseph said to his father, "Not so, father! For this is the first-born. Place your right *hand* on his head." 19. But his father refused and said, "I know, my son; I know[22] *that he is the first-born; I am also aware that* he too will become a *great* people, and he too will multiply. Yet his younger brother will multiply more than he, and *his children will be numerous*[23] among the nations." 20. So he blessed them that day, saying, "By you, *Joseph my son, the house of* Israel shall bless *the infant on the day of circumcision,*[24] saying, 'May *the Lord* make you like Ephraim and *like Manasseh.' And in the numbering of the tribes, the chief of Ephraim will be numbered before the chief of Manasseh."*[25] And (thus) he established that Ephraim would be before Manasseh. 21. Then Israel said to Joseph, "As for me, behold *my end has come! (I am about)* to die. But *the Memra of the Lord will be at your assistance and* will bring you back to the land of your fathers. 22. As for me, *behold* I give you *the city of* Shechem, one *portion*[26] *as a gift* more than your brothers, which I took from the hands of the Amorites *when you went into it, and I arose and assisted you with* my sword and with my bow."[27]

Notes, Chapter 48

[15]See above 47:7 (Ps.-J.) and n. 4 to that verse.

[16]"Bless . . . and Isaac" omitted in Lond.

[17]*kwwry.* Nf, Nfmg, CTg D, and Onq. use the word *nwn.* See above 1:26 and n. 45 to that verse.

[18]Onq.: "may they increase like the fish of the sea." The Targums (Nf, Nfmg, CTg D, Ps.-J., Onq.) derive the Heb. hapax *ydgw,* "let them grow" (RSV), from *dg,* "fish." Similar midrashic interpretations of the biblical text are based on the same popular etymology; cf. *Gen. R.* 97,3; *b. Berak.* 20a (120–121); *Sotah* 36b (179).

[19]Lit.: "it was evil before him."

[20]Lit.: "supported"; = Onq.

[21]= Onq.

[22]Lond. does not repeat "I know."

[23]Onq.: "and his children will rule over."

[24]We know of no traditional rabbinic source for this addition. It is known, however, that Gen 48:20 was used in the ritual of circumcision; see Schmerler, 1932, 327; Shinan, 1979, 2, 333, n. 173a.

[25]*Gen. R.* 97,5 lists several texts (e.g., Num 1:32, 34; 2:18, 20; Josh 16:8) where Ephraim is mentioned before Manasseh.

[26]Nfmg, P, V, N, CTg Z, and Onq. take the obscure Heb. *škm 'ḥd* to mean "one portion." See also the opinion of R. Judah in *Gen. R.* 97,6. Ps.-J. combines this interpretation with an understanding of *škm* as the place-name "Shechem." Nf has this combined interpretation at the end of its rendering of this verse, as well as interpreting *škm* as "portion" at the beginning of its translation. The tradition that the portion given to Joseph was the garment of Adam, a tradition which is found in (Nf, Nfmg, P, V, N, CTg Z) of this verse, is omitted in Ps.-J. But see above 27:15, where Ps.-J., and Ps.-J. alone, refers to the garments of the first man that were available to Rebekah; see above, n. 11 to that verse. On other occasions, too, Ps.-J. attaches a Targumic tradition to a particular verse when the other Targums attach it to a different verse altogether. See Shinan, 1979, 1, 117, n. 16; 156; idem, 1985, 76, n. 20.

[27]*Gen. R.* 80,10; 97,6; *Jubilees* 34,1–8. Ps.-J. and some versions of Onq. (see Sperber, 1959, 1, 84; Grossfeld, 1988, 156, apparatus, note *e*) are the only Targums to interpret the words "with my sword and my bow" literally. Compare Nf, Nfmg, P, V, N, CTg Z. Cf. also *Mekilta* to Exod 14:10 (1, 207); *Gen. R.* 97,6 ("with pious acts and noble deeds"); *b. B. Bat.* 123a (508); Jerome: *arcum hic, et gladium, justitiam vocat* (*Quaest. hebr.* in Gen 48:22).

CHAPTER 49

1. Jacob[1] called his sons and said to them, "*Purify yourselves from uncleanness,*[2] and I will tell you *the concealed secrets, the hidden times,*[3] *the giving of the reward of the righteous, the punishment of the wicked, and what the happiness*[4] *of Eden will be.*" The twelve tribes of Israel were gathered together surrounding the golden bed on which he was lying. But as soon as the Glory of the Shekinah of the Lord was revealed, the time in which the King Messiah was destined to come was hidden from him.[5] Then he said, "Come, and I will relate to you what will befall you at the end of the days. 2. Gather and hear, O sons of Jacob, and *receive instruction from*[6] Israel your father. 3. Reuben, you are my first-born, *the first fruit of* my *virile* might, and the beginning of *the effusion of my heated imagination.*[7] *You would have been worthy of the birthright, the dignity of the priesthood and the kingship. But because you sinned, my son, the birthright was given to Joseph, the kingship to Judah, and the priesthood to Levi.*[8] 4. *I compare you to a little garden into which mighty rushing streams*[9] *entered; it was not able to resist them, and it was swamped. Thus you were ruined, Reuben my son. The sin that you committed do not (commit) again, and that which you sinned will be forgiven you.*[10] For *it is reckoned to you as if you had gone in unto the woman with whom* your father *had lain, when you disarranged my* couch upon which *you* mounted.[11] 5. Simeon and Levi are twin brothers; *sharp* weapons *for robbery is their characteristic.*[12] 6. My soul took no pleasure in their counsel,

Notes, Chapter 49

[1]The Hebrew Text of Gen 49 is often obscure, and the ancient versions translated it rather freely; cf. K. Kohler, *Der Segen Jacob's mit besonderer Berücksichtigung der alten Versionen und des Midrasch* (Berlin, 1867). The Targums of this poetic chapter have been considered at length in several studies. See, e.g., Aberbach-Grossfeld (1976); Bowker (1969, 277–292); Komlosh (1963, 195–206); = idem (1973, 177–193); Pérez Fernández, 1981, 95–169; Syrén (1986).

[2]*Gen. R.* 96; 98,2; *Tanḥ., Wa-Yehi* 8 (151). Ps.-J. is the only Targum to add this phrase. Purification is required as a preparation for revelation; cf. Tg. Lev 9:6 (Nfmg, Ps.-J.). See Pérez Fernández, 1981, 101.

[3]*qyṣ'* lit. "ends." Heb. *qyṣ* and its Aramaic cognate are used as technical terms to refer to end time of redemption; cf., e.g., Tg. Exod 12:42 (Nf); Tg. Jer 8:20; Tg. 1 Chron 7:21. See Le Déaut, 1963, 274–275; Pérez Fernández, 1981, 102–105.

[4]Or: "the tranquility, repose."

[5]*Gen. R.* 98,2; *b. Pesaḥ.* 56a (279).

[6]= Onq. Ps.-J.'s version of this verse is identical with that of Onq. See, on the other hand, the expanded versions of Nf, P, V, N, CTg Z.

[7]Compare Ps.-J.'s phrase, "the beginning . . . imagination," (see also Ps.-J. Deut 23:11), with *Gen. R.* 98,4 and *b. Yeb.* 76a (512), which say that Jacob did not experience an emission of semen before the conception of Reuben.

[8]Cf. *Gen. R.* 98,4; *Tanḥ.* B., *Wa-Yehi* 11, (1,218). See also 1 Chron 5:1 and the Targum of that verse. Deut 33:17 (Ps.-J.) says that the birthright was taken from Reuben and given to Joseph. See also Jerome, *Quaest. hebr.* in Gen 49:3. The midrash and Targums explain why Reuben lost the prerogatives that should have been his as first-born; cf. Syrén, 1986, 129. On the interpretation of Gen 49:3 in the ancient versions (including the Targums) and in Jewish literature, see Chiesa, 1977, 417–440.

[9]Lit.: "rushing mighty streams." The Targums and the ancient versions interpret the unusual phrase *pḥz kmym*, "unstable as water" (RSV), in different ways; cf. Syrén, 1986, 39–40. Onq. reads: "Since you followed your own direction just like water."

[10]*Gen. R.* 98,4.

[11]See above, 35:22 (Ps.-J.) and n. 22 to that verse. In spite of the rabbinic injunction (cf., e.g., *m. Meg.* 4,10), Onq. and Ps.-J. render the whole verse in Aramaic. Ps.-J. acknowledges the guilt of Reuben but also speaks of his being forgiven.

[12]Onq.: "mighty men; in the land of their sojourning did they perform mighty feats." All the Targums (Nf, V, N, CTg Z, Onq.) except Ps.-J. give a positive interpretation to the words "weapons of violence." With Ps.-J.'s version compare *Gen. R.* 98,5 and 99,7, where "weapons of violence" are taken to be weapons that were stolen. For a positive interpretation, see *PRE* 38 (289). Ps.-J. linked *mkrtyhm*, "their swords" (RSV), with *nkr* (Hif.), "to recognize"; hence "their characteristic."

and when they gathered at Shechem to destroy it, my honor was not involved; for in their anger they killed *the king and his ruler,*[13] and at their whim *they demolished the wall of their enemies."*[14] 7. *Jacob said, "Cursed was the city of Shechem*[15] *when they went into it to destroy it in* their anger that was fierce, and (cursed was) their wrath *against Joseph, for it was cruel." "If,"* said Jacob, *"these two dwell together, there will be no king or ruler who can withstand them.*[16] I will divide *the inheritance of the sons of Simeon into two portions; one portion will be given to him within the inheritance of the sons of Judah,*[17] *and another portion among the rest of the tribes* of Jacob.[18] And I will scatter *the tribe of Levi among all the tribes of* Israel." 8. "Judah, *you confessed concerning the incident of Tamar; therefore* your brothers will praise you,*[19] and they will be called Jews after your name.*[20] Your hands will *avenge you of* your enemies *by throwing arrows at them*[21] *when* they *turn* their back[22] before you; and your father's sons will come forward to salute you. 9. I[23] *compare you,* Judah *my son,* to a whelp, *the young of* lions, *because your soul remained aloof from the murder of* my son Joseph,[24] *and from the judgment of Tamar*[25] *you shall be delivered. You rest and you are at ease in strength,* like a lion, and like a lioness;[26] *when he rests,* who will rouse him? 10. *Kings and rulers*[27] shall not cease from *those*

Notes, Chapter 49

[13]HT has *'yš,* "a man," which must be understood as a collective, "men." Nf, V, N, and CTg Z translate in the plural, "kings (and rulers)," while Ps.-J. retains the singular. *Gen. R.* 98,5 takes "a man" to refer to Hamor, the father of Shechem. See Klein, 1986, 2, 52.

[14]Onq.: "they razed the wall of the enemy." Not surprisingly, the Targums refer the violence attributed to Simeon and Levi in our present verse to the violence perpetrated against Shechem by these two brothers (cf. Gen 34:25-29). Nf, Ps.-J., and Onq. (see also CTg Z) read HT *šwr (šhôr),* "ox," as *šûr,* "wall"; cf. *Gen. R.* 98,5. On the application of the term *šhôr* to Joseph (Nfmg, V, N), see Pérez Fernández, 1981, 155–158. See further Böhl, 1987, 128–129.

[15]The Pal. Tgs. (Nf, Nfmg, P, V, N, CTg Z) have Jacob direct his curse, not at the anger and the wrath of Simeon and Levi, as is the case in HT, but at the city of Shechem, which angered the brothers. Ps.-J. also directs the curse at Shechem, but then goes on to curse the brothers' wrath, which, according to Ps.-J., was directed at Joseph.

[16]*PRE* 38 (289).

[17]Cf. Josh 19:1,9.

[18]Ps.-J.'s statement is not based on fact. The clans of Simeon listed in 1 Chron 4:24-43 are described as nomadic.

[19]Onq.: "Judah, you confessed and were not ashamed; (therefore) your brothers shall praise you." Onq. and Ps.-J. interpret Heb. *ywdwk,* "shall praise," according to its twofold meaning, "confess, praise." The confession to which these two Targums refer explicitly (Ps.-J.) or implicitly (Onq.) is recorded in Gen 38:26. Cf. *Gen. R.* 99,8.

[20]*Gen. R.* 97; 98,6.

[21]"By throwing arrows at them": Ps.-J. is the only Targum of this verse to add this specification; see *b. Abod. Zar.* 25a (126); *j. Sotah* 1,17c.

[22]Lit.: "their neck"; = Onq.

[23]Onq. takes the word "lion" in this verse as a symbol of the king, and then introduces a messianic theme into the verse. The Pal. Tgs., including Ps.-J., do not follow this procedure. Cf. Pérez Fernández, 1981, 119–122. On the symbolism lion-king, cf. also Tg. Jer 2:15, and see Hayward, 1987, 51, n. 15.

[24]Cf. Gen 37:26.

[25]*Gen. R.* 98,7 (Theodor-Albeck, 1258): ". . . from the tearing (*mṭrpw*) of my son (Joseph) . . . from the tearing (*mṭrph*) of Tamar. . . ." The midrash plays on *mṭrp,* "from the prey" (RSV), in our present verse.

[26]*lyt',* = Onq. In reality this is another word for "lion"; cf. Levy, 1, 410.

[27]Onq.: "The ruler." The Targums take Heb. *šbṭ,* "sceptre," to refer to a ruling figure (or figures). See also the Targums (Nf, P, V, N, Ps.-J.; cf. also Onq.) of Num 24:17. See *Gen. R.* 97; *b. Sanh.* 5a (16), and the prayer of R. Aḥa recorded in *b. Yoma* 53b (251).

of the house of Judah, nor *scribes teaching the Law* [28] *from his descendants*, until the time *the King Messiah* [29] comes, *the youngest of his sons*, [30] *because of whom* the people will *pine away*. [31] 11. *How beautiful* [32] *is the King Messiah who is to arise from among those of the house of Judah.* He girds *his loins and comes down arranging battle lines against his enemies and slaying kings together with their rulers; and there is no king or ruler who can withstand him.* He makes the mountains red with *the blood of the slain;* [33] his garments *are rolled* in blood; *he is like a presser of grapes.* 12. *How beautiful* [34] *are* the eyes *of the King Messiah, like pure* wine, *for they have not seen* [35] *the uncovering of nakedness or the shedding of innocent blood.* His teeth are whiter than milk *because he has not eaten what has been robbed or taken by force. His mountains and his press will be red from wine, and his hills white from the harvest and from the flocks.* 13. Zebulun shall dwell by the seashores; *he shall control the harbors, subduing the provinces of the sea with* ships. [36] *His territory shall extend as far as* Sidon. 14. Issachar *is loaded with the Law.* [37] *He is a strong tribe, knowing the determinations of the times;* [38] and he lies down between *the territories of his brothers.* 15. He saw that the repose *of the world to come* was good, [39] and that

Notes, Chapter 49

[28]Onq.: "nor the scribe from his children's children." See *Gen. R.* 97; *b. Sanh.* 5a (16). The Targums derive the word *mḥqq*, "ruler's staff," of HT from *ḥq*, "law," and they take *mbyn rglyw*, "from between his feet," to refer to future descendants. On the interpretation of these words in the ancient versions, in Qumran, in rabbinic literature, and in the Targums, see Syrén, 1986, 53–56, 130–131. On the interpretation of *mḥqq* in particular, see Vermes, 1961, 49–55.

[29]*Gen. R.* 98,8; *b. Sanh.* 98b (667); On the interpretation of Heb. *šylh*, "Shiloh" (see RSV), cf. Pérez Fernández, 1981, 127–133; Aberbach-Grossfeld, 1976, 14–16.

[30]The specification "the youngest of his sons," which is found in Ps.-J. alone, may be due to the fact that the author connected *šylh* (see preceding note) with Shelah, the name of Judah's youngest son (cf. Gen 38:5), or with the phrase "her afterbirth (*šlyth*) that comes out from between her feet" (RSV), in Deut 28:57, which Onq. renders as "the youngest (*z'yr*; the word used by Ps.-J. in our present verse) of her children that emerges from her." See A. Caquot, 1976, 20, n. 1; Levey, 1974, 9.

[31]Ps.-J. is alone in rendering *yqht*, "the obedience" (RSV), as *ytymswn*, "pine away," lit., "melt away." The different renderings of this word in the Targums show that the *meturgemanim* did not understand it. See further Syrén, 1986, 47.

[32]The Pal. Tgs. of this verse bear little resemblance to the text being translated. The verb *'sr*, "bind," which the biblical verse uses with the meaning of tethering (an ass), is understood by the *meturgemanim* in another meaning which it has, namely, "gird on (a sword)." This allows them to go on to describe a warrior Messiah. On the influence of Isa 63:1-6 on the Pal. Tgs. of Gen 49:11-12, cf., e.g., P. Grelot, 1963, 371–380; McNamara, 1966A, 230–233; Pérez Fernández, 1981, 135–144. Gen 49:11 is given a Messianic interpretation, e.g., in *Gen. R.* 98,9 and in *b. Berak.* 57a (352).

[33]Tg. Isa 63:2.

[34]The Targums of this verse, like those of the preceding verse, bear little relationship to the text being translated. The Pal. Tgs., including Ps.-J., first describe the physical beauty of the Messiah, and then go on to describe the age of prosperity he will inaugurate. The image of the peaceful Messiah given in this verse complements the picture of the warrior Messiah that is given in v. 11. Cf. Pérez Fernández, 1981, 141–144.

[35]Lit.: "from to see." The same phrase occurs in V, N, and CTg Z.

[36]Onq.: "he shall conquer provinces with ships, and the best of the sea he shall consume." Nf (our only genuine Pal. Tg. of this verse), Ps.-J., and Onq. celebrate the maritime power and military achievements of Zebulun (cf. *Lev. R.* 25,2) and go on to record the material prosperity of that tribe. See further Syrén, 1986, 131–132.

[37]I.e., loaded with knowledge of the law; cf. Jastrow, 477 (under *ḥmyr*). See *Gen. R.* 98,12, and especially 99,10, which reads: ". . . as an ass bears burdens, so does Issachar bear [the yoke of] the Torah." Ps.-J. is the only Targum of this verse to draw attention to Issachar's knowledge of the law. See also above, Ps.-J. 30:18 and n. 19 to that verse.

[38]See above 46:13 (Ps.-J.) and n. 11 to that verse. See also Jerome, *Quaest. hebr.* in Gen 49:14-15.

[39]Ps.-J. is the only Targum to introduce the idea of "the world to come" into this verse. We know of no source for this interpretation.

(his) portion of the land *of Israel* was pleasant; *therefore* he bent his shoulder *to labor in the Law, and his brothers offered him gifts.* [40] 16. *From those of the house of* Dan *there shall arise a man who* will judge his people *with true judgments.* [41] As one, [42] the tribes of Israel will *obey him.* 17. There will be *a man who will be chosen and who will arise from those of the house of* Dan. *He will be comparable to* the adder *that lies at the cross*roads and to the *heads of the* serpents that *lie in wait* by the path, biting the horses in the heel, and out of fear of it the rider falls, *turning* backwards. *Thus shall Samson, son of Manoah,* [43] *kill all the warriors of the Philistines, both horsemen and foot soldiers. He will hamstring their horses and throw their riders* [44] *backwards."* 18. *When Jacob saw Gideon, son of Joash,* [45] *and Samson, son of Manoah, who were arising as redeemers, he said, "I have not yearned for the redemption of Gideon, nor have I waited for the redemption of Samson, for their redemption is the redemption of an hour. But* for your redemption I yearn *and wait,* O Lord, *because your redemption is an eternal redemption."* [46] 19. *"The tribe of* Gad, *armed, will cross the wadis of the Arnon* [47] *with the rest of the tribes, and they will suppress before them the pillars* [48] *of the land.* [49] *In the end* [50] *they will return, armed, with great possessions, and they will dwell securely beyond the Jordan. For so they chose, and they were pleased* [51] *when they received their inheritance.* 20. *Happy* [52] *is* Asher! *How* rich *are his fruits! His land produces spices and aromatic roots, and his territory produces* the delicacies of kings, *and he gives thanks and praise for them before the Lord of the world.* 21. Naphtali is *a swift messenger, like* a hind [53] *that runs on the tops of the mountains, announcing good tidings."* He announced that Joseph

Notes, Chapter 49

[40]See above 46:14 (Ps.-J.) and n. 12 to that verse. On Issachar's zeal for the study of the Torah as indicated in the Targums of vv. 14 (Ps.-J.) and 15 (Nf, P, V, N, CTg Z, Ps.-J.), see Syrén, 1986, 132–133.

[41]*Gen. R.* 99,11; *b. Sotah* 10a (45). The midrash reads HT as "Dan shall judge his people as One." The "One" is taken to be God, whose judgments are true, i.e., just. Ps.-J. says that Dan, like God, will judge justly.

[42]Taking HT *k'hd* to mean "as one" rather than "as one of," the Targums (Nf, P, CTg Z, Ps.-J.) understand HT to say that Dan will administer justice, not "as one of the tribes," but "over the tribes."

[43]*Gen. R.* 98,13; 99,11; *b. Sotah* 10a (45). Samson, son of Manoah, was of the tribe of Dan; cf. Judg 13:2, 21-24.

[44]Reading *rkbyhwn* (= Onq.) rather than *dbbyhwn,* "their enemies," which is the reading in Lond. and *ed. pr.*

[45]Gideon, son of Joash, who was not from the tribe of Dan but from that of Manasseh (cf. Josh 17:2; Judg 6:11), is not mentioned in the sources referred to in the next note, except *Midrash Psalms* 60,9; see Schmerler, 1932, 343.

[46]*Gen. R.* 98,14; 99,11; *Midrash Psalms* 31,2 (1, 393); 60,9 (1, 515-516). On the Targums of this verse, see further Pérez Fernández, 1981, 145–154. Syrén, 1986, 113–115.

[47]Heb. *nhl,* "wadi, torrent," in the idiom *nhl 'rnwn* "the wadi Arnon," can be rendered by Ps.-J. in the plural (cf. Deut 2:24; 3:8, 16; 4:48) or in the singular (cf. Deut 2:36; 3:12). It is not surprising, then, to find Ps.-J. use the plural "wadis" in our present verse and in Exod 15:16 and Num 34:11 in additions to the biblical text. In Num 21:28 Ps.-J. refers to *"the wadis of* the Arnon," where the biblical text has "the Arnon." In Num 21:14, where HT has *nhlym,* "wadis," in the plural, Ps.-J. reads "the wadis *near* the Arnon."

[48]See above 46:28 (Ps.-J.) and n. 28 to that verse.

[49]*Gen. R.* 97; 98,15; *Num. R.* 13,20. Cf. Deut 33:20.

[50]The word *'qb,* "heel," "end" (cf. Jastrow, 1104) of HT gave occasion for this addition.

[51]Reading *hnh lhwn* with Lond. (Rieder and Clarke read *hwh lhwn*) rather than *hwh lhwn* of *ed. pr.* Bowker (1969, 280) translates the text of Lond. as "so will it be to them."

[52]The only words of this verse in *ed. pr.* are "spices and aromatic roots." Haggadic texts praised the fertility of the territory of Asher; cf., e.g., *Gen. R.* 98,16. See further Syrén, 1986, 133.

[53]*b. Sotah* 13a (67); *Testament of Naphtali* 2,1.

was still alive;[54] *he hurried and went to Egypt and brought the title deeds of the field of the double (cave) in which Esau has no portion.*[55] *When he opened his mouth to praise (God) in the assembly of Israel, he could choose from all languages.*[56] 22. *"Joseph, my son, you have become great;*[57] *my son, you have become great*[57] *and you have become mighty; and it was your destiny*[58] *to become mighty, because you subdued your inclination*[59] *in the incident with your mistress and in the incident with your brothers.*[60] *I compare you to a vine planted by springs of water, that sends forth its roots and splits the sharp rocks,*[61] *and overshadows*[62] *with its branches all barren trees. Even so, Joseph my son, you subdued with your wisdom and your good deeds all the Egyptian sorcerers. And when the people were crying out before you,*[63] the daughters *of rulers were walking* on the walls *and throwing rings and necklaces of gold before you, so that you might lift up your eyes toward them.*[64] *But you did not lift up your eyes towards any one of them, so as to become guilty because of them on the day of great judgment.* 23. *All the Egyptian sorcerers* embittered[65] him *and quarreled with him,*[66] *and they also informed on him before Pharaoh, hoping to discredit him,*[67] *speaking against him with a slanderous tongue*[68] *that is as harsh as arrows."*[69] 24. *The strength of his member returned to its former state*[70] *so that he might not have intercourse with his mistress, and his hands were withheld*[71] *from voluptuous thoughts. And he subdued his inclination because of the* strict *instruction he*

Notes, Chapter 49

[54]See above, 46:17 (Ps.-J.) and n. 15 to that verse.

[55]*Gen. R.* 98,17; *b. Sotah* 13a (67); *PRE* 39 (309).

[56]Compare the claim that a Sanhedrin should not be established in a city unless at least two people there were conversant with the seventy languages (*b. Sanh.* 17b [87–88]), and the view that Mordecai understood seventy languages (cf. *b. Meg.* 13b [78–79]; Tg. 1 Esther 1:22). The midrashic interpretation (cf. *Gen. R.* 98,17) and the Targums (Nf, Nfmg, P, V, N, Ps.-J.) of our present verse understood *'mry špr,* "comely fawns," to mean "beautiful words," and so they attribute the gift of beautiful speech to Naphtali.

[57]Lit.: "who hast become great." See *Gen. R.* 78,10; 98,18.

[58]Lit.: "the end was upon you," reading *swp* with *ed. pr.* rather than *ṭwp* (read *ṭwb?*) of Lond.

[59]*PRE* 39 (305); cf. *b. Sanh.* 19b (103–104); *LAB* 43,5; 4 Macc 2,2.

[60]The "incident with your mistress" refers to the events narrated in Gen 39:7–13, and the "incident with your brothers" refers to the fact that Joseph did not take revenge on his brothers who sold him.

[61]Lit.: "the teeth of the rocks."

[62]Lit.: "conquers, subdues"; = Nf, P, V, N.

[63]Lit.: "when they were crying out (*hww mqlsyn*) "before you." See above, 41:43.

[64]*Gen. R.* 98,18; *PRE* 39 (307); cf. also *Gen. R.* 97.

[65]Or perhaps: "they afflicted (*'mryrw,* or *mmryrw* [= *ed. pr.*])." The same form of the verb (*mrr.* [Af.]) is used by Ps.-J. in Exod 1:14, where it is said that the Egyptians embittered the lives of the Hebrews. See *Gen. R.* 98,19, which, in a comment on our present verse (v. 23), speaks of different people that caused suffering to one another.

[66]Cf. LXX, "reproached him," deriving Heb. *rbw,* "shot at" (RSV), from *ryb,* "contend."

[67]Lit.: "to bring him down from his honor"; = V, N.

[68]See above, 1:16 (Ps.-J.) and n. 29 to that verse.

[69]HT *ḥṣym,* "arrows," is taken to refer to slander, which, like an arrow, smites at a distance; cf. *Gen. R.* 98,19.

[70]Ps.-J. takes Heb. *tšb,* "remained" (RSV), to be derived from *šwb,* "return," and Heb. *qšt,* "bow," is taken to refer to the *membrum virile.* Cf. *Gen. R.* 87,7; 98,20; *b. Sotah* 36b (180); *j. Hor.* 2,46d. Ps.-J. is the only one of the Targums to give this rather indelicate interpretation of the biblical words. On Ps.-J.'s readiness to refer to indelicate matters see above, Introduction, p. 7.

[71]Lit.: "were scattered." Ps.-J.'s text is not very clear. The author seems to take Heb. *wypzw,* "were made agile" (RSV), to be derived from *pwṣ,* "spread," as do the texts from *Gen. R.* and *j. Hor.* mentioned in the preceding note.

had received from Jacob.[72] Thus *he was found worthy of becoming administrator*[73] *and of having his name engraved with theirs on* the stones of Israel.[74] 25. "May your help *be* from *the Memra of* the God of your father, and may *He who is called* Shaddai bless you with the blessings *that come down with*[75] *the dew* of heaven above, *and with the best of* the blessings *of the springs* of the deep *that come up and make the plants grow from* below. *Blessed be* the breasts *from which you sucked* and the womb *in which you lay!*[76] 26. May the blessings of your father *be added*[77] *to* the blessings *with which my fathers Abraham and Isaac have blessed me, (and) which the princes of* the world, *Ishmael and Esau, and all the children of Kethurah desired.*[78] *Let all these blessings be gathered, and let them form a crown*[79] *of greatness* for Joseph's head, for the brow of *the man who was master and ruler*[79] *in Egypt and (who) was sensitive to the honor of* his brothers.[80] 27. Benjamin is *a mighty tribe, like* a wolf (with) his prey. *The Shekinah of the Lord of the world will dwell in his land,*[81] *and in his inheritance the Temple will be built.*[82] In the morning the *priests will offer the regular lamb (of sacrifice) until the fourth hour,*[83] *and at twilight they will offer a second lamb,*[84] *and in the evening they will divide what is left of the remainder of the offerings,*[85] *and each* will eat *his portion.*" 28. All these are the twelve

Notes, Chapter 49

[72]Like the texts mentioned in n. 70, and like *PRE* 39 (305), Ps.-J. allows us to understand that Joseph had to struggle to resist the attentions of his mistress. Ps.-J. takes "from the hands of the Mighty One of Jacob" (RSV) to refer to the mighty teaching which Joseph received from Jacob. All the other Targums of this verse (Nf, P, V, N, Onq.) correctly refer "the Mighty One of Jacob" to God.

[73]Cf. *b. Sotah* 36b (181): "from there was he worthy to be made a shepherd." See Onq.: "by whose (God's) *Memra* he (Joseph) sustains fathers and children, the seed of Israel." Like Onq. and the text from *Sotah*, Ps.-J. applies the term Shepherd of the biblical verse to Joseph.

[74]*b. Sotah* 36b (180-181). Cf. Exod 28:21.

[75]Lit.: "from"; = Onq. The phrase "blessings that descend from the dew of heaven above" in Onq. and in Ps.-J. has probably been modeled on Gen 27:28: "May God give you of the dew (*mṭl*) of heaven."

[76]*Gen. R.* 98,20. Cf. McNamara, 1966A, 131–133.

[77]Since the words of Jacob as recorded in the biblical text—"The blessings of your father surpass . . ."—might seem to favor Joseph more than his brothers, the Targums (Nf, P, V, N, Ps.-J., Onq.) change "surpass" to "be added."

[78]Nf, Ps.-J., and Onq. take the Heb. *t'wt,* "bounties" (RSV), in its usual meaning, "desire," and they understand *gb't 'wlm,* "the everlasting hills," as "the princes of the world." Nf and Ps.-J. explain that these princes are Ishmael and Esau, who represent the Arab and Roman-Christian worlds respectively. Cf. Splansky, 1981, 94–96.

[79]Nf, P, V, N, and Ps.-J. understand *nzyr,* "separate form" (RSV), first as "crown" (*nzr*), and later as "leader." See also Deut 33:16 (Nf, P, V, N, L, Ps.-J.). Cf. Syrén, 1986, 60–65. With regard to Joseph's "crown of greatness," see *Testament of Benjamin* 4,2, where the readers are urged to imitate Joseph's virtue so that they too "may wear crowns of glory."

[80]*Testament of Joseph* 17,1.

[81]Onq. "The Shekinah will dwell in his territory." Cf. Tg. Deut 33:12 (Nf, V, N, Ps.-J., Onq.); *Mekilta de R. Shimon b. Yohai* to Exod 14:22 (edition Epstein-Melamed, 63); *b. Meg.* 26a (157).

[82]Since it was believed that at least part of the temple was in the territory of Benjamin, it was reasonable for the Targums of our present verse (Nf, P, V, N, Ps.-J., Onq.) to glorify Benjamin in terms of the Temple and its worship. See *Gen. R.* 99,1; *b. Yoma* 12a (53); *Meg.* 26a (157); *Zebah.* 54a (270–271); *ARN* A 35. See further Aberbach-Grossfeld, 1976, 63–67.

[83]". . . until the fourth hour": This is the opinion of R. Judah as expressed in *b. Berak.* 26b (160).

[84]*Gen. R.* 99,3; cf. Exod 29:39; Num 28:4. See also Jerome, *Quaest. hebr.* in Gen 49:27.

[85]HT speaks of dividing (spoil). Since the two daily regular sacrifices were completely consumed, the Targums, including Onq., had to refer to other sacrifices besides these to give meaning to HT "dividing" in their text; cf. Aberbach-Grossfeld, 1976, 67. To allow for this addition the Targums, which had already translated the word "evening" as "twilight" (Nf, P, Ps.-J.) or "sunset" (V, N) or "towards evening" (Onq.), now translate it as "evening."

tribes of Israel, *all of them equally righteous,* [86] and this is what their father said to them as he blessed them, blessing each with an appropriate blessing. 29. Then he commanded them, saying to them, "I am about to be gathered to my people. Bury me with my fathers in the cave that is in the field of Ephron the Hittite, 30. in the cave that is in the field of the double (cave) which is facing Mamre, in the land of Canaan, the field that Abraham bought from Ephron the Hittite as a burial possession. 31. There they buried Abraham and Sarah his wife; there they buried Isaac and Rebekah his wife; and there I buried Leah. 32. The field and the cave that is in it were bought from the sons of *the Hittite.*" 33. When Jacob finished commanding his sons, he drew his feet into the bed, and he expired and was gathered to his people.

CHAPTER 50

1. *Joseph* [1] *laid his father in a bed of ivory overlaid with pure gold, inlaid with precious stones, and reinforced with linen cords. There they poured out foaming wines, and there they burned the best of spices;* [2] *there stood the heroes of those of the house of Esau, and the heroes of those of the house of Ishmael;* [3] *there stood Judah the lion—the hero among his brothers. He spoke up* [4] *and said to his brothers, "Come, let us weep* [5] *over our father, a tall cedar whose top will reach towards the heavens and* [6]

Notes, Chapter 49 (Cont.)

[86]Lit.: "all of them righteous as one." See *Gen. R.* 99,4; *Tanḥ., Wa-Yehi* 16 (157). These texts point out that when Jacob had blessed the tribes individually, attributing special qualities and privileges to each one of them, he went on and blessed all of them together, lest one tribe be considered greater than another. This view is based on the words "he blessed *them*" in the biblical verse.

Notes, Chapter 50

[1]There is no parallel in rabbinic literature for the long midrash which Nf, Nfmg 1 and 2, P, V, N, Ps.-J. and the Targum Tosefta (CTg FF) place at the beginning of this verse; cf. Schmerler, 1932, 352–353; Brayer, 1950, 92; Shinan, 1979, 1, 71–72.

[2]Cf. *Sefer Ha-Yashar* 59 (192): "And they put Joseph in a coffin filled with spices and all sorts of perfume." The mention of spices in Ps.-J.s version of our present verse may have been prompted by the fact that Jacob was embalmed (cf. v. 2).

[3]How these representatives of the houses of Esau and Ishmael came to be in Egypt is not explained. They disappear from the scene after this verse, and are not said to accompany Jacob's sons who took their father to Canaan for burial (vv. 7-9). Verse 13 (Ps.-J.) mentions Esau and his associates, but in a very different context.

[4]Lit: "answered."

[5]Reading *nybky* with Lond. This is also the reading (with orthographical variations) in P, V, and N. In these texts Judah invites his brothers to weep over Jacob, who is compared to a cedar. Cf. 1 *QGenApoc.* 19,14-17, where Abraham is compared to a cedar. See the rabbinic parallels given by Fitzmyer, 1971, 111, and by M.R. Lehmann, 1958–1959, 249–263, especially 257–259. *Ed. pr.*, Nf, and Nfmg 2 read *nbny*, "let us build." Nfmg 1 has "and build." But the idea of "building a cedar" is strange, and the reading "let us weep over" is probably the correct one. The image of the cedar as developed in the Targums of this verse is similar to Ezek 31:3-9.

[6]Lit.: "but, besides, surely." The same conjunction is used in P, V, N and one reading in Nfmg. Nf and a reading in Nfmg use "and."

whose branches cover all the inhabitants of the earth; and its roots reach to the bottom of the deep. From him there arose twelve tribes, and from him there are destined to arise kings and rulers, as well as the priests in their divisions to offer sacrifices; and from him (there shall arise) the Levites in their groupings to sing." Behold, then Joseph *inclined* upon his father's face and wept over him and kissed him. 2. Joseph commanded his servants the physicians to embalm his father. So the physicians embalmed Israel. 3. Forty days were spent *in embalming* him, for so many days are spent in embalming, and the Egyptians wept for him seventy days, *saying to one another, "Come, let us weep over Jacob the righteous, for whose merit the famine passed from the land of Egypt." For it had been decreed that there would be a famine for forty-two years. But for the merit of Jacob forty years were withheld from Egypt, and there was famine for two years only.*[7] 4. When the days of weeping for him passed, Joseph spoke to *the chiefs of* Pharaoh's house, saying, "If, I pray, I have found mercy in your eyes, speak, I pray, in the hearing of Pharaoh, saying, 5. 'My father made me swear, saying, "Behold, I am about to die; in the grave which I dug for myself in the land of Canaan, there you shall bury me." ' And now, let me go up, I pray, to bury my father, and I will return." 6. And Pharaoh said, "Go up and bury your father as he made you swear." 7. So Joseph went up to bury his father; and with him went up all the servants of Pharaoh, the elders of his house, and all the elders of the land of Egypt, 8. and all the *men of* Joseph's house, his brothers and his father's house; only their little ones, their flocks, and their oxen did they leave in the land of Goshen. 9. Chariots and horsemen went up with him too; it was a very great company. 10. When they came to the threshing floor of Atad, which is beyond the Jordan, there they lamented with a very great and solemn lamentation; and he observed seven days' mourning for his father. 11. When the Canaanite inhabitants of the land saw the mourning at the threshing floor of Atad, *they loosed the girdles of their loins in honor of Jacob, and pointing with their hands,*[8] they said, "This is a solemn mourning on behalf of the Egyptians." Therefore *the place* was called Abel-Mizraim, which is beyond the Jordan. 12. Thus his sons did for him as he had commanded them. 13. When his sons carried him to the land of Canaan, *Esau*[9] *the wicked heard of the matter, and he set out from the mountain of Gabla with many legions and came to Hebron and would not allow Joseph to bury his father in the double cave. Then Naphtali went immediately, and running down to Egypt, he came (back) that same day.*[10] *He brought the title deeds concerning the di-*

Notes, Chapter 50

[7]*Gen. R.* 89,9. See above, 47:7 (Ps.-J.) and n. 6 to that verse. In our present verse Ps.-J. does not take into account the fact that Joseph foretold that there would be seven years of famine (cf. Gen 41:27, 30)

[8]*Gen. R.* 100,6; *j. Sotah* 1,17b; *Tanḥ., Wa-Yehi* 17 (158).

[9]The closest parallel to Ps.-J.'s long addition to this verse is found in *PRE* 39 (309–310). Essentially the same material is recorded in *b. Sotah* 13a (66–67) and in *Gen. R.* 97. A similar tradition is recorded briefly in *Gen. R.* 98,17, where the children of Heth are said to have tried to prevent the burial of Jacob in Machpelah.

[10]Compare Gen 24:61 (Ps.-J.), where it is said that the way was shortened for Abraham's servant, and see n. 37 to that verse. See also Exod 19:4, where Ps.-J., and Ps.-J. alone, says that God transported the Israelites from Pelusium to Jerusalem and back in one day.

vision of the double cave which Esau had written for Jacob his brother.[11] *And immediately Joseph beckoned to Hushim, son of Dan, who took a sword and cut off the
head of Esau the wicked. Esau's head went on rolling until it went into the cave and
rested in the bosom of Isaac his father. The sons of Esau buried his body in the field
of the double (cave).*[12] *Afterwards his sons* buried *Jacob* in the cave of the field of the
double (cave) facing Mamre, the field which Abraham had purchased as a burial
possession from Ephron the Hittite. 14. After he had buried his father, Joseph returned to Egypt, he and his brothers and all who had gone up with him to bury his
father. 15. When Joseph's brothers saw that their father was dead, *and that (Joseph)*
[13] *did not sit*[14] *together with them to eat bread,*[15] they said, "Perhaps Joseph *bears
hatred* against us, and he will surely pay us back for all the evil that we have done to
him." 16. So they commanded *Bilhah*[16] to say to Joseph, "Before his death your father commanded (us) to say *to you,* 17. 'Thus shall you say to Joseph, "Please pardon, I pray, the guilt of your brothers and their sins, although[17] they have done evil
to you," ' and now, pray, pardon the guilt of the servants of the God of your father."
And Joseph wept as they[18] spoke with him. 18. His brothers also went and *inclined*
before him and said, "Behold, we are your servants." 19. Joseph said to them, "Do
not be afraid, *because I will not do you evil but good, for I fear and am humbled before the Lord.*[19] 20. As for you, you thought evil *thoughts* against me, *supposing that
when I did not sit*[14] *with you to eat, it was because I bear enmity towards you. But
the Memra of the Lord* intended it for good *for me. For my father had me sit at the
head, and out of respect for him I accepted (that). But now, I do not accept (it),*[20] so

Notes, Chapter 50

[11]The tradition that Naphtali ran to Egypt for the title deeds is recorded in 49:21 (Nf, P, V, N, Ps.-J.), but Ps.-J. is the
only Targum to repeat this tradition in our present verse. On Ps.-J.'s tendency to repeat traditions, see above, Introduction, p. 6. In 31:4 Ps.-J., and Ps.-J. alone, mentions that Naphtali was a swift messenger: see above, n. 3 to that verse.

[12]*PRE* 39 (310) says that Esau's head was taken into the cave of Machpelah and that his body was taken to Mount Seir.
Rieder, in his edition of Pseudo-Jonathan (1984, vol. 1; Hebrew section, p. 100, n. 13), notes that it is surprising that Ps.-
J. says that Esau's body was buried in Machpelah. Shinan (1979, 1, 173, n. 9) suggests that Ps.-J. may originally have read
Mount Seir, and that a copyist replaced this with "the field of the double (cave)." The copyist may have been influenced
by HT, which says that Jacob's sons buried their father "in the cave of the field at Machpelah."

[13]*Gen. R* 100,8; *Tanḥ.* B., *Shemoth* 2 (2,2).

[14]See above, 27:19 (Ps.-J.) and n. 12 to that verse.

[15]Reading *lḥm'* rather than *lḥd'* of *ed. pr.* and Lond. In v. 20 Ps.-J. explains why Joseph did not sit with his brothers
after Jacob's death. Thus, Ps.-J.'s additions to vv. 15 and 20 form a coherent unity. On Ps.-J.'s tendency to attach elements of a tradition to different verses of the biblical text, see above, Introduction, p. 5.

[16]*Tanḥ.* B., *Shemoth* 2 (2,2); *Tanḥ.*, *Ṣav* 7 (378). See Gen 37:2, which tells of Joseph's closeness to the sons of Bilhah
and Zilpah.

[17]Lit.: "because, for."

[18]The author of Ps.-J. ignores the fact that he had earlier said (v. 16) that Bilhah had been appointed spokesperson for
the brothers.

[19]Onq.: "Do not be afraid, for *I am one who fears the Lord.*" The Targums (Nf, P, V, Ps.-J., Onq.) cannot tolerate
Joseph's rhetorical question "Am I in the place of God"? See above 30:2, where the Targums modify the same question
which HT puts on the lips of Jacob.

[20]*Gen. R.* 100,8 explains that although Jacob placed Joseph above Judah, who was a king, and above Reuben, who was
the first-born, Joseph did not feel that it was right for him to sit above these after their father's death. See above, v. 15 and
n. 15 to that verse. It may be noted that if one did not know the tradition which is recorded in the *Gen. R.* passage just referred to, Ps.-J.'s haggadic addition would not be very clear. On Ps.-J.'s tendency to make allusions to well-known
traditions, see above, Introduction, p. 6.

that *I may merit that a deliverance* be brought about *for us* this day, to keep alive many people *from the house of Jacob.* 21. And now do not be afraid. I will sustain you and your little ones." And he comforted them and spoke *comforting* (words)[21] to their hearts. 22. Joseph dwelt in Egypt, he and his father's house. Joseph lived a hundred and ten[22] years. 23. Joseph saw children of the third *generation* of Ephraim; also, *when* the children of Machir, son of Manasseh, were born, Joseph *circumcised them.*[23] 24. Joseph said to his brothers, "*Behold,* I am about to die; but *the Lord* will surely *remember*[24] you and bring you up from this land which he swore to Abraham, to Isaac, and to Jacob." 25. Then Joseph made the sons of Israel swear that they would say *to their children,*[25] "*Behold, you will be enslaved in Egypt, but do not make plans to go up out of Egypt until the time that two deliverers come and say to you, 'The Lord surely remembers* you,'[26] *and at the time that you go up*[27] you shall bring up my bones from here." 26. Joseph died at the age of a hundred and ten years. And they embalmed him *and decorated him*[28] and placed him in a coffin,[29] *which they sank in the middle of the Nile*[30] of Egypt.

Notes, Chapter 50

[21]= P, Onq. Cf. *Gen. R.* 100,9.

[22]Lond. and *ed. pr.* read "twenty" by mistake. In v. 26 they correctly read "ten."

[23]Onq.: "*reared* (them)." Onq. and Ps.-J. both interpret the metaphorical expression "born upon Joseph's knees." See also above, 30:3 and n. 4 to that verse.

[24]Onq.: "remembers." HT: "will visit." See v. 25, where Ps.-J. agrees with Onq. in its translation of the same Hebrew idiom.

[25]Cf. *Mekilta* to Exod 13:19 (1, 181).

[26]The two deliverers were, of course, Moses and Aaron; see *Tanh., Shemoth* 24 (178–179). Cf. also *Gen. R.* 97,6; *b. Sotah* 13a (68). See Exod 13:17 (Ps.-J.), which tells of the punishment meted out to those who left Egypt before the appointed time.

[27]*Gen. R.* 100,11.

[28]Possibly with a crown and with royal garments. Or, the verb used (*'tr*) might be translated as "crown," so that the text means that the brothers crowned Joseph with a royal crown; cf. Schmerler, 1932, 358. We know of no source for Ps.-J.'s addition.

[29]*glwsqm';* = Gr. *glôssokomon* = Nfmg, P, V.

[30]*Mekilta* to Exod 13:19 (1,176); *b. Sotah* 13a (67). For other parallels see Bowker, 1969, 297. Ps.-J.'s haggadic addition about the sinking of the coffin is completed in Exod 13:19 (Ps.-J.), where it is said that Moses took the coffin out of the Nile. On Ps.-J.'s practice of adding elements of a particular haggadah to different biblical verses, see above, Introduction, p. 5.

SELECT BIBLIOGRAPHY

Manuscripts of the Palestinian Targums

Neofiti

Biblioteca Apostolica Vaticana, Codex Neofiti 1.

Fragment Targums

Paris, Bibliothèque Nationale, MS Hébr. 110, fol. 1–16 (=P);

Biblioteca Apostolica Vaticana, Ebr. 440, fol. 198–227 (=V);

Nürnberg, Stadtbibliothek Solger 2.2o, fol. 119–147 (=N);

Leipzig, Universitätsbibliothek B.H., fol. 1 (=L);

New York, Jewish Theological Seminary (Lutzki) 605, (E.N. Adler 2587), fol. 6, 7 (=Jr);

London, British Library Oriental 10794, fol. 8 (=Br.);

Moscow, Günzburg 3 (copied from MS Nürnberg);

Sassoon Private Collection 264, fol. 225–267 (copied from 2nd *Biblia Rabbinica*).

Cairo Genizah Manuscripts of the Palestinian Targums

Principally in libraries in:
>Cambridge, University Library (Taylor-Schechter Collection);
>Oxford, Bodleian Library;
>Leningrad, Saltykov-Schedrin Library (Antonin Collection);
>New York, Jewish Theological Seminary (Adler Collection).

Pseudo-Jonathan

London, British Library, Additional 27031.

EDITIONS OF TEXTS

Neofiti I

Díez Macho, A. *Neophyti* I. Targum Palestinense. MS de la Biblioteca Vaticana. Vols. 1–5. Madrid-Barcelona: Consejo Superior de Investigaciones Científicas; 1 *Génesis*, 1968; 2 *Éxodo*, 1970; 3 *Levitico*, 1971; 4 *Numeros*, 1974; 5 *Deuteronomio*, 1978.

Genizah Fragments

Kahle, P. *Masoreten des Westens II.* Stuttgart: Kohlhammer, 1930; reprint Hildesheim: Olms, 1967.

Klein, M. L. *Genizah Manuscripts of Palestinian Targum to the Pentateuch.* 2 vols. Cincinnati: Hebrew Union College, 1986.

Fragment Targums

Ginsburger, M. *Das Fragmententhargum.* Berlin: Calvary, 1899; reprint, Jerusalem: Makor, 1969.

Klein, M. L. *The Fragment-Targums of the Pentateuch According to their Extant Sources.* 2 vols. Analecta Biblica 76. Rome: Biblical Institute Press, 1980.

Pseudo-Jonathan

Clarke, E. G., with Aufrecht, W. E.; Hurd, J. C.; Spitzer, F. *Targum Pseudo-Jonathan of the Pentateuch: Text and Concordance.* Hoboken, N.J.: Ktav, 1984.

Díez Macho, A. *Biblia Polyglotta Matritensia.* Series IV. *Targum Palaestinense in Pentateuchum.* Additur Targum Pseudojonatan ejusque hispanica versio. Editio critica curante A. Díez Macho, adjuvantibus L. Díez Merino, E. Martínez Borobio, T. Martínez Saiz. Pseudojonatan hispanica versio: T. Martínez Saiz. Pseudojonathan hispanica versio: T. Martínez Saiz. Targum Palaestinensis testimonia ex variis fontibus: R. Griño., Madrid: Consejo Superior de Investigaciones Científicas. L. 1, *Genesis*, 1989; L. 2, *Exodus*, 1980; L. 3, *Leviticus*, 1980; L. 4, *Numeri*, 1977; L. 5, *Deuteronomium*, 1980.

Ginsburger, M. *Pseudo-Jonathan.* (Thargum-Jonathan ben Usiël zum Pentateuch). Nach der Londoner Handschrift (Brit. Mus. Add. 27031). Berlin: Calvary, 1903.

Rieder, D. *Pseudo-Jonathan*: Thargum Jonathan ben Uziel on the Pentateuch copied from the London MS. (British Museum Add. 27031). Jerusalem: Salomon's, 1974. Reprinted with Hebrew translation and notes; 2 vols. Jerusalem, 1984–85.

Onqelos

Berliner, A. *Targum Onkelos.* Herausgegeben und erläutert von A. Berliner. Berlin: Gorzelanczyk, 1884.

Sperber, A. *The Bible in Aramaic.* Vol. 1, *The Pentateuch according to Targum Onkelos.* Leiden: Brill, 1959.

Other Targum Texts

Díez Macho, A. "Nueva Fuente para el Targum Palestino del Dia Septimo de Pascua y Primero de Pentecostes," in *Escritos de Biblia y Oriente.* Miscelánea conmemorativa del 25° aniversario del Instituto Español Bíblico y Arqueológico (Casa de Santiago) de Jerusalén. Bibliotheca Salmanticensis, Estudios 38; ed., R. Aguirre, F. García López. Salamanca-Jerusalem: Universidad Pontificia, 1981, 233–257.

idem: "Nuevos Fragmentos de Tosefta Targumica," *Sefarad* 16 (1956) 313–324.

idem: "Deux nouveaux fragments du Targum palestinien à New York," in *Studi sull' Oriente e la Bibbia offerti a P. Giovanni Rinaldi.* Genoa: Studio e Vita, 1967, 175–178.

Hurwitz, S. *Machsor Vitry,* nach der Handschrift im British Museum (Cod. Add. No. 27200 u. 27201). Leipzig, 1899; 2nd edition Nürnberg: Bulka, 1923; reprint Jerusalem: Aleph, 1963, 305–344.

Kasher, R. "A Targumic Tosefta to Genesis 2:1-3," *Sinay* 78 (1976–77) 9–17.

Klein, M. "The Targumic Tosefta to Exodus 15:2," *JJS* 26 (1975) 61–67.

Komlosh, Y. "The Targum Version of the Crossing of the Red Sea," *Sinay* 45 (1959) 223–228.

Translations of the Palestinian Targums of the Pentateuch

Etheridge, J. W., *The Targums of Onkelos and Jonathan ben Uzziel on the Pentateuch: With Fragments of the Jerusalem Targum: From the Chaldee,* by J. W. Etheridge. 2 vols. London: Longman, Green Longman, 1862, 1865; reprint in 1 vol., New York: Ktav, 1968.

Le Déaut, R. with J. Robert. *Targum du Pentateuque. Traduction des deux Recensions Palestiniennes complètes.* 4 vols. Trans. R. Le Déaut with J. Robert. Sources Chrétiennes 245, 256, 261, 271. Paris: Cerf. Vol. 1, *Genèse,* 1978; vol. 2, *Exode et Lévitique,* 1979; vol. 3, *Nombres,* 1979; vol. 4, *Deutéronome,* 1980.

Codex Neofiti 1: Spanish translation by A. Díez Macho; French translation by R. Le Déaut; English translation by M. McNamara and M. Maher in the *editio princeps,* ed. A. Díez Macho.

Pseudo-Jonathan: Spanish translation by T. Martínez Saiz in the Díez Macho edition in *Biblia Polyglotta Matritensia.* See above. French translation in Le Déaut-Robert; see above. Hebrew translation in Rieder, 1984–85; see above.

Rabbinic Sources

Mekilta de-Rabbi Ishmael. 3 vols; edited and translated by J. Z. Lauterbach. Philadelphia: JPS 1933–35; reprint 1949. (We give volume and page reference to this edition.)

Mekilta de-Rabbi Shimon bar Yohai, eds. J. N. Epstein and E. Z. Melamed. Jerusalem: Hillel Press, (no date).

Midrash Bereshit Rabba. Critical edition with notes and commentary. 3 vols., eds. J. Theodor and Ch. Albeck. Jerusalem: Wahrmann, 1965.

Midrash Tanḥuma. Vilna, 1833; reprint Israel, no date. (Referred to as *Tanḥ.*).

Midrash Tanḥuma. 2 vols., ed. S. Buber. Vilna, 1885; reprint Jerusalem, 1964. (Referred to as *Tanḥ. B.*).

Midrash Tehillim, ed. S. Buber. Vilna, 1891; reprint Jerusalem, 1984.

Pesikta de Rab Kahana. 2 vols., ed. B. Mandelbaum. New York: Jewish Theological Seminary, 1962.

Pirke de Rabbi Eliezer, ed. D. Luria. Warsaw, 1852.

Sifre on Deuteronomy, ed. L. Finkelstein. Berlin, 1939; reprint New York: JPS, 1969.

Sifre on Numbers, ed. H. S. Horovitz. Leipzig: Fock, 1917; reprint Jerusalem: Wahrmann, 1966.

Talmud Yerushalmi. Krotoschin, 1866; reprint Jerusalem, 1960.

Tosefta, ed. M. S. Zuckermandel. Jerusalem: Wahrmann, 1963.

Translations of Rabbinic Works

The Babylonian Talmud. Translated into English with notes, glossary and indices. Ed. I. Epstein. 18-vol. edition. London: Soncino, 1978. (When referring to texts from the Babylonian Talmud, we give the page number of this edition in brackets).

Los Capítulos de Rabbí Eliezer. Versión crítica, introducción y notas por M. Pérez Fernández. Biblioteca Midrásica 1. Valencia: Institución S. Jerónimo para la Investigación Bíblica, 1984.

The Fathers According to Rabbi Nathan. Trans. J. Goldin. Yale Judaica Series 10. New Haven: Yale University Press, 1955. (Referred to as *ARN* A).

The Fathers According to Rabbi Nathan (Abot de Rabbi Nathan), Version B. Trans. A. J. Saldarini. Studies in Judaism in Late Antiquity 11. Leiden: Brill, 1957. (Referred to as *ARN* B).

Mekilta de Rabbi Ishmael. See above under "Rabbinic Sources."

The Midrash on Psalms. Translated from the Hebrew and Aramaic by W. G. Braude. 2 vols. Yale Judaica Series XIII. New Haven: Yale University Press, 1959. [We refer to this work as *Midrash Psalms*, giving the page references in brackets.]

The Midrash Rabbah. Ed. H. Freedman and M. Simon. New Compact Edition in 5 vols. London: Soncino, 1977. (Referred to as *Gen. R., Exod. R.*, etc.).

The Mishnah. Trans. H. Danby. Oxford: University Press, 1939.

Pesikta de-Rab Kahana. Trans. W. G. Braude and I. J. Kapstein. Philadelphia: JPS, 1975.

Pesikta Rabbati. 2 vols. Trans. W. G. Braude. Yale Judaica Series XVIII. New Haven-London, 1968.

Pirke de Rabbi Eliezer. The Chapters of Rabbi Eliezer the Great. Translated and Annotated by G. Friedlander. New York: Sepher-Hermon, 4th ed. 1981.

Sefer ha-Yashar, or *The Book of Jasher. Referred to in Joshua and Second Samuel.* Trans. M. M. Noah. New York: Noah and Gould, 1840. (We give the page numbers of this edition in brackets.)

Tanna debe Eliyyahu—The Lore of the School of Elijah. Translated from the Hebrew by W. G. Braude and I. J. Kapstein. Philadelphia: JPS, 1981.

General

Aberbach, M.: 1969, "Patriotic Tendencies in Targum Onkelos," *The Journal of Hebraic Studies* 1, 13–24.

Aberbach, M., and Grossfeld, B.: 1976, *Targum Onqelos on Genesis 49.* SBL Aramaic Studies 1. Missoula, Mont.: Scholars Press.

Aberbach, M., and Grossfeld, B.: 1982, *Targum Onkelos to Genesis.* New York: Ktav.

Alexander, P.S.: 1972, "The Targumim and Early Exegesis of 'Sons of God' in Genesis 6," *JJS* 23 (1972) 60–71.

idem: 1974, *The Toponomy of the Targumim with Special Reference to the Table of Nations and the Boundaries of the Land of Israel.* Dissertation, Oxford University.

idem: 1976, "The Rabbinic Lists of Forbidden Targumim," *JJS* 27, 178–191.

idem: 1985, "The Targumim and the Rabbinic Rules for the Delivery of the Targum," *VTSupp* 36, 14–28.

Allony, N.: 1975, "The Jerusalem Targum Pseudo-Jonathan. Rieder's edition" (in Hebrew), *Beth Miqra* 62, 423–425.

Aptowitzer, A.: 1930–31, "The Heavenly Temple According to the Haggadah" (Hebrew), *Tarbiz* 2, 137–153, 257–287.

Aptowitzer, V.: 1924, "Asenath, the Wife of Joseph. A Haggadic Literary-Historical Study," *HUCA* 1, 239–306.

Aruch Completum sive Lexicon vocabula et res quae in Libris Targumicis, Talmudicis, et Midraschicis continentur, explicans. N. b. Jechielis. Ed. A. Kohut. Vienna: Brög, 1878–92.

Bacher, W.: 1874, "Das gegenseitige Verhältniss der pentateuchischen Targumim," *ZDMG* 28, 59–72.

idem: 1884, 1890, *Die Agada der Tannaiten.* 2 vols. Strasbourg: Tübner.

idem: 1899, 1905, 1965, *Die exegetische Terminologie der jüdischen Traditionsliteratur.* 2 vols. Leipzig, 1899, 1905. 2 vols. in one. Darmstadt: Wissenschaftliche Buchgesellschaft, 1965.

idem: 1906, "Targum," *JE* 12, 57–63.

Bamberger, B.J.: 1975, "Halakic Elements in the Neofiti Targum: A Preliminary Statement," *JQR* 66, 27–38.

Barnstein, H.: 1899, "A Noteworthy Targum MS. in the British Museum," *JQR* 11, 167–171.

Barry Levy, B.: see under Levy, Barry B.

Beer, B.: 1859, *Leben Abraham's nach Auffassung der jüdischen Sage.* Leipzig: Leiner.

Berliner, A.: *Targum Onkelos.* See above under "Editions of Texts: Onqelos."

Beyer, K.: 1984, *Die aramäischen Texte vom Toten Meer.* Göttingen: Vandenhoeck und Ruprecht.

Black, M.: 1967, *An Aramaic Approach to the Gospel and Acts*, 3rd ed. Oxford: Clarendon.

Bloch, R.: 1955A, 1978, "Note Méthodologique pour l'étude de la Littérature Rabbinique," *Recherches de Science Religieuse* 43, 194–227. Also published in English as "Methodological Note for the Study of Rabbinic Literature," trans. W. S. Green and W. J. Sullivan, in *Approaches to Ancient Judaism: Theory and Practice*. Ed. W. S. Green. Brown Judaic Studies I. Missoula, Mont.: Scholars Press, 1978, 51–75.

idem: 1955B, "Note sur l'utilisation des fragments de la Geniza du Caire pour l'étude du Targum Palestinien," *REJ* n.s. 14, 5–35.

idem: 1957, "Juda engendra Pharès et Zara, de Thamar (Matth., 1, 3)," in *Mélanges bibliques rédigés en l'honneur de André Robert*. Travaux de L'Institut Catholique de Paris, no. 4. Paris, pp. 381–389.

Böhl, F.: "Die Metaphorisierung (Metila) in den Targumim zum Pentateuch," *Frankfurter Judaistische Beiträge* 15 (1987) 111–149.

Bowker, J.: 1969, *The Targums and Rabbinic Literature*. Cambridge: University Press.

Bowker, J. W.: 1967, "Haggadah in the Targum Onqelos," *JSS* 12, 51–65.

Brayer, M. M.: 1950, *Studies in the Pseudo Jonathan of the Bible. Book of Genesis*. Unpublished doctoral dissertation. New York: Yeshiva University.

idem: 1963, "The Aramaic Pentateuch Targums and the Question of Avoiding Anthropomorphisms" (in Hebrew), *Talpiyot* 8, 513–525.

idem: 1964, "The Pentateuchal Targum Attributed to Jonathan ben Uzziel—A Source for Unknown Midrashim" (in Hebrew), in *The Abraham Weiss Jubilee Volume*. Ed. M. S. Feldbaum. New York, 201–231.

idem: 1971, "The Debate Between a Sadducee and a Pharisee in the Mouths of Cain and Abel" (in Hebrew), *Beth Miqra* 44, 583–585.

Brock, S.: 1979, "Jewish Traditions in Syriac Sources," *JJS* 30, 212–232.

Burchard, C.: 1970, "Zum Text von 'Joseph and Aseneth'" *JStJud* 1, 3–34.

Caquot, A.: 1976, "La parole sur Juda dans le testament lyrique de Jacob (Gen 49, 8-12)," *Semitica* 26, 5–32.

Cashdan, E.: 1967, "Names and the Interpretation of Names in the Pseudo-Jonathan Targum to the Book of Genesis," in *Essays Presented to Chief Rabbi Israel Brodie on the Occasion of His Seventieth Birthday."* Ed. H.J. Zimmels, J. Rabbinowitz, and L. Finestein. London: Soncino, pp. 31–39.

Cathcart, K.J., and Gordon, R.P.: *The Targum of the Minor Prophets*. The Aramaic Bible 14. Wilmington, Del.: Michael Glazier, 1989.

Charlesworth, J. H., ed.: 1983, 1985, *The Old Testament Pseudepigrapha*. 2 vols. London: Darton, Longman and Todd.

Chester, A.: 1986, *Divine Revelation and Divine Titles in the Pentateuchal Targumim.* Texte und Studien zum antiken Judentum 14. Tübingen: Mohr (Siebeck).

Chiesa, B.: 1977, "Contrasti ideologici del tempo degli Asmonei nella Aggádáh e nelle versioni di Genesi 49, 3," *Annali del Istituto Orientale di Napoli* 37, 417–440.

Churgin, P.: 1933–34, "The Targum and the Septuagint," *AJSL* 50, 40–65.

idem: 1943, "On the Origin of Targumic Formulas" (in Hebrew), *Horeb* 7, 103–109.

idem: 1946, "The Halakah in Targum Onkelos" (in Hebrew), *Horeb* 9, 79–93.

Clarke, E.G.: 1974–75, "Jacob's dream at Bethel as interpreted in the targums and the New Testament," *SR* 4, 367–377.

idem: 1984, *Targum Pseudo-Jonathan of the Pentateuch: Text and Concordance.* See above under "Editions of Texts: Pseudo-Jonathan."

idem: 1986, "Noah: *gbr ṣdyq* or *gbr zky,* in *Salvación en la Palabra,* 337–345. See under Muñoz León.

Cook, E.M.: 1986, *Rewriting the Bible: The Text and Language of the Pseudo-Jonathan Targum.* Unpublished Ph.D. dissertation, University of California, Los Angeles.

Cook, J.: 1983, "Anti-Heretical Traditions in Targum Pseudo-Jonathan," *JNSL* 11, 47–57.

Cowling, G. J.: 1968, *The Palestinian Targum: Textual and Linguistic Investigations in Codex Neofiti I and Allied Manuscripts.* Unpublished doctoral thesis. University of Aberdeen.

Dalman, G.H.: 1897, "Die Handschrift zum Jonathantargum des Pentateuch, Add. 27031 des Britischen Museum," *MGWJ* 41, 454–456.

idem: 1927, 1960, *Grammatik des Jüdisch-Palästinischen Aramäisch. Aramäische Dialektproben.* 2nd ed. Leipzig, 1927; reprint, Darmstadt: Wissenschaftliche Buchgesellschaft, 1960.

Delcor, M.: 1970, "La portée chronologique de quelques interprétations du Targoum Néophyti contenues dans le cycle d'Abraham," *JStJ* 1, 105–119.

Díez Macho, A.: 1956, "Nuevos Fragmentos de Tosefta Targumica," *Sefarad* 16, 313–324.

idem: 1960, "The Recently Discovered Palestinian Targum: Its Antiquity and Relationship with the Other Targums," *VTSupp* 7, 222–245.

idem: 1963, "El Logos y el Espíritu Santo," *Atlántida* 1, 381–396.

idem: 1972, *El Targum. Introducción a las Traducciones Aramaicas de la Biblia.* Barcelona: Consejo Superior de Investigaciones Científicas.

idem: *Neophyti 1.* Targum Palestinense. MS de la Biblioteca Vaticana. Vols. 1–5. Madrid-Barcelona: Consejo Superior de Investigaciones Científicas:
1 *Génesis,* 1968;
2 *Éxodo*; 1970;

3 *Levitico*, 1971;

4 *Numeros*, 1974;

5 *Deuteronomio*, 1978.

idem: 1981, "L'Usage de la troisième personne au lieu de la première dans la Targum," in *Mélanges Dominique Barthélemy.* Études Bibliques offertes à l'occasion de son 60ᵉ Anniversaire. Ed. P. Casetti, O. Kiel, and A. Schenker. Orbis Biblicus et Orientalis 38. Fribourg: Éditions Universitaires; Göttingen: Vandenhoeck und Ruprecht, 61–89.

idem: 1986, *(In memoriam), Salvación en la Palabra*; see under Muñoz León.

Díez Merino, L.: 1976, "El Suplicio de la Cruz en la Literatura Judía Intertestamental," *Liber Annuus Studii Biblici Franciscani* 26, 31–120.

idem: 1984, "El Sintagma *nś' 'ynym* en la tradición aramea," *Aula Orientalis* 2 (1984) 23–41.

Doubles, M.C.: 1968, "Indications of Antiquity in the Orthography and Morphology of the Fragment Targum," in *In Memoriam Paul Kahle.* Ed. M. Black and G. Fohrer. Beihefte zur Zeitschrift für die alttestamentliche Wissenschaft 103. Berlin: Töpelmann, 79–89.

Elbogen, I.: 1931, *Der jüdische Gottesdienst in seiner geschichtlichen Entwicklung.* 3rd ed. Frankfurt am Main, 1931; reprint Hildesheim: Olms, 1962.

Epstein, A.: 1892, "Les Chamites de la Table Ethnographique selon le Pseudo-Jonathan," *REJ* 24, 82–98.

idem: 1895, "Tosefta du Targoum Yerouschalmi," *REJ* 30, 44–51.

Eskhult, M.: 1981, "Hebrew and Aramaic *'älôqîm*," *Orientalia Suecana* 30, 137–139.

Esterlich, P.: 1967, "El Targum Pseudojonathán o Jerosolimitano," in *Studi sull' Oriente e la Bibbia offerti a P. Giovanni Rinaldi.* Genoa: Studio e Vita, 191–195.

Faur, J.: 1975, "The Targumim and Halakha," *JQR* 66, 19–26.

Finkelstein, L., see above (under "Rabbinic Sources") *Sifre on Deuteronomy.*

Fitzmyer, J. A.: 1971, *The Genesis Apocryphon of Qumran Cave 1. A Commentary.* 2nd, rev. ed. Biblica et Orientalia 18a. Rome: Biblical Institute.

Foster, J. A.: 1969, *The Language and Text of Codex Neofiti in the Light of Other Palestinian Sources.* Ph.D. dissertation. Boston University Graduate School.

Geiger, A.: 1928, *Urschrift und Übersetzungen der Bibel.* 2nd ed. Frankfurt am Main: Madda.

Ginzberg, L.: 1900, *Die Haggada bei den Kirchenvätern und in der apokryphischen Literatur*, Berlin: Calvary.

idem: 1909–46, *The Legends of the Jews.* 7 vols. Philadelphia: JPS (referred to as *Legends*).

Ginsburger, M.: 1900, "Verbotene Thargumim," *MGWJ* 44, 1–7.

idem: 1903, *Pseudo-Jonathan.* (See above under "Pseudo-Jonathan").

Goldberg, A. M.: 1963, "Die spezifische Verwendung des Terminus Schekhinah im Targum Onkelos als Kriterium einer relativen Datierung," *Judaica* 19, 43–61.

idem: 1969, *Untersuchungen über die Vorstellung von der Schekhinah in der frühen rabbinischen Literatur.* Studia Judaica V. Berlin: De Gruyter.

Golomb, D. M.: 1983, "Nominal Syntax in the Language of Codex Vatican Neofiti I: Sentences Containing a Predicate Adjective," *JNES* 42, 181–194.

idem: 1985, *A Grammar of Targum Neofiti.* Harvard Semitic Monographs 34. Chico, Calif.: Scholars Press.

Gordon, R. P. See above, Cathcart, K.J., and Gordon, R.P.

Gottlieb, W.: 1944, "Targum Jonathan ben Uzziel to the Torah" (in Hebrew), *Melilah* 1, 26–34.

Grelot, P.: 1959, "Les Targum du Pentateuque. Étude comparative d'après Genèse IV, 3-16," *Semitica* 9, 59–88.

idem: 1963, "L'exégèse messianique d'Isaïe LXIII, 1-6," *RB* 70, 371–380.

idem: 1972, Review of R. Le Déaut-J. Robert, *Targum des Chroniques,* in *Biblica* 53, 132–137.

Gronemann, S.: 1879, *Die Jonathan'sche Pentateuch-Uebersetzung in ihrem Verhältnisse zur Halacha.* Leipzig: Friese.

Grossfeld, B.: 1979, "The Relationship between Biblical Hebrew *brḥ* and *nws* and their Corresponding Aramaic Equivalents in the Targum—*'rq, 'pk, 'zl*: A Preliminary Study in Aramaic-Hebrew Lexicography," *ZAW* 91, 107–123.

idem: 1988, *The Targum Onqelos to Genesis.* The Aramaic Bible 6. Wilmington, Del.: Michael Glazier.

idem: (due) 1990, *An Analytic Commentary of the Targum Neofiti to Genesis: Including Full Rabbinic Parallels.* Hoboken, N.J.: Ktav.

Grossfeld, B., and Aberbach, M.: 1976, *Targum Onqelos on Genesis 49.* SBL Aramaic Studies I. Missoula, Mont.: Scholars Press.

Grossfeld, B., and Aberbach, M.: 1982, *Targum Onkelos to Genesis.* New York: Ktav.

Havazelet, M.: 1976, "Parallel References to the Haggadah in the Targum Jonathan Ben 'Uziel and Neofiti: Genesis, Exodus and Leviticus," *JJS* 27, 47–53.

Hayward, R.: 1974, "The Memra of *YHWH* and the Development of its Use in Targum Neofiti I," *JJS* 25, 412–418.

idem: 1980, "Memra and Shekhina: A Short Note," JJS 31, 210–213.

idem: 1981, *Divine Name and Presence: The Memra.* Totowa, N.J.: Allanheld, Osmun.

idem: 1987, *The Targum of Jeremiah.* The Aramaic Bible 12. Wilmington, Del.: Michael Glazier.

idem: 1989A, "The Date of Targum Pseudo-Jonathan: Some Comments," *JJS* 40, 7–30.

idem: 1989B, "Targum Pseudo-Jonathan and Anti-Islamic Polemic," *JSS* 34, 77–93.

Heinemann, J., *Aggadah and Its Development* (in Hebrew). Jerusalem: Keter, 1974.

Heller, B., "Muhammedanisches und Antimuhammedanisches in den Pirke Rabbi Eliezer," *MGWJ* 69 (1925) 47–54.

Herr, M.D., "Pirkei de-Rabbi Eliezer," *EJ* 13, 558–560.

Isenberg, S. R.: 1968, *Studies in the Jewish Aramaic Translations of the Pentateuch.* Unpublished Ph.D. dissertation. Harvard University.

idem: 1970, "An Anti-Sadducee Polemic in the Palestinian Targum Tradition," *Harvard Theological Review* 63, 433–444.

idem: 1971, "On the Jewish-Palestinian Origins of the Peshitta to the Pentateuch," *JBL* 90, 69–81.

Itzchaky, E.: 1982, *The Halakah in Targum Jerushalmi I.* Pseudo-Jonathan b. Uzziel and its Exegetic Methods (in Hebrew). Unpublished Ph.D. dissertation. Ramat-Gan: Bar-Ilan University.

idem: 1985, "Targum Yerushalmi I and the School of R. Ishmael" (in Hebrew). *Sidra* 1, 45–57.

Jastrow, M.: 1950 (etc.; reprints; preface 1903), *A Dictionary of the Targumim, the Talmud Babli and Yerushalmi, and the Midrashic Literature.* 2 vols. New York: Pardes.

Jaubert, A.: 1963, "L'image de la colonne (1 Timothée 3, 15)," in *Studiorum Paulinorum Congressus Internationalis Catholicus 1961. Analecta Biblica* 17–18. 2 vols. Rome: Pontifical Biblical Institute, vol. 2, 101–108.

Jerome, *Hebraicae quaestiones in Libro Geneseos.* Ed. P. De Lagarde (in CCL 72, 1–56, Turnhout: Brepols, 1959).

Kadari, M.Z.: 1963, "The Use of *d*-clauses in the language of Targum Onkelos," *Textus* 3, 36–59.

Kahle, P.: 1930, *Masoreten des Westens* II. Stuttgart: Kohlhammer.

idem: 1959, *The Cairo Geniza.* 2nd ed. Oxford: Blackwell.

Kasher, M. M.: 1974, *Torah Shelemah.* Vol. 24. *Targumey ha-Torah. Aramaic Versions of the Bible. A Comprehensive Study of Onkelos, Jonathan, Jerusalem Targums and the Full Jerusalem Targum of the Vatican Manuscript Neofiti 1.* Jerusalem.

Kasher, R.: 1976–77, "A Targumic Tosephta to Gen 2:1–3" (in Hebrew), *Sinay* 78, 9–17.

idem: 1986, "Targumic Conflations in the Ms Neofiti I" (in Hebrew). *HUCA* 57, Hebrew section 1–19.

Kasowski, Ch.J: 1940, *Osar Leshon ha-Onkelos. Concordance to Targum Onkelos.* 2 vols. Jerusalem.

Kaufman, S. A.: 1973, review of J.P.M. van der Ploeg *et al.*, *The Job Targum From Qumran*, *JAOS*, 93, 317–327.

idem: 1976 review of G. J. Kuiper, *The Pseudo-Jonathan Targum and Its Relationship to Targum Onkelos*, *JNES* 35, 61–62.

Klein, M. L.: 1974, "Notes on the Printed Edition of MS Neofiti I," *JSS* 19, 216–230.

idem: 1975, "A New Edition of Pseudo-Jonathan," *JBL* 94, 277–279.

idem: 1976, "Converse Translation: A Targumic Technique," *Biblica* 57, 515–537.

idem: 1979, "The Preposition *qdm* ('before'), a Pseudo-Anti-Anthropomorphism in the Targum," *JTS* n.s. 30, 502–507.

idem: 1980, *The Fragment-Targums of the Pentateuch.* 2 vols. Rome: Biblical Institute Press.

idem: 1981, "The Translation of Anthropomorphisms and Anthropopathisms in the Targumim," *VTSupp* 32, 162–177.

idem: 1982, *Anthropomorphisms and Anthropopathisms in the Targumim of the Pentateuch*, with parallel citations from the Septuagint (in Hebrew). Jerusalem: Makor.

idem, 1982A, "Associative and Complementary Translation in the Targumim," *Eretz-Israel*, 16 (H. M. Orlinsky volume), 134*–140*.

idem: 1986, *Genizah Manuscripts of Palestinian Targum to the Pentateuch.* Cincinnati: Hebrew Union College Press.

idem: 1988, "Not to be Translated in Public—*l' mtrgm bṣybwr!*" *JJS* 39, 80–91.

Komlosh, Y.: 1963, "The Aggadah in the Targums of Jacob's Blessing" (in Hebrew), *Bar Ilan* 1, (= P. Churgin memorial volume), 195–206.

idem: 1968, "Characteristic Tendencies in Targum Onkelos" (in Hebrew), *Bar Ilan* 6, 181–190.

idem: 1973, *The Bible in the Light of the Aramaic Translations* (in Hebrew). Tel Aviv: Bar-Ilan University-Dvir.

idem: 1977, "Characteristics of Targum Neophyti of Exodus" (in Hebrew), in *Proceedings of the Sixth World Congress of Jewish Studies.* Jerusalem: Academic Press, 183–189.

Kosmala, H.: 1979, 1963, "At the End of Days," in *Messianism in the Talmudic Era.* Ed. L. Landman. New York: Ktav, 1979, 302–312. This essay was originally published in the *Annual of the Swedish Theological Institute* 2 (1963) 27–37.

Krauss, S., "Die biblische Völkertafel im Talmud, Midrasch und Targum," *MGWJ* 39 (1895), 1–11; 49–63.

Kuiper, G. J.: 1968, "A Study of the Relationship Between *A Genesis Apocryphon* and the Pentateuchal Targumim in Genesis 14, 1-12," in *In Memoriam Paul Kahle.* Beihefte zur Zeitschrift für die alttestamentliche Wissenschaft 103. Eds. M. Black and G. Fohrer, Berlin: Töpelmann, 149–161.

Kuiper, G. J.: 1972, *The Pseudo-Jonathan Targum and Its Relationship to Targum Onkelos.* Studia Ephemeridis "Augustinianum" 9. Rome: Institutum Patristicum "Augustinianum."

Kutscher, E. Y.: 1957, 1965, "The Language of 'Genesis Apocryphon,'" in *Scripta Hierosolymitana* IV. Eds. Ch. Rabin and Y. Yadin. 2nd ed. Jerusalem: Magnes, 1965, 1–35.

idem: 1976, *Studies in Galilean Aramaic.* Bar Ilan Studies in Near Eastern Languages and Culture. Trans. from Hebrew and annotated with additional notes by M. Sokoloff. Jerusalem: Ahva.

Lasry, G.: 1968, "Some Remarks on the Jewish Dialectical Aramaic of Palestine During the First Centuries of the Christian Era," *Augustinianum* 8, 468–476.

Le Déaut, R.: 1963, *La Nuit pascale. Essai sur la signification de la Paque juive à partir du Targum d'Exode XII, 42.* Rome: Pontifical Biblical Institute.

idem: 1966, *Introduction à la Littérature Targumique.* Première partie. Rome: Pontifical Biblical Institute.

idem: 1968, "Lévitique 22:26–23:44 dans le Targum Palestinien. De l'importance des gloses du codex Neofiti I," *VT* 18, 458–471.

idem: 1970, "Aspects de l'intercession dans le Judaïsme ancien," *JStJud* 1, 35–57.

idem: 1974, "The Current State of Targumic Studies," *Biblical Theology Bulletin* 4, 3–32.

idem: with J. Robert: 1978, 1979, 1980, *Targum du Pentateuque. Traduction des deux recensions Palestiniennes complètes.* 4 vols. Trans. R. Le Déaut with J. Robert. Sources Chrétiennes 245, 256, 261, 271. Paris: Cerf. Vol. 1, *Genèse*, 1978; vol. 2, *Exode et Lévitique*, 1979; vol. 3, *Nombres*, 1979; vol. 4, *Deutéronome*, 1980.

idem: 1987, "Quelques usages de la racine *ZMN* das les Targums du Pentateuque," in *La vie de la Parole. De l'Ancien au Nouveau Testament.* Études ... offertes à P. Grelot. Paris: Desclée, 1987, 71–78.

Le Déaut, R., and Robert, J.: 1971, *Targum des Chroniques.* 2 vols. Analecta Biblica 51. Rome: Biblical Institute Press.

Lehmann, M. R.: 1958–59, "1QGenesis Apocryphon in the Light of the Targumim and Midrashim," *Revue de Qumran*, 1, 249–263.

Lentzen-Deis, F.: 1970, *Die Taufe Jesu nach den Synoptikern.* Frankfurt am Main: Knecht.

Levey, S. H.: 1974, *The Messiah: An Aramaic Interpretation.* The Messianic Exegesis of the Targum. Monographs of the Hebrew Union College 2. Cincinnati/New York: Hebrew Union College-Jewish Institute of Religion.

Levine, E.: 1968, "Contradictory Sources in Targum Jonathan ben Uzziel" (in Hebrew). *Sinay* 64, 36–38.

idem: 1969, "Internal Contradictions in Targum Jonathan ben Uzziel to Genesis," *Augustinianum* 9, 118–119.

idem: 1970, "The Aggadah in Targum Jonathan ben 'Uzziel and Neofiti 1 to Genesis: Parallel References," in *Neophyti I.* Ed. A. Díez Macho (see above under "Neofiti"). Vol. 2, *Éxodo*, 537–578.

idem: 1971A, "Some Characteristics of Pseudo-Jonathan Targum to Genesis," *Augustinianum* 11, 89–103.

idem: 1971B, "A Study of Targum Pseudo-Jonathan to Exodus," *Sefarad* 31, 27–48.

idem: 1972, "British Museum Aramaic Additional MS 27031," *Manuscripta* 16, 3–13.

Levy, Barry B.: 1986, 1987, *Targum Neophyti 1. A Textual Study.* Vol. 1, Introduction, Genesis, Exodus; vol. 2, Leviticus, Numbers, Deuteronomy. Lanham, New York, London: University Press of America.

Levy, J.: 1881, 1966, *Chaldäisches Wörterbuch über die Targumim und einen grossen Theil des rabbinischen Schriftthums.* Leipzig; reprint Köln: Melzer, 1966. [Referred to as "Levy."]

idem: 1924, *Wörterbuch über die Talmudim und Midraschim.* 4 vols. Reprint of 2nd ed. (Berlin-Vienna). Darmstadt: Wissenschaftliche Buchgesellschaft, 1963.

Lieberman, S.: 1962, *Hellenism in Jewish Palestine.* New York: Jewish Theological Seminary, 2nd ed.

Loader, J. A.: 1978, "Onqelos Genesis 1 and the Structure of the Hebrew Text," *JStJud* 9, 198–204.

Lund, S., and Foster, J.: 1977, *Variant Versions of Targumic Traditions Within Codex Neofiti I. SBL*, Aramaic Studies 2. Missoula: Scholars Press.

Luzarraga, J.: 1973, *Las tradiciones de la nube en la Biblia y en el judaísmo primitivo.* Analecta Biblica 54. Rome: Pontifical Biblical Institute.

McCarthy, C.: 1981, *The Tiqqune Sopherim and other Theological Corrections in the Masoretic Text of the Old Testament.* Freiburg (Schweiz) and Göttingen.

idem: 1989, "The Treatment of Biblical Anthropomorphisms in the Pentateuchal Targums," *Back to the Sources.* Biblical and Near Eastern Studies in Honour of Dermot Ryan. Ed. K. Cathcart and J. F. Healey. Dublin, 1989.

McNamara, M.: 1966A, *The New Testament and the Palestinian Targum to the Pentateuch.* Analecta Biblica 27. Rome: Pontifical Biblical Institute, 1966; reprint 1978.

idem: 1966B, "Some Early Rabbinic Citations and the Palestinian Targum to the Pentateuch," *Rivista degli studi orientali* 41, 1–15.

idem: 1972, *Targum and Testament.* Aramaic Paraphrases of the Hebrew Bible: A Light on the New Testament. Shannon: Irish University Press.

idem: 1977, "The Spoken Aramaic of First Century Palestine," in *Church Ministry*. Ed. A. Mayes. Proceedings of the Irish Biblical Association 2. Dublin: Dominican Publications.

idem: 1983A, *Palestinian Judaism and the New Testament*. Wilmington, Del: Michael Glazier.

idem: 1983B, *Intertestamental Literature*. Wilmington, Del.: Michael Glazier.

Maher, M.: 1971, "Some Aspects of Torah in Judaism," *Irish Theological Quarterly* 38, 310–325.

idem: 1988, *Targum Pseudo-Jonathan of Exodus 1–4*. Unpublished Ph.D. dissertation, National University of Ireland (University College Dublin).

idem: 1990, "The *Meturgemanim* and Prayer," *JJS* 41, 226–246.

Mann, J.: 1940, *The Bible as Read and Preached in the Old Synagogue*. Vol I. The Palestinian Triennial Cycle: Genesis and Exodus. Cincinnati, 1940. Reprint with Prolegomenon by B. Z. Wacholder. New York: Ktav, 1971.

Maori, Y.: 1975, *The Peshitta Version of the Pentateuch in Its Relation to the Sources of Jewish Exegesis* (in Hebrew). Unpublished Ph.D. dissertation. Hebrew University, Jerusalem.

idem: 1983, "The Relationship of Targum Pseudo-Jonathan to Halakhic Sources" (in Hebrew). *Te'uda* 3, 235–250.

Marmorstein, A.: 1905, *Studien zum Pseudo-Jonathan Targum*. Pozsony: Alkalay.

Martínez Borobio, E.: 1975, *Estudios linguisticos sobre el Arameo del MS. Neofiti I*. Madrid: Universidad Complutense.

idem: 1976, "El Uso de *qdm* y *mn qdm* ante YHWH en la literatura Targumica y las Frases o 'Formulas de Respeto' que se originan," *Miscelánea de Estudios Arabes y Hebräicos* 25, 109–137.

Maybaum, S.: 1870, *Die Anthropomorphien und Anthropopathien bei Onkelos und die spätern Targumim*. Breslau: Schletter.

Moore, G. F.: 1922, "Intermediaries in Jewish Theology: Memra, Shekinah, Metatron," *Harvard Theological Review* 15, 41–85.

idem: 1927–30, *Judaism in the First Centuries of the Christian Era*. 3 vols. Cambridge, Mass.: Harvard University Press.

Muñoz León, D.: 1974A, *Dios-Palabra. Memra en los Targumim del Pentateuco*. Institucion S. Jeronimo 4. Granada.

idem: 1974B, "El 4o de Esdras y el Targum Palestinense," *Estudios Biblicos* 33 (1974) 323–355; 34 (1975) 49–82.

idem: 1977, *La Gloria de la Shekina en los Targumim del Pentateuco*. Madrid: Consejo Superior de Investigaciones Científicas. Instituto "Francisco Suarez."

idem (ed.): 1986, *Salvación en la Palabra. Targum. Derash. Berith.* En memoria del profesor Alejandro Díez Macho, Madrid: Ediciones Cristiandad.

Neubauer, A.: 1868, *La Géographie du Talmud*, Paris: Frères.

Neumark, M.: 1905, *Lexikalische Untersuchungen zur Sprache der jerusalemischen Pentateuch-Targume.* Heft I. Berlin: Poppelauer.

Nickelsburg, G. W. E.: 1984, "The Bible Rewritten and Expanded," in *Jewish Writings of the Second Temple Period.* Ed. M. E. Stone. Assen: Van Gorcum; Philadelphia: Fortress.

Niehoff, M.: 1988, "The Figure of Joseph in the Targums," *JJS* 39, 234–250.

Noah, M. M. (trans.). *Sefer ha-Yashar or The Book of Jasher.* See above under "Translations of Rabbinic Works."

Odeberg, H.: 1939, *The Aramaic Portions of Bereshit Rabba.* With Grammar of Galilean Aramaic. Lunds Universitets Årsskrift. N.F. Avd. 1 Bd. 36. Nr. 4. 2 vols. Lund: Gleerup; Leipzig: Harrassowitz.

Ohana, M.: 1972, *Le Targum Palestinien et la Halaka.* Unpublished doctoral thesis. University of Barcelona.

idem: 1973, "Agneau pascal et circoncision: Le problème de la Halakha Prémishnaïque dans le Targum palestinien," *VT* 23, 385–399.

idem: 1974, "Prosélytisme et Targum palestinien: Données nouvelles pour la datation de Néofiti 1," *Biblica* 55, 317–332.

idem: 1975, "La polémique judéo-islamique et l'image d'Ismaël dans Targum Pseudo-Jonathan et dans Pirke de Rabbi Eliezer," *Augustinianum* 15, 367–387.

Pérez Fernández, M.: 1981, *Tradiciones Mesiánicas en el Targum Palestinense.* Estudios exegéticos Institución San Jerónimo 12. Valencia-Jerusalem: Institución San Jerónimo-Casa de Santiago.

idem: 1984, "Versiones targúmicas de Génesis 3,22-24," in *Simposio Bíblico Español* (Salamanca, 1982). Eds. N. Fernández Marcos, J. Trebolle Barrera, J. Fernández Vallina. Madrid: Universidad Complutense, pp. 457–475.

Petermann, I. H., *De duabus Pentateuchi Paraphrasibus Chaldaicis.* Part I. *De indole paraphraseos, quae Ionathanis esse dicitur.* Berlin: Academic Press, 1829.

Peters, C.: 1934, "Targum und Praevulgata des Pentateuchs," *Oriens Christianus* 31, 49–54.

idem: 1935, "Peschittha und Targumim des Pentateuchs," *Le Muséon* 48, 1–54.

Philo. *Philo with an English Translation.* Ed. and trans. F. H. Colson, and G. H. Whitaker. 10 vols. and 2 supplementary vols. Loeb Classical Library. London: Heinemann; Cambridge, Mass.: Harvard University Press, 1929–41. Reprint 1956–62.

Prigent, P.: 1974, "*In Principio.* A propos d'un livre récent," *RHPR* 54, 391–397.

Pseudo-Philo. *Pseudo-Philo's Liber Antiquitatum Biblicarum.* Ed. G. Kish. Publications in Mediaeval Studies. Notre Dame, Ind.: University of Notre Dame, 1949.

Rappaport, S.: 1930, *Agada und Exegese bei Flavius Josephus.* Vienna: Alexander Kohut Memorial Foundation.

Rashi, *Pentateuch with Targum Onkelos, Haphtaroth and Rashi's Commentary.* Hebrew text with trans. by M. Rosenbaum and A. M. Silbermann with A. Blashki and L. Joseph. 5 vols. Jerusalem: Silbermann Family, 1973.

Revel, D.: 1924–25, "Targum Jonathan to the Torah" (in Hebrew). *Ner Ma'aravi* 2, 17–122.

Ribera, J.: 1983, "La expresión aramaica *mn qdm* y su traducción," *Aula Orientalis* 1, 114–115.

Ribera i Florit, J.: 1983, "Evolución morfológica y semántica de las partículas *k'n* y *'ry* en los diversos estadios del arameo," *Aula Orientalis*, 1, 227–233.

idem: 1984, "Elementos comunes del Targum a los Profetas y del Targum Palestinense," in *Simposio Biblico Español.* Salamanca, 1982. Ed. N. Fernández Marcos, J. Trebolle Barrera, J. Fernández Vallina. Madrid: Universidad Complutense, pp. 477–493.

Rieder, D.: 1965, "Comments and Clarifications on Targum Jonathan ben Uzziel" (in Hebrew), *Sinay* 56, 116–119.

idem: 1968, "On the Ginsburger Edition of the 'Pseudo-Jonathan' Targum of the Torah" (in Hebrew), *Leshonenu* 32, 298–303.

Rodríguez Carmona, A.: 1978, *Targum y Resurrección. Estudio de los textos del Targum Palestinense sobre la resurrección.* Granada.

idem: 1980, "Nota sobre el vocabulario sacredotal en el Targum Palestinense," *Cuadernos Bibliocos* 4, 71–74.

Sandmel, S.: 1955, "Philo's Place in Judaism: A Study of Conceptions of Abraham in Jewish Literature, II," *HUCA* 26, 151–332.

Schäfer, J. P.: 1970, "Die Termini 'Heiliger Geist' und 'Geist der Prophetie' in den Targumim und das Verhältnis der Targumim zueinander," *VT* 20, 304–314.

Schäfer, P.: 1971, "Berešit Bara' 'Elohim. Zur Interpretation von Genesis 1,1 in der rabbinischen Literatur," *JStJ* 2, 161–166.

idem: 1971–72, "Der Grundtext von Targum Pseudo-Jonathan. Eine synoptische Studie zu Gen 1." Das Institutum Judaicum der Universität Tübingen, 1971–72, 8–29.

idem: 1972, *Die Vorstellung vom Heiligen Geist in der rabbinischen Literatur.* Munich: Kösel.

idem: 1975, *Rivalität zwischen Engeln und Menschen.* Untersuchungen zur rabbinischen Engelvorstellung. Berlin-New York: de Gruyter.

Schmerler, B.: 1932, *Sefer Ahavat Yehonathan. Genesis* (in Hebrew). Bilgary.

Schulthess, F.: 1924, *Grammatik des Christlich-Palästinischen Aramäisch.* Tübingen: Mohr (Siebeck).

Schürer, E.: 1973, 1979, 1987, *The History of the Jewish People in the Age of Jesus Christ (175 B.C.–A.D. 135).* A new English version revised and edited by G. Vermes, F. Millar, M. Black. Literary editor P. Vermes. 3 vols. Edinburgh: Clark.

Seligsohn, H.: 1858, *De duabus Hierosolymitanis Pentateuchi paraphasibus.* Particula 1: De origine hierosolymitanae utriusque paraphasis ex onkelosiana Pentateuchi versione ducenda. Bratislava.

Seligsohn, H., and Traub, J.: 1857, "Ueber den Geist der Uebersetzung des Jonathan ben Usiel zum Pentateuch und die Abfassung des in den Editionen dieser Uebersetzung beigedruckten Targum jeruschalmi," *MGWJ* 6, 96–114, 138–149.

Shinan, A.: 1975, "'Their Prayers and Petitions.' The Prayers of the Ancients in the Light of the Pentateuchal Targums" (in Hebrew), *Sinay* 78, 89–92.

idem: 1975–76, "*lyšn byt qwdš'* in the Aramaic Targums of the Torah" (in Hebrew), *Beth Miqra* 21, 472–474.

idem: 1976, "'And the Lord put a mark on Cain.' On Targum Pseudo-Jonathan to Gen 4:15" (in Hebrew), *Tarbiz* 45, 148–150.

idem: 1977A, "Midrashic Parallels to Targumic Traditions," *JStJ* 8, 185–191.

idem: 1977B, "The Aramaic Targums of the Creation Story and Ps 104" (in Hebrew), *Shnaton* 2, 228–232.

idem: 1979, *The Aggadah in the Aramaic Targums to the Pentateuch* (in Hebrew). 2 vols. Jerusalem: Makor.

idem: 1982, "A Word to the Wise Is Sufficient" (in Hebrew), *Criticism and Interpretation* 18, 69–77.

idem: 1982–83, "On the Theoretical Principles of the Meturgemanim" (in Hebrew), *Jerusalem Studies in Jewish Thought* 2, 7–32.

idem: 1983A, "Folk Elements in the Aramaic Targum Pseudo-Jonathan" (in Hebrew), in *Studies in Aggadah and Jewish Folklore.* Presented to Dov Noy on his 60th Birthday, Ed. I. Ben-Ami and J. Dan. Jerusalem: Magnes, 139–155.

idem: 1983B, "Miracles, Wonders and Magic in the Aramaic Targums of the Pentateuch" (in Hebrew), in *Essays on the Bible and the Ancient Near East.* Festschrift I. L. Seeligman. 2 vols. Ed. A. Rofé and Y. Zakovitch. Jerusalem: Rubinstein, 2, 419–426.

idem: 1983C, "The Angelology of the 'Palestinian' Targums on the Pentateuch," *Sefarad* 43, 181–198.

idem: 1985, "The 'Palestinian' Targums—Repetitions, Internal Unity, Contradictions," *JJS* 36, 72–87.

idem: 1986, "On the Characteristics of Targum Pseudo-Jonathan to the Torah" (in Hebrew), in *Proceedings of the Ninth World Congress of Jewish Studies*. Jerusalem: World Union of Jewish Studies, 109–116.

idem: 1990, "Dating Targum Pseudo-Jonathan: Some More Comments," *JJS* 41, 57–61.

Silverstone, A. E.: 1931, *Aquila and Onkelos*. Manchester: University Press.

Skinner, J.: 1912, *Genesis*. The International Critical Commentary. Edinburgh: T. & T. Clark.

Sokoloff, M.: 1980, "Notes on the Vocabulary of Galilean Aramaic" (in Hebrew), in *Studies in Hebrew and Semitic Languages*. Dedicated to the Memory of E. Y. Kutscher. Ed. G. B. Safratti, P. Artzi, J. C. Greenfield, and M. Kadarri. Ramat-Gan, Israel: Bar-Ilan University, 166–173.

idem: 1990, *A Dictionary of Jewish Palestinian Aramaic of the Byzantine Period*. Ramat-Gan, Israel: Bar-Ilan University.

Speier, S.: 1966–67, 1969–70, "The Relationship Between the 'Arukh' and 'Targum Neofiti I'" (in Hebrew), *Leshonenu* 31 (1966–67) 23–32; 34 (1969–70) 172–179.

Speiser, E. A.: 1964, *Genesis*. The Anchor Bible. New York: Doubleday.

Sperber, A.: 1934–35, "The Targum Onkelos," *PAAJR* 6, 309–351.

idem, 1959. See above under "Editions of Texts: Onqelos."

Spiegel, S.: 1967, *The Last Trial*. New York: Random House.

Splansky, D. M.: 1981, *Targum Pseudo-Jonathan: Its Relationship to Other Targumim, Use of Midrashim and Date*. Unpublished Ph.D. dissertation, Hebrew Union College, Cincinnati.

Stemberger, G.: 1974, "Die Patriarchenbilder der Katakombe in der Via Latina im Lichte der jüdischen Tradition," *Kairos* 16, 19–78.

Strack, H. L. and Billerbeck, P.: 1922–69, *Kommentar zum Neuen Testament aus Talmud und Midrasch*. 4 vols. Munich: Beck.

Strack, H. L., and Stemberger, G.: 1982, *Einleitung in Talmud und Midrasch*. 7th ed. Beck'sche Elementarbücher. Munich: Beck.

Syrén, R.: 1986, *The Blessings in the Targums. A Study on the Targumic Interpretations of Genesis 49 and Deuteronomy 33*. Acta Academiae Abonensis, ser. A., vol. 64, nr. 1. Åbo: Åbo Akademi.

Tal (Rosenthal), A.: 1974, "MS Neophyti I: The Palestinian Targum to the Pentateuch. Observations on the Artistry of a Scribe," *Israel Oriental Studies* 4, 31–43.

idem: 1975, *The Language of the Targum of the Former Prophets and Its Position within the Aramaic Dialects* (in Hebrew). Texts and Studies in the Hebrew Language and Related Subjects 1. Tel-Aviv: Tel-Aviv University.

idem (Tal, A.): 1979–80, "Studies in Palestinian Aramaic," *Leshonenu* 44, 43–65.

Towner, W. S.: 1973, *The Rabbinic Enumeration of Scriptural Examples.* Leiden: Brill.

Urbach, E. E.: 1975, *The Sages. Their Concepts and Beliefs.* 2 vols. English trans. Jerusalem: Magnes.

Vermes, G.: 1961, *Scripture and Tradition in Judaism.* Studia Post-Biblica 4. Leiden: Brill; 2nd rev. ed. 1973.

idem: 1963A, "The Targumic Versions of Genesis IV 3-16," *Annual of Leeds University Oriental Society* 3 (1961–62) 81–114.

idem: 1963B, 1975, "Haggadah in the Onkelos Targum," *JSS* 8 (1963) 159–169. Reprint in G. Vermes, *Post-Biblical Jewish Studies.* Studies in Judaism in Late Antiquity. Leiden: Brill, 1975, 127–138.

idem: 1978, "The Impact of the Dead Sea Scrolls on Jewish Studies During the last Twenty-Five Years," in *Approaches to Ancient Judaism: Theory and Practice.* ed. W. G. Scott. Brown Judaic Studies I. Missoula: Scholars Press, 201–214.

Voster, W. S.: 1971, "The Use of the Prepositional Phrase *bmymr'* in the Neofiti I Version of Genesis," in *De Fructu Oris Sui.* Essays in Honour of Adrianus van Selms. Pretoria Oriental Series. Ed. I. H. Eybers, F. C. Fensham, et al., Leiden: Brill.

Wieder, A. A.: 1974, "Three Philological Notes," *Bulletin of the Institute of Jewish Studies* 2, 103–109.

York, A. D.: 1974, "The Dating of Targumic Literature," *JStJ* 5, 49–62.

idem: 1979, "The Targum in the Synagogue and in the School," *JStJ* 10, 74–86.

Zunz, L.: 1892, *Die gottesdienstlichen Vorträge der Juden, historisch entwickelt.* 2nd ed. Frankfurt am Main: Kaufmann; this work, supplemented by H. Albeck, has been republished in Hebrew, Jerusalem, 1942.

INDEXES

HEBREW BIBLE

APOCRYPHAL/DEUTEROCANONICAL BOOKS

Tobit		**1 Maccabees**	
12:19	67	15:37	48

NEW TESTAMENT

Matthew		**Luke**		**Titus**	
1:3	130	2:51	125	2:14	39
5:22	30	4:14	118		
18:8–9	30	6:22	118	**Hebrews**	
19:5	25			5–7	58
25:34	23			7:1	58
25:41	30	**Galatians**		7:2	58
		4:29–30	77		
Mark					
6:27	127	**Ephesians**			
6:31	77	2:10	39		

APOCRYPHA AND PSEUDEPIGRAPHA

1 Enoch					
6,3	38	8,19	22	4,9–13	45
6,7	38	10,22–23	50	9,7	26
6–11	37	12,26	49		
8,1	38	15,17	65	**Sibylline Oracles**	
8,1–2	38	16	67	3,24–26	22
9,6	38	18,13	78		
9,7	38	21,12	78	**Testaments of the XII Patriarchs**	
10,8	38	27,8	98		
10,11	38	28,9	103		
60,7–8	19	30,3	118	**Levi**	
60,20	94	31,16	104	23–24	78
70	37	32,1–3	114		
72,37	18	32,3–6	120	**Judah**	
		34,1–8	156	3–7	148
		34,1–9	148		
2 Enoch		39,6	131		
6,1	94	43,15	147	**Zebulun**	
8,1–8	23			3,2	126
30,1	22			10,3	30
30,13	22	**4 Maccabees**			
31,1	23	2,2	161	**Naphtali**	
		12,12	30	2,1	160
Psalms of Solomon				8,4–5	50
14	30	**Ascension of Isaiah**			
		9,9	37	**Joseph**	
				13	130
Jubilees		**2 (Syriac) Baruch**		17,1	162
2,7	20, 22	4,4	61	18,4	124
4,1	31	29,4	19(2)	20,3	58
4,8	31	85,13	30		
4,23	37				
5,1	37	**3 Baruch**		**Benjamin**	
5,19	39	4,8	26	4,2	162

TARGUM PSEUDO-JONATHAN

TARGUM NEOFITI AND NEOFITI GLOSSES

FRAGMENT TARGUMS

CAIRO GENIZAH TARGUMS

TARGUM TOSEFTA

TARGUM ONQELOS

TARGUM NEBI'IM

TARGUM HAGIOGRAPHA

SEPTUAGINT

THEODOTION

PESHITTA

VULGATE

QUMRAN TEXTS

JEWISH WRITERS

CHRISTIAN WRITERS

RABBINIC

I. Tosefta, Mishnah, Talmud

II. Midrash

INDEX OF SUBJECTS

(Page numbers followed by *n.* refer to footnotes; page numbers alone refer to the text of Ps.-J.)

INDEX OF AUTHORS